Daniel López Ridruejo

Ian Kallen

SAMS
Teach Yourself

Apache 2
in 24 Hours

SAMS

800 East 96th St., Indianapolis, Indiana, 46240 USA

Sams Teach Yourself Apache 2 in 24 Hours

Copyright © 2002 by Sams Publishing

International Standard Book Number: 0-67232-355-9

Library of Congress Catalog Card Number: 2001096489

Printed in the United States of America

First Printing: June 2002

06   05   04   4   3   2

Trademarks

Warning and Disclaimer

Bulk Sales

Sams Publishing offers excellent discounts on this book when ordered in quantity for bulk purchases or special sales. For more information, please contact

> **U.S. Corporate and Government Sales**
> **1-800-382-3419**
> corpsales@pearsontechgroup.com

For sales outside of the U.S., please contact

> **International Sales**
> **1-317-428-3341**
> international@pearsontechgroup.com

ACQUISITIONS EDITOR
Shelley Johnston

DEVELOPMENT EDITOR
Heather Goodell

MANAGING EDITOR
Charlotte Clapp

PROJECT EDITOR
Elizabeth Finney

COPY EDITOR
Michael Henry

INDEXER
Mandie Frank

PROOFREADER
Bob LaRoche

TECHNICAL EDITOR
Patrik Grip-Jansson
Allan Liska

TEAM COORDINATOR
Amy Patton

INTERIOR DESIGNER
Gary Adair

COVER DESIGNER
Aren Howell

PAGE LAYOUT
Susan Geiselman

Contents at a Glance

Contents

Hour 17 Setting Up a Secure Server   **263**

Foreword

When I started working on mod_perl back in early 1996, Apache was at version 1.1 or so and Perl at 5.002-ish. At the time, members of the Apache Group[1] were already talking about Apache version 2.0, and Robert Thau, main architect of the original Apache module API, had a prototype in the works. It wasn't until six years later that the first GA release of Apache 2.0 (2.0.35) hit the streets. Why did it take so long? One possible explanation can be found in mod_ssl.h:

```
/* "The Apache Group: a collection of talented individuals who are trying
to perfect the art of never finishing something." — Rob Hartill
*/
```

Whatever the real reasons are, if you are already familiar with Apache 1.3, this book will illustrate the many reasons why Apache 2.0 was worth the wait.

Over the years, Apache has evolved into the dominant Web server platform thanks to its open source license and modular architecture. Apache 2.0, which was finally released in April 2002, brings increased performance and a number of exciting new features. Among those features are filters, which allow modules to process content produced by other modules before delivering it to clients; a multi-protocol architecture that allows Apache to serve other protocols, such as FTP and POP3; and improved support for non-Unix platforms, such as Windows, using the Apache Portable Runtime and platform-specific multi-processing modules.

All these new features come at a price because module authors must modify their software to work with the new internal APIs and support threaded operation. Similarly, system administrators who upgrade to the new version must update their knowledge of the server and how to configure popular third-party modules to work with Apache 2.0. This book makes that transition easier by providing you with a solid foundation on how to manage, extend, and fine-tune Apache 2.0 servers.

As you know, there are many developers who contribute to the Apache httpd and subprojects such as mod_perl, Jakarta, Tcl, XML, and PHP. Beyond those, an endless number of third-party modules extend Apache in various ways. Most developers have experience with only a small subset of these. Through his work with Comanche, Daniel's knowledge of the server and its extensions covers far more area than the average developer. I'm sure you'll find that Daniel's experience is apparent throughout the book, and the many years he's spent building his knowledge is presented in a way that will be apparent to you in a matter of hours.

---

[1] As it was called at the time before the Apache Software Foundation came to be

I'm very excited that Apache 2.0 is finally here. If you're not already excited also, this book will certainly change that quickly!

—Doug MacEachern

Doug MacEachern is a developer at Covalent Technologies, Inc. He is the lead developer of the mod_perl Apache module, an Apache Software Foundation member, and coauthor of the book Writing Apache Modules with Perl and C.

Lead Author

Daniel López Ridruejo is a senior developer with Covalent Technologies, Inc., which provides Apache software, support, and services for the enterprise. He is the author of several popular Apache and Linux guides and of Comanche, a GUI configuration tool for Apache. Daniel is a regular speaker at open source conferences such as LinuxWorld, ApacheCon, and the O'Reilly Open Source Convention. He holds a Master of Science degree in telecommunications from the Escuela Superior de Ingenieros de Sevilla and Danmarks Tekniske Universitet. Daniel is a member of the Apache Software Foundation.

Contributing Author

Ian Kallen is a senior software engineer and product team lead with Covalent Technologies developing enterprise-class management tools for the Apache Web server. Prior to joining Covalent, Ian managed the software and network operations at Salon.com and GameSpot.com. Ian is an instructor at San Francisco State University's Multimedia Studies program, and has been an invited speaker at the O'Reilly Open Source Convention, ApacheCon, and other technology events. In his spare time, Ian plays blues guitar and softball, but he hasn't had any spare time, so the strings are rusty and the mitt is dusty.

Dedication

To my father.

Acknowledgments

I would like to thank my parents, Francisco and Marisol; my brother, Angel; and my sister, Reyes for their support and encouragement while writing this book. My family in Madrid, el abuelo y tio Angel, Olga, Alvaro, Maria, tia Mari, Gregorio, and Veronica who take good care of me during my flights back and forth to the United States.

Special thanks go to the team at Sams that gave me the opportunity to write this book and patiently helped me through the process: Shelley Johnston, Elizabeth Finney, Jennifer Kost, and Heather Goodell. Vicki Harding and Craig Wiley, from Studio B, took care of all the paperwork so that I could concentrate on writing.

I am grateful to Patrik Grip-Jansson and Allan Liska for reviewing early drafts and providing valuable feedback, and to Mike Henry for great copy editing work.

Ian Kallen is the contributing author for the hours on Tomcat, mod_perl, mod_rewrite, and virtual hosting. Ian is a talented and experienced developer, and I enjoyed working with him on this project.

Covalent has given me the opportunity to work with great engineers, many of them core Apache developers, from whom I have learned a great deal and had a lot of fun making Apache enterprise-ready. I would like to thank especially Cody Sherr, Costin Manolache, Doug MacEachern, Jon Travis, Will Rowe, and Ryan Bloom for reviewing my work and answering Apache-related questions. Scott Albro, Mark Douglas, and Fung Yang are some of the other great individuals at Covalent I enjoy working with.

While I am at it, I would like to say hello to my kickboxing buddies, and thank them for providing me with a much-needed physical challenge after long hours in front of my laptop: Jochen, Lars, Mike, and Ken and to my friends in Sevilla, especially Juanpa, Javi, Pablo y Paco. A big hello to Jesús Blanco, wherever in the world you are right now! My friends in Denmark—Finnbjorn, Marco, Kristian, and Leo (yes, you are Danish by now, Leo!)—always encouraged me to "write a book or something" so that I would stop talking about Linux. Here is the result, I hope you like it! I am also grateful to professors Lars Dittman, Jorge Chavez, and Alfredo Navarro, who always encouraged me and provided support to pursue my ideas.

Todd Andersen, Eduardo de Castro, Simon Barber, Roy Petruchska, and Ziv Kimhi are some of the people who will be happy that the book is *finally* done.

And, of course, kudos to the Apache developers who have created the best Web server in the world! Even if they sometimes take a little too much time in doing so, the result is worth waiting for. I hope this book will contribute to the further success of Apache.

—*Daniel López Ridruejo*

I would like to extend a big helping of gratitude to Daniel for inviting me to contribute to this book. Over the years, Daniel's efforts at bringing Apache to the people have really been an inspiration. At last, I have a text to accompany the Apache course I teach at SFSU!

My hat is off to many of the same folks that Daniel mentioned. To the unparalleled group who are my colleagues at Covalent, their talent, patience, and dedication is truly awesome. To the gang at Sams, their guidance, fortitude, and generally putting up with me has been very gracious. To the Apache developers, for making me look good when I've had to operate stable, flexible, and economical high-volume Web sites: You make it all possible.

Special thanks go to my wife, Heidi, and our children, Jessica and Jonah, for their love, inspiration, and support. I don't know if I can ever adequately give what I get, but I'll keep trying.

—*Ian Kallen*

We Want to Hear from You!

As the reader of this book, *you* are our most important critic and commentator. We value your opinion and want to know what we're doing right, what we could do better, what areas you'd like to see us publish in, and any other words of wisdom you're willing to pass our way.

You can e-mail or write me directly to let me know what you did or didn't like about this book—as well as what we can do to make our books better.

Please note that I cannot help you with technical problems related to the topic of this book, and that due to the high volume of mail I receive, I might not be able to reply to every message.

When you write, please be sure to include this book's title and author as well as your name, e-mail address, and phone number. I will carefully review your comments and share them with the author and editors who worked on the book.

E-mail: opensource@samspublishing.com

Mail: Mark Taber
            Associate Publisher
            Sams Publishing
            800 East 96th Street
            Indianapolis, IN 46240 USA

For more information about this book or another Sams title, visit our Web site at www.samspublishing.com. Type the ISBN (excluding hyphens) or the title of a book in the Search field to find the page you're looking for.

Introduction

You don't write because you want to say something, you write because you've got something to say.

—F. Scott Fitzgerald

So, What Does This Book Have to Say?

This book explains in simple, clear terms how to configure, manage, and extend version 2.0 of Apache, the most popular Web server on the Internet.

The main goal of writing this book is to show that Apache is not hard to use or administer[1], at least not as hard as many people seem to think. One of the reasons Apache is so popular with experienced system administrators is because it allows for a great deal of flexibility in how it is built and configured. But that flexibility also means that the server can be intimidating and complex for beginner users. The default Apache distribution has several hundred configuration options. Which of those options are essential and which are used only in obscure situations? How do I perform simple tasks such as password protecting a certain part of my Web site or running CGI scripts?

Although the Apache server documentation has improved greatly over time, it is still mostly a reference for the server configuration options. This book will guide you through those options and take away much of the complexity with simple, easy-to-understand explanations. We will take a practical, hands-on approach and concentrate on how to configure the most popular features and troubleshoot common problems.

For some special cases or truly advanced functionality, the book gives pointers to where you can find additional information.

By the time you finish this book, you will be able to build a custom Apache server, create server-side dynamic pages with PHP and mod_perl, build a secure server with mod_ssl and run Java servlets with Tomcat. You will also learn how to monitor the server, tune Apache for performance and scalability, run a proxy server, and restrict access to certain parts of your Web site.

[1]*Because it didn't take me much to figure out that a technical book is not going to make me rich or get me any hot dates!*

Who Should Read This Book?

This book is intended for beginning and intermediate users of Apache 2.0, such as the following:

- Administrators who are already familiar with Apache 1.3, but want a better understanding of the new 2.0 features. They will find information about the new multi-processing and multiprotocol architecture, the filtering framework, how to configure popular modules such as mod_perl and PHP to work with 2.0, and advice on how to migrate from 1.3 servers.
- Administrators who are familiar with another Web server, such as Microsoft IIS or Netscape/IPlanet, and want to migrate to Apache.
- Unix and Windows administrators who have set up servers in the past for mail or file access, and want to learn how to set up a Web server.
- Web developers who want to gain a better understanding of how Web servers work or to gain valuable Web administration skills.
- Linux users who are curious about Web servers and want to know how to configure the Apache server included in their distribution.

What Is Required to Read This Book?

You must be familiar with Unix or Windows basic shell operation, such as creating and navigating directories, editing files, and executing programs. Previous experience with Web servers is valuable but not required. You will need Internet access for downloading the Apache software, third-party modules, and documentation.

Why Is This Book Better than Other Apache Books?

This book's focus is on providing a *practical* guide to Apache running on Windows and Unix platforms such as Solaris and Linux. To achieve that goal, I draw on my experience over the years working with Apache-related projects. Being the author of the Comanche GUI configuration tool, which is downloaded several thousands of times a month, gets me in contact with people new to Apache and the problems they face trying to get started with the server. On the other end of the spectrum, working for Covalent, which provides commercial Apache software and services, enables me to gain valuable insights and understanding about how Apache is used in enterprise environments. It also gives me the opportunity to work with, and learn from, some of the most talented Apache developers out there, such as Ryan Bloom, Doug MacEachern, and Costin Manolache.

I have been a speaker at several open source conferences, such as ApacheCon and LinuxWorld, and authored several how-to guides on Linux and Apache that have been translated to more than ten languages. This has taught me that it is not only important to know a particular subject, but you must also be able to effectively communicate that experience to your audience. That often means spending a large amount of time of the writing process making sure that the material is well structured, clear, and easy to understand.

This book covers both Windows and Unix. This is important because the 2.0 version of Apache for Windows has reached a level of quality and maturity similar to the Unix versions. This, coupled with the continuous security problems associated with Microsoft IIS, will likely mean an increase in the number of Apache servers deployed on the Windows platform.

Structure of This Book

This book is divided into three parts. The first part (Hours 1 through 10) helps you build, configure, and get started with Apache. After completing the chapters, you will be able to start, stop, and monitor your Web server. You will also be able to serve both static content and dynamic content (via CGIs), customize the logs, and restrict access to certain parts of your Web server.

The second part (Hours 11 through 17) covers advanced administration topics, such as the role of multi-processing modules, filtering, performance tuning, publishing extensions, and secure servers.

The third part (Hours 18 through 24) explains how to build and configure popular Apache modules and related software, such as PHP, `mod_perl`, and Tomcat.

Each hour includes a "Further Reading" section that provides pointers to additional documentation on that hour's topics. The "Related Directives" section provides a summary of the configuration directives discussed in the hour, and you can use this list to look up detailed descriptions in the Apache reference documentation.

Code listings can be found at `http://apacheworld.org/ty24/`.

Conventions Used in This Book

This book uses different typefaces to differentiate between code and regular English. Therefore, code lines, commands, directives, variables, and text you type or see onscreen appear in a `computer typeface`.

Do not type any line numbers that appear at the beginning of lines in code listings. The line numbers are used to reference lines of code during the explanation of the listing.

A Note presents interesting pieces of information related to the surrounding discussion.

A Tip offers advice or teaches an easier way to do something.

A Caution advises you about potential problems and helps you steer clear of disaster.

PART I

Basic Apache

Hour

Hour 1

Apache and the Web

In this hour, you will learn

- Web architecture, understanding the inner workings of the protocols necessary for browser and server communication
- The evolution of the role and capabilities of Web servers over time
- The strengths and weaknesses of the Apache Web server and its history

Internet Protocols

The Web has become part of our everyday life. People use the Internet to get weather reports, buy books, read news, and keep in contact with friends via Web e-mail. Web browsers provide a friendly interface to access the information and to hide the complexity of the underlying protocols. Web servers are the programs that provide the information to the Web browsers.

This section describes a number of protocols used by browsers and servers to communicate, such as TCP/IP (Transmission Control Protocol/Internet Protocol), DNS (Domain Name System), and HTTP (Hypertext Transfer

Protocol). This will provide you with the basic foundation on which later topics such as access control and request information logging will build. Even if you are already familiar with these protocols, you might want to skim through this section for a quick refresher.

TCP/IP

TCP/IP is the basic family of protocols of the Internet. Other protocols, such as those for transmission of mail or Web pages, work on top of TCP/IP.

The Internet started as a military network before it evolved into an academic and commercial network. It was built during the Cold War, and the protocols were designed so that they could keep working even in the event that parts of the network were destroyed by a nuclear attack. TCP/IP is used to transmit packets between machines in a distributed network. Each machine is assigned a unique number (an IP address), and messages are passed from one machine to another (routed) until they reach their destination. An IP address is usually represented in dotted notation, with four numbers between 0 and 255. The Internet is a hierarchical network, as the addressing structure reflects. The initial part of the address identifies the network and the rest identifies the node, as you can see in Figure 1.1. IP addresses are assigned by ICANN (Internet Corporation for Assigned Names and Numbers; `http://www.icann.org`) via the IANA (Internet Assigned Number Authority; `http://www.iana.org`). Certain address ranges, marked as private, are not connected to the Internet and can safely be used by organizations in their internal networks.

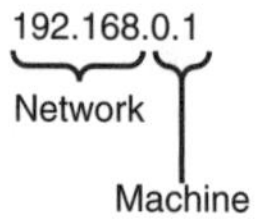

FIGURE 1.1

IP address structure.

Similar to how IP addresses identify uniquely a machine in the network, port numbers uniquely identify services in the machine. Each of the standard protocols has a number assigned by ICANN. HTTP uses port 80 by default. HTTP is the protocol Web browsers and servers use to communicate and is described later in this hour.

You could think of the Internet as a giant telephone network that connects computers instead of people. IP addresses represent the main phone number of an office. IP ports represent the extension of a particular department within that office.

An IP protocol packet is the basic transmission unit. It contains the destination IP address, the origin IP address, and some data. IP packets can be lost or duplicated due to congestion or network failure. TCP works on top of IP and takes care of discarding duplicated packets and retransmitting lost ones, offering a reliable transmission protocol to the application developer.

DNS

IP addresses are difficult to remember. In addition, it would be nice to be able to refer to a particular service or machine without worrying about changes in the underlying IP addressing scheme. This can be accomplished by assigning a name to each machine. Originally the number of machines in the Internet was very limited and the relationship between IP addresses and names was kept in a file that was distributed to system administrators.

As the Internet grew, the system became unpractical and the DNS (Domain Name System) protocol was born. In this system, identifiers are made of a machine name and a domain name (see Figure 1.2). Name servers answer requests for machine names and return the associated IP addresses.

FIGURE 1.2

Domain name structure.

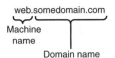

Domain names have different components, and the first one is called the *top-level domain*. Some of the traditional top-level domains are .org for nonprofit organizations, .com for commercial entities, and .net for network-related sites. Additionally, each country is assigned a top-level domain.

The domain name system is hierarchical. Name servers communicate with each other and cache answers. The root name servers know about only the top-level domains. For example, if you are looking for the IP address of www.apache.org, you ask your local name server. If your local name server does not have that name in its cache, it asks an upstream DNS server. The upstream DNS server repeats the process until one of the DNS servers in the hierarchy knows the address of the DNS server for the apache.org domain. The name server for the apache.org domain will eventually be reached and it will reply with the IP address or addresses associated with that particular name.

You can experiment typing the nslookup command in your Unix shell or windows command prompt:

```
nslookup www.apache.org
Server:  ns2.mindspring.com
Address:  207.69.188.186

Non-authoritative answer:
```

```
Name:    www.apache.org
Address: 64.125.133.20
```

Your computer must be connected to the Internet for the nslookup command to work.

Thanks to DNS, a Web site that moves from one colocation facility to another can change its IP address while the name typed by the users in their browsers remains the same.

ICANN administers top-level domains via InterNIC (Internet Network Information Center; http://www.internic.net), which in turn delegates to commercial registers.

There is much more to Internet addressing than what is covered here. Please refer to the "Further Reading" section at the end of this hour for further information.

HTTP

HTTP (Hypertext Transfer Protocol) is used by servers and browsers to communicate with each other. It is a request response protocol based on TCP. The browser sends a request to the server for a particular resource, together with some information (headers) about the browser version, language preferences, and so on.

The server answers with a status code, several headers, and the requested data. The status code indicates whether the request has been processed correctly, the resource has moved to a new location, the access is forbidden, and so on. Headers provide information about the requested resource, such as the content type, last modification time, and more. The data for the requested resource is usually a Web page or an image.

URL

The browser reads the data returned in the response and displays it to the user. Web pages are written in HTML, a text-based language that enables pages to link to other pages, images, and so on. If the data retrieved by the browser contains links, the user can click these links to retrieve new documents. The linked documents can live in the same server or in a different one thousands of miles away. The process of navigating from one server to the other is simple and transparent to the user. The links identify unique resources in the Web via URLs (Uniform Resource Locators). A URL is made of individual components, as shown in Figure 1.3.

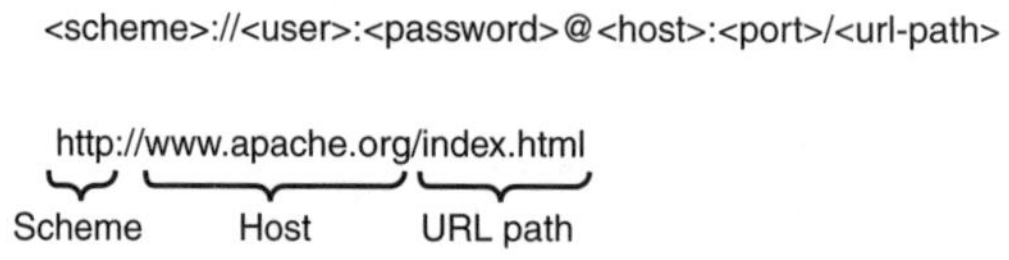

FIGURE 1.3
URL structure.

<scheme>://<user>:<password>@<host>:<port>/<url-path>

http://www.apache.org/index.html
Scheme   Host   URL path

The first component of the URL is the scheme, or protocol, that will be used to access the URL. HTTP and FTP are examples of valid URL schemes. An optional username and password component might be included to access resources that require it. The host component identifies the machine that provides the resource. The port component identifies the specific port the server is listening at. If the port does not appear, the default port for the HTTP scheme (port number 80) is assumed. The final component specifies the resource to be accessed; in Figure 1.3, the resource is the index file for the Web site.

SSL

SSL stands for Secure Sockets Layer and is a protocol to secure communications between clients and servers. The secure version of HTTP is called HTTPS and provides support for encryption and authentication. Encryption is used to prevent an attacker from eavesdropping on requests containing sensitive data (for example, credit card information). Authentication is used to validate that the other end is truly who he claims to be. (When you buy online, you want to make sure the business at the other end is who it claims to be.) The default port for the HTTPS scheme is 443. SSL is covered in Hour 17, "Setting Up a Secure Server."

HTTP Internals

Let's have a closer look at the HTTP protocol. Listings 1.1 and 1.2 show an example of an HTTP request/response pair. The request is made by Internet Explorer 5 running on Windows 2000, and the response is provided by an Apache Web server running on FreeBSD. The user typed http://www.apache.org in the browser. The browser examined the URL and decided to make a request to the www.apache.org Web site. To do so, it first resolved the name to the corresponding IP address (64.125.133.20) using the DNS system. No port was specified in the URL, so the default port for HTTP (port 80) was assumed. After the TCP connection was opened, the browser sent the request and received the response.

The numbers appearing in the listings have been added to make it easy to refer to individual request lines in the text, and are not part of the HTTP protocol.

LISTING 1.1 HTTP Request

```
1: GET / HTTP/1.1
2:Accept: image/gif, image/x-xbitmap, image/jpeg, image/pjpeg,
➥ application/vnd.ms-powerpoint, application/vnd.ms-excel, application/msword,
➥*/*
3:Accept-Language: en-us
4:Accept-Encoding: gzip, deflate
5:User-Agent: Mozilla/4.0 (compatible; MSIE 5.01; Windows NT 5.0)
```

LISTING 1.1   continued

```
6:Host: www.apache.org
7:Connection: Keep-Alive
```

LISTING 1.2   HTTP Response

```
 1: HTTP/1.1 200 OK
 2: Date: Sat, 09 Feb 2002 17:17:23 GMT
 3: Server: Apache/2.0.32-dev (Unix)
 4: Cache-Control: max-age=86400
 5: Expires: Sun, 10 Feb 2002 17:17:23 GMT
 6: Accept-Ranges: bytes
 7: Content-Length: 8667
 8: Keep-Alive: timeout=5, max=100
 9: Connection: Keep-Alive
10: Content-Type: text/html
11:
12: <!DOCTYPE html PUBLIC "-//W3C//DTD XHTML 1.0 Transitional//EN"
13:              "http://www.w3.org/TR/xhtml1/DTD/xhtml1-transitional.dtd">
14: <html>
15:   <head>
16: (...)
```

Figure 1.4 shows how a browser displays the information received in Figure 1.3.

FIGURE 1.4

Page rendered in browser.

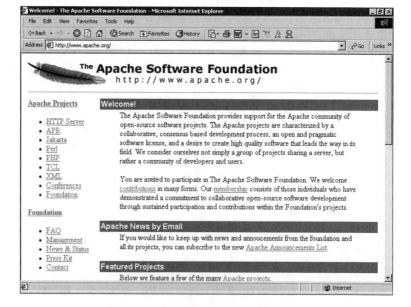

The first line of the request is made of the following components: first, an HTTP method name; in this case, GET, for retrieving a document. Other methods include POST, for posting information to the Web server (in that case, the request contains data that is passed to the server for processing); and HEAD, for retrieving headers without any data (useful to detect whether a document has changed). The next element in the first line is the resource location. A single / indicates to the Web server that you are requesting the front page for the Web site. Finally, the HTTP protocol version number that the client speaks is provided.

Other interesting headers in the request (Listing 1.1):

- **Host:** Indicates the particular host you are making the request to. This is useful when a single instance of the server is hosting different Web sites.
- **Connection: Keep-alive** (line 7) indicates that the client desires to leave the connection open to transmit further requests.
- **Accept-Language: en-us** (line 3) indicates the client preferred language is English, U.S. variant.

The response (Listing 1.2) starts with a status line. The first component identifies the protocol version the server will speak. The second and third components represent the status code of the response in numeric and text modes.

The following are common HTTP status codes returned by Web servers, where xx is a placeholder that stands for the particular response number. For example, 401 means the request was not authorized and 403 means the resource could not be found. They are different status codes, but because both refer to client error codes, they belong to the $4xx$ group.

- **2xx** codes mean the request was successful.
- **3xx** codes mean the resource has moved to a new location.
- **4xx** client error: The request could not be fulfilled because the resource does not exist, access is forbidden, and so on.
- **5xx** server error: The server encountered an error. This can happen because the server malfunctioned, the method is not implemented, and so on.

After the status code, several headers add information about the resource being served:

- **Server** (line 3) identifies the server name and version serving the request.
- **Content-length** (line 7) specifies the size in bytes of the resource being returned.
- **Content-type** (line 10) identifies the MIME-type of the request; in this case, text/html. MIME stands for Multipurpose Internet Mail Extensions, and is a

mechanism used to identify the content type of a certain resource. This allows the browser to display the information correctly.

Other headers (Cache-control, Expires, ETag, and so on) are used, among other things, to control the validity in time of the document and avoid unnecessary network traffic.

After the headers, a blank line precedes the contents of the resource being transmitted. After the resource has been transmitted, the server may decide to leave open the connection to accept further requests from the client. This depends on the protocol version being used and the connection type negotiated by client and server.

Do It Yourself HTTP

HTTP is a simple, text-based protocol. You do not need a browser to issue HTTP requests. You can use a telnet client, a program that allows you to connect directly to the server and port you specify. Most UNIX versions come with a version of telnet preinstalled. Some Windows versions include a telnet client, but it might not be appropriate because it will not echo some of the characters. *Echo* means that the characters will appear in your screen as you type them in addition to being transmitted to the remote end. You can use the free EasyTerm package instead. You can download it from http://www.arachnoid.com/easyterm. Make sure to enable the local echo in the properties configuration.

Connect via telnet to www.apache.org (or your favorite Web site) at port 80, and type GET / HTTP/1.0. Press the Enter key twice. You will get the response shown in Listing 1.3.

LISTING **1.3**   Manual HTTP Request

```
 1: bash-2.04$ telnet www.apache.org 80
 2: Trying 64.125.133.20...
 3: Connected to www.apache.org.
 4: Escape character is '^]'.
 5: GET / HTTP/1.0
 6:
 7: HTTP/1.1 200 OK
 8: Date: Sun, 10 Feb 2002 17:53:31 GMT
 9: Server: Apache/2.0.32-dev (Unix)
10: Cache-Control: max-age=86400
11: Expires: Mon, 11 Feb 2002 17:53:31 GMT
12: Accept-Ranges: bytes
13: Content-Length: 8667
14: Connection: close
15: Content-Type: text/html
16:
```

LISTING 1.3   continued

```
17: <!DOCTYPE html PUBLIC "-//W3C//DTD XHTML 1.0 Transitional//EN"
18:                 "http://www.w3.org/TR/xhtml1/DTD/xhtml1-transitional.dtd">
19: <html>
20:   <head>
21: ...
```

If the request is not transmitted by the client before a certain amount of time (timeout), the server will close the connection.

> By using telnet, you can get a better understanding of the underlying HTTP protocol. A lot of the directives in later hours refer to the configuration of specific HTTP headers. It is very common to use telnet or another command-line tool to debug the settings and see whether the headers are being sent correctly.

If you have the lynx command-line browser installed in your Unix system, you can get a similar result by issuing the command

```
lynx -head -dump http://www.apache.org
```

Web Servers History

Previous sections provided you with an understanding of the underlying Web protocols. This section provides you with an historical perspective on the evolution of Web servers.

How It All Got Started

What we know as the World Wide Web started originally in the CERN research center in Switzerland, although the ideas of hypertext (documents with embedded links to other documents) and markup languages date back to the 1950s and 1960s.

In 1990, Tim Berners-Lee wrote the first prototype of a GUI-based hypertext system. One year later, he made the programs available in the Internet via FTP. In November 1992, there were 26 Web servers. NCSA Mosaic, a popular Web browser, was released in 1993 for Unix and was quickly ported to Windows and Macintosh. In 1994, the authors of NCSA Mosaic and the NCSA Web server, who at the time were working for the University of Illinois at Urbana-Champaign, left their work to join a startup called Netscape.

Apache

The NCSA Web server software was very popular. Because many of the original developers of the server left their work to join Netscape, development slowed and eventually
halted. The NCSA server was open source, and users of the software started exchanging
software patches to fix bugs and improve the functionality of the Web server. Eventually
they got together and created The Apache Group, a group of developers working on "a
patchy server," hence the name. The first official release of Apache, version 0.6.2, happened in April 1995. Version 1.0, a major rewrite with a modular architecture, was
released in November 1995. Three major revisions happened in the 1.x series. Version
1.1 was released in July 1996, 1.2 in June 1997, and 1.3 in June 1998. 1.3 was the first
version of Apache to add support for the Windows platform. In the meantime, several
Apache-based servers appeared, mainly to incorporate SSL support. Due to patents and
encryption regulations in the United States, SSL software could not be freely distributed
with Apache. The first alpha release of Apache 2.0, a major rewrite, happened in March
2000. The first general availability release of Apache 2.0 happened in May 2002.

Apache currently powers more than 60% of all the active sites in the Internet
(`http://www.netcraft.com/survey`), as seen in Figure 1.5.

FIGURE 1.5

*Evolution of Web
server market share.*

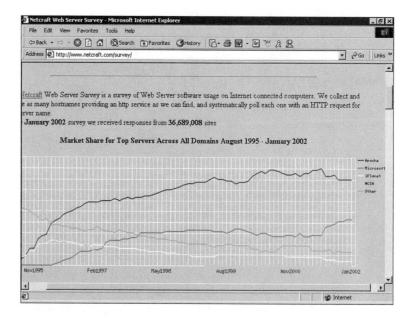

Apache Software Foundation

In 1999, The Apache Group incorporated as the Apache Software Foundation (ASF), a not-for-profit corporation. From the Apache Web site:

> The Apache Software Foundation will provide organizational, legal, and financial support for the Apache open-source software projects. The Foundation ensures the continuity of Apache projects beyond the participation of individual volunteers, enables contributions of intellectual property and financial support on a sound basis, and provides a vehicle for limiting legal exposure while participating in open-source projects.

The Apache Software Foundation provides a common umbrella for a variety of Apache and Web-related technologies. Particularly successful projects are the PHP HTML-embedded language and the Jakarta projects for server-side Java.

Web servers have evolved over time, and Apache and related projects have pioneered many of those advances. Initially the Web server provided only static content. Over time, standards such as CGI (Common Gateway Interface) and Java servlets allowed content to be dynamically generated. Other server-side improvements and languages allowed code to be embedded in HTML pages, which is processed before being sent to the client. Several Apache projects provide support and reference implementations for many of these technologies. The future of the Web seems to be data oriented and will build on technologies such as XML and Web services. Most likely, Apache developers will play an important role in defining those technologies.

Apache Considerations

Like any software product, Apache has advantages and disadvantages. Bear in mind that what makes Apache successful is not so much excelling at one or more specific features, but the right combination of flexibility, performance, and security.

Advantages of Apache

The following are some of the advantages that have contributed to the success of Apache.

Open Source

The Apache license allows for both commercial and noncommercial distribution, modification, and usage. The code is developed by a large, distributed group of talented developers. The open source nature of Apache allows for many other advantages, such as improved stability, security, and customization. You will see how this is so in the following sections.

Stability and Scalability

Apache powers many of the busiest Web sites in the world, such as Amazon.com and MP3.com. These Web sites have strict requirements for uptime and scalability.

Because Apache code is available, and Apache is used widely, the server has been continuously improved and tuned over the years. The underlying operating system is important when running mission-critical Web servers. Apache runs on many flavors of Unix, which is regarded as a stable, dependable OS platform.

Apache 2.0 can be configured as a threaded server, a process-based server, or a mixture of the two. This allows the administrator to balance the performance and stability needs in a particular setup. Process-based servers are stable but scale worse than threaded servers. Well-designed threaded servers can be faster but less stable if a thread misbehaves. Hour 2, "Understanding Apache Internals," explains in detail the differences between threads and processes, and different Web server architectures.

Security

The open source nature of Apache makes it possible for an attacker to analyze the code, searching for possible vulnerabilities or denial-of-services attacks. Fortunately, it also allows developers to do the same. Changes to the source code are watched for insecurities and are subject to extensive peer review. This encourages high coding standards, and security issues are usually detected before they go into the code and become problems.

No serious remote vulnerabilities have been discovered in Apache for years. When problems arise in Apache or one of its modules, fixes are available within hours or days.

If a critical problem or bug is encountered, the availability of source code enables the organization to fix it or hire an expert to fix it. With proprietary servers, depending on the relationship with the vendor, the number of customers affected by the bug, and so on, usually the problem is either solved in future releases of the product, which could be months away, or not solved at all.

Flexibility

Apache can be configured and built in a variety of ways to accommodate different needs. It is possible to create custom builds of Apache that include only the modules needed, reducing server size and increasing security. Additionally Apache allows for dynamic loading of modules, so modules can be compiled as shared libraries and added or removed without the need to recompile the server. It is possible to have several sets of configuration files that can be enabled depending on the role of the server and the load on the network. For example, you can have configuration files for staging and production, and you can control the number of server processes independently.

Performance

Raw performance considerations are relevant in the design of a Web server, but its importance needs to be put in context. An old Pentium machine running Apache and Linux can saturate a ten-megabit network serving static content. Today the bottlenecks are usually in dynamic page generation, application design, and database access. Having said that, Apache performs pretty well even without detailed performance tuning. You can always use Apache for dynamic content generation, and use specific-purpose Web servers for serving the static content such as images.

Multiplatform

Apache runs on nearly every flavor of Unix and Windows, and other operating systems such as OS/390 and BeOS. This allows enterprises and service providers to standardize on a common Web serving platform across a heterogeneous collection of machines, operating systems, and application servers.

Extensible

Apache has a powerful modular API that allows the server to be extended in a variety of ways. Apache 2.0 allows developers to create their own protocol handlers (like FTP or POP3), thus allowing Apache to become a general server framework.

Other modules offer template frameworks, authentication, XML processing, and interfaces to enterprise data sources such as directories and relational databases.

Organizations can leverage the Apache API to build custom modules to interface to their existing infrastructure and legacy systems.

Works with Multiple Languages

Apache works with a variety of development languages, including C, C++, Perl, Python, PHP, Tcl, and Java. It provides a shared, common framework between the languages. Apache 2.0 incorporates the concept of filters, allowing the content generated by a module to be further processed by another before being returned to the browser.

Service Providers

Apache is very popular with Internet and Application Service Providers. This is because Apache provides extensive support for massive virtual hosting, including security features to isolate hosted clients from each other. The text-based configuration and customization make Apache suitable for automated setup and deployment.

Popular; It Is Easy to Get Expertise

Administrative costs are an important part of any software solution. The scarcer certain knowledge and skill sets are, the more expensive it is to hire people with that expertise.

Apache is the most popular server on the Internet. Many Web masters and system administrators are familiar with it. In addition, Apache is commonly used in university projects and research because source code is available. This makes it easy to hire experienced developers and administrators familiar with Apache.

Standards Compliance

One of the goals of Apache is to be standards-compliant, and it has become a reference implementation of the HTTP protocol specification. But the real world is full of buggy browser implementations, incomplete implementations of specification, and so on. Because many Apache developers and users run real-world ISPs and Web sites, Apache has incorporated mechanisms to provide workarounds. The server can behave differently based, for example, on the version of the client browser.

Disadvantages

Apache has its own sets of disadvantages and drawbacks. The following are some of them.

Not a Company

Apache was created by a group of open source developers because they needed a reliable Web server to run their sites. The ASF is a not-for-profit corporation. It does not have support, professional services, or marketing departments. Commercial backing is an important consideration for companies of a certain size that decide to embrace and deploy Apache as their platform of choice across their organization.

Fortunately, companies such as IBM, Red Hat, and Covalent provide the necessary products and services to make Apache ready for the enterprise.

Open Source

Because Apache is open source, the server and related projects are in a continuous state of development. It is difficult to track all libraries and their dependencies. Development pace itself varies greatly over time and there is no product roadmap. Releases of Apache happen only when the server is ready.

Configuration

The learning curve for Apache can be steep. Correct configuration of Apache requires time and skill. There are plenty of Apache books published, several GUI tools are available for configuring Apache, and the Apache reference documentation is quite good.

However, especially for novice users, Apache is still hard to configure and lags behind some of its competitors in ease of use. But as users become experienced with the Apache configuration, they appreciate the ease in which configuration can be replicated and automated.

Performance

There are Web servers that are more lightweight and faster than Apache. The trade-off is usually flexibility and features. Although Apache scales well and can handle high loads, other Web servers might be more appropriate for serving pure static content.

Summary

In this hour, you were introduced to the protocols that enable the World Wide Web, with a special focus on HTTP. You learned a little bit of Internet history and the role of the Apache server. Finally, the advantages and drawbacks of the Apache server were explained. Hour 2 explains the internal architecture of Apache, and provides you with a foundation for your first Apache installation in Hour 3, "Installing and Building Apache."

Q&A

Q Why is it necessary to have timeouts in HTTP?

A The number of simultaneous connections is limited by the operating system resources (process-based servers require one server instance per request). Timeouts are necessary to close inactive connections and avoid denial-of-service scenarios.

Q Can my Web server run on a port other than 80?

A Yes. As an example, in Unix systems, only privileged users can bind to port 80. Ordinary users need to run their Web server on port numbers greater than 1024. This leads to URLs that are a little bit more difficult to remember, such as `http://www.example.com:8080`.

Q Does HTTP need to make a connection for each request?

A HTTP provides mechanisms so that multiple requests can be transmitted via a single TCP connection. This speeds up the process because setting up and closing connections is expensive. In HTTP 1.0, this is done via the `Connection: Keep-Alive` header; in HTTP 1.1, it is the default.

Further Reading

If you want to learn more about the history of the Internet:

`http://www.isoc.org/internet/history`

Two classics to gain a better understanding of the protocols and the design principles behind the Internet:

Interconnections, Second Edition, by Radia Perlman. ISBN 0201634481

Internetworking with TCP/IP Volume I: Principles, Protocols, and Architecture, by Douglas Comer. ISBN 0130183806

The Linux Network Administrator's Guide provides a hands-on introduction to TCP/IP networking:

`http://www.linuxdoc.org/LDP/nag2/index.html`

Making the Web:

`http://www.w3.org/History.html`

The Apache software Foundation:

`http://www.apache.org`

Request For Comments are technical documents describing the various protocols. They can be obtained at `http://www.rfc-editor.org`.

`HTTP: 1954, 2068, 2616, 2145`

`URL: 1738, 1808, 2396`

`SSL/TLS: 2246`

HOUR 2

Understanding Apache Internals

Hour 1, "Apache and the Web," explained how Web servers and browsers communicate with each other. This hour explains how a Web server works internally, with a focus on Apache architecture. Other hours will build on this knowledge. You can find additional information about Apache architecture in Hour 11, "Multi-Processing Modules."

In this hour, you will learn

- How the evolution of the Web affected the design of Web servers
- The modular architecture of the Apache Web server and the benefits that each component provides
- How Apache processes a request internally

Evolution of the Web

Initial Web servers were simple programs. They served only static content, such as images and text. The content of the pages was updated manually or by scripts run periodically. As the popularity of the Web grew, some Web sites found it useful to generate the content dynamically. Dynamic content generation means that the resource being accessed (such as a Web page or an image) is generated on-the-fly, when someone requests it. The generated content usually depends on input provided by the user requesting the page. This enables you to use Web sites to check stock quotes, search for information, buy a book, and send electronic mail via your browser. Dynamic content was generated at first via external programs using the Common Gateway Interface (CGI) protocol. A CGI program accepts requests via its standard input and returns the result via its standard output, which is then transmitted back to the browser. Scripting languages such as Perl quickly emerged as the best choice for CGI development due to their string manipulation and rapid development capabilities. CGI requires starting and stopping a program (for example, a Perl language interpreter) for every request. This overhead can be significant in high-traffic sites, and affects both the load of the server and the speed with which the request can be served.

The next step in Web content generation was to integrate a scripting language as part of the Web server itself. Instead of creating an interpreter every time a request is received (as CGI requires), an interpreter that processes the requests could be embedded in the Web server. The interpreter is persistent between requests, allowing it to keep database connections open, cache frequently requested data, preload required libraries, and so on.

Additionally, an embedded interpreter can process HTML pages before transmitting them back to the client. Scripting code can be embedded directly in the HTML page and executed when the page is requested; the results are then substituted and the final HTML page is returned to the browser.

Java has emerged in the past few years as the preferred Web development language in corporate environments. Servlets are Java programs that can process HTTP requests via a standard API. A Java servlet engine waits for requests, executes the appropriate Java code, and returns the result. Java has its own standard way of embedding code in HTML pages, called JavaServer Pages. In production systems, a Java servlet engine does not usually serve HTTP requests directly, mainly for performance reasons. Servlet engines work in conjunction with Apache. Apache can be configured to serve the static content and forward dynamic content to the servlet engine via a special Apache module called a *connector*.

Apache Architecture

This hour explains how the Apache Web server is internally organized to allow for all the different kinds of Web development approaches mentioned earlier. Apache is not a monolithic server. It is composed of several pieces or modules. New modules can be added to provide enhanced functionality, and existing modules can be removed to reduce the size of the server and improve performance.

Figure 2.1 describes the general architecture of Apache 2.0. The different components are explained in detail in their own sections. The figure is only an outline, but should give you a good idea of the server structure.

Multi-Processing Modules (MPMs) define the basic processing model of Apache (that is, process-based or threaded) and take care of the initial connection setup. Protocol modules implement different protocols like HTTP or FTP. Different extension modules can manipulate the request via filters and hooks. Both mechanisms are explained in detail later on in this hour. Finally, other modules provide the content or relay the request to an external program (such as a CGI or an application server).

Multi-Processing Modules

Multi-Processing Modules (MPMs) specify the execution model of the Apache Web server. They allow Apache to act as a process-based server, a thread-based server, or a combination of both. Performance, scalability, stability, and platform support considerations drive the choice of an MPM. Figure 2.2 shows a comparison of the three server architectures mentioned.

Process-Based Server

In a process-based server, a server forks several children. *Forking* means that a parent process makes identical copies of itself, called *children*.

Each one of the children can serve a request independent of the others. This approach has the advantage of improved stability: If one of the children misbehaves, it can be killed without affecting the rest of the server. For example, if one of the children leaks memory with every request, it can be destroyed after *n* requests have been served and a new child can be spawned. The increased stability comes with a performance penalty: Each one of the children occupies additional memory and there is a certain amount of time spent in context switching. *Context switching* is a procedure that the operating system must carry out to assign processor time to each of the children. Context switching can be an expensive operation in terms of performance, especially in heavily loaded servers with limited memory. Another disadvantage of processes is that they are isolated from each other, making interprocess communication and data sharing difficult.

Apache provides a prefork MPM that allows it to perform as a process-based server. *Prefork* means that children can be forked at startup, instead of when a request comes. The administrator can configure several parameters, such as the number of children to fork at startup and the maximum number of possible children.

Figure 2.1
Apache 2.0 architecture.

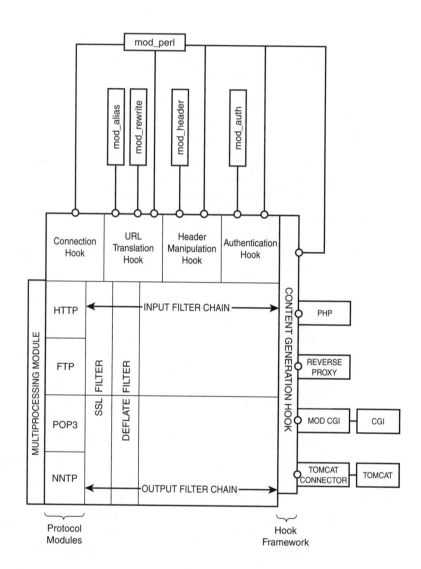

FIGURE 2.2
Server architecture comparison.

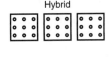

Threaded Server

Threads are similar to processes, but they can share memory and data with other threads. This has the advantage that there is no context switching (threads are part of the same process), and the disadvantage that poorly written code can take the whole server down with it. This is possible because a misbehaving thread can overwrite and corrupt data and code that belongs to other threads.

The Apache MPM for the Windows platform is an example of a threaded server MPM.

Hybrid Server

Both threaded and process-based servers have their own sets of advantages and disadvantages. The Apache developers created a threaded MPM that allows for a mixed approach. A server can spawn different processes, each one of them containing a number of threads.

Additional MPMs

It is possible to create other MPMs, such as the Perchild MPM.

The Perchild MPM maintains several processes running under different user IDs. Each of the processes will serve requests for specific virtual hosts. This allows ISPs to serve different customers with the same server, yet be able to keep their processes and data isolated from each other, mainly for security reasons.

There are additional MPMs to support specific platforms, such as BeOS and OS/2. From time to time, Apache developers create experimental MPMs to test new ideas, such as the leader-follower MPM.

MPM Selection and Compatibility

Although MPM selection depends on many factors, including support for specific third-party modules and functionality, some MPMs perform better in certain platforms. Threaded MPM is preferred in most Unix platforms including Linux and Solaris. Windows has its own MPM.

As a general rule of thumb, third-party modules should run in a similar way, independent of the MPM in place. However, some of the modules being ported from Apache 1.3 might not work well under a threaded MPM. Other modules specifically designed for Apache 2.0 that take advantage of threads might have less functionality when running with a process-based MPM. You can find more information about MPMs in Hours 3, "Installing and Building Apache," and 11.

Hooks

A *hook* is a mechanism that enables Apache modules to modify the behavior of the server or other modules. The server or a module can declare hooks, and other modules can then register interest in them. When the server reaches that point, the registered modules are called one after another until one of them signals successful completion. Hooks correspond to events or phases in the processing of the request.

Some of the hooks that Apache provides are

- **Connection phase:** Client establishing a connection. This can be useful to implement additional protocols in Apache.
- **Authorization:** Protecting access to resources. Different authorization modules can register for this hook. One module can base the authorization decision on network information (such as the IP address of the client). Another module can make the decision based on the type of resource being accessed, and so on.
- **Header modification:** Certain modules might want to analyze or change headers provided by the client or add new headers to the response.
- **Content handling:** The default behavior in Apache is to return the document requested, if it exists on disk. A module can use this hook to provide dynamically generated content.

Each of the modules that registered for a certain hook can return different status codes when it is called. The status code indicates whether everything went okay, there was an error, or the module does not want to handle the request. If a module declines the request, it allows the next module that expressed interest in that hook to be executed. For example, a translation module might want to perform on-the-fly translation of documents stored in disk. If the document is, say, in Spanish, the translation module reads and translates the document to English, returning a success status. If the document is in English, and thus does not need translation, the module can return a declined status code and let the default content handler return the file on disk.

Multi-Protocol Support

Apache 2.0 can be extended to process protocols other than HTTP. Apache provides hooks so that module authors can take over the connection phase. This means that

Apache, since version 2.0, is more than a Web server—it is a generic server framework. By building a server on top of Apache, a developer can take advantage of a solid, portable infrastructure, an extension mechanism, and the possibility of using many other third-party modules that exist for Apache.

`mod_ftp` and `mod_pop3` are two examples of protocol modules currently available for Apache. `mod_ftp` is a proprietary module developed by Covalent technologies that provides the functionality of an FTP server.

`mod_pop3` is an open source implementation of the Post Office Protocol version 3, an Internet protocol used for retrieving mail from a central server.

Please refer to Hour 24 for additional information.

Content-Handling Modules

Content handlers and generators are modules that provide the content that will be returned to the browser. Apache includes a default content handler that returns the content of files on disk. PHP and `mod_perl` are examples of content handler modules. They allow pages to be dynamically generated by embedded scripting engines. In the case of `mod_perl`, applications can be written in the Perl scripting language.

`mod_perl` is discussed in Hour 20. PHP allows HTML pages to contain embedded code. That embedded PHP code is executed and the results are substituted in the page. PHP is described in Hour 19.

PHP and `mod_perl` are not only content-handling modules. `mod_perl` exposes the full Apache API, and full-featured Apache modules can be written entirely in Perl.

PHP can also filter content produced by other modules looking for and executing embedded PHP code, as explained in the "Filters" section later in this hour.

Connector Modules

Sometimes the content is produced not by an Apache module but by an external program, such as an application server or servlet engine. In such cases, a need exists to transfer the request information from Apache to the external application. The external application will process the request and return a response to Apache.

If that external application is in a different machine, there might be additional requirements for encryption or load balancing.

The BEA WebLogic application server and the Tomcat servlet engine are two examples of applications that need a connector module.

Filters

You can think of the filtering architecture in Apache as a factory assembly line. Filters are workers in the factory, and requests and responses are the items traveling in the line. Each filter processes the content and passes the result to the next filter. Filters can process the information in a variety of ways:

- **Encryption:** Secure Sockets Layer (SSL) is a protocol used to encrypt and secure communications between browsers and servers. The SSL protocol is described in detail in Hour 17, "Setting Up a Secure Server." SSL for Apache 2.0 is implemented as a filter. It is possible to add SSL support to other protocols simply by inserting the SSL filter before information is read from or written to the network.

- **Compression:** If the server detects that the browser supports compressed content, it can compress the data before sending it to the browser, reducing network bandwidth. Compression can be optional, to avoid processing already compressed content such as certain image files.

- **Watermarking:** A module could be developed to process word processor documents and add a serial identification number that contains information about the user who downloaded it.

- **Virus scanning:** Documents served by Apache can be scanned for viruses or malicious code. With the multi-protocol nature of Apache, it is possible to use the same code to scan HTML pages served via HTTP and mail messages downloaded via a POP3 module.

- **Session tracking:** A session tracking filter could rewrite URLs on-the-fly to add session information. This can be done independently of how the content was generated (a Java servlet, PHP, CGI program, and so on).

Access/Authentication/Authorization Modules

Access, authentication, and authorization form an important module category.

These modules provide mechanisms to authenticate the identity of a user and to restrict access to specific resources. Modules can restrict access based on the identity of the user, network information (such as the client IP address or protocol used), the type of resource being accessed, or many other parameters.

There are Apache authentication modules for different back ends, including Unix-style password files, LDAP, Berkeley-style databases, Oracle, Network Information Service (NIS), and many others.

You can learn more about access, authentication, and authorization modules in Apache in Hour 7, "Restricting Access." Additional modules can be found in Hour 24, "Apache Software Foundation Projects."

Apache Portable Runtime

Apache runs on a great variety of platforms, ranging from Unix-like operating systems to the latest Windows versions and anything in between, including BeOS and Mac OS X.

Most operating systems offer a similar set of capabilities for networking, interprocess communication, shared memory access, and so on, but they are implemented in different ways. Even in the Unix world, the APIs (Application Programming Interfaces) that are supposed to be common vary in subtle and incompatible ways from vendor to vendor and even between releases of the same operating system.

Previous versions of Apache had to deal with this explicitly. Programmers needed to provide different code depending on the platform. This code was surrounded by preprocessor directives so that when Apache was compiled for a specific platform, the right code would be selected and included. This proved not to be the best solution. Code was not as clear as it could be, and changes for one platform tended to break things in another.

Apache developers changed the way they approached the problem with version 2.0 of the server. They abstracted all the platform-dependent functionality into a common library, the Apache Portable Runtime (APR).

Apache programmers can write software using this library, which runs the same regardless of the underlying platform.

This makes the code clearer and easier to maintain. Platform-specific optimizations can be encapsulated into the library. Developers can port Apache to new platforms simply by adding support for APR.

APR is divided into core libraries (fundamental portable functions) and APR util (other code that needs to be portable).

APR core covers the following, among many other areas:

- File creation and manipulation
- Socket programming
- Threads and processes
- String management
- Shared memory

APR util covers these areas:

- DBM database abstraction layer
- XML library
- Digest
- Base64 encoding

APR is used in projects other than Apache, such as the Subversion control system, which can be found in `http://subversion.tigris.org`.

> The Apache developers considered existing portability toolkits before decid-
> ing to write their own. The main candidates were the Netscape Portable
> Runtime (NSPR) and the Adaptive Communication Environment (ACE)
> toolkit. NSPR could not be used because of license conflicts that were not
> resolved until it was too late. Additionally, NSPR covered many other topics
> Apache developers were not interested in. ACE is C++-centric and Apache is
> written in C.

A Day in the Life of a Request

You have seen in previous sections how Apache can act as an FTP server or POP3 server. This section deals with the case in which Apache acts as a pure Web server.

It covers step-by-step what occurs from the time Apache is started until a request is suc-cessfully fulfilled. Figure 2.3 shows a diagram of the request cycle.

FIGURE 2.3
Apache request lifecycle.

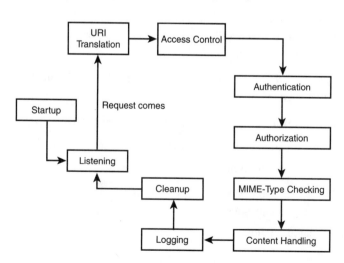

Apache Startup

Apache reads its configuration and loads the specified modules and required libraries. At configuration time, modules register their interest with Apache to act as filters, use certain hooks, and so on. Apache keeps tracks of this information for later use.

Request Process

Apache starts listening for requests on the specified port. At some point in time, a client sends an HTTP request to the Apache server. The Apache MPM module in place selects the thread or process that is going to handle the request and passes the request to it. The HTTP protocol module checks that the request is compliant with the protocol and processes it.

Apache examines the URL being accessed and—based on its configuration—decides on the filters and modules that will process the request.

Checking for Hooks

The request goes through several phases in Apache, each one with associated hooks. Some of these phases and hooks are described in the following list.

- **URI translation phase:** The URI translation phase translates the request from the URI to a server resource. For example, when serving static content, Apache uses that information to determine which file to return. Other modules, such as mod_rewrite, can manipulate the URL in complex ways, as described in Hour 22.

- **Access control phase:** The access control phase determines access to the resource based on network information of the client, such as the remote IP address.

- **Authentication:** The identity of the remote user can be verified against a variety of backend authorization systems such as an LDAP directory or a password file.

- **Authorization:** Determines whether the user is authorized to access the resource.

- **MIME-type checking:** Determines the content type of the resource being accessed. This can usually be determined from the file extension, but is not always the case. This phase is important because other filters or modules can be configured to process all resources of a certain type (such as images or XML files).

- **Filters:** Filters can be inserted to process the incoming request or the outgoing response. For example, an SSL filter could be inserted in the connection phase and at the end of the response phase to provide encryption. Filters can be automatically inserted by modules or explicitly by the system administrator using the configuration file.

- **Content handler:** In this step, a response is constructed and returned to the client. The default behavior in Apache is to look for the requested content on disk. Apache returns the file contents or an error if the file could not be found.

- **Logging:** After the request has been served, logging modules can store information about the request.

- **Cleanup:** In this phase, Apache frees resources used to process the current request and prepares to serve the next one.

Summary

In this hour, you learned about the internal architecture of Apache and its extension mechanisms: filter and hooks. This understanding will be necessary in the hours that cover building Apache, tuning server performance, and filter configuration.

Q&A

Q What are the advantages and disadvantages of using hooks and filters?

A Filters can slow down the processing of the request, but allow modules to process the content created by each other. Hooks allow modules to modify the request URL, headers, and so on, but not the actual content. Certain modules (compression modules) must be implemented as filters, others (authorization modules) need only hooks, and some of them (scripting language engines such as PHP) need both.

Q Do threaded servers scale better than process-based servers?

A In general, yes, but this depends largely on the design of the server architecture, the underlying OS platform, and the specific machine. Threaded servers do not spend time in context switching, but they need to use locking mechanisms. *Locking mechanisms* are software procedures used to synchronize threads and protect them from simultaneously accessing certain resources. A thread will lock a certain resource until it finishes working with it, avoiding another thread interrupting it in mid-process. A well-designed threaded server will minimize the number of locks necessary and its duration. The underlying OS libraries might have better support for processes or threads, influencing the server model choice. Finally, a machine running a process-based server might perform okay, but if that machine runs out of memory it might need to use disk space (swap) to perform context switching. Disk access is several orders of magnitude slower than memory access and should be avoided at all costs.

Q How does Apache architecture compare to other Web servers?

A Both iPlanet (formerly Netscape) and Microsoft provide server-side APIs to build modules, called NSAPI (Netscape Server API) and ISAPI (Internet Information Server API). Both servers provide a mechanism similar to hooks this way.

Other frameworks, such as the Tomcat servlet engine, provide filtering mechanisms so that the output of one servlet can be processed by another one.

Quiz

1. What are the advantages and disadvantages of using CGI versus an embedded interpreter?

2. What are the main processing models available for Apache?

3. What are the extension mechanisms for Apache?

Quiz Answers

1. They are mainly related to performance. Embedded interpreters do not have startup and initialization costs for every request. Data can be cached between requests. In threaded Web servers, resources such as database connections can be shared between scripts. CGI scripts have the advantage that they do not leak resources because they are destroyed after every request and the resources are freed.

2. Process-based server, threaded server, and hybrid server. An additional MPM, per-child, is described in Hour 11.

3. Apache modules can extend the server via hooks and filters. Hooks are well-defined points in the life of a request (such as authorization hook and connection hook). Filters allow modules to modify the content submitted by the client (input filters) or produced by other modules (output filters).

Further Reading

Most technologies mentioned in this hour are covered later in this book: CGIs in Hour 6, Tomcat in Hour 7, PHP in Hour 19, mod_perl in Hour 20, SSL in Hour 17, and so on.

Multi-processing modules are explained in detail in Hour 11. Hour 24 covers multi-protocol modules such as those for FTP and POP3.

Additional information about Apache request cycle:

```
http://httpd.apache.org/docs-2.0/developer/request.html
```

Apache Portable Runtime home page:

`http://apr.apache.org`

Netscape Portable Runtime:

`http://www.mozilla.org/projects/nspr`

Adaptive Communication Environment:

`http://www.cs.wustl.edu/~schmidt/ACE.html`

Apache modules repository:

`http://modules.apache.org`

HOUR 3

Installing and Building Apache

Previous hours introduced you to the architecture of the Web and Apache. At this point, you are ready to install Apache and get to work. In this hour, you will learn

- How to download, compile, and install a basic Apache server on Unix
- How to download and install a basic Apache server on Windows operating systems

This hour also covers binary, source, and prepackaged installations.

Choosing the Appropriate Installation Method

Several options are available to get a basic Apache installation in place. Apache is open source, meaning that you can have access to the full source code of the software, which in turn enables you to build your own custom sever. Additionally, pre-built Apache binary distributions are available for most modern Unix platforms. Finally, Apache comes already bundled with a variety of Linux distributions, and commercial versions can be purchased from software vendors such as Covalent Technologies and IBM.

Building from Source

Building from source gives you the greatest flexibility, enabling you to build a custom server, remove modules you do not need, and extend the server with third-party modules. Building Apache from source code enables you to easily upgrade to the latest versions and quickly apply security patches. Updated versions from vendors usually take days or weeks to appear.

Building Apache from the source code is not that difficult for simple installations, but can grow in complexity when third-party modules and libraries are involved. Hour 18, "Extending Apache," explains how to extend Apache.

Installing a Binary

Unix binary installations are available from vendors and can also be downloaded from the Apache Software Foundation Web site. They provide a convenient way to install Apache for first-time users.

Third-party commercial vendors provide prepackaged Apache installations together with an application server, additional modules, support, and so on.

The ASF provides an installer for Windows systems—a platform where a compiler is not as commonly available as in Unix systems.

Apache Version Naming

Starting with Apache 2.0, Apache server releases are named with three digits and an optional qualifier (*alpha* or *beta*). The first digit refers to the main Apache release version, the second digit to the major revision, and the third digit to the minor revision. A qualifier of *alpha* means that the code has not reached production-level quality and the feature set is subject to change. In general, only developers working on the Apache code base or advanced users curious about the latest features should run alpha code. A *beta* version means that although the code is still not production-ready, the feature set is more or less complete and the server is considered stable enough for general testing. A sample Apache release name is 2.0.28-beta.

As a side note, Apache developers take great pride in the quality of their code. As a result, beta versions of Apache are much more stable and feature-rich than commercial product beta software. The drawback is that sometimes the development cycle takes way too long.

Installing Apache on Unix

This section explains how to install Apache on Unix and Unix-like systems such as Solaris, Linux, and FreeBSD.

Checking Whether Apache Is Already Installed in Your System

If you are running a modern Linux distribution, chances are that Apache is already installed in your system. Try the following at the command-line prompt:

```
# httpd -v
```

Because some distributions name the Apache binary httpd2, you can also try the following:

```
# httpd2 -v
```

If Apache is installed and the binary is in your path, you will get a message with the version and build time:

```
Server version: Apache/2.0.28
Server built:   Dec 29 2001 10:32:01
```

Otherwise, you will get command not found or a similar message. It might be that Apache is already installed but is in a different path or with a different binary name, such as httpd2. Check whether /usr/local/apache2/ or /etc/httpd2 exists and contains a valid Apache 2.0 installation.

This books covers Apache 2.0, so you must make sure that this is the version installed in your server. An existing 1.3 Apache installation is likely to interfere with your new Apache if the older installation runs at startup. Make sure that either the package is removed from the operating system or the startup script, if any, is disabled. For example, in most Linux distributions, this means modifying the startup scripts at /etc/rc.d/. Apache 1.3 and 2.0 can coexist and run simultaneously if they use different IP address and port combinations, as explained in Hour 4.

If Apache 2.0 is already installed in your system, you can skip the following sections and go directly to Hour 4, "Getting Started with Apache." You can always read this hour later if you decide to build your own server.

3

Installing from Source

The steps necessary to successfully install Apache from source are

1. Downloading the software
2. Running the configuration script
3. Compiling the code and installing it

These steps are described now in detail.

Downloading the Apache Source Code

The official Apache download site is located at http://www.apache.org/dist/httpd.
You can find several Apache versions, packaged with different compression methods.
The distribution files are first packed with the Unix tar utility and then compressed
either with the gzip tool or the compress utility. Download the .tar.gz version if you
have the gunzip utility installed in your system. This utility comes installed by default in
open source operating systems such as FreeBSD and Linux. Download the tar.Z file if
gunzip is not present in your system, such as in the default installation of many commercial Unix operating systems.

> The gzip, gunzip, and gtar programs are useful tools. The Gzip Web site at
> http://www.gzip.org provides you with links to the source code and bina-
> ries for Unix platforms such as Solaris, AIX, and HP-UX. If gunzip is not
> installed but gzip is available in your system, you can use gzip -d instead.

The file you want to download will be named something similar to httpd-2_0_ver-
sion.tar.Z or httpd-2_0_version.tar.gz where version is the most recent release
version of Apache.

Uncompressing the Source Code

If you downloaded the tarball compressed with gzip (tar.gz suffix), you can uncompress it using the gunzip utility (part of the gzip distribution).

> *Tarball* is a commonly used nickname for software packed using the tar
> utility.

You can uncompress and unpack the software by typing the following command:

```
# gunzip < httpd-2_0*.tar.gz | tar xvf -
```

If you downloaded the tarball compressed with compress (tar.Z suffix), you can issue the following command:

```
# cat httpd-2_0*.tar.Z | uncompress | tar xvf -
```

Uncompressing the tarball creates a structure of directories, with the top-level directory named httpd-2.0_version. Change your current directory to the top-level directory.

Configuring the Software

You can specify which features the resulting binary will have by using the configure script, in the top-level distribution directory. By default, Apache will be compiled with a set of standard modules compiled statically and will be installed in the /usr/local/apache2 directory. If you are happy with these settings, you can issue the following command to configure Apache:

```
#./configure
```

For the remainder of the book, it is assumed that you compiled Apache with loadable module support and built most of the modules as such. This, combined with the Apache extension utility (apxs), will enable you to extend the server later with third-party modules without the need to recompile, as described in Hour 18.

To configure Apache this way, issue the following command:

```
#./configure --enable-so --enable-mods-shared=most
```

If you are installing Apache as a normal user and you don't have write permissions on /usr/local/, or you simply want to install Apache on a different location, you can specify an alternative location using the --prefix option. For example, the following line:

```
#./configure --enable-so --enable-mods-shared=most
➥   --prefix=/home/username/apache2
```

will compile Apache to be installed in the home directory of the *username* user.

The purpose of the configure script is to figure out everything related to finding libraries, compile time options, platform-specific differences, and so on, and to create a set of special files called *makefiles*. Makefiles contain instructions to perform different tasks, called *targets*, such as building Apache. These files will then be read by the Unix make utility, which will carry on those tasks. If everything goes well, after executing configure, you will see a set of messages related to the different checks just performed and you will be ready to compile the software.

3

Compiling and Installing Apache

The make utility reads the information stored in the makefiles and builds the server and modules. Type make at the command line to build Apache. You will see several messages indicating the compilation progress. After compilation is finished, you can install Apache by typing make install. The Apache distribution files will be copied to /usr/local/apache2 or the target directory specified with the --prefix switch.

Apache Compilation Options

The Apache configuration script, configure, can take additional options. Many of them are irrelevant for most users, either because they are rarely used or they relate to building Apache distribution packages. A number of them deal with enabling or disabling specific modules, and those are explained in detail in Hour 18. Table 3.1 describes the most useful configuration options. You can get a complete listing by issuing the ./configure --help command.

TABLE 3.1 Configuration Options

--with-mpm=*mpm*	Specifies the Apache Multi-Processing Module. If this option is not specified, the default MPM for the platform will be compiled in. In Unix, the value for *mpm* can be either worker, perchild, or prefork. MPMs are discussed in Hour 11, "Multi-Processing Modules."
--enable-so	Enables loadable module support.
--prefix=*path*	Apache will be installed relative to the value of the *path* directory. By default, Apache will be installed in /usr/local/apache2.
--enable-*module* --disable-*module*	Enables or disables the specified *module*. Check Hour 18 for a complete module listing and descriptions.
--enable-modules=*list* --enable-mods-shared=*list*	Another way of specifying which modules to build, either compiled into the server or as shared libraries. Both switches can take either a list of modules, all (all modules bundled with Apache), or most (includes the majority of the modules you will need).

Selecting the Appropriate MPM

Hour 11 explains the role of Multi-Processing Modules. Table 3.2 shows the relationship between platforms and MPMs.

TABLE 3.2 MPMs and Platforms

Platform	Available MPMs
Windows NT/2000/XP	`winnt`
BeOS	`Beos`
OS/2	`mpmt_os2`
Linux	`worker`, `prefork` (default), `perchild`
Solaris	`worker`, `prefork` (default), `perchild`
HP-UX	`worker`, `prefork` (default), `perchild`
AIX	`worker` (recommended), `prefork` (default), `perchild`
Mac OS X	`worker`, `prefork` (default), `perchild`
FreeBSD	`worker`, `prefork` (default), `perchild`
Cygwin	`prefork` (default)

In the Windows, BeOS, and OS/2 platforms, there is no choice of MPM and the appropriate one will be selected. In Unix platforms, the default is the `prefork` MPM, although the `worker` MPM is probably a better choice, except for some platforms such as FreeBSD. The Cygwin platform supported only the `prefork` MPM at the time this book was being written. Table 3.2 gives you information about which MPM modules are available for a specific platform. Further information on which MPM to choose, their advantages and disadvantages can be found in Hour 11.

Installing Binaries

This section explains how to install a pre-built Apache server on Unix platforms.

Binaries from the Apache Web Site

You can download binaries for different platforms from the Apache Web site at `http://www.apache.org/dist/httpd/binaries`. Check whether binaries for your platform are available. You can download and uncompress the tarball as described in the previous section. In this case, the configuration and compilation steps are not necessary. You can install the software by executing the `install-bindist` script. You can pass an optional argument, the target installation directory. Otherwise, the software will be installed in `/usr/local/apache2`.

Distribution-Specific Packages

Operating system vendors recognize that Apache is an important server software component and either include it by default or make it available in a distribution-specific format.

For Linux distributions based on the RPM format, you can query whether Apache 2.0 is already installed by issuing this command:

```
#rpm -q apache2
```

If Apache 2.0 is not available, you can go to the distribution vendor Web site, download the Apache 2.0 RPM, and install it executing the following command as root:

```
#rpm -i apache2*.rpm
```

Apache 2.0 is part of the FreeBSD and other BSD flavors ports collection. Just change to the appropriate directory and type make install. That command will download the source code, and build and install the server.

You can get Apache binaries and packages for Solaris platforms at http://www.sunfreeware.com. Solaris 8 already bundles an Apache 1.3 version, and future releases will likely include Apache 2.0.

Building from CVS

CVS stands for *concurrent versioning system* and is a popular software development tool that enables programmers to simultaneously work on the same code base, keeping track of changes and revisions and helping to resolve conflicts in the code. Apache is an open source project and makes the source code available via a public CVS server. You can check out any particular release of the code or the latest, unreleased version this way. Compiling and building from CVS is an advanced topic and not recommended for beginners. The following sections comprise a step-by-step guide to compiling Apache from CVS.

The CVS Client

You need the cvs command-line utility to connect to the Apache CVS repository. It is available by default in most Linux distributions and other open source operating systems such as FreeBSD. If cvs is not available for your system, check your vendor package repository or download and compile the source from http://www.cvshome.org.

Checking Out the Source

The main Apache CVS repository is at cvs.apache.org. The first step will be to log in to that server:

```
# cvs -d :pserver:anoncvs@cvs.apache.org:/home/cvspublic login
```

You will be prompted for a password; use anoncvs.

To retrieve the Apache source code (*check out* the code in the jargon), issue the following command:

```
# cvs -d :pserver:anoncvs@cvs.apache.org:/home/cvspublic co httpd-2.0
```

The `httpd-2.0` directory that contains the Apache source code will be created. The packaged source tarball for Apache includes a couple of libraries that are not present in CVS `apr` and `apr-util`. Change your directory to `httpd-2.0/srclib/` and execute the following commands:

```
# cvs -d :pserver:anoncvs@cvs.apache.org:/home/cvspublic co apr
```

```
# cvs -d :pserver:anoncvs@cvs.apache.org:/home/cvspublic co apr-util
```

Building the `configure` Script

You need to change your current directory to `httpd-2.0` and execute the `./buildconf` command. That will create a `configure` script. From this step on, you can follow the instructions in the "Building Apache from Source" section earlier in the hour. The `buildconf` script requires the `autoconf` utility, which is either already included with your system or can be downloaded from `http://www.gnu.org/software/autoconf`.

Check Out a Specific Version of Apache

You can check out a specific version of Apache by using the `-r` *tag* option to the `cvs` command-line utility. For example, this line

```
# cvs -d :pserver:anoncvs@cvs.apache.org:/home/cvspublic
➥    co -r APACHE_2_0_28 httpd-2.0
```

will check out the source code for Apache 2.0.28.

Installing Apache on Windows

Apache 2.0 runs on most Windows platforms and offers increased performance and stability over previous 1.3 Windows versions. You can build Apache from source, but because not many Windows users have compilers, this section deals with the binary installer.

Before installing Apache, you probably want to make sure that you are not currently running a Web server in that machine, such as a previous version of Apache, Microsoft Internet Information Server, or Microsoft Personal Web Server. You might want to uninstall or otherwise disable existing servers. You can run several Web servers but they will need to run in different address and port combinations.

You can download an installer in the MSI format from `http://www.apache.org/dist/httpd/binaries/win32`.

After you download the installer, double-click on the file to start the installation process. You will get a welcome screen, as shown in Figure 3.1, and you will be prompted to accept the Apache license. You can also find a copy of the license in the Apache Software Foundation Web site (http://www.apache.org) and in Appendix A, "Apache License," of this book. Basically the license says that you can do whatever you want with the software—including proprietary modifications— except claim that you wrote it.

FIGURE 3.1

Windows installer welcome screen.

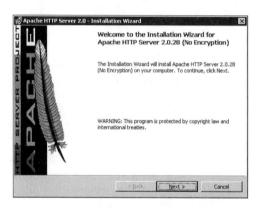

After you accept the license, you are presented with a brief introduction to Apache. Following that, you are asked to provide the installation process with basic information about your computer, as shown in Figure 3.2. This includes the network domain name, the fully qualified domain name (FQDN) for the server, and the administrator's e-mail address. The server name will be the name that your clients will use to access your server, and the administrator e-mail address will be added to error messages so that visitors know how to contact you when something goes wrong. Additionally, you can install Apache as a service or require it to be started manually. Installing Apache as a service will cause it to run every time Windows is started, and you can control it through the usual Windows service administration tools. Choose this option if you plan to run Apache in a production environment or otherwise require Apache to run continuously. Installing Apache for the current user will require you to start Apache manually and set the default port Apache listens to requests to 8080. Choose this option if you use Apache for testing or if you already have a Web server running on port 80. Hour 4 provides further information on the different ways of controlling Apache in Windows.

The following screen enables you to choose the type of installation, as shown in Figure 3.3. *Typical installation* means that Apache binaries and documentation will be installed, but headers and libraries will not. This is the best option to choose unless you plan to compile your own modules.

A *custom installation* enables you to choose whether to install header files or documentation. After selecting the target installation directory, which defaults to c:\Program

Files\Apache Group, the program will proceed with the installation process. If everything goes well, you will be presented with the final screen shown in Figure 3.4.

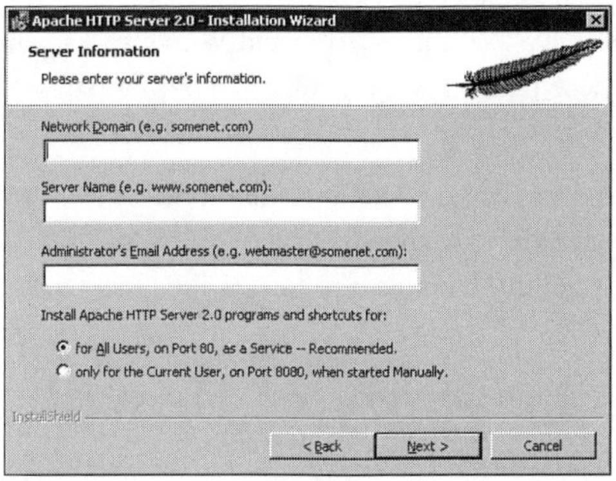

FIGURE 3.2

Basic information screen.

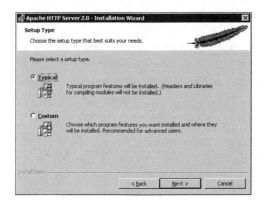

FIGURE 3.3

Installation type selection screen.

FIGURE 3.4

Successful installation screen.

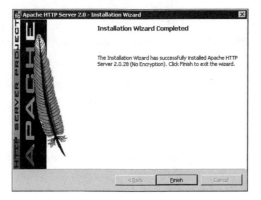

3

Notes About the Windows Installer

At the time this book was written, Apache 2.0 did not support Windows consumer platforms such as Windows 95 and Windows 98. The Apache developers will concentrate on
the server platforms such as Windows 2000 and Windows XP, and when Apache has
been optimized for these platforms, they might attempt to support consumer versions of
Windows.

Additionally, the current releases of the installer at the time of writing did not contain
support for encryption, although future releases will likely include the OpenSSL libraries
by default. Hour 17, "Setting Up a Secure Server," explains the SSL protocol.

Verifying the Integrity of Downloaded Software

When downloading binaries from the Internet, you must make sure that the software is
indeed what you expect it to be. If the Web site has been compromised, the software
could have been replaced by one containing viruses or backdoors. Apache Software
Foundation members digitally sign the released software, so you can check that an
attacker has not modified it. The signatures are contained in the files with asc extensions.
You can find instructions on how to check the validity of the signatures at
http://httpd.apache.org/docs-2.0/install.html#download.

If you are installing Apache from an RPM provided by your vendor, there is a similar
mechanism to check its integrity and authenticity with the -K option, as shown here:

```
# rpm -v -K package.rpm
```

Commercial Alternatives

In addition to the operating-system-vendor-supplied Apache versions, a number of companies offer servers based on Apache.

- **IBM:** The latest IBM HTTP server is based on Apache 2.0 with additional mod-
  ules added (such as encryption). The IBM HTTP server is also part of the
  Websphere Application Server suite. You can find more about this server at
  http://www-4.ibm.com/software/webservers/httpservers.
- **Covalent:** Covalent offers Enterprise Ready Server (ERS), based on Apache 2.0.
  ERS includes support for SSL, FTP, and LDAP, and includes a graphical

management interface component. You can find more about ERS at
`http://www.covalent.net`.

- **Red Hat:** Although at the time this book was written, Red Hat did not offer a 2.0-based Web server, it is likely to do so in the future as part of its secure and commerce servers. More information about Red Hat's Apache products can be found at `http://www.redhat.com/software/apache/index.html`.

Summary

This hour explained different ways of getting an Apache 2.0 server installed on your Unix or Windows machine. It covered both binary and source installation and explained the basic build time options. Hour 16, "Tuning Apache," covers additional build configuration options and tools. The lesson in Hour 4 will guide you through the different steps necessary to get the Apache server you just installed up and running so that you can start serving pages.

Q&A

Q Are there any tools available to help with Apache compilation?

A Several programs, usually referred to as *compilation kits*, are designed to make it easier to compile Apache and additional modules. They present a text interface from which you can specify the desired options and modules to enable. The compilation tool takes care of downloading and patching the necessary software, and configuring and building it. You can find one of these tools at `http://www.apachetoolbox.com`, although it only supports 1.3 at the time of writing this book.

Q Why do some Apache releases seem to be missing?

A When Apache developers agree it is time to make a new release of the server, they mark the sources with the release name and number and proceed to create the source and binary distribution packages, test them, place them in the Web site, and announce it to the world. If a severe problem is found in that testing, the release process is stopped until the problems are fixed. To avoid confusion, a new release name and number will be applied to the next release attempt that includes the new fixes. That is the reason why, for example, there were no public releases between Apache 2.0.16 and 2.0.28. You can always access any version using the CVS repository, as explained earlier in this hour.

Q How can I start a clean build?

If you need to build a new Apache from source and do not want the result of earlier builds to affect the new one, it is always a good idea to run the `make clean` command. That will take care of cleaning up any existing binaries, intermediate object files, and so on.

Quiz

1. Why is it important to make sure that an existing Apache server is not enabled?
2. How can you specify the location to install Apache?

Quiz Answers

1. Only one server can be listening at the same IP and port combination at any given moment. Having previous versions of Apache running will prevent new ones from running and will likely confuse you.
2. You can use the `--prefix` option of the `configure` script. If an existing installation is present at that location, the configuration files will be preserved but the binaries will be replaced.

Further Reading

By far the easiest way to get started with Apache is to use the Apache server included with your operating system (if possible). As you become more experienced with Apache and you need to customize or extend it in particular ways, it is useful to build your own version from source. Hour 18 deals with extending Apache and describes several utilities that can help you do so.

The OpenPKG project provides a consistent way to install server software, including Apache, across a variety of platforms. It is a nice alternative to building Apache from source or using the Apache versions provided by your vendor. The OpenPKG project is open source, supports different operating systems such as Solaris, Linux, and FreeBSD, and it was started by Ralf S. Engelschall, author of several popular Apache modules. You can learn more about OpenPKG at `http://www.openpkg.org`.

The document at this URL describes how to get started compiling and installing Apache on Unix:

`http://httpd.apache.org/docs-2.0/install.html`

In the following URLs, you will find the equivalent information for Windows-based platforms, including compilation from source:

```
http://httpd.apache.org/docs-2.0/platform/windows.html
```

```
http://httpd.apache.org/docs-2.0/platform/win_compiling.html
```

For advanced Apache users, or if you want to become involved in development, the Apache developers' site includes information on CVS access, applying patches, and so on:

```
http://httpd.apache.org/dev/
```

3

Hour 4

Getting Started with Apache

This hour describes the directory layout of Apache installations, the structure of configuration files, and the location and format of error and log files.

In this hour, you will learn

- The steps necessary to have a minimal Apache installation up and running; for example, changing basic server properties such as name and port information
- How to start and stop Apache and how to troubleshoot basic problems

Layout of Server Files and Directories

This section details the location of important Apache server files and programs. The exact location varies depending on the underlying operating system or distribution and how Apache was installed, but they are quite similar. Table 4.1 summarizes the location for different platforms. The rest of the hour provides detailed information about many of the files and programs mentioned here.

TABLE 4.1 Default Locations for Files

Section	Windows	Unix
Default install path	`C:\Program Files\Apache Group\Apache2`	`/usr/local/apache2`
Binaries and support scripts	`bin/apache.exe` `bin/`	`bin/httpd` `bin/`

Log files	`log/error.log`
	`log/access.log`
	`log/httpd.pid`
		`log/error_log`
		`log/access_log`
		`log/httpd.pid`

Proxy	`proxy/`	`proxy/`
Configuration files	`conf/httpd.conf`	`conf/httpd.conf`
CGI scripts	`cgi-bin/test-cgi.bat` `cgi-bin/printenv.pl`	`cgi-bin/test-cgi` `cgi-bin/printenv`
Build information and header files	Does not apply in binary installation	`include/` `build/`
Error messages	`error/`	`error/`
Modules and libraries	`modules/` `bin/`	`modules/` `lib/`
HTML documents	`htdocs/`	`htdocs/`
Icons	`icons/`	`icons/`
Manual	`manual/`	`manual/`

Apache Binary and Support Scripts

The Apache program executable is called `httpd` on Unix and `apache.exe` on Windows. In the same directory you can find support scripts to easily start and stop the server, manipulate password files, and perform benchmarking and log file processing.

Log Files

Apache keeps a log of the requests served, error messages, and so on. You can customize in several ways what gets logged and where it is saved. Apache provides you with two log files by default: `access_log` and `error_log` on Unix and `access.log` and `error.log` on Windows.

Configuration Files

Apache keeps its configuration in text files. The main file is called `httpd.conf`. The configuration language enables you to include additional files to better organize and structure your configuration information.

CGI Scripts Location

This directory is the default location for CGI scripts, first introduced in Hour 1, "Apache and the Web." It contains sample scripts, but they are not enabled by default. This is so because CGI scripts can contain security holes or expose information about the server or files. An attacker could exploit these scripts to run arbitrary commands on the server, display the contents of files, and so on. You can learn more about running CGI scripts in Apache in Hour 6, "Serving Dynamic Content with CGI."

Build Information and Header Files

The build and include directories contain header files and information gathered during the build process. These files are necessary for building additional loadable modules outside the normal Apache build process.

Error Messages

The error messages directory contains information needed to display customizable error messages, as explained in detail in Hour 5, "Using Apache to Serve Static Content."

Manual Pages

The manual directory includes HTML documentation and directive descriptions. The man directory contains manual pages for Apache commands in the Unix man page format.

Modules and Libraries Directory

Dynamic loadable modules, located in the modules directory, provide much of the functionality of Apache. Apart from the modules, Apache requires several libraries that are loaded by the server at runtime (as opposed to being compiled in). This includes the expat XML library and the Apache Portable Runtime library, libapr.

Web Pages and Images

The directory htdocs contains the documents that will be accessible through the Web site. This directory is also called the *document root*. The icons directory contains images that are used in the Apache documentation and icons that are used in directory listings.

Installation Differences

The directory names and locations vary depending on the operating system or distribution vendor. Table 4.1 describes where you can find the files in Unix and Windows. The table should have included the location of Apache 2 files in major Linux distributions such as Red Hat, but at the time of writing this book there were no RPM packages available.

Configuration Files Structure

Apache is configured via text files. The main configuration file is `httpd.conf`.

Please refer to the previous section to learn where this file is located in your system. Apache configuration files contain directives and containers. Directives configure specific settings of Apache, such as authorization, performance, and network parameters. Containers specify the context to which those settings refer. For example, authorization configuration can refer to the server as a whole, a directory, or a single file.

Directives

Apache directives have a simple syntax: the directive name followed by the directive arguments. The directive arguments are separated by spaces. The number and type of arguments vary from directive to directive. Some of the directives do not have any arguments.

Each directive occupies a single line. Directives can be continued in a different line by ending the previous line with a backslash character \.

You can insert comments by preceding them with #. A comment must appear on its own line. It is not possible to append comments at the end of a directive; they will be confused with an argument.

Although Apache end user documentation could be improved (probably one of the reasons you are reading this book!), the reference documentation is comprehensive and accurate. Rather than reproduce it here, you can browse it online at `http://httpd.apache.org/docs-2.0/`.

In the documentation, you can browse the directives by alphabetical order or by the module to which they belong. An entire listing of all the directives would add little or no value to this book. Instead you will find a discussion of the most useful directives because this book concentrates on a practical, task-oriented approach to Apache rather than a simple enumeration of directives.

Figure 4.1 shows an entry from the documentation for the `ServerName` directive description. You can find this entry online at `http://httpd.apache.org/docs-2.0/mod/core.html#servername`.

The schema, as detailed in the documentation at `http://httpd.apache.org/docs-2.0/mod/directive-dict.html`, is the same for all directives:

- **Syntax:** This entry explains the format of the directive options. Compulsory parameters appear in italics, optional parameters appear in italics and brackets.

FIGURE 4.1

Directive description example.

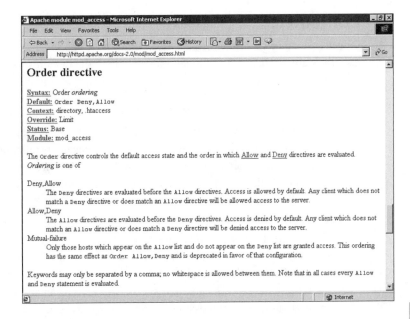

- **Default:** If there is a default value of the directive, it will appear here.

- **Context:** This entry details the containers or sections in which the directive can appear. Containers are explained in the next section. The possible values are `server config`, `virtual host`, `directory`, and `.htaccess`.

- **Status:** This entry refers to whether the directive is built in Apache (`core`), belongs to one of the bundled modules (`base` or `extension`, depending on whether they are compiled by default), part of a Multi-Processing Module (`MPM`), or is bundled with Apache but not ready for use in a production server (`experimental`).

- **Module:** This entry indicates the module to which the directive belongs.

- **Compatibility:** This entry contains information about which versions of Apache support the directive.

- **Override:** Apache directives belong to different categories. The override field is used in specifying which directive categories can appear in `.htaccess` per-directory configuration files. These configuration files are covered in detail in a later section.

A brief explanation of the directive follows these entries in the documentation and finally a reference to related directives or documentation may appear.

Containers

Directive containers, also called *sections*, limit the scope to which directives apply. If directives are not inside a container, they belong to the default server scope (`server config`), applying to the server as a whole.

These are the default Apache directive containers:

- **<VirtualHost>**: A VirtualHost directive specifies a virtual server. Apache enables you to host different Web sites with a single Apache installation. Directives inside this container apply to that particular Web site. This directive accepts a domain name or IP address and an optional port as arguments. Virtual hosts are explained in detail in Hour 14.

- **<Directory>, <DirectoryMatch>**: These containers allow directives to apply to a certain directory or group of directories in the filesystem. Directory containers take a directory or directory pattern argument. Enclosed directives apply to the specified directories and their subdirectories. The DirectoryMatch container allows regular expression patterns to be specified as an argument. You can learn more about regular expressions in the "Further Reading" section of Hour 22, "mod_rewrite."

- **<Location>, <LocationMatch>**: Allow directives to apply to certain requested URLs or URL patterns. They are similar to their Directory counterparts. LocationMatch takes a regular expression as an argument.

- **<Files>, <FilesMatch>**: Similar to Directory and Location containers, Files sections allow directives to apply to certain files or file patterns.

Directory, Files, and Location sections can also take regular expression arguments by preceding them with a ~, as in <Files ~ "\.(gif|jpg)">. However, the DirectoryMatch, LocationMatch, and FilesMatch directives are preferred for clarity.

Containers surround directives, as shown in Listing 4.1.

LISTING 4.1   Sample Container Directives

```
1: <Directory "/some/directory">
2: SomeDirective1
3: SomeDirective2
```

LISTING 4.1   continued

```
 4: </Directory>
 5: <Location "/downloads/*.html">
 6: SomeDirective3
 7: </Location>
 8: <Files "\.(gif|jpg)">
 9: SomeDirective4
10: </Files>
```

Sample directives *SomeDirective1* and *SomeDirective2* will apply to the directory `/www/docs` and its subdirectories. *SomeDirective3* will apply to URLs referring to pages with the `.html` extension under the `/download/` URL. *SomeDirective4* will apply to all files with `.gif` or `.jpg` extensions.

Conditional Evaluation

Apache provides support for conditional containers. Directives enclosed in these containers will be processed only if certain conditions are met.

- **<IfDefine>:** Directives in this container will be processed if a specific command command-line switch is passed to the Apache executable. The directive in Listing 4.2 will be processed only if the `-DMyModule` switch was passed to the Apache binary being executed. You can do this directly or by modifying the `apachectl` script, as described in the "Apache Related Commands" section.

LISTING 4.2   IfDefine Example

```
1: <IfDefine MyModule>
2: LoadModule my_module modules/libmymodule.so
3: </IfDefine>
```

IfDefine containers allow the argument to be negated. That is, directives inside a `<IfDefine !MyModule>` section will be processed only if no `-DMyModule` parameter was passed as a command-line argument.

- **<IfModule>:** Directives in an `IfModule` section will be processed only if the module passed as an argument is present in the Web server. For example, Apache ships with a default `httpd.conf` configuration file that provides support for different MPMs. Only the configuration belonging to the MPM compiled in will be processed, as can be seen in Listing 4.3. The meaning of the individual directives will be explained in Hour 11, "Multi-Processing Modules." The purpose of the example is to illustrate that only one of the directive groups will be evaluated.

LISTING 4.3   IfModule Example

```
 1: <IfModule prefork.c>
 2: StartServers          5
 3: MinSpareServers       5
 4: MaxSpareServers      10
 5: MaxClients           20
 6: MaxRequestsPerChild   0
 7: </IfModule>
 8:
 9: <IfModule worker.c>
10: StartServers          3
11: MaxClients            8
12: MinSpareThreads       5
13: MaxSpareThreads      10
14: ThreadsPerChild      25
15: MaxRequestsPerChild   0
16: </IfModule>
```

ServerRoot

The ServerRoot directive takes a single argument: a directory path pointing to the directory where the server lives. All relative path references in other directives are relative to the value of ServerRoot. The default value for this directive, assuming that you installed Apache from source as described in the previous hour, is /usr/local/apache2.

Including Additional Configuration Files

Apache provides an Include directive that can be used to process additional files containing Apache configuration directives. Include accepts a file or a directory as an argument. If a directory is specified, all files in that directory are read and processed as configuration files. If the file or directory is a relative path, it is assumed it is relative to the value of the ServerRoot directive, as described previously. An example:

```
Include conf/ssl.conf
```

Per-Directory Configuration Files

Apache uses per-directory configuration files to allow directives to exist outside the main configuration file httpd.conf. These special files can be placed in the filesystem. Apache will process the content of these files if a document is requested in a directory containing one of these files or any subdirectories under it. The contents of all the applicable per-directory configuration files are merged and processed. For example, if Apache receives a request for the /usr/local/apache2/htdocs/index.html file, it will look for per-directory configuration files in the /, /usr, /usr/local, /usr/local/apache2, and /usr/local/apache2/htdocs directories, in that order.

Enabling per-directory configuration files has a performance penalty. Apache must perform expensive disk operations looking for these files in every request, even if the files do not exist.

Per-directory configuration files are called .htaccess by default. This is for historical reasons; they were used to protect access to directories containing HTML files.

The directive AccessFileName enables you to change the name of the per-directory configuration files from .htaccess to something else. It accepts a list of filenames that Apache will look for when looking for per-directory configuration files.

If .htaccess is present in the Context: directive syntax field of a directive definition, that directive can be placed in per-directory configuration files.

Apache directives belong to different groups, specified in the Override: field in the directive syntax description. Possible values are

- **AuthConfig:** Authorization directives
- **FileInfo:** Directives controlling document types
- **Indexes:** Directives controlling directory indexing
- **Limit:** Directives controlling host access
- **Options:** Directives controlling specific directory features

You can control which of these directive groups can appear in per-directory configuration files by using the AllowOverride directive. AllowOverride also can take an All or a None argument. All means directives belonging to all groups can appear in the configuration file. None disables per-directory files in that directory and any of its subdirectories. Listing 4.4 shows how to disable per-directory configuration files for the server as a whole. This improves performance and is the default Apache configuration.

LISTING 4.4 Disabling Per-Directory Configuration Files

```
1: <Directory />
2: AllowOverride none
3: </Directory>
```

Merging Rules

When different configuration directives can apply to the same resource, they are processed in the following priority order:

1. <Directory> sections and per-directory files processed simultaneously
2. <DirectoryMatch> and <Directory> sections containing regular expression arguments

3. `<Location>` and `<LocationMatch>` sections

4. `<Files>` and `<FilesMatch>` sections

Directory sections are evaluated starting with the ones with the shortest path (directory components) first. The rest of the sections are evaluated in the order in which they appear in the configuration file. `<VirtualHost>` contents are processed after global scope directives, so they can override their values.

Additional Configuration Files

The `mime.types` configuration file contains information associating file extensions with certain content types. This list is necessary so Apache can set the right HTTP headers when a certain file is requested. MIME type configuration is explained in detail in Hour 5.

Minimal Apache Configuration

You can edit the Apache `httpd.conf` file with your favorite text editor. In Unix, this probably means `vi` or `emacs`. In Windows, you could use Notepad or WordPad. You must remember to save the configuration file in plain text format, which is the only one Apache will understand.

If your machine is properly configured, and you installed Apache from source or are using the Apache that came with your system, you probably do not need to change the default configuration file. There are only two parameters that you might need to change to be able to start Apache for the first time: the name of the server and the address and port to which it is listening. The name of the server is the one Apache will use when it needs to refer to itself; for example, when redirecting requests. Apache usually can figure out its server name from the IP address of the machine, but this is not always the case. If the server does not have a valid DNS entry, you might need to specify one of the IP addresses of the machine. If the server is not connected to a network (you might want to test Apache on a standalone machine), you can use the value 127.0.0.1, the loopback address. The default port value is 80. You might need to change this value if there is already a server running in the machine at port 80, or if you do not have administrator permissions because on Unix systems only the root user can bind to port numbers less than 1024 (privileged ports).

Both listening address and port values can be changed with the `Listen` directive. The `Listen` directive takes either a port number or an IP address and a port, separated by a semicolon. If only the port is specified, Apache will listen at that port in all available IP addresses in the machine. If an additional IP address is provided, Apache will listen at only that address and port combination. For example, `Listen 80` tells Apache to listen for requests at all IP addresses at port 80. Listen `10.0.0.1:443` tells Apache to listen only at 10.0.0.1 at port 443.

The `ServerName` directive, described in detail in the next hour, enables you to define the name the server will report in any self-referencing URLs. The directive accepts a DNS name and an optional port, separated by a colon. Make sure that `ServerName` has a valid value. Otherwise, the server will not function properly; for example, it will issue incorrect redirects.

On Unix platforms, you can specify which user and group IDs the server will run as with the `User` and `Group` directives. The `nobody` user is a good choice for most platforms. There are problems in the HP-UX platform with this user ID, so you must create and use a different user ID, such as `www`.

Log Files

Apache includes two log files by default. The `access_log` file is used to track client requests. The `error_log` is used to record important events, such as errors or server restarts. These files won't exist until Apache is started for the first time. The files are named `access.log` and `error.log` in Windows platforms.

access_log

When a client requests a file from the server, Apache records several parameters associated with the request, including the IP address of the client, the document requested, the HTTP status code, the current time, and so on. Figure 4.2 describes a sample log entry in detail. Hour 8, "Logging and Monitoring," will teach you how to modify which parameters get logged.

FIGURE 4.2
Sample log entry.

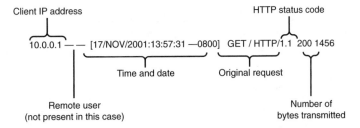

error_log

This file includes error messages, startup messages, and any other significant events in the life cycle of the server. This is the first place to look when you have a problem with Apache. Listing 4.5 shows a sample entry.

LISTING 4.5   Sample Error Log Entry

```
1. [Thu Feb 28 20:57:16 2002] [crit] (48)Address already in use:
2. ↪make_sock: could not bind to address 10.0.0.2:80
3. [Thu Feb 28 20:57:16 2002] [alert] no listening sockets available,
4. ↪ shutting down
```

Additional Files

The pid file contains the process ID of the running Apache server. You can use this number to send signals to Apache manually, as described in the next section.

The scoreboard file, present on Unix Apache, is used by the process-based MPMs to communicate with their children.

In general, you do not need to worry about these files.

Apache-Related Commands

The Apache distribution includes several executables. This section covers only the server binary and related scripts. Hours 7, "Restricting Access," 8, and 16, "Tuning Apache," cover user management, log management, and benchmarking utilities, respectively.

Apache Server Binary

The Apache executable is named httpd in Unix and apache.exe in Windows. It accepts several command-line options, which are described in Table 4.2. You can get a complete listing of options by typing /usr/local/apache2/bin/httpd -h on Unix or apache.exe -h on Windows.

TABLE 4.2   httpd Options

Option	Meaning
-D	Allows you to pass a parameter that can be used for <IfDefine> section processing
-l	Lists compiled-in modules
-v	Shows version number and server compilation time
-f	Allows you to pass the location of httpd.conf if it is different from the compile-time default
-d	Allows you to specify an alternate initial ServerRoot

After Apache is running, you can use the Unix `kill` command to send signals to the parent Apache process. Signals are a mechanism to send commands to a process. To send a signal, you execute the following command:

```
kill -SIGNAL pid
```

where *pid* is the process ID and *SIGNAL* is one of the following:

- **HUP:** Stop the server
- **USR1** or **WINCH:** Graceful restart; which signal to use depends on the underlying operating system
- **SIGHUP:** Restart

If you make some changes to the configuration files and you want them to take effect, it is necessary to signal Apache that the configuration has changed. You can do this by stopping and starting the server or by sending a restart signal. This tells Apache to reread its configuration.

A normal restart can result in a momentary pause of service. A graceful restart takes a different approach. Each thread or process serving a client will keep processing the current request, but when it is finished, it will be killed and replaced by a new thread or process with the new configuration. This allows seamless operation of the Web server with no downtime.

Controlling Apache on Windows

On Windows, you can signal Apache using the `apache.exe` executable:

- **Apache.exe -k restart:** Tells Apache to restart
- **Apache.exe -k graceful:** Tells Apache to do a graceful restart
- **Apache.exe -k stop:** Tells Apache to stop

You can access shortcuts to these commands in the Start menu entries that the Apache installer created. If you installed Apache as a service, you can start or stop Apache by using the Windows service interface: In Control Panel, select Administrative Tasks and then click on the Services icon.

Additionally, Apache 2.0 can place a program, Apache Monitor, in the system tray. It is a simple GUI that you can use to start and stop the server directly or as a service. It is either installed at startup or you can launch it from the Apache entry in the Start menu.

Apache Control Script

Although it is possible to control Apache on Unix using the `httpd` binary it is recommended that you use the `apachectl` tool. The `apachectl` support program wraps common functionality in an easy-to-use script. To use `apachectl`, type

`./apachectl command`

where *command* is `stop`, `start`, `restart`, or `graceful`. You can also edit the contents of the `apachectl` script to add extra command-line options.

Some OS distributions might provide you with additional scripts to control Apache.

Starting Apache for the First Time

To start Apache on Unix, change to the directory containing the `apachectl` script and execute the following command:

`./apachectl start`

To start Apache on Windows, click on the Start Apache link in the Control Apache section in the Start menu. If you installed Apache as a service, you must start the Apache service instead (as described in the previous section).

If everything goes well, you can access Apache using a browser. The default installation page will be displayed, as shown in Figure 4.3. If you cannot start the Web server or an error page appears instead, please consult the "Troubleshooting" section later in this hour. Make sure that you are accessing Apache in one of the ports specified in the `Listen` directive—usually 80 or 8080. If you do not have a browser handy, you can also use the telnet command-line tool as explained in Hour 1 and displayed in Listing 4.6.

LISTING 4.6　Testing Apache Manually

```
1: bash-2.04$ telnet 127.0.0.1 80
2: Trying 127.0.0.1...
3: Connected to 127.0.0.1.
4: Escape character is '^]'.
5: GET / HTTP/1.0
6: HTTP/1.1 200 OK
7: Date: Mon, 22 Oct 2001 05:40:44 GMT
8: Server: Apache/2.0.18 (Unix)
9: .. .
```

FIGURE 4.3

Apache default installation page.

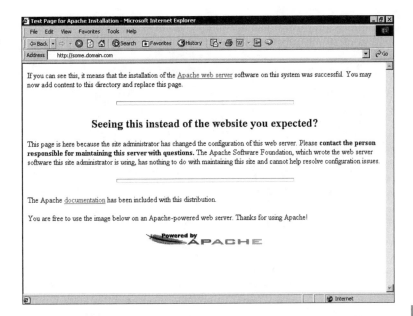

You can now check the log files. If the server started successfully, the error log file will contain a message noting the event:

```
[Thu Feb 28 20:56:44 2002] [notice] Apache/2.0.27 (Unix) configured
➥ -- resuming normal operations
```

The access log will contain a log of the request you just made to make sure that Apache was running.

Troubleshooting

There are several common problems that you might encounter the first time you start Apache.

Existing Web Server

If there is already a server running in the machine and listening to the same IP address and port combination, Apache will not be able to start successfully. You will get an entry in the error log file indicating that Apache cannot bind to the port:

```
[crit] (48)Address already in use: make_sock: could not bind to
➥address 10.0.0.2:80
[alert] no listening sockets available, shutting down
```

To solve this problem, you need to stop the running server or change the Apache configuration to listen in a different port.

No Permission to Bind to Port

You will get an error if you do not have administrator permissions and you try to bind to a privileged port (between 0 and 1024):

```
[crit] (13)Permission denied: make_sock: could not bind to address 10.0.0.2:80
[alert] no listening sockets available, shutting down
```

To solve this problem, you must either become administrator before starting Apache or change the port number (8080 is a commonly used non-privileged port).

Access Denied

You might not be able to start Apache if you do not have permissions to read the configuration files or to write to the log files. You will get an error similar to the following:

```
(13)Permission denied: httpd: could not open error log file
   ➥ /usr/local/apache2/logs/error_log.
```

This problem can happen if Apache was built and installed by a different user than the one trying to run it.

Wrong Group Settings

You can configure Apache to run under a certain username and group. Apache has default values for the running server username and group. Sometimes the default value is not valid, and you will get an error containing setgid: unable to set group id.

To solve this problem, you must change the value of the Group directive in the configuration file to a valid value. Check the /etc/groups file for existing groups.

Summary

This hour provided you with enough understanding of Apache configuration and server control to have a basic server installation up and running. The following hours will build on that knowledge, providing further information on configuration and monitoring of the server.

Q&A

Q Why are per-directory configuration files useful?

A Although per-directory configuration files have an impact on server performance, they can be useful for delegated administration.

Because per-directory configuration files are read every time a request is made, there is no need to restart the server when a change is made to the configuration.

You can allow users of your Web site to add configuration on their own without granting them administrator privileges. In this way, they can password protect sections of their home pages, for example.

Q What do you mean by a valid `ServerName` directive?

A As explained in Hour 1, the DNS system is used to associate IP addresses with domain names. The value of `ServerName` is returned when the server generates a URL. If you are using a certain domain name, you must make sure that it is included in your DNS system and will be available to clients visiting your site.

Quiz

1. What is the main difference between Location and Directory sections?
2. What is the difference between a restart and a graceful restart?

Quiz Answers

1. Directory sections refer to file system objects; Location sections refer to elements in the request URI.
2. During a normal restart, the server is stopped and then started, causing some requests to be lost. A graceful restart allows Apache children to continue to serve their current requests until they can be replaced with children running the new configuration.

Related Directives

This section contains directives mentioned in this hour or that are related to topics discussed in this hour. You can consult the Apache reference documentation for comprehensive syntax information and usage.

-   **`PidFile`, `ScoreBoardFile`:** Change default name and location of `pid` and `scoreboard` files.

- **Listen:** Specify IP addresses and ports the server will listen at.
- **ServerName:** Specify the DNS name and port the server will use for self-referential URLs.
- **AccessFilename:** Change the name of the per-directory configuration files.
- **ErrorLog**, **AccessLog:** Change the default name and location of error and access log files. Logging is covered in detail in Hour 8.
- **<VirtualHost>**, **<Directory>**, **<Location>**, **<Files>:** Container directives. Directives included in these sections will apply only to the specified scope.
- **<IfDefine>**, **<IfModule>:** Process files included in this section if a certain parameter is present or a module has been compiled in.
- **Include:** Include external files containing configuration directives.
- **User, Group:** Specify the Unix user and group ID Apache will run as.
- **AllowOverride:** Specify which options can be present in per-directory configuration files.

Further Reading

The Apache documentation project can be found at

http://httpd.apache.org/docs-2.0/

Information on starting and stopping Apache can be found at

http://httpd.apache.org/docs-2.0/invoking.html

http://httpd.apache.org/docs-2.0/stopping.html

HOUR 5

Using Apache to Serve Static Content

This hour covers directives and modules that are commonly used to administer static content in Apache installations.

In this hour, you will learn

- How to configure Apache to listen on different IP addresses and ports
- How to organize the URL space with directory aliasing and redirection
- How to customize the server information and error messages

Addresses, Ports, and Server Names

Apache needs to know which IP addresses and ports to listen to while waiting for incoming requests. You can use the `Listen` directive for that purpose. The general syntax is `Listen` *ipaddress:port*. The IP address is optional. If it is not present, it means Apache should listen on all IP addresses available in the machine. For example, `Listen 80` means listen at port 80 at all available IP addresses. `Listen 10.0.0.1:8080` means listen at address 10.0.0.1 and port 8080. In Unix systems, only users with administrator privileges can bind to privileged ports (ports below 1024). Because port 80 is a privileged port, if you are using Apache as a normal user, you must bind to a different port, such as 8080.

You can use multiple `Listen` directives to specify multiple IP addresses and ports to listen to. This directive is usually placed at the beginning of the `httpd.conf` file.

The `ServerName` Directive

The `ServerName` directive accepts a fully qualified domain name and an optional port. If the port is not specified, it is assumed to be 80 for HTTP and 443 for HTTPS connections. (The HTTPS protocol is described in Hour 17, "Setting Up a Secure Server.") The value of the `ServerName` directive will be used when Apache needs to construct URLs that refer to themselves; for example, when issuing certain HTTP redirects, as explained later in the hour.

> The HTTP/1.1 protocol allows different Web sites to be associated with a single IP address. The browser specifies which particular site it is addressing by using the `Host:` HTTP header.

In certain situations, this might not be the preferred behavior, and you will want to construct the URL based on the `Host:` header provided by the HTTP/1.1 protocol. You can use the `UseCanonicalName` directive for this purpose. It accepts one argument, which can be `on`, `off`, or `dns`. `UseCanonicalName` on instructs Apache to use `ServerName`, which is the default behavior. Setting the value to `off` tells Apache to look at the `Host:` header provided by the client. If this header is not present—for example, because of an older browser—Apache will use the value of `ServerName`. Setting the argument to `dns` will make Apache try to infer the valid server name by a reverse lookup from the IP address of the request. This is useful in certain virtual hosting setups. Virtual hosts are described in detail in Hour 14, "Virtual Hosting." However, you need to take into account that DNS lookups can be expensive in terms of performance, and can slow down the server response.

If `ServerName` is not present, Apache will try to infer a valid server name by performing a reverse DNS lookup on the server's IP address.

Usually you make queries to a DNS server to find the IP associated with a hostname. A reverse DNS lookup means that you query the DNS server for the names associated with a particular IP address.

Customizing the Web Server

Apache is used in a great variety of environments. One of the reasons for its success in so many different scenarios is that nearly every aspect of the server can be customized. This section covers customization of error messages and information related to the server.

Error Messages

Apache returns an error response when it can't find a requested document, finds out the user does not have permission to read it, encounters an error in processing, and so on. These responses are technically accurate, including mentions of HTTP error codes, but are not necessarily very useful to the end user visiting your Web site. An example of a default Apache error message is shown in Figure 5.1.

FIGURE 5.1
Sample Apache error message.

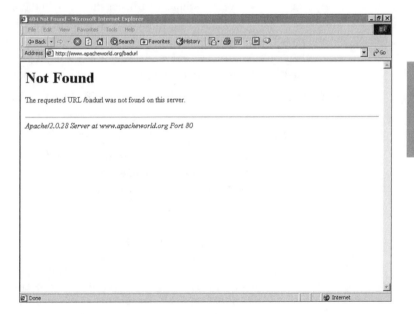

The standard Apache responses can be replaced with custom pages that have the same look and feel of your Web site, are written in the preferred language of the visitor, or present him with a search or feedback form. To do this, you can use the `ErrorDocument` directive.

The `ErrorDocument` Directive

`ErrorDocument` accepts a three-digit HTTP status code as described in Hour 1, "Apache and the Web," and allows you to replace the default error message with one of the following options:

- **Customized Message:** You can provide a string to display in the error document to replace the default message:

  ```
  ErrorDocument 500 "Our server encountered an internal problem, \
  please wait a few minutes and try again"
  ErrorDocument 404 "Oops, we couldn't find your document!"
  ```

- **Internal URL:** You can redirect the user to another page in the same Web server. The destination can be a static page or can be generated dynamically, for instance, via a CGI script. The internal URL must be absolute and start with a /. For example, the following directive instructs Apache to send all failed requests to a CGI program that provides the search page for the Web site:

  ```
  ErrorDocument 404 /cgi-bin/search.cgi
  ```

  Apache creates new environment variables that contain the information about the original request that otherwise would be lost, such as the URL that caused the problem. These variables are prefixed with `REDIRECT`, `REDIRECT_URL`, `REDIRECT_QUERY_STRING`, and so on. The destination program generating the page can use this information to determine what went wrong with the original request.

- **External URL:** You can provide a fully qualified URL pointing to another Web site:

  ```
  ErrorDocument 404 http://search.example.com
  ```

  In this case, Apache will issue a redirect to the client (HTTP code 302) to point to the new URL (`http://search.example.com`). As a side effect, the client will not get the original 404 Document Not Found error code.

> Recent versions of the Internet Explorer browser won't display error documents with size less than 512 bytes, and will substitute its own error messages. You can disable this behavior by selecting Tools, Internet Options, Advanced, and deselecting the Show Friendly HTTP Error Messages option. You cannot rely on your users turning off this feature, so if you want to make sure that your users can read your error messages, you must make them bigger than 512 bytes.

International Error Messages

Apache 2.0 offers a predefined mechanism to provide error documents in different lan-
guages, depending on the configuration of the browser. It uses Server Side Includes
(SSIs) from `mod_include` and the content negotiation features from `mod_negotiation`.
You can find more information at `http://httpd.apache.org/docs-`
`2.0/misc/custom_errordocs.html`.

Handling URL Errors: `mod_speling`

`mod_speling` is a useful Apache module that recognizes misspelled URLs and redirects
the user to the correct location for the document. `mod_speling` is able to correct URLs
with the wrong capitalization or with one letter missing or incorrect. Capitalization problems usually arise when serving content that has been generated in a case-insensitive
environment such as Windows through a Web server on a case-sensitive platform such as
Unix. Users misspelling the URL while typing it in the browser usually cause letters to
be missing or incorrect.

For example, if a user requests the file `file.html` and it is not present, `mod_speling` will
see whether there is a similar document such as `FILE.HTML`, `file.htm`, and so on, and
will return it, if present.

To enable spelling checks, you can add `CheckSpelling` onto your Apache configuration.
The `mod_speling` module is included with Apache but is not compiled by default if you
installed Apache from source. Hour 18, "Extending Apache," explains how to enable
modules for compilation. Before using this module, you must bear in mind that searching
for the appropriate misspelled file has performance implications.

> If there are several documents that can match the misspelling, the module
> will return a list of these documents. This could have security implications
> because you might not want to make some of those files visible.

Customizing Server Information

Responses generated by Apache may include information about the server and its compiled modules. You can configure the amount of information included because revealing
too much information about your server is probably not a good idea.

Server Identification

Apache returns a `Server:` header with every request. By default, this header includes
information about the server name, version, and platform. Other modules present in the

server, such as SSL, PHP, or mod_perl, may add additional entries to the server string containing the module name and version:

```
Server: Apache/2.0.28-dev (Unix) SSL/2.0.0
```

You can use the ServerTokens directive to restrict the information included in this header. Table 5.1 presents each one of the possible settings and sample output, together with a directive description and sample output. The default value is ServerTokens Full.

TABLE 5.1   ServerTokens Options

Settings	Output
ServerTokens ProductOnly	Apache
ServerTokens Minimal	Apache/2.0.28
ServerTokens OS	Apache/2.0.28 (Unix)
ServerTokens Full	Apache/2.0.28 (Unix) SSL/2.0. 0

Contact Information

When Apache returns a self-generated document, such as a directory listing or an error page, it adds a trailing footer including server information and, optionally, a contact e-mail address.

ServerSignature *On/Off* enables or disables generation of this footer.

ServerAdmin *admin@email.example.com* sets the e-mail address included in the footer.

Figure 5.2 shows a sample ServerSignature footer.

FIGURE 5.2
Sample Apache
ServerSignature
footer.

Aliasing and Mapping of Resources

The structure of your Web site might not necessarily match the layout of your files on disk. You can use the Alias and AliasMatch directives to map directories on disk to specific URLs. For example, the following directive:

```
Alias /icons/ /usr/local/apache2/icons/
```

will cause a request for `http://www.example.com/icons/image.gif` to make Apache look for the `/usr/local/apache2/icons/image.gif` file.

The trailing slashes in the `Alias` directive are significant. If you include them, the client request must include the slash as well or the `Alias` directive won't take effect. For example, if you use the following directive:

```
Alias /icons /usr/local/apache2/icons
```

and request `http://www.example.com/icons`, the server will return a 404 Document Not Found error response.

The `AliasMatch` directive provides a similar behavior, but enables you to specify a regular expression for the URL. The matches can be substituted in the destination path. For example, the directive

```
AliasMatch ^/help(.*) /usr/local/apache/htdocs/manual$1
```

will match any URL under `help` to filesystem paths under the `manual` directory.

URL Redirection

The structure of a typical Web site keeps changing over time. You might not be able to control other sites that link to you, such as search engines with stale links. People accessing your Web site through such links will receive an error. To avoid that, you can configure Apache with the `Redirect` directive to redirect those requests to the correct resource, whether it is in the current server or a different one.

The `Redirect` directive takes several arguments: an optional status parameter containing the redirect code, the origin URL location, and the destination URL. The status can be a numeric HTTP status code, but for common cases it is also possible to use one of the following labels:

- **permanent:** Permanent redirect status (301)
- **temp:** Temporary redirect status (302)
- **seeother:** The document has been replaced (303)
- **gone:** The document has been permanently removed (401)

A 302 temporary redirect is probably all you need in practice and that is the default value if no status code is provided. If the status code is not a redirect, such as 401, the destination URL can be omitted. Redirect codes are 300 to 399.

5

A sample `Redirect` directive is

```
Redirect temp /news/ http://example.com/latest/news/
```

A request for `http://example.com/news/index.html` will be redirected to `http://example.com/latest/news/index.html`.

The `RedirectMatch` directive is similar to `Redirect`, but allows the origin URL path to be a regular expression.

The `RedirectTemp` and `RedirectPermanent` directives have the same effect as `Redirect` with a `temp` or `permanent` status code.

The `mod_rewrite` module allows complex redirection rules and is explained in Hour 22, "mod_rewrite."

MIME Types

MIME stands for Multipurpose Internet Mail Extensions. MIME is a set of standards that defines, among other things, a way to indicate the content type of a document, its MIME type. Examples of MIME types are `text/html` and `audio/mpeg`.

The first component of the MIME type is the main category of the content (text, audio, image, video) and the second component is the specific type.

Apache uses MIME types to determine which modules or filters will process certain content, and to add HTTP headers to the response to identify its content type. These headers will be used by the client application to identify and correctly display the contents to the end user.

This section explains how to associate files with their MIME type.

Defining MIME Types

Apache has a file called `mime.types` that includes the most common media types and their associated file extensions. Listing 5.1 shows sample entries from this file.

LISTING 5.1 Sample `mime.types` Entries

```
audio/mpeg              mpga mp2 mp3
video/mpeg              mpeg mpg mpe
text/html               html htm
text/plain              asc txt
```

Each entry contains a MIME type and, optionally, associated file extensions.

The `TypesConfig` directive allows you to specify alternate files containing MIME type definitions.

You can add new MIME type extensions by editing this file or by using the `AddType` directive. `AddType` accepts a MIME type and a list of file extensions.

For example, `AddType text/xml xml` will associate the `text/xml` MIME type with files ending with the `xml` extension.

The `DefaultType` directive defines the MIME type for files whose MIME type could not be determined from the configured mappings. The default value for this setting is `text/plain`.

The official MIME type list is maintained by IANA (Internet Assigned Numbers Authority) and can be found at the following URL: `http://www.isi.edu/in-notes/iana/assignments/media-types/media-types`.

MIME Magic

Most Unix operating systems include a `file` command-line utility that determines the type of a file by peeking at its first few bytes.

The Apache module `mod_mime_magic` emulates that behavior and can determine the MIME type of a file on-the-fly.

The `MimeMagicFile` directive enables this behavior and specifies the location of the configuration file containing the information necessary to make the MIME type determination. Apache includes the `magic` configuration file in the `conf` directory. You need to be aware that enabling `mod_mime_magic` can affect the performance of your server. `mod_mime_magic` is included with Apache, but is not compiled by default.

The `ForceType` Directive

You can use the `ForceType` directive to establish the MIME types for all files in a particular directory or location, overriding any other settings. For example, the directive

```
<Location /images/>
    ForceType image/gif
</Location>
```

will force Apache to treat all files in that directory as GIF image files, independent of their name or extension.

Content Handlers

Handlers are a way Apache determines which actions to perform on the requested content. Modules provide handlers and you configure Apache to associate certain content with specific handlers. For example, a language translation module might provide a translation handler. You could then associate this handler with the files you want to translate before sending them back to the browser. This section explains the common mechanism for configuring handlers in Apache. This information will be useful in other hours that deal with dynamic content generation.

The AddHandler directive associates a certain handler with filename extensions. RemoveHandler can be used to remove previous associations. For example, AddHandler cgi-script .cgi .pl will tell Apache to treat all documents with cgi or pl extensions as CGI scripts.

The SetHandler directive enables you to associate a handler with all files in a particular directory or location. The Action directive enables you to associate a particular MIME type or handler with a CGI script. Both directives are explained further in Hour 6, "Serving Dynamic Content with CGI."

Apache includes a number of built-in and default handlers, including

- **default-handler:** The default behavior by Apache is to send the file back to the client, adding additional headers.
- **send-as-is:** This handler is provided by the mod_asis module. Apache will send the contents directly to the client, without adding headers of its own. The file thus must include HTTP headers of its own, and you must be careful to ensure that they are correct.
- **cgi-script:** Process the file as a CGI script, as described in Hour 6.
- **server-info:** Get the server's configuration information or the server's status report, as described in Hour 8, "Logging and Monitoring."

Directory Listings

When Apache receives a request that translates into a directory on disk, you can configure the server to act in different ways.

Default Document Index

Apache can look for a special document, called the *directory index*, and return it. You can use the DirectoryIndex directive to specify a list of possible index files:

```
DirectoryIndex index.html index.htm
```

The directory index can live in a different directory. For example, you could use a CGI script that generates a different index depending on the directory requested:

```
DirectoryIndex /cgi-bin/index.cgi
```

Directory Indexing

If no directory index document is present, a default page containing the directory listing will be presented. The listing is automatically generated by the mod_autoindex module, which is compiled in by default.

Figure 5.3 shows a sample directory listing.

FIGURE 5.3

Sample Apache directory listing.

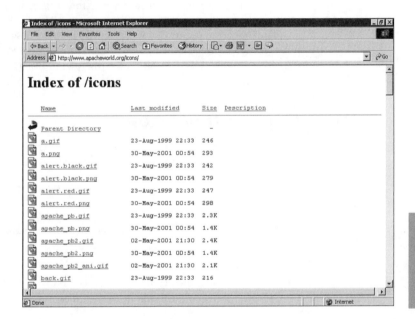

You can modify the icon and text associated with specific files depending on file extensions, MIME encoding, and MIME types. You can add images via the AddIcon, AddIconByEncoding, and AddIconByType directives. Similar directives exist to add text in place of images for text-based browsers: AddAlt, AddAltByEncoding, and AddAltByType. The AddDescription directive adds a text description for a specific file.

The IndexOption directive allows you fine-grained control over the layout and display of the files: whether to include date and size information, display ordering, and other formatting options.

5

The IndexOrderDefault directive allows you to control the order of directory listing. It takes two arguments: The first is either Ascending or Descending, and the other is the criterion, one of Name, Date, Size, or Description.

You can learn more about these directives in the mod_autoindex module documentation page.

You can designate header and footer files to be added to the directory listings via the HeaderName and ReadmeName directives.

> All these options and directives for directory listings are probably useful only if you have a download area or otherwise need to distribute a collection of files. That is the reason this section covers only the basic mechanism and refers you to the Apache documentation for the specific options. The icons and description texts can ease the navigation of the tree structure.

Forbidding Directory Access

You might want to prevent access to directory listings, mainly for security reasons. As a general rule, the less information you give to a possible attacker, the better.

You might also have other files you are working on and you are not ready yet to link from the main site.

To disable directory listings, you can either disable the mod_autoindex module or use the Options -Indexes directive. You can disable listings for the server as a whole or for specific directories. The Options directive controls which server features are available in a particular directory, such as directory indexing or, as you will see in Hour 6, CGI program execution. Please refer to the Apache documentation for additional details.

If you do not want specific files to show up in the directory listing, you can use the IndexIgnore directive. The IndexIgnore directive takes a list of filenames or wildcard expressions that will not be shown. For example, IndexIgnore .htaccess *~ will hide .htaccess per-directory configuration files and backup files created by Unix editors, which usually end on ~.

Trailing Slash

When you are referring to a directory, you need to make sure that the URL contains a trailing slash because that is the correct syntax. It is a common mistake for the user to forget it while typing the URL (http://example.com/downloads instead of http://example.com/downloads/), which in normal circumstances will result in an error page and a confused user. The mod_dir Apache module provides functionality that addresses this common problem. If mod_dir is present in the server, and a request for a directory missing the trailing slash is received, the server will send a redirect back to the browser with the correct URL. That is, if the user requests http://example.com/ downloads, and the directory downloads exists in the document root, a redirect response will be returned pointing to http://example.com/downloads/. Make sure that ServerName is set correctly because the redirect response will use that value.

Icons for Bookmarks

Many modern browsers, such Internet Explorer, Mozilla, and Konqueror, allow you to associate an icon with a Web site. You can see an example in Figure 5.4. When you access a Web site for the first time, the browser sends a request for a favicon.ico file. Older browser versions may send a request whenever you bookmark a page to the same location containing the bookmarked document. The favicon.ico file is an icon in the Windows icon format. You can use the AliasMatch directive described in this hour to redirect all requests for a favicon.ico to a single location containing the icon for your site:

AliasMatch /favicon.ico /usr/local/apache2/icons/site.ico

This avoids placing one file in each subdirectory that the user bookmarks.

Icon

FIGURE 5.4
Favorites icon in browser.

5

Summary

This hour explained how to use Apache as a traditional Web server serving static content such as HTML pages and images. You learned how to customize Web server responses, and how to use redirects and aliasing to present a consistent URL namespace even when the site structure changes over time. You have also learned how to configure Apache to listen to specific IP addresses and ports.

Q&A

Q **Why would I want to remove information from the `Server:` header?**

A The main reason is security. The less information you provide to a potential attacker regarding specific server versions or the Apache modules you are running, the better off you are.

Q **What makes a good error document?**

Good additions for an error page are a site map, a search form, and a link to contact the system administrator.

You can visit `http://www.plinko.net/404/custom.asp#good` for other ideas on creating good error documents.

Quiz

1. When are trailing slashes in a URL important?
2. Can you name some of the handlers included with Apache?
3. Which HTTP codes do you use to indicate that a document has moved to a different location?

Quiz Answers

1. When creating a URL mapping with the `Alias` directive or accessing a URL that references a directory in disk.
2. The content handlers described in this hour are `default-handler`, `send-as-is`, `cgi-bin`, and `server-info`.
3. The `3xx` family of HTTP codes, such as `301`, `302`, `303`, and so on.

Related Directives

This section contains directives mentioned in this hour or that are related to topics discussed in this hour. You can consult the Apache reference documentation for comprehensive syntax information and usage.

Listening and Hostname

- **`Listen`**: Addresses and ports to listen to.
- **`ServerName, UseCanonicalName`:** How to determine the server name to use for redirects and other self-referential URLs.

Customization

- **ServerTokens, ServerSignature:** Customization of server headers and footers on generated pages.
- **ErrorMessage:** Custom error messages.

Site Structure

- **Alias, AliasMatch:** Associate directory or file on disk with URL.
- **CheckSpelling:** Enable checking of request for URL for simple errors and correcting them when possible.
- **Redirect, RedirectMatch, RedirectTemp, RedirectPermanent:** Redirection of URLs.

Directory Listings

- **IndexOptions:** Fine-grained directory listing control.
- **IndexIgnore:** Ignore certain files.
- **DirectoryIndex:** Index files.
- **HeaderName, ReadmeName:** Descriptions to display in directory listings.
- **AddIcon, AddIconByEncoding, AddIconByType:** Associate icons with files.
- **AddAlt, AddAltByEncoding, AddAltByType:** Associate files with text to display instead of icons.
- **AddDescription:** Add a description to a file.
- **Options:** Controls which server features are available in a particular directory.

MIME and File Handlers

- **TypesConfig:** Point to a file containing MIME type definition.
- **MimeMagicFile:** File containing magic MIME types.
- **AddHandler, RemoveHandler, SetHandler:** Associate or remove handlers with resources.
- **ForceType:** Associate a MIME type with all files in a directory or location.
- **AddType:** Associate MIME type with file extensions.

Further Reading

The following URL covers Apache handlers in depth:

```
http://httpd.apache.org/docs-2.0/handler.html
```

You can find additional information on the Apache URL mapping directives mentioned in this hour at

`http://httpd.apache.org/docs-2.0/urlmapping.html`

Hour **6**

Serving Dynamic Content with CGI

This hour's lesson covers the configuration of Apache to allow execution of CGI scripts. CGI is a simple and well-understood protocol for generating dynamic content.

In this hour, you will learn

- How the CGI protocol works
- How to configure Apache to run CGI scripts, on both Unix and Windows
- How to troubleshoot common errors

Common Gateway Interface

CGI stands for Common Gateway Interface. It is a standard protocol used by Web servers to communicate with external programs. The Web server provides all the necessary information about the request to the external program, which processes it and returns a response. The response is then transmitted back to the client.

CGI Protocol

The creation of the CGI protocol can be traced back to two of the original Web servers: the CERN and NCSA HTTP servers. Both servers provided mechanisms to invoke external programs and scripts to create dynamic content. These two solutions were incompatible, so the developers agreed on a common protocol to allow programs to work with any Web server that implemented this protocol.

The CGI 1.1 specification can be found at http://hoohoo.ncsa.uiuc.edu/cgi.

CGI Operation

The basic process by which an external CGI program serves a request is the following:

1. Apache receives a request and determines that it needs to be served by the CGI program.
2. Apache starts an instance of the CGI program.
3. Apache passes information about the request to the CGI.
4. Apache receives the response from the CGI, optionally processes its headers and contents, and sends it to the client.
5. The CGI program finishes and all resources associated with it are recalled by the operating system.

Apache communicates with the CGI script via a pipe. A *pipe* is a mechanism that connects two programs. The programs can send and receive data to and from each other by writing and reading from the pipe.

CGI Environment Variables

Apache passes additional information about the request and the server to the CGI program via environment variables.

Table 6.1 shows some of the environment variables. A complete listing can be obtained at http://hoohoo.ncsa.uiuc.edu/cgi/env.html.

TABLE 6.1 CGI Environment Variables

Variable Name	Variable Description
SERVER_NAME	Hostname or IP address of the server
REQUEST_METHOD	HTTP request method: HEAD, GET, POST, and so on

TABLE 6.1 continued

Variable Name	Variable Description
REMOTE_ADDR	Client IP address
CONTENT_TYPE	MIME type of any client data being passed by a POST or PUT request
CONTENT_LENGTH	Size of the client data

If the client is using SSL to connect to the server, additional environment variables are available, as described in Hour 17, "Setting Up a Secure Server."

CGI Response

The CGI response includes optional HTTP headers separated from the response body by an additional carriage return. Any valid HTTP header can be returned by the CGI, including the following:

- **Location:** Instructs Apache that the CGI is not going to answer the request and that the client should be redirected to the specified URL.
- **Status:** This is not a valid HTTP header and it is not transmitted back to the client, but it indicates the HTTP status code for the request to Apache.
- **Content-Type:** Specifies the type of data returned in the request. For example, if you are returning a Web page, the header value should be text/html.

Advantages and Disadvantages of CGI Scripts

This section describes some of the advantages and drawbacks of using CGI programs to provide dynamic content. Advantages of CGI development include portability, simplicity of the protocol, available code, ability to distribute CGI programs as binaries, and robustness against memory leaks. The main disadvantages of CGI development are related to performance and the mixing of code and presentation.

Portability

CGI programs can be written in any language and will work with Web servers that support the CGI interface (which is virtually all of them). Perl is the language of choice for CGI development because of its string processing capabilities and cross-platform support.

6

Simplicity

Programming CGIs is extremely simple. There is no need to learn a new language or specific APIs: Everything that is written to the standard output will be sent to the browser. Several libraries are available for Perl, C, and other languages that provide support for argument parsing, HTML formatting, and so on. These libraries make CGI development even easier.

Existing Code

The CGI protocol has been around for a long time and there are plenty of books, tutorials, and Web sites providing information about CGI programming. There are many commercial and freely available scripts that provide shopping carts, credit card processing, template systems, discussion forums, and so on.

Source Hiding

CGI supports many development languages, including those that can be compiled to executable code. This is important for companies that need to distribute software applications for the Web, but do not want to distribute their source code.

Memory Leaks

Programmers need to be careful with memory allocation and management when programming processes that will be running continuously for a long time. This is not usually an issue with CGI programs because they have a limited lifetime, and resources such as memory are freed when the process is eliminated.

Performance

Apache needs to start and stop a process for each CGI request (either the CGI binary or an interpreter, in the case of scripts). This has several drawbacks.

- If the number of requests increases, the number of process creation and destruction operations also increases and can impact performance. If the number of processes grows to occupy the available memory, the operating system will need to swap some of them to disk, slowing down the response time significantly.

- CGI programs usually need to load additional libraries and establish connections to remote resources such as databases. These steps must be repeated over and over because a process is created and destroyed for every request and the connections to the database are lost.

- There is no way of caching frequently accessed data. CGI scripts need to use databases or other external means to store any kind of information.

Code and Presentation

CGI favors a style of development in which code and presentation are tied to each other. Print statements in the CGI program generate the HTML output.

This makes it difficult to change the look and feel or structure of the Web site and requires designers to understand CGI programming. If the development language is compiled and not interpreted, even a simple change such as correcting a typo will require a new compilation of the application, slowing down the development cycle.

Configuring Apache

Apache provides support for executing CGI scripts through two modules: mod_cgi and mod_cgid. Although they are very similar from the point of view of the server administrator, they vary in their internal operation. mod_cgi is used with process-based MPMs and mod_cgid is used with threaded MPMs. mod_cgid works around some limitations in forking new processes from threaded applications by creating a CGI daemon. This process is created at startup time and is in charge of accepting requests for CGIs, processing them, and returning the results to the main Apache server. The differences between the architectures are illustrated in Figure 6.1.

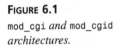
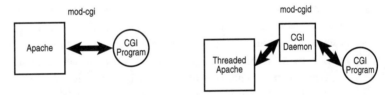

FIGURE 6.1
mod_cgi *and* mod_cgid *architectures.*

The appropriate Apache CGI module for your particular platform is compiled by default when you build Apache. The only difference from the administrator's point of view is that mod_cgid has an extra directive, ScriptSock, to specify a socket to connect to the CGI daemon. You do not need to modify the value for this directive; the default is usually okay.

6

CGI Content

You can use several Apache directives to mark specific files or directories as containing CGI scripts.

ScriptAlias

This directive is similar to the `Alias` directive explained in Hour 5, "Using Apache to Serve Static Content." It associates a directory on disk with a certain URL. Apache will treat any file requested in that directory as a CGI.

```
ScriptAlias /usr/local/apache2/cgi-bin/ /cgi-bin/
```

A request for the `/cgi-bin/example.cgi` URL will make Apache look for the `/usr/local/apache2/cgi-bin/example.cgi` file and execute it as a CGI. You can use the `ScriptAliasMatch` directive to match directories using regular expressions.

 Remember that all files in the target directory will be treated as CGI scripts, regardless of their extensions or contents.

Fine-Grained Control

The Apache CGI processing modules provide the content handler `cgi-script`. You can associate specific files or directory contents with this handler. When one of those files is requested, Apache processes it as a CGI script.

You can use `<Files>`, `<Directory>`, or `<Location>` sections and use the `SetHandler` directive, as described in Listing 6.1. You can associate specific file extensions as described in Listing 6.2. In all cases, you need to provide additional configuration to specify that CGI execution is allowed. This is done via the `ExecCGI` parameter to the `Options` directive. That is, a file must be both marked as a CGI and placed in a directory that allows CGI execution for it to be processed as a CGI script.

LISTING 6.1   SetHandler Directive

```
1: # Any files accessed thru the /cgi-bin/ url will execute as CGI scripts.
2: <Location "/cgi-bin/">
3: Options +ExecCGI
4: SetHandler cgi-script
5: <Location>
```

LISTING 6.2   Associating CGI Processing with File Extensions

```
1: # Any files ending in .pl will be executed as CGI scripts
2: <Files *.pl>
3: Options +ExecCGI
4: SetHandler cgi-script
```

LISTING 6.2 continued

```
 5: </Files>
 6:
 7: # Any files ending in .cgi in the /usr/local/apache2/htdocs/scripts
 8: # will be executed as CGI scripts
 9: AddHandler cgi-script .cgi
10:
11: <Directory "/usr/local/apache2/htdocs/scripts">
12: Options +ExecCGI
13: </Directory>
```

Action and Script

Apache provides additional directives that simplify associating specific MIME types, file extensions, or even specific HTTP methods with a particular CGI. The mod_actions module, included in the base distribution and compiled by default, provides the Action and Script directives:

- The Action directive accepts two arguments. The first argument is a handler or a MIME content type; the second points to the CGI program to handle the request.
- The Script directive associates certain HTTP request methods with a CGI program.

Listing 6.3 shows how to use the Action directive to process all GIF images via the process.cgi script, and the Script directive to process all uploads to the Web server. The information about the original requested document is passed to the CGI via the PATH_INFO (document URL) and PATH_TRANSLATED (document path) environment variables.

LISTING 6.3 Action and Script Directives

```
Action image/gif /cgi-bin/process.cgi

Script PUT /cgi-bin/upload.cgi
```

6

The directory containing the destination CGI must be marked as allowing CGI scripts execution. You can do this with the ScriptAlias directive or the ExecCGI parameter to the Options directive.

CGI Security

The ability to execute CGI programs in the Web server poses a security risk. An attacker could exploit poorly written scripts to gain access to the Web server. By restricting the execution to certain directories and files, the administrator can have tighter control over the code that is executed in the server. In some cases, it might be necessary to allow users to execute their own CGI programs in a safe manner. Hour 14, "Virtual Hosting," covers this topic.

Non Parse Headers (NPH) Scripts

When the CGI returns its content, the Web server can process the headers returned and add some of its own. Apache provides a mechanism to bypass this processing and to send the output of the CGI directly to the client. These CGIs are called Non Parse Headers (NPH) CGIs. There are no Apache configuration directives dealing with this; you just need to prefix the name of the CGI with nph- (for example, nph-example.cgi), and Apache will treat it as an NPH CGI program.

Debugging CGI Execution

Apache provides several directives to aid in debugging CGI programs. The ScriptLog directive allows you to define a special file that contains debugging information, including the headers and data received and the output of the CGI. The size of the file can grow quickly, so two additional directives are provided: ScriptLogLength limits the maximum size of the file and ScriptLogBuffer limits the maximum number of bytes saved for POST request logging. As noted in the Apache documentation, CGI debugging is off by default and should be enabled only when troubleshooting specific problems because it can slow the execution speed significantly.

Unix Configuration

Apache includes two sample CGI scripts that you can use to test that CGI support in Apache is working properly. The exact location of the files in your system is described in Hour 4, "Getting Started with Apache." One of the examples is a shell script, which can run with the default system shell. The other is written in Perl.

Testing Shell Script CGIs

The Apache distribution includes a simple shell script CGI, test-cgi. The first step is to make the script executable. You can do this with the chmod a+x test-cgi command.

You can now use your browser to access the /cgi-bin/test-cgi URL. Figure 6.2 shows the resulting page.

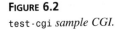

FIGURE 6.2

test-cgi *sample CGI.*

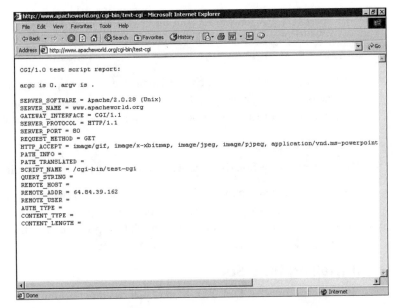

If you have problems running the CGI script, refer to the troubleshooting section.

Perl Installation

You need to follow certain steps to run CGI scripts with Perl on Unix. Perl is the language of choice for CGI development. The following sections explain how to get Perl installed in your Unix operating system.

Preinstalled Perl

If you are using a recent Linux, FreeBSD distribution or any other Open Source Unix OS, chances are good that Perl came already installed with your system. You can test so by typing which perl at the command prompt. You can check the Perl interpreter version installed by issuing the perl -v command. The Perl interpreter is usually placed in the /usr/bin or /usr/local/bin directory.

Installing Binaries

Installing a Perl binary distribution varies from system to system.

Linux

You need to use the package management tools included with your distribution to check whether the Perl package has already been installed or to install it otherwise. If you are running Red Hat Linux or another RPM-based distribution such as SuSE or Mandrake,

6

you can use the `rpm` command-line tool to install the appropriate RPM after you have downloaded it:

```
# rpm -i perl*.rpm
```

Other Linux distributions, such as Debian, use different package management utilities, but the procedures are similar. In any case, so many scripts and utilities depend on Perl that most modern Linux distributions already come with it preinstalled.

Solaris Packages

Newer versions of Solaris come with Perl preinstalled by default in `/usr/bin`.

You can download binary packages of Perl at `http://www.perl.com/CPAN-local/ports/index.html#solaris`. Some of the packages are in the standard Solaris `pkg` format. You can find information on Solaris package installation at `http://www.sunfreeware.com/pkgadd.html`.

Installing from Source

If you want to install Perl from source, you can download it from

`http://www.perl.com/pub/a/language/info/software.html#sourcecode`

Perl includes its own build environment. You can configure the build with the following commands:

```
# rm -f config.sh Policy.sh
# sh Configure -de
```

You will be prompted for several questions and afterwards the appropriate building files will be created. You can then issue the following commands:

```
# make
# make test
# make install
```

This process will install Perl in the default location for the platform, usually `/usr/local/`.

Testing Perl CGI Scripts

The Apache distribution includes a simple Perl script, `printenv`, that you can use for testing purposes. You need to make sure that the script allows execution. You can do this with the `chmod a+x printenv` command. You might need to change the first line of the script (it will look something like `#!/usr/local/bin/perl`) to point to the exact location of your Perl interpreter.

You can now use your browser to access the /cgi-bin/printenv URL. Figure 6.3 shows the resulting page.

FIGURE 6.3

printenv *sample CGI.*

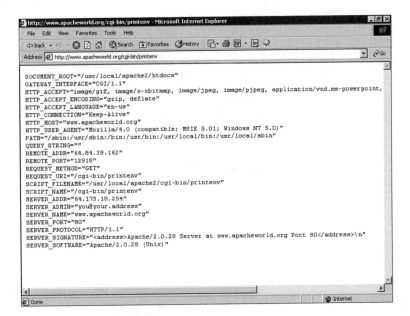

Windows Configuration

The Apache distribution includes two sample CGI scripts for Windows. One of them is a batch file and the other is a Perl script; they are counterparts of the Unix script described in the previous section.

Testing Batch File CGIs

You can access the test-cgi.bat example by requesting the /cgi-bin/test-cgi.bat URL through your browser. Figure 6.4 shows the resulting page.

The test-cgi.bat program is a simple text file that you can edit with Notepad or any other Windows text editor.

Perl on Windows

Windows does not come with a version of Perl preinstalled, so you must install it first, and then configure Apache to recognize and execute Perl scripts.

The easiest way to install Perl on Windows is by downloading the free ActivePerl distribution from the ActiveState Web site at http://www.activestate.com.

6

When the installer is launched, you will be presented with the software license, followed by a screen that enables you to choose which packages to install (see Figure 6.5).

FIGURE 6.4

`test-cgi.bat` *sample CGI.*

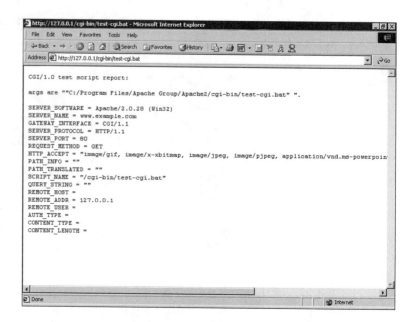

FIGURE 6.4

`test-cgi.bat` *sample CGI.*

FIGURE 6.5

Perl installer package selection.

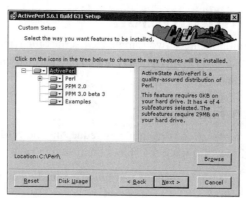

By default, the software will be installed in `C:\Perl`. Then you will be presented with the options of adding an environment variable that contains the path to the Perl installation, and associating Perl script extensions (such as `.pl`) with the Perl interpreter, as shown in Figure 6.6.

FIGURE 6.6

Perl installer environment variable creation.

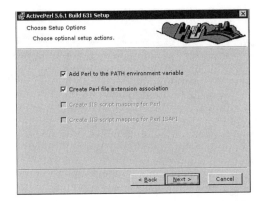

If everything goes well, you will see the Installation Complete screen shown in Figure 6.7.

FIGURE 6.7

Final installation screen.

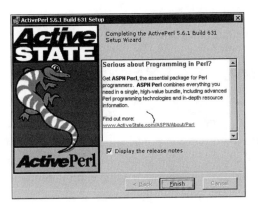

Testing Perl Scripts

There are two ways that you can configure a Perl script to run under Windows. The first one is to modify the first line of the script to point to your Perl interpreter; in this case, `C:\Perl\bin\perl.exe`.

Alternatively, you can let Apache select the interpreter from the file extension by using the Windows registry. You can do so with the `ScriptInterpreterSource` directive. A setting of `ScriptInterpreterSource registry` makes Apache use the registry. `ScriptInterpreterSource script` tells Apache to take a look at the first line of the script.

You can then access the `/cgi-bin/printenv.pl` URL to run the script and see the results, as shown in Figure 6.8.

6

FIGURE 6.8

Sample Perl script output on Windows.

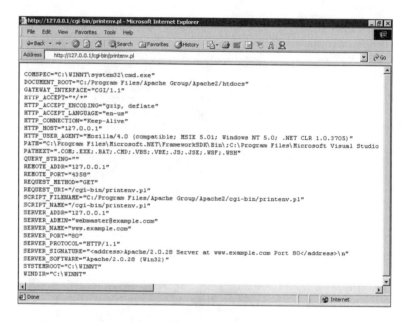

Enhancing Your CGI Performance

One of the main drawbacks of CGI development is the performance impact associated with the requirement to start and stop programs per every request.

mod_perl and FastCGI are two possible solutions for this problem. Both require careful examination of existing code because you can no longer assume in your CGIs that all resources will be automatically freed by the operating system after the request is served.

mod_perl

mod_perl is a module that embeds a Perl interpreter inside the Apache Web server. In addition to a powerful API to Apache internals, mod_perl includes a CGI compatibility mode that provides an environment that allows existing CGIs to run with little or no modification. mod_perl is covered in detail in Hour 20.

FastCGI

FastCGI is a standard that allows the same instance of the CGI program to answer several requests over time. You can read the specs and download software development kits at http://www.fastcgi.com.

At the time of this writing, there is no support for the FastCGI protocol on Apache 2.0. The authors of the previous version mention that a 2.0 version is under development and might have already released by the time you are reading this. Refer to the Fast CGI Web site mentioned earlier for more information.

Common CGI Problems

This section describes common problems you might face when developing with CGI and how to troubleshoot them.

Forbidden Error

If you get a 403 Forbidden error page when trying to access the CGI, the problem is likely due to filesystem permissions or execute permissions.

Filesystem Permissions

This error occurs because Apache has insufficient permissions to read or execute the program. You will find an error log entry similar to the following:

```
[error] [client 10.0.0.3] (13)Permission denied:
➥ access to /cgi-bin/test-cgi denied
```

To fix this, make sure that the user Apache runs as (normally user nobody) has read and execute permissions in the directory containing the CGI and its parent directories.

CGI Execute Permissions

If the directory containing the CGI program has not been marked as allowing CGI execution, you will get an entry like the following in your error log file:

```
[client 10.0.0.2] Options ExecCGI is off in this directory:
➥ /usr/local/apache2/cgi-bin/testcgi
```

To fix this error, use any of the directives described in this hour, such as `ScriptAlias`, `Action`, `Script`, `Options`, and so on. For example:

```
Scriptalias /cgi-bin/ /usr/local/apache2/cgi-bin
```

Internal Server Error

If you get a 500 Internal Server Error message, it means that Apache found an error while trying to execute the CGI script. This can be due to program permissions, interpreter location, or malformed headers, among other reasons.

6

Program Permissions

The error might be caused because the CGI is not executable by the user Apache is running as. You will get an entry in the error log similar to the following:

```
[error] [client 10.0.0.3] Premature end of script headers:
➥ /usr/local/apache2/cgi-bin/test-cgi
```

You can fix this issuing the following command:

```
chmod a+x  program.cgi
```

program.cgi is the name of your CGI script.

Interpreter Location

If your CGI program is a script and Apache cannot find the appropriate interpreter, you will get an error log entry similar to the following:

```
[error] [client 10.0.0.3] Premature end of script headers:
➥ /usr/local/apache2/cgi-bin/printenv
```

To fix this problem, you must edit the source code for the script and make sure that the first line points to the correct interpreter. For example, the sample script might point to `/usr/local/bin/perl`, but the Perl interpreter in that system might be located in `/usr/bin/perl`.

Malformed Headers

The server expects the response from the script as zero or more headers, followed by an empty line, followed by the data requested. If the headers are not in the appropriate format (usually because of an error in the CGI programming logic), you will get an entry like the following in your error log:

```
[error] [client 10.0.0.3] malformed header from script.
➥ Bad header=xxx: /usr/local/apache2/cgi-bin/example.cgi
```

Other Causes

In general, if you get a "premature end of headers" entry in the error log, it is due to an abnormal program termination. The program failure could be caused by a variety of reasons, such as errors in your code, missing libraries that the program is linked to, or the reasons described in the previous sections. In some cases, the operating system or Apache might terminate the process if its resource usage (memory, CPU time) exceeds a certain limit. Hour 16, "Tuning Apache," deals with some of these issues.

Source Code in the Browser

If you see the source code of your script instead of the intended output, it means that Apache did not identify the file as a CGI program. Use a directive explained in this hour, such as `ScriptAlias` or `AddHandler`, to make the association.

Summary

This hour introduced the CGI protocol and the steps necessary to use CGIs with Apache. It has given you an overview of CGI development advantages and disadvantages. In general, you should use CGIs only if you are maintaining existing CGI code or are using existing commercial or open source ready-to-run CGI applications such as user forums, poll systems, shopping carts, and so on. There are plenty of other technologies for generating dynamic content with Apache, such as `mod_perl` and PHP, which are described in later hours. These other technologies provide similar or superior functionality and do not suffer the performance problems associated with CGI.

Q&A

Q How do I enable CGI in home directories?

A In a Unix system, you can use the `<Directory>` directive to enable CGI execution in the home directory of your users:

```
<Directory /home/*/public_html/cgi-bin>
    Options +ExecCGI
    SetHandler cgi-script
</Directory>
```

Users will be able to execute CGI scripts placed in the `public_html/cgi-bin/` subdirectory of their home directory. Allowing users to run CGI scripts has security implications.

Q Can I process the output of my CGI script?

A Yes, the filtering mechanism in Apache 2.0 allows you to process both the headers and the data generated by the CGI script before sending it back to the client. This allows the inclusion of dynamic headers, URL rewriting for user tracking, and so on. Hour 12, "Filtering Modules," introduces filter configuration.

6

Quiz

1. What are the most common causes of "premature end of headers" errors?
2. Where can you look for error messages related to CGI scripts?

Quiz Answers

1. The most frequent causes are related to permissions in the files or parent directories leading to the file, or the path to the interpreter being incorrectly provided in the first line of the script.
2. The normal Apache error log will contain those error messages. Additionally, the ScriptLog directive enables you to specify an additional file that will contain extensive debugging information.

Related Directives

This section contains directives mentioned in this hour or that are related to topics discussed in this hour. You can consult the Apache reference documentation for comprehensive syntax information and usage.

Associating Resources as CGI

- **Script, Action:** Associate MIME types, handlers, and HTTP methods with a specific CGI for processing
- **AddHandler:** Associate file extensions with a specific content type
- **ScriptAlias, ScriptAliasMatch:** Associate directory with URL and mark its contents as containing CGI programs
- **Options:** The ExecCGI option allows CGI execution in a specific container

Debugging and mod_cgid

- **ScriptLog:** Location of the CGI error log
- **ScriptLogBuffer, ScriptLogLength:** Control size of the logged data
- **ScriptSock:** Location of the socket used to communicate with CGI daemon if using mod_cgid module

Further Reading

This section contains additional resources covering CGI programming and Apache configuration.

Apache CGI howto:

`http://httpd.apache.org/docs-2.0/howto/cgi.html`

Perl is the most popular CGI development language. The base Perl distribution already includes a powerful CGI library: `http://stein.cshl.org/WWW/software/CGI`.

CGI category in the Comprehensive Perl Archive Network (CPAN):

`http://www.cpan.org/modules/by-`
`category/15_World_Wide_Web_HTML_HTTP_CGI/CGI`

Comprehensive CGI resource index, including ready-to-run scripts:

`http://www.cgi-resources.com`

CGI Programming with Perl, by Scott Guelich, Shishir Gundavaram, and Gunther Birznieks, is a good written reference.

6

HOUR 7

Restricting Access

This hour explains how to restrict access to parts of a Web site based on the identity of the user or on information about the request.

In this hour, you will learn

- How to restrict access based on the user, client IP address, domain name, and browser version
- How to enable and configure Apache authentication modules
- How to use the user management tools provided with Apache

Authentication

Authorization and authentication are common requirements for many Web sites. Authentication establishes the identity of parties in a communication. You can authenticate yourself by something you know (a password, a cookie), something you have (an ID card, a key), something you are (your fingerprint, your retina), or a combination of these elements. In the context of the Web, authentication is usually restricted to the use of passwords and certificates. Certificates are explained in Hour 17, "Setting Up a Secure Server."

Authorization deals with protecting access to resources. You can authorize based on several factors, such as the IP address the user is coming from, the user's browser, the content the user is trying to access, or who the user is (which is previously determined via authentication).

Apache includes several modules that provide authentication and access control and that can be used to protect both dynamic and static content.

You can either use one of these modules or implement your own access control at the application level and provide customized login screens, single sign-on, and other advanced functionality. Those topics are application- and development language–specific and are not covered in this book, which only deals with authentication and authorization at the Web server level.

Client Authentication

You authenticate users of your Web site for tracking or authorization purposes. The HTTP specification provides two authentication mechanisms: basic and digest. In both cases, the process is the following:

1. A client tries to access restricted content in the Web server.

2. Apache checks whether the client is providing a username and password. If not, Apache returns an HTTP 401 status code, indicating user authentication is required.

3. The client reads the response and prompts the user for the required username and password (usually with a pop-up window).

4. The client retries accessing the Web page, this time transmitting the username and password as part of the HTTP request. The client remembers the username and password and transmits them in later requests to the same site, so the user does not need to retype them for every request.

5. Apache checks the validity of the credentials and grants or denies access based on the user identity and other access rules.

In basic authentication, the username and password are transmitted in clear text, as part of the HTTP request headers. This poses a security risk because an attacker could easily peek at the conversation between server and browser, learn the username and password, and reuse them freely afterwards.

Digest authentication provides increased security because it transmits a digest instead of the clear text password. The digest is based on a combination of several parameters, including the username, password, and request method. The server can calculate the digest on its own and check that the client knows the password, even when the password itself is not transmitted over the network.

> A *digest algorithm* is a mathematical operation that takes a text and returns another text, a digest, which uniquely identifies the original one. A good digest algorithm should make sure that, at least for practical purposes, different input texts produce different digests and that the original input text cannot be derived from the digest. MD5 is the name of a commonly used digest algorithm.

Unfortunately, although the specification has been available for quite some time, only very recent browsers (Internet Explorer 5, Opera 4.0, Konqueror) support digest authentication. This means that for practical purposes, digest authentication is restricted to scenarios in which you have control over the browser software of your clients, such as in a company intranet.

In any case, for both digest and basic authentication, the requested information itself is transmitted unprotected over the network. A better choice to secure access to your Web site involves using the HTTP over SSL protocol, as described in Hour 17, "Setting Up a Secure Server."

User Management

When the authentication module receives the username and password from the client, it needs to verify that they are valid against an existing repository of users. The usernames and passwords can be stored in a variety of backends. Apache bundles support for file- and database-based authentication mechanisms. Third-party modules provide support for additional mechanisms such as LDAP (Lightweight Directory Access Protocol) and NIS (Network Information Services) .

Apache Authentication Modules

This section describes three authentication modules bundled with Apache: mod_auth, mod_auth_dbm, and mod_auth_digest. A fourth module, mod_auth_anon, is also mentioned. You can refer to Hour 18, "Extending Apache," for details on how to enable these modules.

Common Functionality

Apache provides the basic framework and directives to perform authentication and access control. The authentication modules provide support for validating passwords

7

against a specific backend. Users can optionally be organized in groups, easing management of access control rules.

Apache provides three built-in directives related to authentication that will be used with any of the authentication modules: AuthName, AuthType, and Require.

AuthName accepts a string argument, the name for the authentication realm. A *realm* is a logical area of the Web server that you are asking the password for. It will be displayed in the browser pop-up window.

AuthType specifies the type of browser authentication: basic or digest.

Require enables you to specify a list of users or groups that will be allowed access. The syntax is Require user followed by one or more usernames, or Require group followed by one or more group names. For example:

```
Require user joe bob
```

or

```
Require group employee contractor
```

If you want to grant access to anyone who provides a valid username and password, you can do so with

```
Require valid-user
```

With the preceding directives, you can control who has access to specific virtual hosts, directories, files, and so on. Although authentication and authorization are separate concepts, in practice they are tied together in Apache. Access is granted based on specific user identity or group membership. Some third-party modules, such as certain LDAP-based modules, allow for clearer separation between authentication and authorization.

Apache 1.3 offers file-owner and group-owner arguments for the Require directive. In those cases, the username or group must be valid and be the same as the file being accessed in order to gain access to it.

Module Functionality

The authentication modules included with Apache provide

- **Backend storage:** Provide text or database files containing the username and groups information

- **User management:** Supply tools for creating and managing users and groups in the backend storage
- **Authoritative information:** Specify whether the results of the module are authoritative

> Sometimes a user will not be allowed access because it is not found in the user database provided by the module or because no authentication rules matched it. In that case, one of two situations will occur:
>
> - If the module specifies its results as authoritative, the user will be denied access and Apache will return an error.
> - If the module specifies its results as not authoritative, other modules can have a chance of authenticating the user.
>
> This enables you to have a main authorization module that knows about most users, and to be able to have additional modules that can authenticate the rest of the users.

File-Based Authentication

The `mod_auth` Apache module provides basic authentication via text files containing usernames and passwords, similar to how traditional Unix authentication works with the `/etc/passwd` and `/etc/groups` files.

Backend Storage

You need to specify the file containing the list of usernames and passwords and, optionally, the file containing the list of groups.

The users file is a Unix-style password file, containing names of users and encrypted passwords. The entries look like the following, on Unix, using the crypt algorithm:

```
admin:iFrlxqg0Q6RQ6
```

and on Windows, using the MD5 algorithm:

```
admin:$apr1$Ug3.....$jVTedbQWBKTfXsn5jK6UX/
```

The groups file contains a list of groups and the users that belong to each one of them, separated by spaces, such as in the following entry:

```
web: admin joe daniel
```

The `AuthUserFile` and the `AuthGroupFile` directives take a path argument, pointing to the users file and the groups file. The groups file is optional.

7

User Management

Apache includes the htpasswd utility on Unix and htpasswd.exe on Windows; they are designed to help you manage user password files. Both versions are functionally identical, but the Windows version uses a different method to encrypt the password. The encryption is transparent to the user and administrator. The first time you add a user, you need to type the following:

```
htpasswd -c file userid
```

where *file* is the password file that will contain the list of usernames and passwords, and *userid* is the username you want to add. You will be prompted for a password and the file will be created. For example:

```
htpasswd -c /usr/local/apache2/conf/htusers admin
```

will create the password file /usr/local/apache2/conf/htusers and add the admin user.

The -c command-line option tells htpasswd that it should create the file. When you want to add users to an existing password file, do not use the -c option or the file will be overwritten.

It is important that you store the password file outside the document root and thus make it inaccessible via a Web browser. Otherwise, an attacker could download the file and get a list of your usernames and passwords. Although the passwords are encrypted, once you have the file, it is possible to perform a brute force or dictionary attack to try to guess them.

Authoritative

The AuthAuthoritative directive takes a value of on or off. By default it is on, meaning that the module authentication results are authoritative. That is, if the user is not found or does not match any rules, access will be denied.

Using mod_auth

Listing 7.1 shows a sample configuration, restricting access to the private directory in the document root to authenticated users present in the htusers password file. Note that the optional AuthGroupFile directive is not present.

LISTING 7.1   File-Based Authentication Example

```
1: <directory /usr/local/apache2/htdocs/private>
2: AuthType Basic
3: AuthName "Private Area"
4: AuthUserFile /usr/local/apache2/conf/htusers
```

LISTING 7.1   continued

```
5: AuthAuthoritative on
6: Require valid-user
7: </directory>
```

Database File-Based Access Control

Storing usernames and passwords in plain text files is convenient, but it does not scale well. Apache needs to open and read the file sequentially to look for a particular user. When the number of users grows, this becomes a very time-consuming operation. The mod_auth_dbm module enables you to replace the text-based files with indexed database files, which can handle a much greater number of users without performance degradation. mod_auth_dbm is included with Apache, but is not enabled by default.

Backend Storage

The mod_auth_dbm module provides two directives, AuthDBMUserFile and AuthDBMGroupFile, that point to the database files containing the usernames and groups. Unlike plain text files, both directives can point to the same file, which combines both users and groups.

User Management

Apache provides a Perl script (dbmmanage on Unix and dbmmanage.pl on Windows) that allows you to create and manage users and groups stored in a database file. Under Unix, you might need to edit the first line of the script to point to the location of the Perl interpreter in your system. If you do not have Perl installed, Hour 6, "Serving Dynamic Content with CGI," covers Perl installation on both Unix and Windows. On Windows, you need to install the additional MD5 password package. If you are using ActiveState Perl, start the Perl package manager and type

```
install Crypt-PasswdMD5
```

To add a user to a database on Unix, type

```
./dbmmanage dbfile adduser userid
```

On Windows, type

```
perl ./dbmmanage.pl dbfile adduser userid
```

You will be prompted for the password, and the user will be added to the existing database file or a new file will be created if one does not exist.

7

When adding a user, you can optionally specify the groups it belongs to as comma-separated arguments. The following command adds the user daniel to the database file /usr/local/apache2/conf/dbmusers and makes it a member of the groups employee and engineering:

```
dbmmanage /usr/local/apache2/conf/dbmusers adduser daniel employee,engineering
```

If you ever need to delete the user daniel, you can issue the following command:

```
dbmmanage dbfile delete daniel
```

The dbmmanage program supports additional options. You can get complete syntax information in the dbmmanage manual page or by invoking dbmmanage without any arguments.

 Recent versions of Apache 2.0 provide an additional utility, htdbm, that does not depend on Perl and provides all the functionality that dbmmanage does.

Authoritative

The AuthDBMAuthoritative directive takes an argument of on or off. By default it is on, meaning that the module authentication results are authoritative and if the user is not found or does not match any rules, access will be denied.

Using mod_auth_dbm

Listing 7.2 shows a sample configuration, restricting access to Unix home directories to members of the student and faculty groups. As you can see, both users and groups are stored in the same database file.

LISTING 7.2   Database File-Based Authentication Example

```
1: <directory /home/*/public_html>
2: AuthType Basic
3: AuthName "Private Area"
4: AuthDBMUserFile /usr/local/apache2/conf/dbmusers
5: AuthDBMGroupFile /usr/local/apache2/conf/dbmusers
6: AuthDBMAuthoritative on
7: Require group student faculty
8: </directory>
```

Digest-Based Authentication

The mod_auth_digest Apache module is an experimental module that provides support for digest authentication. Only part of its functionality is implemented.

Backend Storage

The `mod_auth_digest` module provides two directives, `AuthDigestFile` and `AuthDigestGroupFile` that point to the files containing the usernames and groups.

User Management

Apache provides a utility, `htdigest` on Unix and `htdigest.exe` on Windows, which provides equivalent functionality to that of `htpasswd`, but with an additional argument: the realm to which the user belongs.

Authoritative

The `AuthDigestAuthoritative` directive takes a value of `on` or `off`. By default it is `on`, meaning that the module authentication results are authoritative and if the user is not found or does not match any rules, access will be denied.

Additional Directives

`AuthDigestDomain` takes a list of URLs that share the same realm and username password protection. This directive is not mandatory, but it helps speed up the internal working of `mod_auth_digest`. The URLs can be absolute (indicating scheme, port, and so on) or relative.

The `mod_auth_digest` module is considered experimental code. This means it is still in development and some of the functionality is not implemented, at least at the time this book was written. The missing functionality deals with the inner workings of the protocol and is not required for normal operation.

Using `mod_auth_digest`

Listing 7.3 shows an example similar in purpose to Listing 7.1, this time using digest authentication. This example uses a `<Location>` container, the value of the `AuthType` directive is `Digest`, and the optional `AuthDigestDomain` directive is present, specifying additional URLs.

LISTING 7.3   Database File-Based Authentication Example

```
1: <Location /private>
2: AuthType Digest
3: AuthName "Private Area"
4: AuthDigestFile /usr/local/apache2/conf/digestusers
5: AuthDigestDomain /private /private2 /private3
6: AuthDigestAuthoritative on
7: Require valid-user
8: </Location>
```

7

Additional Authentication Modules

Apache provides an additional authentication module, mod_auth_anon, that allows anonymous user logins. The user provides his e-mail address as authentication credentials. This does not provide any security, but allows a convenient user tracking mechanism.

Access Control

The mod_access module, enabled by default, enables you to restrict access to resources based on parameters of the client request, such as the presence of a specific header or the IP address or hostname of the client.

Access Rules

You can specify access rules using the Allow and Deny directives. Each of these directives takes a list of arguments such as IP addresses, environment variables, and domain names.

IP Addresses

You can deny or grant access to a client based on its IP address:

```
Allow from 10.0.0.1 10.0.0.2 10.0.0.3
```

You can also specify IP address ranges, with a partial IP address or a network/mask pair.

A Partial IP Address

You can specify the first one, two, or three bytes of an IP address. Any IP address containing those will match this rule. For example, the rule

```
Deny from 10.0
```

will match any address starting with 10.0, such as 10.0.1.0 and 10.0.0.1.

A Network/Mask Pair

The IP address specifies the network and the mask specifies which bits belong to the network prefix and which ones belong to the nodes.

```
Allow from 10.0.0.0/255.255.255.0
```

will match IP addresses 10.0.0.1, 10.0.0.2, and so on, to 10.0.0.254.

You can also specify the network mask via high-order bits. For example, the previous rule could be written as

```
Allow from 10.0.0.0/24
```

Domain Name

You can control access based on specific hostnames or partial domain names. For example, `Allow from example.com` will match `www.example.com`, `foo.example.com`, and so on.

 Enabling access rules based on domain names will force Apache to do a reverse DNS lookup on the client address, bypassing the settings of the `HostNameLookups` directive. The `HostNameLookups` directive is described in Hour 8, "Logging and Monitoring." This has performance implications.

Environment Variables

You can specify access rules based on the presence of a certain environment variable, prefixing the name of the variable with `env=`. You can use this feature to grant or deny access to certain browsers or browser versions, to prevent specific sites from linking to your resources, and so on. Listing 7.4 shows you how to implement browser blocking.

LISTING 7.4   Using Environment Variables to Restrict Access

```
BrowserMatch MSIE iexplorer
Deny from env=iexplorer
```

Note that, for this example to work as intended, the client needs to transmit the User-Agent header. Because the client sends this header, it could be omitted or manipulated, but most users will not do so and the technique will work in most cases.

How to set environment variables is explained in Hour 9, "Content Negotiation and Environment Variables."

All Clients

The keyword `all` matches all clients. You can specify `Allow from all` or `Deny from all` to grant or deny access to all clients.

Access Rules Evaluation

You can have several `Allow` and `Deny` access rules. You can choose the order in which the rules are evaluated by using the `Order` directive. Rules that are evaluated later have higher precedence. `Order` accepts one argument, which can be `Deny,Allow`, `Allow,Deny`, or `Mutual-Failure`. `Deny,Allow` is the default value for the `Order` directive. Note that there is no space in the value.

7

Deny,Allow

Deny,Allow specifies that Deny directives are evaluated before Allow directives. With Deny,Allow, the client is granted access by default if there are no Allow or Deny directives or the client does not match any of the rules. If the client matches a Deny rule, it will be denied access unless it also matches an Allow rule, which will take precedence because Allow directives are evaluated last and have greater priority.

Listing 7.5 shows how to configure Apache to allow access to the /private location to clients coming from the internal network or the domain example.com and deny access to everyone else.

LISTING 7.5   Sample Access Control Configuration

```
1: <location /private>
2:   Order Deny,Allow
3:   Allow from 10.0.0.0/255.255.255.0  example.com
4:   Deny from all
5: </location>
```

Allow,Deny

Allow,Deny specifies that Allow directives are evaluated before Deny directives. With Allow,Deny, the client is denied access by default if there are no Allow or Deny directives or if the client does not match any of the rules. If the client matches an Allow rule, it will be granted access unless it also matches a Deny rule, which will take precedence.

Note that the presence of Order Allow,Deny without any Allow or Deny rules will cause all requests to the specified resource to be denied because the default behavior is to deny access.

Listing 7.6 allows access to everyone except a specific host.

LISTING 7.6   Sample Access Control Configuration

```
1: <location /some/location/>
2:   Order Allow,Deny
3:   Allow from all
4:   Deny from host.example.com
5: </location>
```

Mutual-Failure

In this case, the host will be granted access only if it matches an Allow directive *and* does not match any Deny directive.

Combining Access Methods

In previous sections, you learned how to restrict access based on user identity or request information. The Satisfy directive enables you to determine whether both types of access restrictions must be satisfied in order to grant access. Satisfy accepts one parameter, which can be either all or any.

Satisfy all means that the client will be granted access if it provides a valid username and password *and* passes the access restrictions. Satisfy any means the client will be granted access if it provides a valid username and password *or* passes the access restrictions.

Why is this useful? For example, you might want to provide free access to your Web site to users coming from an internal, trusted network address, but require users coming from the Internet to provide a valid username and password. Listing 7.7 demonstrates just that.

LISTING 7.7 Mixing Authentication and Access Control Rules

```
1: <Location /restricted>
2: Allow from 10.0.0.0/255.255.255.0
3: AuthType Basic
4: AuthName "Intranet"
5: AuthUserFile /usr/local/apache2/conf/htusers
6: AuthAuthoritative on
7: Require valid-user
8: Satisfy any
9: </Location>
```

Access control based on connection or request information is not completely secure. Although it provides an appropriate level of protection for most cases, the rules rely on the integrity of your DNS servers and your network infrastructure. If an attacker gains control of your DNS servers, or your routers or firewalls are incorrectly configured, he can easily change authorized domain name records to point to his machine or pretend he is coming from an authorized IP address.

Limiting Access Based on HTTP Methods

In general, you want your access control directives to apply to all types of client requests and this is the default behavior. In some cases, however, you want to apply authentication and access rules to only certain HTTP methods such as GET and HEAD.

7

The <Limit> container takes a list of methods and contains the directives that apply to requests containing those methods. The complete list of methods that can be used is GET, POST, PUT, DELETE, CONNECT, OPTIONS, TRACE, PATCH, PROPFIND, PROPPATCH, MKCOL, COPY, MOVE, LOCK, and UNLOCK.

Many of these methods are WebDAV methods. WebDAV is a publishing protocol that is based on and extends HTTP. It is covered in Hour 13, "Publishing Extensions."

The <LimitExcept> section provides complementary functionality, containing directives that will apply to requests not containing the listed methods.

Listing 7.8 shows an example from the default Apache configuration file. The <Limit> and <LimitExcept> sections allow read-only methods, but deny requests to any other methods that can modify the content of the file system, such as PUT.

LISTING 7.8   Restricting Access Based on Rule

```
 1: <Directory /home/*/public_html>
 2:     AllowOverride FileInfo AuthConfig Limit
 3:     Options MultiViews Indexes SymLinksIfOwnerMatch IncludesNoExec
 4:     <Limit GET POST OPTIONS PROPFIND>
 5:         Order allow,deny
 6:         Allow from all
 7:     </Limit>
 8:     <LimitExcept GET POST OPTIONS PROPFIND>
 9:         Order deny,allow
10:         Deny from all
11:     </LimitExcept>
12: </Directory>
```

Summary

This hour explained how to restrict access to your Web site based on the identity of the remote user and information from the HTTP request or network connection. It also covered the authentication modules included with Apache and additional tools that you can use to create and manage your user and group databases.

Q&A

Q I have a Unix system. Can I use /etc/passwd as my user database?

A Although it might seem convenient, it is advisable that you do not use the existing /etc/passwd file for authenticating users of your Web site. Otherwise, an attacker who gains access to a user of your Web site will also gain access to the system. Keep separate databases and encourage users to choose different passwords for their system accounts and Web access. Periodically run password checkers that scan for weak passwords and accounts in which the username is also the password.

Q Why am I asked for my password twice in some Web sites?

A Your browser keeps track of your password so that you do not have to type it for every request. The stored password is based on the realm (`AuthName` directive) and the hostname of the Web site. Sometimes you can access a Web site via different names, such as `domain.com` and `www.domain.com`. If you are authorized to access a certain restricted area of `domain.com` but you are redirected or follow a link to `www.domain.com`, you will be asked again to provide the username and password because your browser thinks it is a completely different Web site.

Quiz

1. Can you configure Apache to prevent a certain Web site from linking to yours? (Hint: You can use the `Referer:` HTTP header for this.)

2. What are the advantages of database files over plain text files?

3. Can you name some disadvantages of HTTP basic authentication?

Quiz Answers

1. For example, if you want to deny the example.org Web site access to your site, you can add the following to your configuration file:

```
SetEnvIfNoCase Referer "^http://www.example.org/" evil_site=1
Order Allow,Deny
Allow from all
Deny from env=evil_site
```

2. They are much more scalable because they can be indexed. This means that Apache does not need to read the file sequentially until a match is found for a particular user, but rather can jump to the exact location.

3. One disadvantage is that it is transmitted in clear text over the network. This means that unless you are using SSL (explained in Hour 17), it is possible for an attacker to read the packets your browser sends to the server and steal your password. Another disadvantage is that HTTP authentication does not provide a means for customizing the login (except the realm name). It is very common for Web sites to implement custom login mechanisms using HTML forms and cookies.

7

Related Directives

This section contains directives mentioned in this hour or that are related to topics discussed in this hour. You can consult the Apache reference documentation for comprehensive syntax information and usage.

Common Authentication

- **AuthName:** Name for authentication realm
- **AuthType:** Basic or digest authentication
- **Require:** Users or groups that are allowed access
- **<Limit>, <LimitExcept>:** Limit access control and authentication based on the request method
- **Satisfy:** Require both authentication and access control

File-Based Authentication

- **AuthAuthoritative:** Whether authentication results are authoritative
- **AuthUserFile:** File containing users
- **AuthGroupFile:** File containing groups

Database File-Based Authentication

- **AuthDBMAuthoritative:** Whether authentication results are authoritative
- **AuthDBMUserFile:** File containing users
- **AuthDBMGroupFile:** File containing groups

Digest Authentication

- **AuthDigestAuthoritative:** Whether authentication results are authoritative
- **AuthDigestFile:** File containing users
- **AuthDigestGroupFile:** File containing groups
- **AuthDigestDomain:** List of URLs that share the same realm and username password protection

Access Control

- **Allow, Deny:** Allow or deny access based on IP, hostname, and environment variable
- **Order:** Access rules

Further Reading

Hour 17 covers access control based on certificates and parameters of an SSL connection.

A great number of modules provide access control against various databases, NT domains, Pluggable Authentication Modules (PAMs), and so on. Most of the modules run on Apache 1.3, but they are being ported to work with Apache 2.0. Hour 24, "Additional Apache Modules and Projects," mentions some of them, such as mod_auth_ldap.

Digest authentication is described in RFC 2617. The MD5 algorithm is described in RFC 1321. You can download both RFCs at http://www.rfc-editor.org.

7

HOUR 8

Logging and Monitoring

This hour describes how the logging system in Apache works and how to customize it—which information to store and where to do it. In this hour, you will learn how to

- Understand log formats and logging levels
- Rotate and analyze logs
- Interpret common errors that might appear in your logs
- Monitor Apache resource usage and performance using mod_status

Logging HTTP Requests

You can keep track of who visits your Web sites by logging accesses to the servers hosting them. You can log every aspect of the requests and responses, including the IP address of the client, the user, and the resource accessed. You need to take three steps to create a request log:

1. Define **what** you want to log; your log format
2. Define **where** you want to log it; your log files, a database, an external program
3. Define **whether** or not to log; conditional logging rules

What Do You Want to Log?

You can log nearly every aspect associated with the request. You can define how your log entries look by creating a log format. A log format is a string that contains text mixed with log formatting directives. Log formatting directives start with a % and are followed by a directive name, usually a letter indicating the piece of information to be logged. When Apache logs a request, it scans the string and substitutes the value for each directive. For example, if the log format was This is the client address %a, the log entry will be something like This is the client address 10.0.0.2. That is, the logging directive %a was replaced by the IP address of the client making the request. You can get a comprehensive list of all formatting directives in Table 8.1.

TABLE 8.1   Log Formatting Directives

Formatting Options	Explanation
Data from the Client	
%a	Remote IP address, from the client.
%h	Hostname or IP address of the client making the request. Whether the hostname is logged depends on two factors: The IP address of the client must be able to resolve to a hostname using a reverse DNS lookup, and Apache must be configured to do that lookup using the HostNameLookups directive, explained later in this hour. If these conditions are not met, the IP address of the client will be logged instead.
%l	Remote user, obtained via the identd protocol. This option is not very useful because this protocol is not supported on the majority of the client machines, and the results can't be trusted anyway because the client provides them.
%u	Remote user from the HTTP basic authentication protocol.
Data from the Server	
%A	Local IP address, from the server.
%D	Time it took to serve the request in microseconds.
%{env_variable}e	Value for an environment variable named env_variable.
%{time_format}t	Current time. If {time_format} is present, it will be interpreted as an argument to the Unix strftime function. See the logresolve Apache manual page for details.
%T	Time it took to serve the request, in seconds.
%v	Canonical name of server that answered the request.

8

TABLE 8.1   continued

Formatting Options	Explanation
%V	Server name according to the UseCanonicalName directive.
%X	Status of the connection in the server. A value of 'x' means the connection was aborted before the server could send the data. A '+' means the connection will be kept alive for further requests from the same client. A '-' means the connection will be closed.
Data from the Request	
%{cookie_name}C	Value for a cookie named cookie_name.
%H	Request protocol, such as HTTP or HTTPS.
%m	Request method such as GET, POST, PUT, and so on.
%{header_name}i	Value for a header named header_name in the request from the client. This can be useful, for example, to log the names and versions of your visitors' browsers.
%r	Text of the original HTTP request.
%q	Query parameters, if any, prefixed by a ?.
%U	Requested URL, without query parameters.
Data from the Response	
%b, %B	Size, in bytes, of the body of the response sent back to the client (excluding headers). The only difference between the options is that if no data was sent, %b will log a '-' and %B will log '0'.
%f	Path of the file served, if any.
%t	Time when the request was served.
%{header_name}o	Value for a header named header_name in the response to the client.
%>s	Final status code. Apache can process several times the same request (internal redirects). This is the status code of the final response.

Common Log Format (CLF) is a standard log format. Most Web sites can log requests using this format and the format is understood by many log processing and reporting tools. Its format is the following: "%h %l %u %t \"%r\" %>s %b". That is, hostname or IP address of the client, remote user via identd, remote user via HTTP authentication, time when the request was served, text of the request, status code, and size in bytes of the content served.

You can read the common log format documentation of the original W3C server at http://www.w3.org/Daemon/User/Config/Logging.html.

The following is a sample CLF entry:

```
10.0.0.1 - - [19/Nov/2001:11:34:56 -0800] "GET / HTTP/1.1" 200 1456
```

Note that you cannot trust the value of the username for HTTP authentication if the status code is 401, which means the user needs to authenticate itself.

Each of the formatting directives accepts extra options based on the status of the response. Check the "Conditional Logging" section later in the hour for a detailed explanation.

You are now ready to learn how to define log formats using the LogFormat directive. This directive takes two arguments: The first argument is a logging string, and the second is a nickname that will be associated with that logging string.

For example, the following directive from the default Apache configuration file defines the Common Log Format and assigns it the nickname common:

```
LogFormat "%h %l %u %t \"%r\" %>s %b" common
```

You can also use the LogFormat directive with only one argument, either a log format string or a nickname. This will have the effect of setting the default value for the logging format used by the TransferLog directive, explained in the following section.

Additional Logging Parameters

Other modules can add additional log formatting directives to the LogFormat directive. One example is the SSL module for Apache, described in Hour 17, "Setting Up a Secure Server."

Where Do You Want to Log the Information?

You can log request data to different places, including files, databases, and arbitrary programs for further processing.

Logging to Files

Logging to files is the default way of logging requests in Apache. You can define the name of the file using the TransferLog and CustomLog directives.

The TransferLog directive takes a file argument and will use the latest log format defined by a LogFormat directive with a single argument (the nickname or the format string). If no log format is present, it defaults to the Common Log Format.

The following example shows how to use the LogFormat and TransferLog directives to define a log format that is based on the CLF but that also includes the browser name:

```
LogFormat "%h %l %u %t \"%r\" %>s %b \"%{User-agent}i\""
TransferLog logs/access_log
```

The CustomLog directive enables you to specify the logging format explicitly. It takes at least two arguments: a logging format and a destination file. The logging format can be specified as a nickname or as a logging string directly.

For example, the directives

```
LogFormat "%h %l %u %t \"%r\" %>s %b \"%{User-agent}i\"" myformat
CustomLog logs/access_log myformat
```

and

```
CustomLog logs/access_log "%h %l %u %t \"%r\" %>s %b \"%{User-agent}i\""
```

are equivalent.

The CustomLog format can take an optional environment variable as a third argument, as explained in the "Environment Variables" section later in the hour.

Logging to a Program

Both TransferLog and CustomLog directives can accept a program, prefixed by a pipe sign |, as an argument. Apache will write the log entries to the standard input of the program. The program will, in turn, process them by either logging the entries to a database, transmitting them to another system, and so on.

If the program dies for some reason, the server makes sure that it is restarted. If the server stops, the program is stopped as well.

The rotatelogs utility, bundled with Apache and explained later in this hour, is an example of a logging program.

As a general rule, unless you have a specific requirement for using a particular program, it is easier and more reliable to log to a file on disk and do the processing, merging, analysis of logs, and so on, at a later time, possibly on a different machine.

You need to make sure that the program you use for logging requests is secure because it runs as the user Apache was started with. On Unix, this

> usually means root because the external program will be started before the
> server changes its user ID to the value of the User directive, typically nobody.

Logging to Databases

Apache provides modules that can log requests directly to a backend database such as
MySQL, PostgreSQL, or Oracle. Unfortunately, at the time I am writing this book, those
modules are available only for the 1.3 version of the server.

Additionally, instead of an Apache module, it is possible to use a command-line program
as explained in the previous section. The command-line utility will, in turn, insert the
logs into the database. See the pglogd utility in the "Logging to Databases" section later
in the hour.

Cluster Logging

You can run into scalability and management problems when administering logs from a
great number of machines or a single server receiving a lot of requests. The simple act of
logging to a file on disk can have a significant performance impact on a heavily loaded
server.

There is an Apache module called mod_log_spread that can facilitate cluster logging.
mod_log_spread is based on the Open Source Spread library for reliable distributed communication.

mod_log_spread does not store logs to disk but transmits them over the network using
the spread protocol. The logs are multicasted to multiple log receivers and logging agents
can be added or removed on the fly. The resulting system is highly reliable and can scale
to hundreds of Web servers.

You can find more about mod_log_spread at
http://www.lethargy.org/mod_log_spread/, and about the spread library and protocol
at http://www.spread.org.

At the time of this writing, there is only an Apache 1.3 module, but a version for Apache
2.0 will likely be available soon.

Covalent Technologies (http://www.covalent.net) provides a proprietary logging
framework for Apache 2.0 as part of its enterprise Apache offering.

Conditional Logging

In certain situations, you might want to avoid logging a certain request. For example, you could configure Apache to log requests for only HTML pages, not icons or images, thus easing the load on a busy server. Or you could configure Apache not to log requests from the internal network, so they do not affect the statistics of the site.

The `HostNameLookups` Directive

When a client makes a request, Apache knows only the IP address of the client. Apache must perform what is called a *reverse DNS lookup* to find out the hostname associated with the IP address. This can be a time-consuming operation and can introduce a noticeable lag in the request processing. The `HostNameLookups` directive allows you to control whether to perform the reverse DNS lookup.

`HostNameLookups` can take one of the following arguments: `on`, `off`, or `double`.

The default is `off`. The `double` lookup argument means that Apache will find out the hostname from the IP and then will try to find the IP from the hostname. This is necessary if you are really concerned with security, as described in `http://httpd.apache.org/docs-2.0/dns-caveats.html`. If you are using hostnames as part of your `Allow` and `Deny` rules (described in Hour 7, "Restricting Access"), a double DNS lookup is performed regardless of the `HostNameLookups` settings.

If `HostNameLookups` is enabled (`on` or `double`), Apache will log the hostname; otherwise, it will log only the associated IP address. There are plenty of tools to resolve the IP addresses in the logs later. Refer to the Managing Logs section later in the hour. Additionally, the result will be passed to CGI scripts via the environment variable `REMOTE_HOST`.

The `IdentityCheck` Directive

At the beginning of the hour, it is explained how to log the remote username via the `identd` protocol using the `%l` log formatting directive. The `IdentityCheck` directive takes a value of `on` or `off` to enable or disable checking for that value and making it available for inclusion in the logs. Since the information is not reliable and takes a long time to check, it is switched off by default and should probably never be enabled. The only reason that `%l` is mentioned is because it is part of the Common Log Format.

Environment Variables

The `CustomLog` directive, described previously, accepts an environment variable as a third argument. If the environment variable is present, the entry will be logged; otherwise, it will not. If the environment variable is negated by prefixing an `!` to it, the entry will be logged if the variable is *not* present.

The following example shows how to avoid logging images in GIF and JPEG format in your logs:

```
SetEnvIf Request_URI "(\.gif|\.jpg)$" image
CustomLog logs/access_log common env=!image
```

Status Code

You can specify whether to log specific elements in a log entry. At the beginning of the hour, you learned that log directives start with a %, followed by a directive identifier. In between, you can insert a list of status codes, separated by commas. If the request status is one of the listed codes, the parameter will be logged; otherwise, a - will be logged.

For example, the directive identifier %400,501{User-agent}i will log the browser name and version for malformed requests (status code 400) and requests with methods not implemented (status code 501). This can be useful for tracking which clients can be causing problems.

You can precede the method list with an ! to log the parameter if the methods are implemented:

```
%!400,501{User-agent}i
```

Error Messages

Apache can be configured to log error messages and debug information. In addition to errors generated by Apache itself, CGI errors also will be logged.

Each error log entry is prefixed by the time the error occurred and the client IP address or hostname, if available. As with HTTP request logging, you can log error information to a file or a program. On Unix systems, you can also log to the syslog daemon. There are modules for Apache 1.3 that allow you to log to the Windows event log and will likely be ported to Apache 2.0 over time.

You can use the ErrorLog directive to define where you want your logs to go. It takes one argument, which can be a file, a program, or the syslog daemon.

Logging to a File

A file argument indicates the path to the error log file. If the path is relative, it is assumed to be relative to the server root. By default, the error log file will be located in the logs directory and will be named error_log on Unix and error.log on Windows. The following is an example:

```
ErrorLog logs/my_error_log
```

Logging to a Program

You can specify the path to a program, prefixed by a pipe |. Apache will log errors to the standard input of the program and the program will further process them. The following is an example:

```
ErrorLog "|/usr/local/bin/someprogram"
```

The `syslog` Daemon Argument

On a Unix system, if you specify `syslog` as an argument, you can log error messages to the Unix system log daemon `syslogd`. By default, log errors are logged to the `syslog` facility `local7`. The facility is the part of the system generating the error. You can specify a facility by providing `syslog:facility` as an argument. Examples of `syslog` facilities are `mail`, `uucp`, `local0`, `local1`, and so on. For a complete list, you need to have a look at the documentation for `syslog` included with your system (try `man syslogd` or `man syslogd.conf` at the command line). The following is an example of logging to `syslog`:

```
ErrorLog syslog:local6
```

The `LogLevel` Directive

The error information provided by Apache has several degrees of importance. You can choose to log only important messages and disregard informational or trivial warning messages. The `LogLevel` directive takes an error level argument. Only errors of that level of importance or higher will be logged.

Table 8.2 specifies the valid values for the `LogLevel` directive, as specified by the Apache documentation. By default, the `LogLevel` value is `warn`. That should be enough for most Apache installations. If you are trying to troubleshoot a specific configuration, you can lower the level to `debug`.

TABLE 8.2 `LogLevel` Options as Described in the Apache Documentation

Setting	Description	Example
emerg	Emergencies—system is unusable	`Child cannot open lock file. Exiting.`
alert	Action must be taken immediately	`getpwuid: couldn't determine user name from uid.`
crit	Critical conditions	`socket: Failed to get a socket, exiting child.`
error	Error conditions	`Premature end of script headers.`
warn	Warning conditions	`Child process 1234 did not exit, sending another SIGHUP.`

TABLE 8.2   Continued

Setting	Description	Example
notice	Normal but significant condition	httpd: caught SIGBUS, attempting to dump core in...
info	Informational	Server seems busy, (You may need to increase StartServers, or Min/MaxSpareServers)...
debug	Debug-level messages	Opening config file...

Monitoring Apache

The Apache distribution contains two modules that allow you to monitor its configuration and real-time behavior and performance.

The mod_info module provides information about the configuration of the server and modules installed. Figure 8.1 shows a sample report page. This module is included with Apache, but is not compiled by default.

FIGURE 8.1

Sample mod_info *page.*

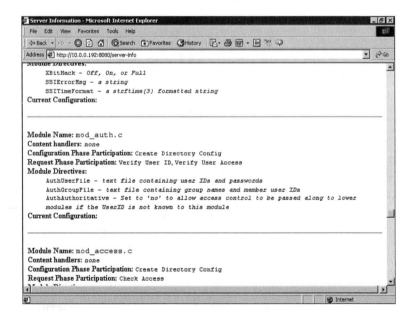

The mod_status module provides real-time information about Apache, as shown in Figure 8.2. The page shows the number of current children, how many of them are idle, which requests are being answered, the traffic served by Apache so far, the server uptime, and so on.

FIGURE 8.2
Sample mod_status
page.

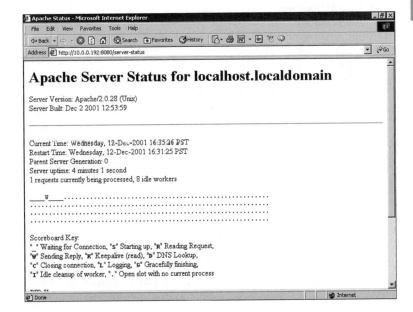

Configuring Modules

Both mod_info and mod_status provide Apache handlers. You must run the handler in a <Location> block to access the content provided by the modules. Because the information contains sensitive data, it is a good idea to protect the access to that location by using a password or IP-based access control, as explained in Hour 7.

Listings 8.1 and 8.2 show sample settings for enabling mod_info and mod_status and restricting access to them, as included in the default Apache configuration file. You must replace .example.com with the domain name for your particular network.

LISTING 8.1 Enabling mod_status

```
<Location /server-status>
    SetHandler server-status
    Order deny,allow
    Deny from all
    Allow from .example.com
</Location>
```

LISTING 8.2 Enabling `mod_info`

```
<Location /server-info>
    SetHandler server-info
    Order deny,allow
    Deny from all
    Allow from .example.com
</Location>
```

After the modules are compiled into the server (or loaded as shared modules), the capability to display the information is available across all configuration files, including per-directory configuration files. This can pose a security risk because the information provided by the modules, such as the complete configuration for the server, contains sensitive data.

Additional Configuration

You can use the `AddModuleInfo` directive to provide a snippet of additional information for a specific module. It takes two arguments: The first argument is a module name, and the second is an HTML string that will be added to the `mod_info` page.

The `ExtendedStatus` directive can be used to provide additional information in the `mod_status` information page. It is set to `off` by default.

The `log_status` Perl script in the `support` subdirectory of the Apache distribution can be used to periodically monitor the status of the server.

Additional Log Files

Other modules, such as `mod_rewrite` (Hour 22), SSL (Hour 17), and `mod_cgi` (Hour 6), have their own log files. You can learn more about them in their respective hours.

Managing Logs

Apache provides several tools for managing your logs. Other Apache-specific third-party tools are available and are mentioned here. Because Apache can log requests in the Common Log Format, most generic log processing tools can be used with Apache as well.

Resolving Hostnames

Earlier in the hour, you learned how to use the `HostNameLookups` directive to enable or disable hostname resolution at the time the request is made. If `HostNameLookups` is set to `off` (the default), the log file will contain only IP addresses. Later, you can use the command-line `logresolve` utility on Unix or `logresolve.exe` on Windows to process the log file and convert the IP addresses to hostnames.

`logresolve` reads log entries from standard input and outputs the result to its standard output. To read to and from a file, you can use redirection, on both Unix and Windows:

```
logresolve < access.log > resolved.log
```

Log resolving tools are efficient because they can cache results and they do not cause any delay when serving requests to clients.

Fastresolve is an alternative, freely available log resolving utility that can be found at `http://www.pix.net/staff/djm/sw/fastresolve/`.

Log Rotation

In Web sites with high traffic, the log files can quickly grow in size. It is necessary to have a mechanism to rotate logs periodically, archiving and compressing older logs at well-defined intervals.

Log files cannot be removed directly while Apache is running because the server is writing directly to them. The solution is to use an intermediate program to log the requests. The program will, in turn, take care of rotating the logs.

Apache provides the `rotatelogs` program on Unix and `rotatelogs.exe` on Windows for this purpose. It accepts three arguments: a filename, a rotate interval in seconds, and an optional offset in minutes against UTC (Coordinated Universal Time).

For example,

```
TransferLog "|bin/rotatelogs /var/logs/apachelog 86400"
```

will create a new log file and move the current log to the `/var/logs` directory daily. (86400 is the number of seconds in one day.)

> If the path to the program includes spaces, you might need to escape them by prefixing them with a \ (backslash). This is especially common in the Windows platform.

If the name of the file includes % prefixed options, the name will be treated as input to the strftime function that converts the % options to time values. The manual page for rotatelogs contains a complete listing of options, but just as an example:

```
TransferLog "|bin/rotatelogs /var/logs/apachelog%m_%d_%y 86400"
```

will add the current month, day, and year to the log filename.

If the name does not include any %-formatted options, the current time in seconds is added to the name of the archived file.

cronolog and httplog are additional log rotating programs. httplog adds support for additional compression of log files. You can find them at http://www.cronolog.org/ and http://nutbar.chemlab.org/downloads/.

Merging and Splitting Logs

When you have a cluster of Web servers serving similar content, maybe behind a load balancer, it is often necessary to merge the logs from all the servers in a unique log stream before passing it to analysis tools.

Similarly, if a single Apache server instance handles several virtual hosts, sometimes it is useful to split a single log file into different files, one per each virtual host.

Logtools is a collection of log manipulation tools that can be found at http://www.coker.com.au/logtools/.

Apache includes the split-file Perl script for splitting logs. It can be found in the support subdirectory of the Apache distribution.

Logging to Databases

Apache itself does not include tools for logging to databases, but a few third-party scripts and programs are available.

pglogd collects logs and stores them in a PostgreSQL database. It can be found at http://www.digitalstratum.com/pglogd/.

The Eureka tool allows you to import existing log files into a database and do interactive, on-the-fly querying. It can be found at http://sourceforge.net/projects/eureka/.

Log Analysis

After you have collected the logs, you can analyze them and gain information about traffic and visitor behavior.

There are many commercial and freely available applications for log analysis and reporting. Two of the most popular open source applications are Webalizer (`http://www.mrunix.net/webalizer/`) and awstats (`http://awstats.sourceforge.net`).

Wusage is a nice, inexpensive commercial alternative and can be found at `http://www.boutell.com/wusage/`.

Monitoring Error Logs

If you run Apache on a Unix system, you can use the `tail` command-line utility to monitor, in real time, log entries both to your access and error logs. The syntax is

```
tail -f logname
```

`logname` is the path to the Apache log file. It will print on screen the last few lines of the log file and will continue to print entries as they are added to the file.

There are additional programs that enable you to quickly identify problems by scanning your error log files for specific errors, malformed requests, and so on, and reporting on them:

- Logscan can be found at `http://www.garandnet.net/security.php`
- ScanErrLog can be found at `http://www.librelogiciel.com/software/`

Common Errors

As you run your Web site day to day, you might find several common kinds of errors, some of which are described in this section. Most of them can be safely ignored.

Connection Reset by Peer

This is a harmless error that appears when a client disconnects before completing the request, usually because the user closed the browser or pressed the Back button while a request was in process.

File `favico.icon` Not Found

When a user bookmarks a page using a browser such as Internet Explorer or Konqueror, the program requests a file, `favico.icon`, that contains an icon to be displayed next to the bookmark entry. If that file does not exist, you will get this error. You can learn more about this icon in Hour 5, "Using Apache to Serve Static Content."

File `robots.txt` Not Found

Another harmless error. This file is requested by Web crawlers, also known as *Web spiders*. They are programs, usually associated with search engines, that scan the Internet searching and indexing content. Well-behaved Web spiders will request this file and use its contents to learn which parts of the Web site they are allowed to connect to and which parts they should stay away from. You can learn more about this file in Hour 16, "Tuning Apache."

`httpd.pid` Overwritten

This message appears if the previous Apache did not have a clean shutdown. This means that it had to be killed manually or crashed before it had time to remove its `pid` file, as occurs during a normal shutdown.

In addition to the errors detailed in this section, you might find common CGI errors in the error logs, usually related to script permissions, abnormal termination, and buggy scripts. They are described in Hour 6, "Serving Dynamic Content with CGI." You might also see errors related to the multi-processing modules (MPMs).

These are errors related to Apache reaching the maximum number of possible connections, processes, threads, and so on. They are explained in Hour 11, "Multi-Processing Modules."

Summary

This hour's lesson explained how to log specific information about the requests and errors generated by Apache. You can store the logs in files or databases, or pass them to external programs.

You learned about the different utilities available for managing, processing, and analyzing logs, both the ones included with Apache and those available from third parties.

Finally, the hour introduced two Apache modules commonly used to monitor the state and configuration of the server.

Q&A

Q Why wouldn't I want to log images?

A In this hour, you learned how to avoid logging certain types of files, such as images. But why would you like to do that? In heavily loaded servers, logging can become a bottleneck. If the purpose of logging is to count the number of visitors

and analyze their usage of the Web site, this can be achieved by logging only the HTML pages, not the images contained in them. This reduces the number of hits stored in the logs and the time spent writing them.

Q What are those weird log entries?

A From time to time, you might find a multitude of requests looking for `cmd.exe`, `root.exe`, or similar programs. They are usually preceded by a long string of character and path components. They probably belong to an Internet worm, such as Red Code. A worm is a malicious program that exploits vulnerabilities of Web servers such as Microsoft IIS. After the program gains control of the server, it uses your server to launch attacks on other servers. At the time of writing this book, Apache is not vulnerable to any of those attacks and you can safely ignore those entries.

Quiz

1. How would you avoid logging hits from a client accessing your Web site from a particular network?

2. How can you log images to a different file?

Quiz Answers

1. How would you avoid logging hits from a client accessing your Web site from a particular network?

   In some situations, it is desirable to ignore requests coming from a particular network, such as your own, so that they do not skew the results. This can be done either by post-processing the logs and removing them or by using the SetEnvIf directive:

   ```
   SetEnvIf Remote_Addr 10\.0\.0\. intranet
   CustomLog logs/access_log "%h %l %u %t \"%r\" %>s %b" !intranet
   ```

2. How can you log images to a different file?

   Earlier in the hour, you learned how to avoid logging images. Instead of ignoring images altogether, you can easily log them to a separate file, using the same environment variable mechanism:

   ```
   SetEnvIf Request_URI "(\.gif|\.jpeg)$" image
   CustomLog logs/access_log common env=!image
   CustomLog logs/images_log common env=image
   ```

Related Directives

This section contains directives mentioned in this hour or that are related to topics discussed in this hour. You can consult the Apache reference documentation for comprehensive syntax information and usage.

- **TransferLog:** Log requests to a file or program.
- **CookieLog:** Deprecated directive included for compatibility purposes. You should use CustomLog instead.
- **LogFormat:** Define a log format for use with other directives such as TransferLog or CustomLog.
- **CustomLog:** Log to a file or program with a custom log format.
- **ErrorLog:** File or program where to log errors.
- **LogLevel:** Establish error-reporting threshold.
- **AddModuleInfo:** Add additional information to mod_info reports.
- **ExtendedStatus:** Provide additional information in mod_status reports.
- **SetEnvIf:** Set environment variables based on the request.

Further Reading

This hour mentions a variety of tools for processing and managing logs. You can find additional tools at two popular open source Web sites: http://freshmeat.net and http://sourceforge.net.

Several tutorials on logging are available from http://httpd.apache.org/docs-2.0/misc/tutorials.html.

Additional Apache documentation on logging can be found at http://httpd.apache.org/docs-2.0/logs.html.

HOUR 9

Content Negotiation and Environment Variables

This hour will show you how to configure Apache so that it can serve different versions of a Web site's content based on the client settings. It will also cover what environment variables are and how to use them, for example, to work around browser bugs. In this hour, you will learn

- What content negotiation is and how to configure Apache to provide support for it
- How to use environment variables to modify Apache behavior

Environment Variables

Environment variables are variables that can be shared between modules and are also available to external processes such as CGIs and server side include (SSI) documents. (See Hour 12, "Filtering Modules," for more information about SSI documents.) Environment variables also can be used for inter-module communication and to flag certain requests for special processing.

You can set environment variables with the SetEnv directive. This variable will be available to CGI scripts and SSI pages, and can be logged or added to a header. For example,

```
SetEnv foo bar
```

will create the environment variable foo and assign it the value bar. You can then access this variable from a Perl script with

```
print $ENV(foo)
```

or from a SSI page with

```
<!--#echo var="foo" -->
```

You can log its value with the %{foo}e formatting option, as explained in Hour 8, "Logging and Monitoring." Or you can add it to a header, as explained later in this hour, with

```
Header set X-Foo "%{foo}e"
```

You can remove specific variables using the UnsetEnv directive. For example,

```
UnsetEnv foo
```

will remove the environment variable foo so that it is not available to scripts or SSI pages.

The PassEnv directive enables you to expose variables from the server process environment. The server process environment contains information about the operating system version, the location of important files and libraries, the current path, and so on. For example,

```
PassEnv LD_LIBRARY_PATH
```

will make the environment variable LD_LIBRARY_PATH available to CGI scripts and SSI pages. This variable contains the path to loadable dynamic libraries in some Unix systems, such as Linux.

Standard Environment Variables

A set of environment variables is available for every request and passed to CGI scripts. This set is defined at http://hoohoo.ncsa.uiuc.edu/cgi/env.html. Table 9.1 provides a listing of their names and meaning.

TABLE 9.1   Standard Environment Variables

Environment Variable	Meaning
SERVER_SOFTWARE	Name of the server (Apache, in this case) and version number.
SERVER_NAME	Hostname or IP address of the Apache server.
GATEWAY_INTERFACE	Version of the CGI specification, such as CGI/1.1.
SERVER_PROTOCOL	Request protocol, such as HTTP/1.1.
SERVER_PORT	Port that the request was addressed to.
REQUEST_METHOD	HTTP request method, such as GET or POST.
PATH_INFO	Additional path information in the URL, after the path to the script.
PATH_TRANSLATED	Resultant path from adding PATH_INFO to the document root path.
SCRIPT_NAME	Location path to the CGI script; for example, /cgi-bin/script.pl.
QUERY_STRING	Any query parameters passed in the URL.
REMOTE_ADDR	Client IP address.
REMOTE_HOST	Client hostname, if available; otherwise, the client IP address.
AUTH_TYPE	HTTP authentication method, such as basic authentication, as explained in Hour 7, "Restricting Access."
REMOTE_USER	HTTP authentication username.
REMOTE_IDENT	Username according to the identd protocol. Not used for a variety of reasons explained in Hour 8.
CONTENT_TYPE	Content type of requests with attached data, such as POST requests.
CONTENT_LENGTH	Size of the attached data, if any.

The value of an HTTP header can be accessed via an environment variable by prefixing the header name with HTTP_ and converting any dashes to underscores. For example, the User-Agent: header can be accessed via the HTTP_USER_AGENT environment variable.

Certain modules, such as SSL, which is described in Hour 17, "Setting Up a Secure Server," provide additional environment variables.

> The directives described in this hour cannot overwrite the values of standard environment variables.

Setting Environment Variables Dynamically

The SetEnvIf directive enables you to set environment variables based on request information, such as the username, the file being requested, or a specific HTTP header value.

This directive takes a request parameter, a regular expression, and a set of variables that will be modified if the parameter matches the expression.

For example, you can match Internet Explorer browsers with this line:

```
SetEnvIf HTTP_USER_AGENT MSIE iexplorer
```

This line will set the environment variable `iexplorer` to the value 1. You can also set the variable to an arbitrary value:

```
SetEnvIf HTTP_USER_AGENT MSIE iexplorer=true
```

or even use a negated expression:

```
SetEnvIf HTTP_USER_AGENT MSIE !javascript
```

Later, you can check the existence and value of this variable to perform a variety of actions:

- You can provide different content based on the browser. For example, simplified HTML pages for text browsers such as Lynx, or for PDA and cell phone browsers.
- Decide whether to log a specific request, as explained in Hour 8.
- Rewrite the URL request with `mod_rewrite`, which is explained in Hour 22, "Dynamic URI Resolution with `mod_rewrite`."

In fact, checking for the client user agent is so common that `mod_setenvif` provides the `BrowserMatch` directive. The previous directive could be rewritten as

```
BrowserMatch MSIE iexplorer=1
```

 Both `SetEnvIf` and `BrowserMatch` have case-insensitive versions, `SetEnvIfNoCase` and `BrowserMatchNoCase`, that can be used to simplify the regular expressions in certain situations.

Special Environment Variables

Apache provides a set of special environment variables. If one of those variables is set, Apache will modify its behavior. They are commonly used to work around buggy clients. Table 9.2 provides a list of those environment variables and the meaning of each one.

TABLE 9.2 Special Environment Variables

Environment Variable	Meaning
downgrade-1.0	The client request will be interpreted as an HTTP/1.0 request.
force-no-vary	The Vary: header, explained later in the hour, is not correctly interpreted by some browsers and the presence of this environment variable will remove them from the served requests.
force-response-1.0	Some clients do not behave correctly when an HTTP/1.1 response is returned. When this variable is set, Apache will return an HTTP/1.0 response.
nokeepalive	Certain clients have problems with keep-alives; setting this variable disables support for them.
redirect-carefully	Certain clients have problems handling redirects, and setting this variable works around those problems. This is the case for DAV clients, as explained in Hour 13, "Publishing Extensions."
ssl-unclean-shutdown, ssl-accurate-shutdown	These environment variables are used to work around buggy client-side SSL protocol implementations. SSL is covered in Hour 17.
no-gzip	You can use this environment variable to indicate to mod_deflate not to perform content compression.

Header Manipulation

The Header and RequestHeader directives, provided by the mod_headers module, can be used to add and remove arbitrary headers in HTTP requests and responses.

You can add a response HTTP header, deleting any other HTTP headers with the same name that might be present by using

Header set *header-name header-value*

If you want to add a new header instead of replacing an existing one, you can use

Header add *header-name header-value*

If you want to append the value to an existing header, you can use

`Header append header-name header-value`

You can remove certain headers by using the following directive:

`Header unset header-name`

You can modify the request headers by using `RequestHeader` instead of `Header`.

You can add the content of environment variables to the `header-value` argument by using the format string `%{variable-name}e`; this is similar to how the `LoggingFormat` directive works, as explained in Hour 8. This could be useful when you are using Apache as a reverse proxy so that you can pass client information to the backend server. Information such as client address and hostname is lost because from the point of view of the backend server, the request seems to be coming from the reverse proxy. Hour 15, "Apache as a Proxy Server," covers using Apache as a reverse proxy.

Content Negotiation

Users accessing your Web site do so using a variety of browsers, and each one has different capabilities. The HTTP protocol provides mechanisms that enable you to maintain different versions of a certain resource and return the appropriate content. For example, you might want to maintain photo images with different resolutions and formats, and deliver the lower-resolution images to browsers with limited display capabilities and the higher-resolution images to more-capable browsers. Content negotiation is also commonly used to maintain multilingual sites. Before moving into the details of how content negotiation works, the following two sections explain the concepts of encoding and character sets.

Content Encoding

Hour 5, "Using Apache to Serve Static Content," introduced the concept of MIME types, which can be used to specify the content type of a resource such as text, video, image, and so on.

Encoding is the format in which a resource is stored or represented. You can think of it as a wrapper around the resource. Encoding usually relates to compression (such as files compressed with `gzip`), encryption, and UUencode (Unix-to-Unix encode, which is used to represent binary content using ASCII characters). The encoding information will appear in the `Content-Encoding:` header.

Encoding can usually be determined from the file extension. For example, `listing.txt.gz` has a MIME type of `text/plain` and a `gzip` encoding. You can use the

`AddEncoding` directive to associate file extensions with specific encodings. For example, `AddEncoding gzip .gz .gzip` adds the `gzip` encoding to the `gz` and `gzip` file extensions.

> To support older browsers, it is recommended that you use `AddEncoding x-gzip .gz .gzip` instead. Consult the `AddEncoding` Apache manual page for additional information.

You can use `RemoveEncoding` to remove any MIME type association from specific file extensions.

Character Sets

In addition to the encoding, it is important to specify the language and character set for a resource. The language will be specified in the `Content-Language:` HTTP header and the character set appended to the `Content-Type:` header, together with the MIME type. For example:

```
Content-Language: en
Content-Type: text/plain; charset=ISO-8859-1
```

You can use `AddCharset` to associate character sets with specific file extensions, and `RemoveCharset` to remove those associations. For example:

```
AddCharset UTF-8 .utf8
```

Similarly, you can use `AddLanguage` and `RemoveLanguage` to associate languages with file extensions, as in

```
AddLanguage en .en
```

You can specify a default language with the `DefaultLanguage` directive. For a Web site in English, that would be

```
DefaultLanguage en
```

You can specify a default character set for documents without one associated by using the `AddDefaultCharset` directive:

- **AddDefaultCharset On** will add the `iso-8859-1` character set, which is the default.
- **AddDefaultCharset Off** will disable this behavior.
- **AddDefaultCharset *charset*** enables you to set a specific default character set.

You can find additional information about character sets and language codes at
`http://www.w3.org/International/O-charset.html`.

Negotiation

This section explains how HTTP negotiation works from the perspective of both the
client and the server.

Client Negotiation

Clients express their preferences using a variety of headers, and it is Apache's job to provide the resource that best matches those preferences for languages, file formats, and
so on.

The `Accept-Encoding:` header specifies the encodings that the browser understands,
such as compressed content. The `Accept-Language:` header specifies the preferred languages. The `Accept-Charset:` header allows the client to specify the character sets that
the client supports.

Finally, with the `Accept:` header, the client lists the MIME types it understands and its
preferences. The following line is a sample `Accept:` header from an Internet Explorer
browser:

```
Accept: image/gif, image/x-xbitmap, image/jpeg, image/pjpeg,
➥ application/vnd.ms-powerpoint, application/vnd.ms-excel,
➥ application/msword, */*
```

The client can provide a quality factor for each MIME type, language, character set, and
so on that it supports. This is a number between 0 and 1 that can be used to establish a
preference. For example,

```
Accept-Language: en; q=1.0, fr; q=0.8
```

tells the server the client prefers documents written in English, but also will accept documents written in French.

Server Configuration

There are two main ways to configure content negotiation in Apache: multiviews and
type maps.

Multiviews

You can turn on the multiviews negotiation mechanism by adding an

```
Options +Multiviews
```

directive to your configuration. Whenever a document is requested, Apache will look for
similar documents with additional extensions. For example, if a document named `index`

is requested, Apache will look for files such as index.en.html and index.txt in that directory. It will construct a list of such files and use the extensions to determine the content encoding and character set, and deliver the appropriate content to the client.

If the client does not provide a language preference, you can use LanguagePriority to determine the preferred language order. For example,

```
LanguagePriority en fr de
```

means that if a document in English is found, it will be served. Otherwise, Apache will look for a document in French, and if that is not found, Apache will look for a document in German.

The MultiviewsMatch directive enables you to fine-tune the behavior of Apache. It can take several options: NegotiatedOnly means that only those extensions associated with a MIME type will be taken into account in the negotiation process. You can also add the Handlers and Filters options to include extensions associated with handlers and filters. Finally, you can specify Any to include any extension. This is not recommended because it could allow unintended access to, for example, backup files ending in .bak.

Type Maps

Type maps are special files that contain a mapping between filenames and metadata about those files, such as their MIME type and language. You can configure a type map for a certain resource by creating a file with the same name and the .var extension, and adding AddHandler type-map .var to your configuration file. The final step is to tell Apache about the .var extension with

```
AddHandler type-map .var
```

The file can contain several entries. Each entry starts with a URI: that is the name of the document, followed by several attributes such as Content-Type:, Content-Language:, and Content-Encoding:. Listing 9.1 shows a sample type map file.

LISTING 9.1   Sample Type Map page.var File

```
URI: page.html.en
Content-type: text/html
Content-language: en

URI: page.html.fr
Content-type: text/html; charset=iso-8859-2
Content-language: fr
```

Whenever a document is requested, Apache will look for a type map file and try to match the resource, taking into account the following factors, in this order: media type, language, media type level, character set, content encoding, and the smallest content length. If a single document cannot be selected, the user will be presented with a page containing a choice of the available documents.

The Vary: Header

The Vary: response header is set automatically by the server to specify the factors (dimensions) that were taken into account when negotiating the document that was finally delivered. The Vary: header also will be provided when no acceptable variant was found. Browsers and proxies can use this information to make caching decisions.

Summary

This hour explained how to configure Apache so that it can serve different content based on the language or file format preferences of your client's browsers. You learned what environment variables are and how they can be used to modify Apache behavior, usually to work around specific browser bugs. This hour also explained how to use Apache configuration directives to alter the content of request and response headers.

Q&A

Q What are valid names for environment variables?

A Environment variables can contain only letters of the English alphabet, numbers, and underscores and cannot begin with a number. Any other characters, such as dashes in HTTP headers, will be converted to underscores.

Q Which content negotiation configuration method is better?

A The multiviews method is easier to configure, but could affect performance because Apache must access the disk for every request to look for available files. Type maps require more effort, but the performance and flexibility are greater.

Q Does the order of the elements in Accept:, Accept-language:, and other negotiation headers imply preference?

A No, preferences are specified using quality factors. However, not that many browsers report quality factors, so in those cases, Apache applies an algorithm that assigns a greater preference to more specific MIME types. For example, text/html will be assigned a quality factor of 1.0, and */* a factor of 0.01. You can refer to the Apache documentation for further information.

Quiz

1. What directive would you use to add a request header with the protocol used to serve the request?

2. Which special environment variable is used to request that the content being served not be compressed?

Quiz Answers

1. You can do so with the following directive:

   ```
   RequestHeader set X-Protocol "${SERVER_PROTOCOL}e"
   ```

   This type of configuration directive is particularly useful when you need to pass client information to a backend server in a reverse proxy situation, as explained in Hour 15.

2. You can use the `no-gzip` environment variable. You can refer to Hour 12 for additional information about compression.

Related Directives

This section contains directives related to topics discussed in this hour. You can consult the Apache reference documentation for comprehensive syntax information and usage.

Environment Variables

- **SetEnv:** Set an environment variable.
- **UnsetEnv:** Unset an environment variable.
- **PassEnv:** Make available a variable of the server's own environment.
- **BrowserMatch, BrowserMatchNoCase:** Set an environment variable if the browser user agent matches a special pattern.
- **SetEnvIf, SetEnvIfNoCase:** Set an environment variable based on client information.

Header Manipulation

- **Header:** Set, unset, or manipulate response headers.
- **RequestHeader:** Set, unset, or manipulate request headers.

Content Negotiation

- **AddCharset, RemoveCharset:** Establish or remove associations between character sets and file extensions.

- **AddLanguage, RemoveLanguage:** Establish or remove associations between language codes and file extensions.

- **LanguagePriority:** Specify a language priority in case the client did not provide one.

- **DefaultLanguage:** Default language for documents.

- **AddDefaultCharset:** Specify whether to add a default character set when serving documents without one specified.

- **Options +Multiviews:** Enable multiviews negotiation method.

- **MultiviewsMatch:** Fine-tuning of multiviews negotiation method.

- **AddEncoding, RemoveEncoding:** Establish or remove associations between language codes and file extensions.

- **AddType, RemoveType, ForceType, TypesConfig:** Manipulate MIME type associations. These directives are covered in Hour 6, "Serving Dynamic Content with CGI."

Further Reading

You can find additional information about content negotiation and Apache at

http://httpd.apache.org/docs-2.0/content-negotiation.html

The mod_charset_lite module enables you to perform character set conversions. This is an experimental module included with Apache.

RFC 1766 specifies tags for identification of languages.

Hour **10**

Apache GUIs

This hour presents several graphical configuration tools that you can use to manage the configuration of your Apache server. In this hour, you will learn

- The advantages and disadvantages of using GUIs and how they compare to text-based configuration
- How to install and use the Comanche and Webmin GUI tools for configuring Apache

GUIs and Text-Based Configuration

There seems to be a never-ending debate about which is a better method for configuring a server: editing text files or using a GUI?

Well, it depends. And, in many cases, these approaches don't exclude each other.

Using Text Files for Configuration

Configuring Apache via text-based configuration files has several advantages. You don't need special software to make configuration changes, just a simple text editor. This enables remote configuration in Unix systems, via `telnet` or `ssh` (a secure version of the Unix remote shell command). These tools don't require much bandwidth, and remote configuration can occur over slow links such as modem connections. Configuration files can be easily backed up or put under a source control system.

The Apache configuration file allows comments to be inserted next to directives. You can document specific settings, either as a reminder for the next time you edit the file or to help other system administrators.

If you must administer a great number of Web sites, you can benefit greatly from a text-based configuration system. You can keep a configuration file template and populate it with the appropriate values for each new Web site.

Using a GUI for Configuration

Although text-file-based configuration is useful in many situations, there are other situations in which GUIs could be appropriate. Well-designed GUIs can provide significant ease of use. It seems each Unix program has its own different configuration file format and directives. Each time you need to configure a new type of server, there's a significant learning curve, especially with the great number of configuration options possible in Apache. What's more, with a configuration system based on text files, there's no easy way to distinguish which of the options are really important and which ones are accessory. A well-designed GUI can provide a consistent and well-organized interface to a variety of programs. The interface can help the user distinguish which features are important, provide context-sensitive help, and guide the user with task wizards.

Badly designed GUIs can provide confusing configuration screens, a limited set of functionality, and not play nicely with the underlying configuration files; for example, by not preserving comments introduced by hand.

The following sections explain how to install two popular GUI applications: Comanche and Webmin. Before installing any of the applications, it's important to take the time to back up your `httpd.conf` file and any other files referenced via the `Include` directive.

Webmin

Webmin is a Web-based administration system for Unix-like servers, including Linux and Mac OS X. It can configure nearly every aspect of the operating system and a variety of servers, such as file servers, mail servers, and, of course, Apache. Webmin is written in Perl, has an open source license, and is extensible via modules. The Webmin Web site can be found at `http://www.webmin.com/webmin/`.

In this section, you will learn how to download, install, and configure Webmin. You will also learn how the Webmin interface works and how to perform basic tasks.

Installing Webmin

Most modern Linux distributions include a Webmin package. If your system is `rpm`-based, such as the Red Hat, SuSE, and Mandrake distributions, you can check whether Webmin is installed by issuing the `rpm -q webmin` command. If Webmin isn't installed, you can use the package from your distribution, the `rpm` available at `http://www.webmin.com`, or install from source as explained in this section.

 Because Webmin is written in Perl, you need a Perl interpreter in the system. Refer to Hour 6, "Serving Dynamic Content with CGI," for instructions on how to install Perl.

You can download the Webmin sources from `http://www.webmin.com/webmin/download.html`. In addition to finding the download `rpm` packages for Linux there, you can also find `pkg` packages for Solaris. The downloaded package will be named `webmin-version.tar.gz`.

To uncompress the sources and start the installation process, type the following:

```
# gunzip < webmin-version.targ.gz | tar xvf -
# cd webmin-version
# ./setup.sh
```

Make sure to substitute `version` for the appropriate Webmin version. You will then be prompted for the following information:

- **Config file directory:** This is where Webmin will store the configuration information for all the programs it can configure and for Webmin itself. The default location is `/etc/webmin`. The rest of the hour assumes that Webmin is installed there.

- **Log file directory:** This is where Webmin will store its log files; the default location is `/var/webmin`.

- **Full path to Perl:** This is the path to the Perl interpreter. The default location is `/usr/bin/perl`. Webmin will test to make sure that the Perl interpreter version is appropriate.

- **Operating system:** You must provide the specific vendor name and version for your operating system. This is necessary because each operating system distribution places configuration files in a different place. Webmin will present you with a list of operating systems that you can choose from.

- **Web server settings:** You provide values for the Webmin server such as the listening ports and the username and password required to protect the pages. You will also be prompted as to whether you want Webmin to run at startup. Webmin listens on port 10000 by default. The Web server will additionally allow for secure access via SSL if the appropriate libraries are installed. You can learn more about SSL in Hour 17, "Setting Up a Secure Server." You might want to change this port number if you are concerned about people scanning your computer for services at specific ports. This information will be stored in /etc/webmin/miniserv.conf by default.

  To change the password later, you need to use the changepass.pl script in the base directory of the distribution:

  ```
  # ./changepass.pl /etc/Webmin/ admin newpassword
  ```

  If you are using the Webmin that came with your distribution, the script may be placed in an alternative location, such as /usr/share/webmin/changepass.pl.

Managing Webmin

You can start or stop Webmin with the following commands:

```
/etc/webmin/start
```

```
/etc/webmin/stop
```

After you start Webmin, you can access it by typing the following URL in your browser:

```
http://example.com:port
```

Substitute *example.com* for your machine hostname and *port* for the port you specified in the installation process (the default port is 10000).

You will be presented with a login page. After providing your username and password, you will access the main Webmin page, as shown in Figure 10.1.

Configuring Apache Settings

Webmin can configure a variety of programs. You can get to the Apache section by clicking first on Servers and then on Apache Server.

Because Webmin knows your operating system version, if an Apache server is already present, Webmin will automatically detect it and you will be able to configure it. Otherwise, you will be presented with the screen shown in Figure 10.2. You must fill in the appropriate paths. If you installed Apache from source as explained in Hour 3, "Installing and Building Apache," the server root is /usr/local/apache2, the Apache binary is /usr/local/apache2/bin/httpd, and the path to the apachectl script is /usr/local/apache2/bin/apachectl.

10

FIGURE 10.1

The main Webmin page.

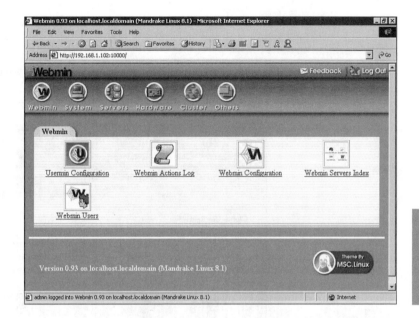

FIGURE 10.2

The initial Apache configuration screen.

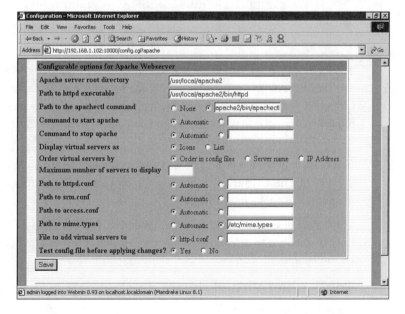

After Webmin knows where Apache is located, you can configure it. Figure 10.3 shows the main Apache configuration screen. One of the tabs in the upper zone of the screen enables you to start the server. If Apache is running, another tab will appear that enables you to stop the server.

FIGURE 10.3

The main Apache configuration screen.

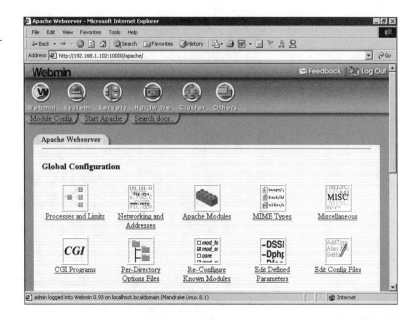

The icons on the screen enable you to configure settings that affect the server as a whole. The default settings are usually appropriate for most situations. In the Processes and Limits section, you can configure the number of Apache processes and the number of requests these servers will process. You can define which modules the Web server will load in the Apache Modules section.

If you scroll down the page, you will see the screen shown in Figure 10.4, which enables you to add a new virtual host. You need to provide the IP address to listen to, the port, the document root, and the name.

The virtual host will be added to the screen and you can configure it by following its link. If you need to delete the server, you can select Server Configuration and press the Delete button.

Configuring Virtual Hosts

When configuring a virtual host, you will be presented with several icons, each one leading to a section that enables you to configure a set of related options. If certain modules are enabled, such as PHP or SSL, new icons will be added that enable you to configure their settings. The options relate to topics covered in previous hours. For example, the Error Handling section covers how to customize error responses and the Aliases and Redirects section explains how to redirect certain URLs to other locations and to map directories in disk to URLs, as explained in Hour 5, "Using Apache to Serve Static Content." The Log Files section enables you to specify files for logging Web requests and server errors, as shown in Hour 6. The CGI section allows you to configure Apache to run CGI scripts, as explained in Hour 8, "Logging and Monitoring."

FIGURE 10.4

Adding a virtual host.

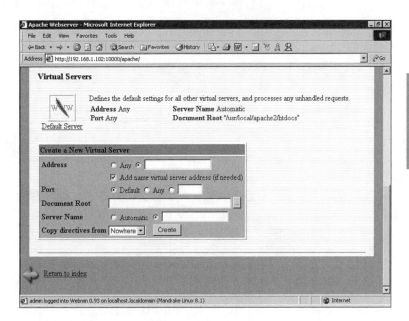

10

Editing Configuration Files Directly

Webmin lets you have a look at the underlying native configuration, edit the configuration directives by hand, and even add new directives that Webmin does not know how to configure. This is useful to configure in-house modules or modules not supported by Apache. Figure 10.5 shows an example.

Configuring Containers

You can create directory, location, and file sections in each of the virtual servers. When each is created, a new link will appear in the page. By following that link, you will be presented with a page covering that section's configuration. Figure 10.6 shows the access control screen for a directory section called `protected`.

FIGURE **10.5**

Editing configuration files directly.

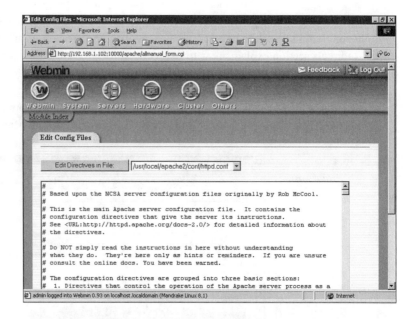

FIGURE **10.6**

An access control screen.

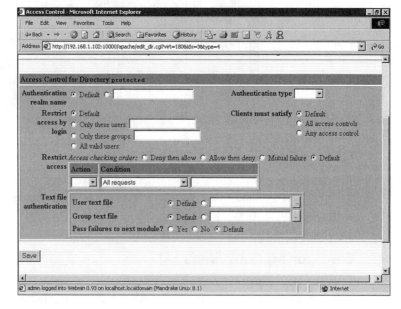

Delegated Administration

Webmin supports delegated administration for Apache. This means that you can restrict certain configuration tasks to a selected user or group of users. You can restrict the ability of the users to start or stop the server, change addresses, pipe logs to programs, or manage only a certain virtual Web server, as shown in Figure 10.7.

FIGURE 10.7

Restricting configuration on a per-user basis.

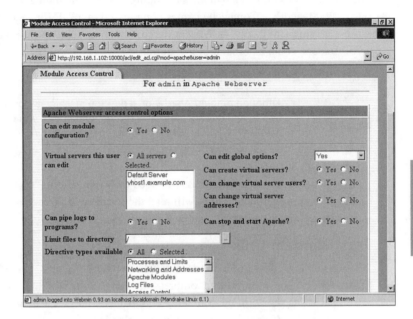

In previous sections, you logged in to the server as a system administrator. To create a user with restricted access, go to the main Webmin screen, select Webmin Users, and choose Create a new Webmin user. As part of the creation process, you can select the modules this user will have access to, such as Apache. After the user is created, clicking on his link will take you to a screen from which you can configure fine-grained access permissions.

Comanche

Comanche stands for *Configuration Manager for Apache*, and is an open source GUI for configuring Apache. Comanche is cross-platform and runs on most Unix, Windows, and Mac operating systems. Comanche has a modular architecture and can be easily extended to configure other types of servers.

Installing Comanche

You can download Comanche from http://www.comanche.org. Binaries for both Unix and Windows are available. Alternatively, you can download the source and run it using a Tcl/Tk interpreter with the [incr Tcl] object-oriented extension. ActiveState (http://www.activestate.com) provides an ActiveTcl distribution that you can use.

Installing on Windows

Comanche runs on most Windows operating systems, including Windows 95, 98, NT, ME, 2000, and XP. Comanche comes compressed in a ZIP file, and you must uncompress it using a tool such as WinZip (http://www.winzip.com). Windows XP supports ZIP folders, so no external tool is required.

 Although running Apache on a desktop machine is possible and useful for testing and development, it is recommended that you run production Web sites only on server versions of the operating system.

After you have extracted the files, you need only double-click on the Comanche icon to launch the program. Comanche will read the location of your Apache installation from the registry and automatically show it to you so that you can start configuring the server.

Installing on Unix

When you have downloaded the Comanche software package, named comanche-version.tar.gz, you must uncompress it, change your working directory, and launch Comanche, as shown in the following commands. You will need to substitute version for the specific Comanche version you downloaded.

```
# gunzip < comanche-version.tar.gz | tar xvz -
# cd comanche-version
# ./comanche-version
```

Because Comanche is a desktop GUI, you need to be running an X-Window based graphical environment, such as KDE or GNOME, to successfully start and use Comanche.

Because Unix does not have a central registry where the location of Apache installations can be stored, you must indicate the location of your Apache servers to Comanche. The first time you start Comanche, you will be presented with a screen telling you that no Apache installations have been found and that you can add a new one by following the New Apache Installation link. You will be prompted for a name to identify the installation and then you will be presented with several options, as shown in Figure 10.8.

You can choose to configure an Apache server installed from source, the Apache bundled with your OS, or a custom Apache installation with files in nonstandard locations. After the new server has been added, you will be able to configure it as explained in the next section.

FIGURE 10.8

Adding a new Apache installation.

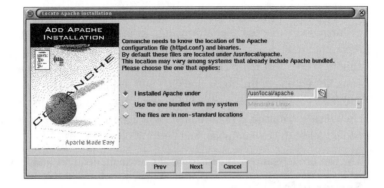

 Comanche supports configuration of several Apache installations simultaneously. You can add new ones by repeating the procedure described in this section.

10

Using Comanche

The Comanche interface is divided in two main areas, as shown in Figure 10.9. The left side of the interface is a tree structure that allows easy access to the server functionality.

FIGURE 10.9

The Comanche user interface.

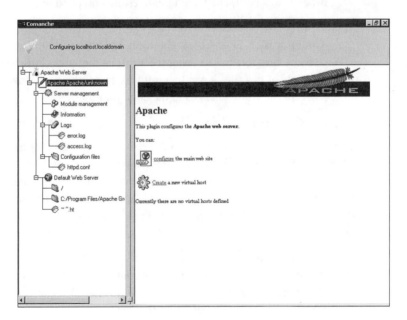

The nodes are organized hierarchically and logically. Each Apache installation node has children nodes that provide information about the server, allow access to error logs, and represent virtual hosts belonging to that server. Each of the virtual host nodes has in turn children nodes that represent directory containers, location containers, and so on. When you click on one of the nodes, the GUI will display an HTML-like page with information and links to access other nodes and perform actions on the current node. If you right-click on a given node, a pop-up menu will appear and enable you to add new children nodes, delete the current node, and perform other actions.

The rest of the section explains several Comanche features and how to access them.

Server Information

Several nodes provide you information about the server or related files:

- **Module management:** This node enables you to set the modules that Comanche will configure in the current Apache installation, as shown in Figure 10.10. Enabling a module here means that Comanche will present you with configuration options related to that module. Disabling a module means that although the module might be active and working in the Apache server, Comanche will not make any attempt to configure it, preserving the settings already present.

- **Information:** This node provides information about the server, such as its version, when it was built, and which modules are compiled in.

- **Logs:** This node offers access to the error and access log files through Comanche.

- **Configuration files:** Comanche reads and writes to the Apache httpd.conf file and any files referenced using the Include directive. This node can display the contents of this file. It can be useful for learning how changes made through the GUI translate into changes in the configuration file.

Server Configuration

Comanche provides a node for default server configuration for each virtual host. Virtual hosts will inherit the settings in the default server. You can launch the configuration pages either by right-clicking on the server node and selecting Properties, or by clicking the configuration link in the right-side HTML display. Figure 10.11 shows how to configure basic settings that correspond to the DocumentRoot, ServerName, and ServerAdmin directives described earlier in the book.

You can add container nodes to each server. Those nodes correspond to <Directory>, <Location>, and <Files> sections in the configuration file. After container nodes are created, you can configure the associated settings, such as access control. Figure 10.12 shows the server access configuration screen.

FIGURE 10.10

Apache module management.

FIGURE 10.11

Basic server settings.

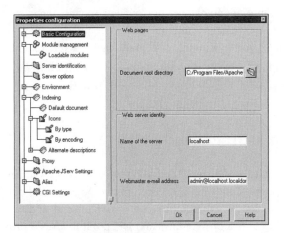

10

FIGURE 10.12

Configuring directory access configuration.

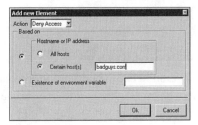

Extending Comanche

The Comanche user interface and directive definition is stored in XML-based files. It's possible to add support for new Apache modules by writing an XML module definition, as explained at the Comanche Web site. It's also possible to write plug-in modules to configure programs other than Apache.

Additional GUI Tools

Comanche and Webmin are popular GUI configuration tools, but are by no means the only ones. The following are some other GUI tools for Apache:

- **Linuxconf:** This is a general configuration tool like Webmin, and includes an Apache configuration module. It provides textual, graphical, and Web-based interfaces. You can find more information about Linuxconf at `http://www.solucorp.qc.ca/linuxconf/`.
- **Covalent management portal:** Covalent Technologies (`http://www.covalent.net`) provides a commercial Web-based configuration tool that enables you to manage multiple Apache servers remotely.
- **ApacheOnHand:** This is a Windows-specific tool for configuring and monitoring Apache servers, both 1.3- and 2.0-based. You can learn more about ApacheOnHand at `http://apache.mappingsoft.com`.

Summary

In this hour, you learned some of the advantages and disadvantages of using a GUI for configuring Apache. You were introduced to two popular GUI configuration tools: Webmin and Comanche. Webmin runs on Unix platforms and can configure a variety of servers. Comanche runs on Windows and Unix, but focuses on Apache configuration.

Q&A

Q Will I still be able to edit the configuration files by hand?

A Yes, both Comanche and Webmin use the underlying Apache configuration files, preserving comments and recognizing any configuration changes you introduce by editing the files directly.

Q What are the advantages of Webmin and Comanche being open source and extensible?

A You can extend Webmin using Perl and Comanche using Tcl. In this way, you can add support for new Apache modules or integrate these configuration tools with other parts of your infrastructure, such as a customer database.

Quiz

1. Are GUI configuration tools such as Webmin more secure than editing the configuration file directly?

2. Can you mention some advantages of editing the configuration files directly as opposed to using a GUI?

3. What are some advantages of using a GUI as opposed to editing the configuration files directly?

Quiz Answers

1. Webmin can offer increased security, especially in shared hosting or administration scenarios. Apache provides delegation of administration tasks via per-directory configuration files, but this approach has performance problems and is not very flexible. Webmin allows delegation so that you can restrict other administrators' access to specific parts of the configuration. However, because Webmin also allows for remote access, it increases the risk of a remote compromise, which can be mitigated by using SSL and a good password.

2. The following are some of the benefits: remote administration, inline comments, revision control, and easy automation.

3. Some of the advantages of using a GUI configuration tool include an easier learning curve, delegated administration, and context-sensitive help. GUIs can also provide sanity checks and validation for your configuration information.

Further Reading

The Web sites for each of the tools described here provide additional information, documentation, and the latest releases of the software. The `http://gui.apache.org` Web site provides a listing of Apache GUIs. You can find additional projects at `http://freshmeat.net` and `http://sourceforge.net`.

10

PART II
Advanced Apache

Hour

HOUR **11**

Multi-Processing Modules

This hour provides an in-depth explanation of multi-processing modules (MPMs) that allow Apache to run as a process-based, threaded, or hybrid server. It analyzes the architecture and goals of the modules and covers their advantages and disadvantages as well as their configuration. This hour provides a necessary foundation for later hours dealing with performance and scalability. In this hour, you will learn

- The available Apache MPM modules, and the advantages and disadvantages of each
- How to configure each of the MPM modules

Overview of Apache MPM Architecture

Hour 2, "Understanding Apache Internals," describes the overall Apache architecture. This hour explains in detail how multi-processing modules define the way Apache serves requests. An MPM is responsible for taking incoming requests and assigning them to the Apache components for further processing. These components can be processes or threads. As explained in Hour 2, processes are isolated from each other. This makes them more robust in case of misbehavior due to a bug in Apache or in the user's code, but they are *heavy* in terms of space and processing time. That is, they take more space because every process keeps its own memory and data independent of the other processes, and more processing time because the operating system takes a certain amount of time to switch execution from one process to the next one (context switching).

Threads are *lighter* because they can share memory and data with other threads and there is no context switching because threads live inside the same process. Threads are more fragile, however, because a misbehaving thread can easily corrupt data or code belonging to other threads. Additionally, because threads share resources, they need synchronization mechanisms (such as software locks) to arbitrate access to those resources. Threaded servers tend to be faster than process-based ones. However, a badly designed threaded server, where threads are continuously waiting around for other threads to release their locks, can be slower than a well-designed process-based server.

Apache offers you a wide range of options, and it can be configured as a threaded server, a process-based server, or a mixture of both so that you can balance your own needs for speed and reliability.

The following sections offer you a description of the three main MPMs provided with Apache, including their configuration. Three of them, Prefork, Worker, and Perchild, are Unix MPMs, and the fourth one is specific to the Windows platform.

The Prefork MPM

The Prefork MPM implements a process-based Web server. Process-based servers are typically used in Unix environments because of their reliability. In this model, a parent process listens for incoming requests. When a new request arrives, the server forks itself and creates a new child that will service that request. The forking mechanism allows a process to create an identical copy of itself, including code and data. The original process is called the *parent* process and the newly created process is named the *child* process. Typical Web servers answer requests simultaneously and thus require several children to be running at the same time. If a new child process has to be spawned every time a request comes, the client will experience a delay. The delay might be minimal if the original process is lightweight (does not take up much memory) or the server is not very loaded, but it could be significant if the processes are heavy, the server is under load, or many requests arrive simultaneously. This can be avoided if, on startup, the server forks several children and keeps them around. Every time a request comes, the server will look to see whether any of the existing children are free and can service the request. Otherwise, the server will create a new child and add it to the pool. Because the children have been created before the requests arrive, this MPM model is named Prefork.

The Prefork MPM enables you to specify the number of children the server creates at startup, the maximum number of children that can be created, and so on. You can learn more in the "Prefork MPM Configuration" section later in this hour.

Because each of the processes keeps its own data and code, if a process starts growing out of control or taking too much CPU time, it can be killed. This will affect the request that child was processing, but will leave all other clients and processes unaffected. You can also limit the number of requests that a particular child will service until a new one replaces it. This is useful, if for example, a third-party module leaks a little bit of memory per every request, which can add up over time. By creating a new, fresh child every certain number of requests, you can keep the memory used by the server under control. This is particularly useful if you do not have access to the source code of the Apache module causing the problem.

The increased stability comes with a performance and memory penalty. If the processes include a scripting engine or cache frequently accessed data, the size of an individual process can be significant. Because most of this information is replicated for each of the children, it adds up quickly. If the size of the processes exceeds that of the physically available memory, the processes are swapped temporarily to disk, slowing down significantly the responsiveness of the Web server.

Prefork MPM Configuration

This section describes the different configuration options for the Prefork module. Many of these configuration options are shared by other MPMs.

Controlling the Number of Processes

You can control the number of processes that will be created at startup by using the StartServers directive. It takes a single argument, indicating the amount of servers to fork when the server starts. The default value is 5 (StartServers 5) and is appropriate for most Web sites. You should change this setting only if you run a very busy Web site.

Apache and the operating system limit the maximum number of processes. The operating system setting varies for each operating system version, vendor, and platform. You can learn more about these settings in Hour 16, "Tuning Apache." Apache has two directives for limiting the number of children. The ServerLimit directive restricts the maximum number of processes that can be created. This directive affects all MPMs; it is set by default to a very high number, and cannot be changed between server restarts. You should usually leave `ServerLimit` unchanged and change `MaxClients` instead. The default setting for the Prefork MPM is `ServerLimit 256`.

`MaxClients` enables you to control the maximum number of processes spawned, but can be changed between restarts. This limit will be necessarily equal or lower than the operating system limits or the value of the `ServerLimit` directive. The default value for the `MaxClients` directive in the Prefork MPM is `MaxClients 256`, which should be enough for most Web sites. This is the maximum number of client requests that can be served simultaneously. Additional requests will be queued, and will be served as the children finish processing the current ones. You can modify the length of the pending connection queue by using the `ListenBacklog` directive. It accepts a single argument, the size of the queue. The default value for `ListenBacklog` is appropriate for most cases. Refer to Hour 16 for additional details and tuning information.

> Please refer to the "Q&A" section to learn the differences between `ServerLimit` and `MaxClients` and the reason both are needed.

So far, you have learned how to control the number of processes at startup and the maximum number of simultaneous processes. Two additional directives allow you fine-grained control over the number of processes at runtime.

The `MinSpareServers` directive defines the minimum number of processes that can be idle (not serving any request) at any time. If the number of idle servers goes below the setting of `MinSpareServers`, Apache will spawn additional servers at the rate of one per second until this limit is reached. The default value is `MinSpareServers 5`, and should be appropriate for most systems. Conversely, `MaxSpareServers` sets the maximum number of idle processes allowed. If the number of idle servers grows beyond this setting, some of them will be killed. The default value is `MaxSpareServers 10`.

> A decreasing number of idle servers means that the number of simultaneous requests is growing. By increasing the number of processes when this occurs, Apache adapts to the load and improves the response time of the server. An increasing number of idle servers means that the number of simultaneous users is diminishing, and as a result, not as many processes are necessary anymore and can be eliminated to preserve system resources.

Finally, you can limit the number of requests that a specific process will serve using the MaxRequestsPerChild directive. It does not count multiple requests reusing the same connection. As explained earlier in the hour, this is useful to prevent memory leaks from becoming an issue with processes running for a long time. The server will kill the process and replace it with a new one after the specified number of requests. The default value is MaxRequestsPerChild 10000, and is appropriate for most Web sites. You can set MaxRequestsPerChild to 0 if you do not want processes to be killed after a specific number of requests.

Server Identity

You can specify the Unix user and group that the server runs as by using the User and Group directives, as explained in Hour 4, "Getting Started with Apache." They can take either a numeric value prefixed by a #, indicating the user ID or group ID, or a name indicating the username or group name. The default value is User #-1 and a common value is User nobody.

The User and Group directives are necessary for security purposes. If Apache is started as root, it performs only a few operations, such as binding to a privileged port and opening logs, and then changes its user ID and group ID.

This way, processes created by the server, such as CGI scripts and embedded interpreters, will not run with administrator privileges. Additionally, if an attacker compromises the server, he will not automatically gain root access in the machine.

> By now, you probably have figured out that running a Web server on Unix as a system administrator is a bad idea. In fact, it is so bad that to enable this behavior, you need to rebuild the server passing the -DBIG_SECURITY_HOLE flag to the compiler.

Network-Related Directives

The Listen directive specifies the IP addresses and ports Apache will listen to for incoming HTTP requests. It is described in detail in Hour 4.

The SendBufferSize directive sets the size in bytes of the TCP buffer. The default settings vary from operating system to operating system. It is a good idea to increase this setting for high-speed, high-latency networks. *Latency* is the time it takes for a packet to reach the client and the acknowledgement response to reach the server.

The ListenBackLog directive allows you to specify the maximum length of the queue of pending connections. The default value is okay for most cases. Check the Apache documentation for additional information.

The ListenBackLog directive allows you to specify the maximum length of the queue of pending connections. The default value is okay for most cases. Check the Apache documentation for additional information.

11

Coordinating Children

Apache can use several mechanisms to control how Apache children accept requests. The `AcceptMutex` directive takes one argument, which can be one of the following:

- `default`: Uses the default compiled-in method
- `flock`: Uses the `flock` system call
- `fcntl`: Uses the `fnctl` system call
- `sysvsem`: Uses semaphores
- `proc_pthread`: Uses POSIX mutexes

> The best locking mechanism is dependent on your operating system and platform and whether you have multiple processors. Please refer to Hour 16 for pointers to documentation on tuning this parameter.

The first two options, `flock` and `fcntl`, require a special file for coordination and process locking. By default, this file is called `accept.lock` and is placed in the `logs/` directory. The `LockFile` directive enables you to specify an alternative location for this file. It takes a single argument, the path to the locking file. The scoreboard file is a mechanism used in some architectures for communication between a parent process and its children. Its default location is `logs/apache_status`, and it can be changed using the `ScoreBoardFile` directive.

> The default values for `LockFile` and `ScoreBoardFile` are usually okay, unless they reside on a file system mounted via the NFS (Network File System) protocol. These files must be placed in a local directory; otherwise, Apache will not perform correctly and will hang.

Keeping Track of Processes

When Apache starts on Unix, it records the process ID into a file, the so-called `pid` file. The process ID is a numeric identifier of the process that can be used to send signals to it, either directly on the command line or with the help of scripts, as seen in Hour 4. The default value for the `PidFile` directive is `logs/httpd.pid`.

> Apache is usually started as root, performs a few critical operations, such as binding to the appropriate port, opening log files, and so on. Afterward, it switches to the user and group specified in the configuration file. It is important that the files Apache modifies or executes and the directories that contain them are owned by root and cannot be overwritten or modified by other users. Otherwise, an attacker could exploit this to gain control of the system. This applies to directives such as `PidFile`, `LockFile`, `ScoreBoardFile`, and `CoreDumpDirectory`.

The `CoreDumpDirectory` Directive

When an Apache process misbehaves, such as trying to write in memory space belonging to other processes or some other serious problem, the operating system will kill the process. It will usually "dump core," writing a snapshot of the running program just as it died, into a binary file named `core`. This file can be used later to find out what went wrong. Please refer to Hour 16 for details on how to extract information from a `core` file.

The `CoreDumpDirectory` directive takes one argument: the directory where to store the `core` file. If the directive is not present, the default behavior is to store the file in the directory specified by `ServerRoot`, but it is usually not a good idea to give write permissions for this directory to the user that Apache runs as.

The Worker MPM

The Worker MPM implements a hybrid server. At startup, Apache creates a number of processes, each one of them in turn containing several threads. You can even create a pure threaded server by restricting the MPM to a single process with multiple threads. Threaded servers tend to scale better and be faster than process-based servers because the overhead of creating and managing threads is much lower. As explained earlier in the hour, this comes at a price of reduced robustness because threads are not protected from each other and a programming mistake in one thread can corrupt data or code of other threads.

On the other hand, the ability to have easy access to common data and code is useful for modules that embed language engines into Apache, such as `mod_perl`. The latest version of `mod_perl` takes extensive advantage of the new threaded architecture of Apache 2.0 to create efficient, lightweight processes with embedded Perl interpreters. Hour 20 covers `mod_perl` for Apache 2.0.

11

Worker MPM Configuration

This section covers the configuration of the Worker MPM.

Processes and Threads

You can specify the number of processes that will be created at startup by using the StartServers directive, as with the Prefork MPM. Each of the processes will have several threads, its number specified by the ThreadsPerChild directive. The default settings are 5 initial processes and 50 threads per process.

The number of threads in each process is fixed, but processes are created or destroyed to maintain the total number of threads between specified limits. Those limits can be configured using MinSpareThreads and MaxSpareThreads. These directives are the counterparts of the MaxSpareServers and MinSpareServers directives in process-based servers. Apache monitors the total number of threads across all processes and creates or destroys processes accordingly.

As in Prefork, MaxClients specifies the maximum number of processes. In the Worker MPM, each process has several threads in turn, so the maximum number of simultaneous clients is MaxClients times the setting of ThreadsPerChild. That is, in the default configuration for the worker MPM.

MaxClients equals 5 and ThreadsPerChild is 50, so the maximum number of simultaneous connections in the default configuration is 250.

MaxThreadsPerChild specifies the maximum number of threads per process and can be changed between restarts. ThreadLimit specifies an upper limit that cannot be changed between restarts. The default value for ThreadLimit is 64 and should be appropriate for most servers. Please refer to the "Q&A" section to learn the difference between these directives. Both directives are also constrained by the underlying operating system settings, as described in Hour 16.

Common Directives

The StartServers, MaxClients, User, Group, Listen, ListenBacklog, LockFile, PidFile, CoreDumpDirectory, ScoreBoardFile, MaxRequestsPerChild, and SendBufferSize directives are identical to the ones described in the Prefork module section.

Perchild MPM

In some situations, such as in shared hosting scenarios, it is desirable to run Apache processes under different user identities for security and performance reasons. The

Perchild MPM provides an efficient method for achieving this with a single Apache server.

An obvious method is to run different server installations, each with its own IP addresses and user identity. This quickly becomes impractical in terms of management and resources for a large number of servers, and simply is not possible for name-based virtual hosts, covered in Hour 14, "Virtual Hosting."

The Perchild MPM creates different processes, each one under a specific user ID and containing a predefined number of threads. The parent process listens for incoming requests, and passes them to the appropriate process, which then takes over from there.

Perchild MPM Configuration

The Perchild MPM regulates the number of children with a mechanism that is the opposite of the Worker MPM. The Worker MPM has a fixed number of threads per process and creates or destroys processes. The Perchild MPM starts a fixed number of processes and varies the number of threads within them to adapt to the server load. Thus, many of the Worker MPM directives for controlling the number of processes have thread-related counterparts in the Perchild MPM.

The NumServers directive specifies the number of processes, and StartThreads specifies the initial number of threads in each process. The number of threads will be increased if the number of idle threads is less than specified by MinSpareServers or decreased if it is greater than the MaxSpareThreads setting.

MaxThreadsPerChild specifies the maximum number of threads that can be created in a process, although this number may be limited too by the settings of the operating system or by the ThreadLimit directive discussed earlier in the Worker MPM section.

Assigning Requests to Processes

Currently, the only way of mapping requests to processes is by virtual host assignments. You can configure processes to run under specific IDs and then associate virtual hosts with those IDs. When a request comes for a virtual host, it will be mapped to the right process.

As mentioned earlier, the Perchild MPM creates a fixed number of children processes. Apache assigns a server ID to each of the processes. So, if NumServers is set to 5, the available children are 1, 2, 3, 4, and 5. You can assign specific user and group IDs to each child process with the ChildPerUserId directive. This directive takes three arguments: the user name or ID, the group name or ID, and the process ID. For example:

```
ChildPerUserId 501 501 1
```

will run the process number 1 with user ID 501 and group ID 501. Processes without an associated `ChildPerUserId` directive will use the settings of the `User` and `Group` directives.

The `AssignUserId` directive associates a `<VirtualHost>` section with a certain user and group ID. Requests for this virtual host will be mapped to the process running the same user ID. Listing 11.1 shows a sample Perchild configuration, with two different servers, each one running under a different user and group ID.

Listing 11.1   Sample Perchild Configuration

```
NumServers 2
ChildperUserID 501 501 1
ChildperUserID 502 502 2

<VirtualHost www.domain1.com>
AssignUserID 501 501
Other directives here...
</VirtualHost>

<VirtualHost www.domain2.com>
AssignUserID 502 502
 Other directives here...
</VirtualHost>
```

If a `<VirtualHost>` does not contain an `AssignUserId` specific user and group ID, the ones Apache is running as will be used instead.

Common Directives

The `User`, `Group`, `Listen`, `ListenBacklog`, `LockFile`, `PidFile`, `CoreDumpDirectory`, `ScoreBoardFile`, `MaxRequestsPerChild`, and `SendBufferSize` directives are identical to the ones described in the "Prefork MPM" section.

Windows MPM

The `mpm_winnt` module is the MPM for the Windows family of operating systems. It uses a control process that launches a single child process that, in turn, creates threads to handle requests. This MPM, together with the underlying Apache Portable Runtime library, makes Apache run better on Windows operating systems such as Windows NT, Windows 2000, and Windows XP. Desktop versions of Windows will likely be supported in the future as was done in the past with Apache 1.3 versions. Although running production servers in desktop platforms is not encouraged, they are very useful for developers, who can develop and test their code locally.

Windows MPM Configuration

The ThreadsPerChild directive sets the number of threads. This number will be constant through the life of Apache, so it is desirable to change it to a value high enough to handle the expected load and any peaks that might occur. By default, ThreadsPerChild is set to 50.

The Windows MPM lacks many of the directives of its Unix counterparts, such as those related to users and groups and process management. The following directives are supported and are identical to the ones described for previous MPMs: CoreDumpDirectory, PidFile, Listen, ListenBacklog, and SendBufferSize. The MaxRequestsPerChild directive has a greater impact because there is only one process. After this limit is reached, the process will be replaced; in the meantime, the clients might experience a delay. Setting MaxRequestsPerChild to 0 means the process will never be replaced.

A current side effect of restarting the server when the MaxRequestsPerChild is reached is that Apache on Windows will reread the configuration file. If you have made changes in the configuration file, you might find problems. That may change in future versions of the server.

11

Which MPM Is Best for Me?

Certain MPMs, such as Perchild, are complex and less tested, if only because the target audience is smaller than for other MPMs. Threaded MPMs, such as the one for Windows and the Worker MPM, require modules to be thread safe. Many of the Apache modules were originally designed for Apache 1.3, which is a process-based server. As the modules are ported to work with Apache 2.0 threaded MPMs, they must account for thread safety and could possibly require a rewrite of parts of the code. This will take some time to implement and debug and, at least initially, some modules will be available only for the Prefork MPM or will be more stable in that platform. This might limit your choices.

However, there are big performance gains and feature advantages for modules designed to work with threaded MPMs, like mod_perl 2.0, described in Hour 20.

Choosing an MPM also depends on the quality of the operating system support for threads and processes, which varies among different Unix flavors. For example, processes in Linux are lightweight and processes on AIX are rather heavy. A process-based Web server does not scale as well on AIX. This is one of the reasons that IBM was one of the first commercial vendors to migrate from Apache 1.3 to Apache 2.0. The

FreeBSD platform didn't have good threading support for a long time and the Prefork MPM was the only MPM available.

In any case, the best approach might be just to try different MPMs and see which one performs better for a specific scenario. Hour 16 introduces you to several tools that you can use to perform the comparison. Bear in mind that MPMs cannot be loaded at runtime and must be compiled in, so you might need to implement several Apache installations for your tests. Modules need to be compiled for a specific MPM as well.

Selecting an MPM

You can select the MPM at compile time with the `--with-mpm` switch to the configure script. MPMs cannot be selected at runtime; they must be compiled into the server.

In certain platforms, such as in Windows and OS/2, only one MPM is available. Check Hour 3 to learn the available options and the default MPM for each platform.

Additional MPMs

There are additional OS-specific MPMs distributed with Apache, such as those for OS/2, BeOS, and NetWare. There are also experimental MPMs that developers create from time to time to explore different ideas, such as the leader-follower MPM. Their configuration is very similar to the modules described in this hour. Check the Apache reference documentation for additional information.

Configuration Limits

If you reach the maximum number of children processes or threads, Apache will leave an informative note in the log file, such as `Server reached MaxClients setting, consider raising the MaxClients setting`. You might want to check what caused the increase in connections and increase the settings as indicated. In some situations, for example, the increase might be due to a misbehaving Web crawling program from a search engine, in which case you should restrict access to the Web site for that particular program.

Summary

This hour introduced you to different Apache MPMs. You learned their strengths and weaknesses and the different configuration options, including those related to performance and scalability. It described the different scenarios in which a particular MPM is preferred over others, depending on factors such as module availability and operating system support.

Q&A

Q Why do I need a `MaxClients` and a `ServerLimit` directive?

A The problem lies in the way Apache currently handles graceful restarts. It requires that the size of the scoreboard file remains constant. The size of this file also limits the maximum number of simultaneous clients.

Let's suppose there is only a single directive, `MaxClients`, and that you want to increase its value in a running server because of a sudden load spike. The preferred method is to perform a graceful restart, which keeps the server answering requests while replacing children with the new configuration. You would not be able to do so because the size of the scoreboard depends on the original value of the `MaxClients` directive. Your only alternative is to stop and start the server or perform a normal restart. But you would be doing that in the worst possible moment, when your load is at the highest, causing many requests to fail.

By having two directives, you can solve this problem. `ServerLimit` sets the hard limit in the number of processes and fixes the size of the scoreboard. `MaxClients` varies the number of processes and can be changed during a restart, but cannot be greater than `ServerLimit`. In most cases, the value of `ServerLimit` is appropriate and you should have to change only the `MaxClients` settings.

In any case, having two directives with apparently the same purpose and that limit each other is confusing. Their syntax or naming might change over time to solve the issue. The reasoning for `ThreadLimit` and `MaxThreadsPerChild` is the same.

Q Are there additional benefits to a threaded architecture?

A Yes. Slow clients, such as modem users downloading big files, can tie up a child for a long period of time, and during that time the child cannot answer other requests. In process-based servers delivering dynamic content, each process has an embedded interpreter whether or not a particular request requires it. Having many such heavy processes serving slow clients is expensive. Threaded servers allow for a shared pool of interpreters that will be used only if the request requires them. Lightweight threads can serve pure static content.

Threaded MPMs offer additional benefits for scalability in the backend. Most Web applications developed with PHP or `mod_perl` require connections to databases. These databases might have license restrictions on the number of simultaneous clients, and have scalability and performance problems when the number of open connections grows. In process-based servers, each child had to open a database connection, which could be reused by later requests in the same child, but not across children. The number of possible connections to the backend server limits the number of server processes.

11

A threaded MPM allows a pool of database connections that can be shared across all threads, thus allowing for a more scalable architecture.

Quiz

1. In a working configuration, reorder the values that will have the following configuration directives from smaller to greater: MaxServers, MaxSpareServers, MinSpareServers, StartServers, ServerLimit.

2. What directive do you use to specify the number of processes to be created at startup? Why is this useful?

3. Which MPM enables you to assign different user IDs to different Apache processes? Why is this useful?

Quiz Answers

1. MinSpareServers < StartServers < MaxSpareServers < MaxServers < ServerLimit

2. The directive is StartServers. This can be useful for very busy Web sites because you want the server to start ready to serve many requests simultaneously.

3. The Perchild MPM. This is useful in hosting situations so that you can isolate virtual hosts belonging to different customers from each other.

Related Directives

This section contains directives mentioned in this hour or that are related to topics discussed in this hour. You can consult the Apache reference documentation for comprehensive syntax information and usage.

- **AcceptMutex:** Define locking mechanism.
- **AssignUserId:** Associate a virtual host with a process ID.
- **ChildPerUserId:** User and group for a specific child process.
- **CoreDumpDirectory:** Directory where to store debugging information when Apache crashes.
- **Group:** Operating system group ID or name the Apache processes run as.
- **Listen:** Specify IP addresses and ports Apache will listen for requests.

- **ListenBacklog:** Length of the queue of requests waiting to be served.
- **LockFile:** Location of the file required for two of the locking mechanisms specified by AcceptMutex.
- **MaxClients:** Maximum number of requests that can be served simultaneously. It equals the number of processes in the Prefork MPM and number of processes times the number of threads in threaded or hybrid MPMs.
- **MaxRequestsPerChild:** Maximum number of requests a child will serve before being replaced.
- **MaxSpareServers:** Maximum number of spare processes to keep around in case of a sudden load spike.
- **MaxSpareThreads:** Maximum number of spare threads to keep around in case of a sudden load spike.
- **MaxThreadsPerChild:** Maximum number of threads allowed in a process.
- **MinSpareServers:** Minimum number of spare processes to keep around in case of a sudden load spike.
- **MinSpareThreads:** Minimum number of spare threads to keep around in case of a sudden load spike.
- **NumServers:** Number of processes to start in the Perchild MPM.
- **PidFile:** Location of the file where the process ID of the main Apache process is stored.
- **ScoreBoardFile:** Location of the scoreboard file used for inter-process communication in some architectures.
- **SendBufferSize:** Size of the TCP buffer in bytes.
- **ServerLimit:** Hard limit for number of processes.
- **StartServers:** Number of processes to create at startup.
- **StartThreads:** Number of threads to create at startup.
- **ThreadLimit:** Hard limit for number of threads per process.
- **ThreadsPerChild:** Number of threads per process.
- **User:** Operating system user ID or name the Apache processes run as.

11

Further Reading

This hour introduced several topics that will be explained in detail in later hours. Tuning Apache for optimal performance involves configuration of the right MPM parameters and is covered in Hour 16. Hour 14 covers configuration of Apache for multiple hosts, and the Perchild MPM is an interesting option for hosting companies with security concerns. Hour 20 covers installation and configuration of `mod_perl`, one of the modules that better takes advantage of the new capabilities of Apache 2.0.

The Apache 2.0 reference documentation covers in detail the syntax of the different MPMs and can be found at `http://httpd.apache.org/docs-2.0/mpm.html`.

Hour **12**

Filtering Modules

This hour describes the available filtering modules for Apache and how to configure them. *Filters* are Apache modules that take input content, modify it, and return it for further processing or delivery to the client. In this hour, you will learn how to

- Configure `mod_deflate` to speed up page downloads from your Web site
- Configure `mod_include` to add dynamic content easily
- Configure `mod_ext_filter` to use external programs as filters

Apache Filtering Architecture

Hour 2, "Understanding Apache Internals," introduced the extension mechanisms of the Apache server, hooks, and filters.

Hooks are appropriate for making decisions based on the request information or manipulating headers. Filters, on the other hand, are appropriate for manipulating content being served or accepted by Apache in a streaming manner. Filters are organized in filter chains. The content of HTTP requests or responses is split in discrete pieces, *buckets*, which are grouped in *bucket brigades*.

Buckets are passed through the filter chain like materials in a factory assembly line. Filters process the content; modifying, removing, or inserting buckets in the brigade. The output of one filter is fed to the input of the next filter. The diagram in Figure 12.1 shows how filters work.

FIGURE 12.1
Filters in Apache.

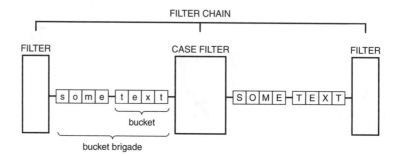

Apache has two filter chains: an input chain and an output chain. Input filters process incoming content (requests) from the client, and output filters process outgoing content (responses) generated by the server.

> The proxy module, described in Hour 15, "Apache as a Proxy Server," might add additional filter chains for processing requests to and from a remote site. At the time this book was written, this feature was not yet implemented in the proxy code. But requests and responses can still be processed, via the input and output filter chains just described, in the browser side of the connection.

Filter Configuration

Filters can be automatically added by modules at runtime or set up in the configuration file. This can be illustrated with the example of the PHP module described in Hour 19. The PHP module for Apache 2.0 is implemented as a filter that processes Web pages containing a mixture of HTML and code, which then executes the code and replaces the result.

You can associate certain file extensions or content types with the PHP module by using the AddHandler directive. When this content is being served, the PHP module will automatically insert the filter that will process that content. Alternatively, you could explicitly associate the filter with specific files, file extensions, and so on. This section explains how to do the latter.

Configuration Directives

You can use the `SetOutputFilter` directive inside any container directive or per-directory access file to configure the chain of filters that will process requests for that location.

The `SetOutputFilter` directive takes one or more filter names, separated by semicolons (;). The order in which the filters appear is the order in which they will process the content.

For example, Listing 12.1 shows how to configure all content in the `/some/path` location to be processed by `mod_include` and the PHP module. `mod_include` is explained in a later section in this hour.

LISTING 12.1 `SetOutputFilter` Example

```
1: <Location /some/path/>
2: SetOutputFilter INCLUDES;PHP
3: </Location>
```

The `AddOutputFilter` directive can be used to associate one or more filters with a set of extensions. The `AddOutputFilter` directive takes one or more filters, separated by semicolons and a list of file extensions to which those filters will apply. For example,

```
AddOutputFilter INCLUDES .inc .shtml
```

tells Apache to process any files ending in `inc` or `shtml` extensions using `mod_include`. If both an `AddOutputFilter` and a `SetOutputFilter` directive apply to the same file, the filter lists from both directives will be merged.

Input filters can be configured via the `AddInputFilter` and `SetInputFilter` directives, which have identical syntax to their output filter counterparts.

Compressing Content with `mod_deflate`

The `mod_deflate` filtering module provides a new filter, `DEFLATE`, that can compress outgoing data. Compressing can be expensive in terms of CPU, but has the advantage of minimizing the amount of data that will be transferred to the client. This is useful when clients connect to the Internet via slow links and the content can be compressed significantly, such as with HTML pages.

12

Other content that is already compressed, such as ZIP files or JPEG images, will benefit very little (if at all) from additional compression.

Of course, for content compression to work, the client must support the opposite functionality: decompression. This is true for most modern browsers, with certain restrictions mentioned in the "Limitations" section later in this hour.

Configuring `mod_deflate`

If you compile Apache from source, you can enable `mod_deflate` by using `--enable-module=mod_deflate`, as explained in Hour 18, "Extending Apache." If the module is compiled as a dynamic extension, you must make sure that the module is loaded using the following directive:

```
LoadModule deflate_module modules/mod_deflate.so
```

This module provides the `DEFLATE` filter that you can use with the `SetOutputFilter` and `AddOutputFilter` directives described at the beginning of the hour. For example, to compress by default all HTML documents in a site, you could add the following configuration line to the main server:

```
SetOutputFilter DEFLATE
```

`mod_deflate` provides three configuration directives:

- **`DeflateFilterNote`:** Internally sets a note that can be read by other modules, indicating the *compression ratio*; that is, the percentage of the file that was compressed before being sent to the browser. A *note* is an attribute associated with a particular request. For example

  ```
  DeflateFilterNote comp_ratio
  ```

  will create the `comp_ratio` note. You can then log this value in your log files by using the `%{comp_ratio}n` format option, as explained in Hour 8, "Logging and Monitoring."

- **`DeflateWindowSize`:** A smaller window size means that the compression process will consume less memory, but the level of compression will be less. The acceptable values can range from 0 to 15, with the default being 15.

- **`DeflateMemLevel`:** A smaller memory level means that the compression process will consume less memory, but the level of compression will be less. The acceptable values are 1 to 9, with the default being 9.

Limitations

Even if the `DEFLATE` filter is enabled for the current request using `SetOutputFilter` or `AddOutputFilter`, `mod_deflate` will deliver compressed content to a client only if two conditions are met. The first condition is that the browser provides an `Accept-encoding:` `gzip` header, indicating that it can understand compressed content. The second condition is that the content being transmitted is of the type `text/html`. This is because current browsers and browser plug-ins do not work correctly with other compressed content types.

Many problems with browser support have been reported on the Apache developer's list. For example, Netscape browsers have trouble understanding compressed JavaScript or Cascading Style Sheets (`application/x-javascript` and `text/css` content types). Macromedia Flash players, depending on the platform and the content requested, have trouble with `text/plain`, `text/xml`, and `application/x-shockwave-flash`. Microsoft browsers can correctly understand compressed Office document formats such as `application/msword`, `application/vnd.ms-excel`, and `application/vnd.ms-powerpoint`, but Netscape has problems. As you can see, figuring out which browser supports what content can be quite difficult. With so many issues, the practical solution to guarantee compatibility with all browsers is to support compression of `text/html` content only.

Additionally, if you know that a specific client has trouble processing compressed content, you can set up the environment variable `no-gzip` by using the `SetEnvIf` or `BrowserMatch` directive, as explained in Hour 9, "Content Negotiation and Environment Variables." This will prevent `mod_deflate` from compressing the content delivered to the client.

For example, most proxies do not handle compressed content correctly. *Proxies* are programs that perform HTTP requests on behalf of other browsers, as explained in Hour 15. Problems arise when clients use a proxy and the proxy caches the compressed version of the content, and serves it to browsers that might or might not support compression.

The following example disables compression for proxy requests, identified as those requests that include a `Via:` header:

```
SetEnvIf Via .* no-gzip
```

mod_deflate is an experimental module. At the time this book was written, there were talks among the Apache developers about providing extra configuration options so that it can compress content types in addition to `text/html` if the client supports it. For example, this is needed for the Subversion project (`http://subversion.tigris.org`), which uses the DAV protocol to transmit revision control information and benefits greatly from compression when transmitting large files.

12

Server Side Includes

Hour 6, "Serving Dynamic Content with CGI," explained how to provide dynamic content using CGI programs. Server Side Includes (SSI) provides an alternative solution by embedding processing instructions into HTML pages. Those instructions will be parsed by the SSI filter and the results substituted in the content. Like CGI, SSI is an "old school" Web technology and a predecessor to other HTML embedded languages such as PHP. SSI provides a simple and effective mechanism for adding pieces of dynamic content with very little overhead; for example, a common footer for each page that includes the date and time the page was served. As another example, the Apache 2.0 distribution uses SSI to provide a custom look and feel for error messages.

SSI is implemented by the filtering module mod_include. If you compile Apache from source, you can enable this module by using --enable-module=mod_include, as explained in Hour 18. If the module is compiled as a dynamic extension, you need to make sure that the module is loaded using the following directive:

```
LoadModule include_module modules/mod_include.so
```

Configuring SSI

As you learned in Hour 6, CGI execution permissions can be granted in a particular context using the Option +ExecCGI directive. Similarly, you can allow SSI parsing with an Option +Includes directive.

The next step is to specify which files the SSI engine will parse. Parsing every single HTML page will have an unnecessary performance impact on the server, so it is better to explicitly differentiate which files need to be parsed for SSI content. Traditionally, the .shtml extension has been used for this purpose. This behavior can be enabled with the configuration options in Listing 12.2 or the ones in Listing 12.3, depending on whether you want to set up the filter manually or let the module set it up automatically.

LISTING 12.2   Associating SSI to Files with the .shtml Extension

```
1: AddType text/html .shtml
2: <FilesMatch "\.shtml(\..+)?$">
3:     SetOutputFilter INCLUDES
4: </FilesMatch>
```

LISTING 12.3   Alternative Configuration for SSI Association

```
1: AddType text/html .shtml
2: AddHandler server-parsed .shtml
```

An alternative way of specifying which files to process is with the XBitHack directive and by setting the execute permission bit in Unix. If the directive XBitHack on is present in the configuration file, Apache will parse any file with the execute bit set. You can set that bit with the following command:

```
chmod +x filename
```

In this case, there is no filter to configure, as mod_include will automatically add it to the filter chain. This is not a very clean solution, but rather a "hack," as the name of the directive indicates. I recommend that you explicitly set the files to be parsed via file extensions, as explained previously.

 The XBitHack directive affects only files with the MIME type text/html.

As you will see in the following section, SSI allows execution of external programs. You can restrict execution privileges with the IncludesNoExec argument to the Options directive: Options -IncludesNoExec prevents the use of the SSI #exec command.

SSI Directives

The general syntax for an SSI directive is the following:

```
<!--#directive argument1=value1 argument2=value2 ... -->
```

directive is the name of the SSI command, and is followed by pairs of arguments and values. The arguments allowed vary depending on the SSI directive.

To test that SSI is working correctly, create an example.shtml file that contains the following:

```
This document, <!--#echo var="DOCUMENT_NAME" -->,
was last modified <!--#echo var="LAST_MODIFIED" -->
```

Configure SSI support as explained earlier, either explicitly setting the filter or using the server-parsed handler. Restart Apache and request the file. The result will be something similar to

```
This document, example.shtml,
was last modified Sunday, 24-Feb-2002 22:06:16 PST
```

12

The following are some of the available SSI commands:

- **config:** The `config` command enables you to specify various SSI-related settings, such as the error message to show to the user when Apache finds an error processing SSI directives.

- **echo:** The `echo` command enables you to output the value of an environment variable. The normal CGI environment variables are available to SSI-parsed files.

- **exec:** This command enables you to execute CGI scripts or commands and include the result in the document.

- **include:** The `include` command enables you to include the content of other files or URLs in the current document.

Additional commands enable you to set variables and even provide primitive `if/else` control flow statements. You can find a complete description of SSI commands, and their syntax and options, at `http://httpd.apache.org/docs-2.0/mod/mod_include.html`.

Additional Configuration Directives

If you do not want SSI commands to be delimited using HTML comment tags (`<!-- -->`), you can change those tags using the `SSIStartTag` and `SSIEndTag` directives.

When an SSI directive cannot be executed successfully, an error message is presented instead. You can change that error message using the `SSIErrorMsg` directive. If you do not want users to see the error in their browsers, you can do so with one of the following directives: `SSIErrorMsg ""` or `SSIErrorMsg "<!-- -->"`.

External Filtering

Apache includes a module, `mod_ext_filter`, that allows filtering of response content using an external program. It starts an external program, feeds the content to the program, reads the response, and inserts it back in the filter chain. The external program reads data from its standard input and writes the result to standard output. This is a common model to many Unix utilities and enables you to use them unmodified. External filters have a performance impact, so they are not recommended for busy sites, but they do allow for interesting possibilities of integration with existing programs.

If you are compiling Apache from source, you can enable this filter with the `--enable-mod-ext-filter` option to the `configure` command, or by using the `apxs` utility, as explained in Hour 18.

If the module was compiled dynamically, you need to make sure that the appropriate LoadModule directive is present:

```
LoadModule ext_filter_module modules/mod_ext_filter.so
```

Configuring External Filtering

The first step is to define (by using the ExtFilterDefine directive) the program that will be used as a filter, the type of content the filter will process, and any additional command-line options that might be required. The complete syntax for the directive is the following:

```
ExtFilterDefine filtername argument1=value1 argument2=value2 ...
```

filtername is the name of the filter that can be used later on by the SetOutputFilter or AddOutputFilter directive.

The arguments are the following:

- **cmd:** External program to execute. You can include any necessary arguments to the program, but in that case, you must enclose the whole command line in quotation marks.
- **mode:** Can be output for output filters and input for input filters. Currently, mod_ext_filter supports only output filters and that is the default value.
- **intype:** By default, the filter will process all requests. The intype argument enables you to specify a MIME type. If intype is present, only requests for that MIME type will be processed.
- **outtype:** If the output content from the filter has a different MIME type than the input content, you can specify it here. Otherwise, the MIME type of the input content will be used for the output content. For example, if the filter takes XML (input MIME type text/xml) and outputs HTML, you must set intype=text/xml and outtype=text/html.

If the filter preserves the content length (the amount of input data matches the amount of output data), you must add an additional PreservesContentLength argument.

Listing 12.4 shows a sample configuration of an external filter with the Unix sort utility. This program takes input text and outputs the sorted result. The filter is defined and then applied to all text files in the /usr/local/apache2/htdocs directory and subdirectory.

12

LISTING 12.4 Associating SSI to Files with .shtml Extension

```
1: ExtFilterDefine sort cmd=/usr/bin/sort intype=text/plain
➥PreservesContentLength
2: <Directory "/usr/local/apache2/htdocs/">
3: SetOuputFilter sort
4: </Directory>
```

To test that it is working, create a file called /usr/local/apache2/htdocs/example.txt with the following content:

```
red
blue
green
yellow
black
white
```

When you request the file, you should get the following in return, with the content ordered alphabetically:

```
black
blue
green
red
white
yellow
```

The ExtFilterOptions configuration directive enables you to specify debugging options for mod_ext_filter. It can take two arguments: DebugLevel and either LogStderr or NoLogStderr. DebugLevel=n specifies the level of debug messages generated by mod_ext_filter and has a default value of DebugLevel=0. LogStderr tells Apache to save error output from the external command, and NoLogStderr (the default) tells Apache not to do it.

DebugLevel specifies the level of debug messages emitted. You must configure the LogLevel setting as well, as described in Hour 8.

Additional Filtering Modules

Other Apache modules are implemented as filters, such as SSL and PHP, which are described in Hour 17, "Setting Up a Secure Server," and Hour 19. Filters can be shared between protocols, so the SSL module can be reused easily when Apache is used as a POP3 or FTP server, as described in Hour 24, "Additional Apache Modules and Projects."

Apache includes two additional filtering modules: `mod_charset_lite` allows charset translations, and `mod_case_filter` is a sample module intended to be an example for module developers.

There are commercial modules that take advantage of the Apache filtering architecture. Covalent's `mod_usertrack` allows tracking of users with cookies and URL rewriting. *URL rewriting* means that the content is scanned as it is served and tracking information is embedded in the HTML links.

Filtering is a feature introduced for the first time in Apache 2.0, and it opens new possibilities for module development: A watermarking module could introduce unique identifiers, an antiviral module could scan downloads for viruses, XML content can be processed and converted to other formats on the fly, and so on.

Scripting modules such as `mod_snake` and `mod_perl` provide support at the script level, exposing the filter API in Python and Perl. Doing so allows a whole new level of flexibility in filter development.

Filtering is also common in other Web technologies, such as Java servlets. The latest servlet specification supports chaining of servlets, a concept of filtering similar to the one explained in this hour.

Summary

This hour explained the filtering infrastructure of Apache and how to configure three of the filter modules included with Apache: `mod_deflate`, `mod_include`, and `mod_ext_filter`.

12

Q&A

Q Does filtering impact performance?

A Filters increase the functionality of Apache, but they have an impact on the performance of the server, depending on the type of filter and the content being filtered. Having said that, the filter framework has been designed and optimized for performance and minimizes the duplication of the data being filtered.

Q How much compression can I expect from `mod_deflate` for HTML pages?

A Around 50% on average. Actual values vary between 20% and 70%, depending on the size of the document.

Quiz

1. mod_deflate is a processor-intensive filtering module. What are the factors that determine whether it can increase performance?

2. Why is compression not enabled for content types other than HTML?

3. How does the XBitHack directive determine whether to process a file?

Quiz Answers

1. Performance gains are achieved if the time to compress the content and transmit the compressed content is less than the time to transmit the original uncompressed content. The bigger the files and the slower the user connections, the more attractive using mod_deflate becomes.

2. Compression is not enabled for content types other than HTML for compatibility reasons because of the problems many browsers have with specific content-types. HTML is the only content-type that most browsers understand correctly when compressed.

3. The XBitHack directive takes a look at the execution permission bit of the file, and works only on Unix.

Related Directives

This section contains directives mentioned in this hour or that are related to topics discussed in this hour. You can consult the Apache reference documentation for comprehensive syntax information and usage.

General Directives

- **AddOutputFilter:** Associate output filters with file extensions
- **SetOutputFilter:** Set response output filters
- **AddInputFilter:** Associate input filters with file extensions
- **SetInputFilter:** Set request input filters

mod_deflate

- **DeflateFilterNote:** Save compression ratio achieved on request note
- **DeflateWindowSize:** Modify compression algorithm window's size to balance memory usage and performance
- **DeflateMemLevel:** Specify memory usage in compression algorithm

mod_include

- **SSIStartTag, SSIEndTag:** Modify tags for SSI command
- **SSIErrorMsg:** Error message when SSI directives cannot execute correctly
- **SSITimeFormat:** Specify how to display dates
- **XBitHack:** Alternative way of identifying SSI files by using the execute bit

mod_ext_filter

- **ExtFilterDefine:** Define filter name and associated external program
- **ExtFilterOptions:** Debugging settings

Further Reading

You can learn more about the compression protocol used by mod_deflate here:

`http://www.gzip.org/zlib/zlib_tech.html`

Apache 2.0 documentation on filtering can be found at

`http://httpd.apache.org/docs-2.0/filter.html`

Server Side Includes are covered in the following addresses:

`http://www.wdvl.com/Authoring/SSI/`

`http://httpd.apache.org/docs-2.0/howto/ssi.html`

12

HOUR 13

Publishing Extensions

Authors of Web content require a means of managing that content and
uploading it to the server. One of the protocols used for this purpose is DAV
(Document Authoring and Versioning). DAV enables users and applications
to publish and modify Web content. In this hour, you will learn

- What publishing solutions are available
- How to build and configure the DAV extension for Apache
- How to configure DAV clients to work with Apache

The Need for a Publishing Protocol

In the early days of the Web, the Webmaster or system administrator traditionally edited the content of Web pages directly in the system hosting the
Web site. The Webmaster logged in to the system remotely, via the telnet or
rsh protocol, and used conventional text editors to edit the HTML code.

As the Web became more popular, several factors described in the following
sections made this approach impractical in many situations.

Windows as a Web Server Platform

A number of Windows-based Web servers appeared, such as Microsoft Internet Information Server. Although not necessarily more robust or secure than their Unix counterparts, these Web servers were definitely easier to use and set up and quickly grew in popularity. However, Windows servers lacked extensive remote access capabilities, and content was copied by hand or by sharing folders in the same local area network.

Separation of Tasks

As Web sites grew in complexity and refinement, a series of new roles emerged. The Webmaster was in charge of administering the Web server, analyzing the logs for errors, updating the software, and so on. Web programmers dealt with providing dynamic features in the Web site, such as personalization, processing forms, and content searching. Designers and editors provided content and graphics for the Web site. This separation of tasks required access restriction policies and easy-to-use methods for updating the Web site content by nontechnical individuals. The tools for generating Web content evolved from simple text editors to sophisticated publishing tools, closer to word processors in features and ease of use.

These tools run on the desktop machine and need a way to upload their content to the Web server.

Web Hosting

Eventually, third-party companies started providing Web-hosting services to corporate customers. Internet service providers and Internet portals provided personal home pages to their users. This increased even more the need for a secure, standard, easy-to-use mechanism for transferring and updating Web pages.

Earlier solutions to this problem were based on different protocols and were not entirely satisfactory. These solutions included:

- **FTP protocol:** Files could be uploaded and deleted using the File Transfer Protocol (FTP) protocol. This was cumbersome for system administrators, who needed to maintain and configure a separate server and user database, and for users, who required an additional tool to upload their changes. The software providers started integrating FTP clients with their publishing products to make it easier for the end user.

- **File uploads via forms:** Some hosting providers allowed clients to upload pages via a form interface. This allowed upload of only one file at a time, and thus was suitable only for simple Web sites such as home pages.

- **File mirroring software:** Tools such as rsync and custom mirroring scripts can compare a local repository with a remote one and make the necessary changes to synchronize them. These are command-line tools commonly used by administrators and advanced developers.

- **HTTP PUT:** This method was eventually introduced in the HTTP specification and allowed clients, such as Netscape Composer, to upload files directly to the server.

- **Proprietary protocols:** This includes protocols such as those from the Microsoft FrontPage publishing tool. They required modifications to the server to support these protocols.

In summary, the existing solutions were difficult to use and administer, nonstandard, and usually required setting up a special, separate server. A new protocol based on HTTP was developed to address these shortcomings: Document Authoring and Versioning, also known as DAV or WebDAV. This hour covers the installation and configuration of the DAV protocol and mentions Microsoft FrontPage server extensions because of their popularity.

The DAV Protocol

The DAV protocol extends HTTP with new methods that allow a DAV client to create, modify, and update files and directories in the server. The client can also access metadata about the resource, such as the author and the date of creation, and lock resources for editing. The integration with HTTP allows DAV to take advantage of existing features, such as SSL for encryption and certificate-based authentication, HTTP basic authentication, proxy servers, and so on. Integration with Apache allows many other possibilities, such as sharing access control mechanisms and interaction with scripting engines such as mod_perl and PHP.

The DAV protocol itself is extensible. Although the resources accessed via DAV usually live in the file system, DAV can act as a standards-based front end to a variety of back-end repositories such as databases, version control systems, and proprietary document management frameworks.

For example, DAV has the concept of collections, which are groups of files. This usually translates to a directory in the server, but it might have a completely different meaning for other backends.

The DAV protocol defines the following new HTTP methods:

- **COPY:** Copy files or collections (equivalent to file system directories). Additional headers enable you to specify the recursive copy of nested collections.

13

- **MOVE:** Move files and collections.
- **MKCOL:** Creates a new collection. If parent collections do not exist, an error is raised. Parent collections must be explicitly created using the PUT method.
- **PROPFIND:** You learned earlier that DAV resources could have metadata information associated with them. The PROPFIND method enables you to query this information.
- **PROPPATCH:** This method enables you to delete, create, and modify resource metadata.
- **LOCK** and **UNLOCK:** These methods allow you to lock a resource. This is useful, for example, for preventing modification to a resource while you are editing it.

The DAV protocol extends existing HTTP methods such as GET and PUT, mainly to make them aware of the new locking features. The OPTIONS method is extended to report DAV capabilities.

Apache and DAV

Apache 2 provides DAV support via the mod_dav module. This module is included with the standard Apache distribution, but it is not compiled by default. You can enable DAV support by using the --with-dav option at compile time, and add support for the file system backend with the --enable-dav-fs option.

If you are using Windows or a Unix binary installation that has loadable module support, you need to add or uncomment the appropriate lines that load the DAV module and the file system backend:

```
LoadModule dav_module modules/mod_dav.so
LoadModule dav_fs_module modules/mod_dav_fs.so
```

Configuring DAV

The first step is defining a lock database using the DavLockDB directive. This directive takes one argument: the path to the database file that will be used to coordinate lock acquisition and release when multiple clients are working on the same resources. A sample setting is

```
DavLockDB logs/dav_lock_db
```

The path to the file can be absolute or relative to your Apache installation (as in the example). The DavLockDB directive must be placed either at the top level of the configuration file or in a <VirtualHost> container.

The next configuration step is to specify the directories and locations you want to make available via the DAV protocol by using the DAV directive. DAV on enables the DAV protocol in a given container and DAV off disables it.

Listing 13.1 shows how simple it is to add DAV support for a specific directory.

LISTING 13.1 Enabling DAV Support

```
<Directory /usr/local/apache2/htdocs/davdocs>
Dav On
</Directory>
```

A Dav directive placed in a <Directory> section enables or disables DAV support for that directory and its subdirectories. Placing a Dav directive inside a <Location> section enables or disables DAV support for URLs prefixed with that location.

Finally, if your DAV server will be accessed via Windows Web folders, you need to add the following configuration file to work around some buggy Microsoft behavior:

```
BrowserMatch "Microsoft Data Access Internet Publishing Provider"
➥ redirect-carefully
```

This directive is already included commented out in the configuration file, so you need only to uncomment it.

Restricting Access

Because mod_dav is an Apache module, it can take advantage of the access control mechanisms of Apache. As Hour 7, "Restricting Access," explained, you can control access based on IP address or hostname, the request method, whether the user has successfully been authenticated, and so on.

In addition, the DAV protocol adds new HTTP method protocols that can be used for fine-grained access control. For example, you can allow read access for most users but restrict updating of information to a few authenticated users.

You can use the <Limit> and <LimitExcept> containers to restrict access based on the HTTP method. Listing 13.2 enables read-only DAV access to the /usr/local/apache2/htdocs/davdocs directory.

13

LISTING 13.2 Enable Read-Only DAV Access

```
<Directory /usr/local/apache2/htdocs/davdocs>
Dav On
<LimitExcept GET POST OPTIONS PROPFIND>
```

LISTING **13.2** continued

```
Order allow,deny
Deny from all
</LimitExcept>
</Directory>
```

Advanced Configuration

The DAV module for Apache provides additional directives for some advanced configuration tuning.

DAVMinTimeout

This DAVMinTimeout directive specifies the minimum time in seconds before a lock expires. This setting overrides the lock timeout value requested by a client if it is less than the specified value. This is useful in certain situations to reduce the network traffic or reduce the possibility of clients being dropped out constantly because the timeout setting is not big enough. For example, DAVMinTimeout 120 will set the timeout value to two minutes.

You can disable this feature by setting its value to 0, which is the default.

LimitXMLRequestBody

This directive is built in to Apache and enables you to specify a maximum allowed size for an XML body request, such as the ones used by mod_dav. By default, it is set to a value of LimitXMLRequestBody 1000000 (1 million bytes). You can disable the size limit by setting the value of LimitXMLRequestBody to 0. This directive can appear in the top level of the configuration file, virtual hosts, and directory and location containers.

The main reason you want to limit the size of requests is to avoid denial of service attacks because the server needs to parse and process the submitted XML. You might also want to have a look at LimitRequestBody and similar directives, which will be described in Hour 16, "Tuning Apache."

DavDepthInfinity

The DAV protocol allows clients to request meta information about all objects in a DAV repository, recursively. If the number of objects is big enough, this can cause performance problems and could be used as a denial of service attack. To avoid this, mod_dav disables this feature by default. You can enable it with the following configuration directive:

```
DavDepthInfinity On
```

DAV Clients

Setting up a DAV server is of little use if you do not have clients to connect to it. This section provides you with information on how to configure different DAV clients to connect to your DAV server.

It assumes that the directory davdocs exists under the document root (/usr/local/apache2/htdocs for a default Unix installation), has write permissions for the user Apache runs as, and has been configured for DAV access:

```
DavLockDB logs/dav_lock_db
BrowserMatch "Microsoft Data Access Internet Publishing Provider"
➥ redirect-carefully
<Location /davdocs/>
Dav On
</Location>
```

Microsoft Clients

Recent versions of Microsoft operating systems, such as Windows 2000 and Windows XP, provide support for DAV via Web folders. Web folders allow transparent access to DAV-enabled servers, by presenting them as Windows desktop folders. Windows users can then drag and drop files into the folders, double-click to edit them, and so on.

You can access davdocs as a Web folder on a Windows 2000 machine directly from Explorer or by using a wizard.

Adding a Web Folder from Explorer

Click on the File menu entry and select Open. A pop-up window will appear, as shown in Figure 13.1.

Type the following URL, http://hostname/davdocs/, where hostname is the name of your server. Check the Open as Web Folder option and click OK. Explorer will connect to the resource, and you should now be able to create directories, drag and drop files, and edit them as shown in Figure 13.2.

The location will be added automatically to the My Network Places folder. You can access this folder by clicking the desktop icon with the same name.

Adding a Web Folder Using a Wizard

To add a Web folder using a wizard, you can go to the My Network Places folder mentioned in the previous section and click on the Add Network Place icon. You will be prompted to provide a URL to the Web folder, and then a description for it, as shown in Figure 13.3.

13

FIGURE **13.1**

Opening a Web folder from Explorer.

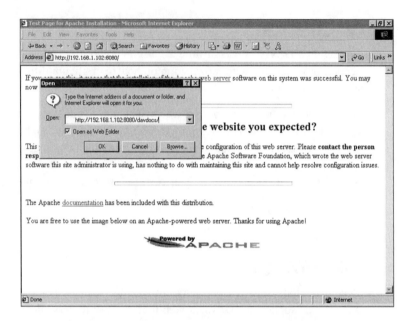

FIGURE **13.2**

Newly created Web folder.

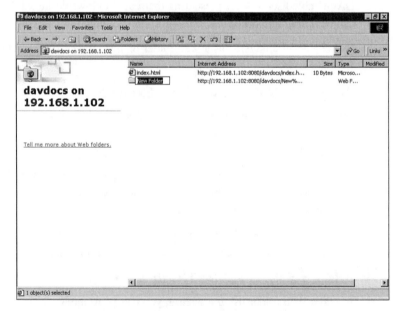

If everything goes well, you can access the Web folder as explained in the previous section.

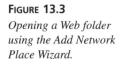

Figure 13.3

Opening a Web folder using the Add Network Place Wizard.

Editing a File Directly from Office

Recent versions of Microsoft Office, such as Office 2000, enable you to open and edit documents directly from DAV-enabled servers. You can simply specify a URL in the Open dialog of the application.

Unix Clients

Several Unix applications are available to connect to a DAV server, as described in the resource section at the end of this hour. This section covers installation of the cadaver command-line utility, which was chosen because it provides an interface similar to an FTP client and is easy to use.

Installation

You can download the latest version of Cadaver from
`http://www.webdav.org/cadaver/`.

Uncompress the tarball by typing the following command:

```
# gunzip < cadaver*.tar.gz | tar xvf -
```

Change to the newly created directory, and run the `configure` script.

```
# ./configure
```

Then build and install the software:

```
# make
# make install
```

You should be able now to use the `cadaver` command-line utility.

Usage

To connect initially to the DAV server, type the following command:

```
# cadaver URL
```

13

where *URL* is the identifier of the server to access, such as `http://hostname/davdocs/`. If `cadaver` was compiled with SSL support, it can open URLs starting with `https://`.

You will be able now to explore the DAV file system by using commands similar to those of an FTP client, as shown in Table 13.1.

TABLE 13.1 Partial List of FTP-Like Commands

Command	Description
`cd` *directory*	Change the current remote directory
`lcd` *directory*	Change the current local directory
`get` *file*	Download a remote file
`put` *file*	Upload a file
`ls` *path*	List the contents of the *path* directory, or the current directory if *path* is not specified

In addition, `cadaver` provides additional commands to manipulate connections, check and modify resource properties, manipulate locks, and so on. Check the manual page for a complete listing of all the options.

Additional DAV Projects

DAV is getting deployed widely, both in commercial products from vendors such as Microsoft, Apple, Adobe, and Xerox, and in a variety of open source projects. You can find a comprehensive list at `http://www.webdav.org/projects/`.

The following sections describe some interesting DAV projects.

Subversion

In previous sections, it was mentioned how `mod_dav` allows backend abstraction. The bundled Apache module provides access to the file system, but the Subversion project provides a front end to a source control system. It provides a CVS replacement using DAV as the transport protocol. You can learn more about Subversion at `http://subversion.tigris.org`.

DAV File Systems

Similar to Microsoft Web folders, Mac OS X provides support for DAV-mounted file systems, as described in `http://www.apple.com/creative/webpro/technology/webdav/`.

A Linux kernel module enables you to mount a DAV server as a local drive. It can be found at `http://dav.sourceforge.net`.

Slide

Slide is a project from the Apache Software Foundation that provides a Java-based content management framework that uses DAV extensively. You can learn more about Slide at `http://jakarta.apache.org/slide/index.html`.

Future Enhancements for DAV

Development of the `mod_dav` Apache module for Apache is currently targeting two areas: support for version control and access control lists.

The official Web DAV site is `http://www.webdav.org`, and the `mod_dav`-specific portion can be found at `http://www.webdav.org/mod_dav/`.

Common Error Messages

This section describes common error messages that you might find in the error log during `mod_dav` installation:

Lock Database

If you find a message similar to the following:

```
(2)No such file or directory: A lock database was not specified with the
➥DAVLockDB directive. One must be specified to use the locking functionality.
➥  [500, #401]
```

The message means that, as the text says, you need to provide a `DavLockDB` directive in the configuration file. If the directive is specified, but the directory containing the lock file cannot be written to; you will get a message like the following:

```
The lock database could not be opened, preventing access to the various
lock properties for the PROPFIND.  [500, #0]
```

Fix the permissions so the path of the `DavLockDB` directive has write permission for the user Apache runs as.

Web Folders

If you can't connect to your DAV server via a Microsoft Web folder and you find something similar to

```
"OPTIONS /davdocs HTTP/1.1" 301
```

13

in the access log, it means that Apache is sending a redirect (HTTP code 301) to the Microsoft client, but the client is getting confused. Apache provides a workaround against this buggy behavior, as explained in earlier sections. Make sure that the following line is present in your configuration file:

```
BrowserMatch "Microsoft Data Access Internet Publishing Provider"
➥ redirect-carefully
```

Microsoft FrontPage

The Microsoft FrontPage publishing tool uses a proprietary protocol. Microsoft provides a set of CGIs and an Apache module (FrontPage extensions) that allow Apache Web servers running on Unix to work with FrontPage clients. At the time this book was written, there was no version of FrontPage extensions for Apache 2.0. You can find more information about FrontPage on Apache at the following Web site:

```
http://www.rtr.com/Ready-to-Run_Software/frontpage_server_extensions.htm
```

Should I Use DAV or FrontPage Extensions?

Microsoft itself seems to be moving away from the FrontPage protocol and favoring the DAV protocol. In addition, FrontPage extensions for Unix are regarded as highly insecure because they require running certain parts with root user privileges. This means that if the Web server is compromised, the attacker automatically gains complete control over the machine. Even with those drawbacks, FrontPage remains one of the most popular Apache modules, running in nearly 20% of all Apache 1.3 servers.

DAV enables you to take advantage of all the other Apache and HTTP protocol features, such as SSL, caching, authentication mechanisms, and so on.

So, unless you need to support older clients that understand only the FrontPage protocol, using mod_dav is likely the better choice.

Summary

This hour explained how to install and configure the mod_dav module, which provides Apache with support for the DAV protocol. This protocol enables publishing and file sharing over the Web. The DAV protocol can take advantage of other Apache features, such as SSL and authentication, to provide secure content access and modification. The DAV protocol is quickly evolving and being embedded in a variety of programs and servers and being extended to support versioning and access control lists.

Q&A

Q **Should I use `<Limit>` or `<LimitExcept>` sections?**

A Both are equivalent for practical purposes. The `<Limit>` directive requires an explicit enumeration of all the methods being restricted, but a `<LimitExcept>` directive will automatically restrict methods that are added in the future.

Q **What are these strange entries in the error log?**

A When Microsoft clients, such as Web folders, connect to your DAV server, they might initially look to see whether it supports FrontPage extensions. They do so by asking for specific files such as `_vti_inf/shtml.exe` and `_vti_inf.html`. You can safely ignore these entries.

Q **Does DAV support symbolic links?**

A No, because they are not supported by all underlying platforms. There is a working group on WebDAV bindings, which will provide that functionality at the DAV protocol level. It can be found at `http://www.webdav.org/specs/`.

Quiz

1. How do you limit DAV write access to a DAV-enabled location to only authenticated users?

2. What is the `DAVMinTimeout` directive used for?

3. Name some of the features of Apache that `mod_dav` can take advantage of.

Quiz Answers

1. Response:

```
<Directory /usr/local/apache2/htdocs/davdocs>
Dav On
<LimitExcept GET POST OPTIONS PROPFIND>
Authtype basic
Authname "DAV write access"
AuthUserFile/usr/local/apache2/conf/htusers
Require valid-user
</LimitExcept>
</Directory>
```

13

2. The `DAVMinTimeout` directive is used to specify minimum timeouts after which locks will expire. This is useful if the client specifies a timeout that is too low, or if your clients access the server via modem and require additional time to reconnect if their connections fail.

3. Some of the advantages include

- SSL for secure access
- Authentication modules for access control
- Logging modules
- Filtering modules for processing content as it is retrieved or uploaded
- High-performance HTTP server framework

Related Directives

This section contains directives mentioned in this hour or that are related to topics discussed in this hour. You can consult the Apache reference documentation for comprehensive syntax information and usage.

- `DAV:` Enable or disable the DAV protocol in a specific container
- `DAVLockDB:` Specify a database file for locking
- `DAVMinTimeout:` Specify a minimum timeout setting for lock expiration
- `DavDepthInfinity:` Enable or disable recursive metadata requests
- `LimitXMLRequestBody:` Limit the size of certain requests to avoid denial of service attacks

Further Reading

RFC 2518, *HTTP standards for distributed authoring*, is the main DAV specification. A number of other specifications deal with revision control, access control lists, bindings (similar to symbolic links), searching of metadata, and so on. A comprehensive list can be found at `http://www.webdav.org/specs/`.

Several papers and talks by Greg Stein, the original author of `mod_dav`, and Jim Whitehead, chairman of the DAV standardization effort, can be found at `http://www.webdav.org/papers/`.

Hour **14**

Virtual Hosting

Apache allows Web administrators the possibility of hosting multiple domains with a single physical installation of Apache. This is called *virtual hosting* and it is the focus of this hour. The lesson covers name-based, IP-based virtual hosting, and DNS and client issues. It explains different mechanisms that can be used to isolate clients from each other and the associated security tradeoffs. When multiple users share a single Web server installation (personal homepages, virtual hosting), there is a need to provide security and user isolation. In this hour, you will learn

- How to configure name-based virtual hosts, IP-based virtual hosts, and the difference between the two
- About the dependencies virtual hosting has on DNS
- How to set up scaled-up cookie-cutter virtual hosts

The Case for Virtual Hosts

Early Web servers were designed to handle the contents of a single site. The standard way of hosting several Web sites in the same machine was to install and configure different, and separate, Web server instances. As the Internet grew, so did the need for hosting multiple Web sites and a more efficient solution was developed: virtual hosting. Virtual hosting allows a single instance of Apache to serve different Web sites, identified by their domain names. *IP-based* virtual hosting means that each of the domains is assigned a different IP address; *name-based* virtual hosting means that several domains share a single IP address. As is explained later in the hour, name-based virtual hosting requires HTTP/1.1 support.

DNS and Virtual Hosting

Web clients use the domain name server system (DNS) to translate hostnames into IP addresses, and vice versa. Several mappings are possible:

- **One to one:** Means that each hostname is assigned a single, unique IP address. This is the foundation for IP-based virtual hosting.

- **One to many:** Means that a single hostname is assigned to several IP addresses. This is useful for having several Apache instances serving the same Web site. If each of the servers is installed in a different machine, it is possible to balance the Web traffic among them, improving scalability.

- **Many to one:** Means that you can assign the same IP address to several hostnames. The client will specify the Web site it is accessing by using the Host: header in the request. This is the foundation for name-based virtual hosting.

When a many-to-one mapping is in place, a DNS server usually can be configured to respond with a different IP address for each DNS query, which helps to distribute the load. This is known as round robin DNS.

Network Interfaces and IP Aliases

A *network interface* is a device that a machine's operating system can use to transmit and receive data over a network with a low-level wire protocol such as TCP. I'm using the term *device* generically, but it's generally a card (such as an Ethernet card) that fits in a computer's expansion slot; thus, the term *network interface card* or *NIC* is commonly used. Attaching a network address to a device is referred to as a *network binding*. Similarly, processes running inside an operating system can bind to network addresses.

This section explains how you can assign one or multiple IP addresses to network interfaces. The examples are Linux-based, so check your operating system documentation for details on how to do the same on your system. You need system administrator privileges to run the examples. Let's take a simple example first: a machine with one network interface, say eth0, with one address (192.168.128.10) bound to it. The syntax used by Linux for binding the IP address to the device is shown in this example:

```
ifconfig eth0 inet 192.168.128.10 netmask 255.255.255.0 up
```

If you subsequently typed

```
ifconfig eth0
```

you would see output similar to Listing 14.1.

LISTING 14.1   Output from the `ifconfig` Command

```
eth0      Link encap:Ethernet  HWaddr 00:50:56:C0:00:C0
          inet addr:192.168.128.10  Bcast:192.168.128.255  Mask:255.255.255.0
          UP BROADCAST RUNNING MULTICAST  MTU:1500  Metric:1
          RX packets:478 errors:0 dropped:0 overruns:0 frame:0
          TX packets:175 errors:0 dropped:0 overruns:0 carrier:0
          collisions:0
          RX bytes:0 (0.0 b)  TX bytes:0 (0.0 b)
```

An Apache server can now bind to any port associated with the IP address by specifying an IP:port combination with the `Listen` directive:

```
Listen 192.169.128.10:80
```

The `Listen` directive in this example is bound to the only ethernet device that the system has. Most modern operating systems support binding multiple IP addresses to one device, a practice referred to as *IP aliasing*. The syntax for defining IP aliases varies with each operating system. For example, Linux systems accomplish this with options to the `ifconfig` command:

```
ifconfig eth0:0 192.168.128.11
```

The Linux syntax for bringing up an additional address bound to the same device is shown here. Now, if you type

```
ifconfig -a
```

the output will include bindings for all network devices, including the real device eth0 as well as our new virtual device eth0:0, as shown in Listing 14.2.

14

LISTING 14.2 Output of `ifconfig` After Adding an IP Alias

```
eth0      Link encap:Ethernet  HWaddr 00:50:56:C0:00:C0
          inet addr:192.168.128.10  Bcast:192.168.128.255  Mask:255.255.255.0
          UP BROADCAST RUNNING MULTICAST  MTU:1500  Metric:1
          RX packets:478 errors:0 dropped:0 overruns:0 frame:0
          TX packets:175 errors:0 dropped:0 overruns:0 carrier:0
          collisions:0
          RX bytes:0 (0.0 b)  TX bytes:0 (0.0 b)

eth0:0    Link encap:Ethernet  HWaddr 00:50:56:C0:00:C0
          inet addr:192.168.128.11  Bcast:192.255.255.255  Mask:255.0.0.0
          UP BROADCAST NOTRAILERS RUNNING  MTU:1500  Metric:1
```

Additional routing configuration might be necessary (with the `route` command), depending on the operating system. Windows systems use the network Control Panel to define additional IP address bindings; the panels are laid out and are accessed differently depending on whether you are using Windows NT 4.0, 2000, or XP.

The same technique used to add a second IP address can generally be applied to add more. The limitations on how many IP aliases can be defined are operating system–specific, but it's not uncommon for Unix systems to support hundreds of IP aliases.

Another way to give a machine multiple IP addresses is to install additional network interfaces. Suppose that a machine has two network interfaces. To configure the second NIC, the `ifconfig` command can be used as we did with the first:

```
ifconfig eth1 inet 192.168.129.10 netmask 255.255.255.0 up
```

If we configure the second interface as shown here:

```
ifconfig -a
```

our output will look like Listing 14.3, which doesn't show any IP aliases.

LISTING 14.3 Output of `ifconfig` After Configuring an Additional Interface

```
eth0      Link encap:Ethernet  HWaddr 00:50:56:C0:00:C0
          inet addr:192.168.128.10  Bcast:192.168.128.255  Mask:255.255.255.0
          UP BROADCAST RUNNING MULTICAST  MTU:1500  Metric:1
          RX packets:478 errors:0 dropped:0 overruns:0 frame:0
          TX packets:175 errors:0 dropped:0 overruns:0 carrier:0
          collisions:0
          RX bytes:0 (0.0 b)  TX bytes:0 (0.0 b)
```

LISTING 14.3   continued

```
eth1      Link encap:Ethernet   HWaddr 00:50:56:C0:00:C1
          inet addr:192.168.129.10  Bcast:192.168.129.255   Mask:255.255.255.0
          UP BROADCAST RUNNING MULTICAST   MTU:1500   Metric:1
          RX packets:0 errors:0 dropped:0 overruns:0 frame:0
          TX packets:0 errors:0 dropped:0 overruns:0 carrier:0
          collisions:0
          RX bytes:0 (0.0 b)   TX bytes:0 (0.0 b)
```

Listing 14.3 shows the two NICs on separate networks. Putting them on the same network is generally done only for specialized applications such as NIC failover in a load-balancing configuration.

IP-Based Virtual Hosting

The simplest virtual host configuration is when each host is assigned a unique IP address. Each IP address maps the HTTP requests that Apache handles to separate content trees in their own VirtualHost containers, as shown in the following snippet:

```
Listen 192.168.128.10:80
Listen 192.168.129.10:80
<VirtualHost 192.168.128.10:80>
    DocumentRoot /usr/local/www-docs/host1
</VirtualHost>
<VirtualHost 192.168.129.10:80>
    DocumentRoot /usr/local/www-docs/host2
</VirtualHost>
```

If a DocumentRoot is not specified for a given virtual host, the global setting, specified outside any <VirtualHost> section, will be used. In the previous example, each virtual host has its own DocumentRoot. When a request arrives, Apache will use the destination IP address to direct the request to the appropriate host. For example, if a request comes for IP 192.168.128.10, Apache will return the documents from /usr/local/www-docs/host1. If the host operating system cannot resolve an IP address used as the VirtualHost container's name and there's no ServerName directive, Apache will complain at server startup time that it can't map the IP addresses to hostnames. This complaint is not a fatal error. Apache will still run, but the error indicates that there might be some work to be done with the DNS configuration so that Web browsers can find your server. A fully qualified domain name (FQDN) can be used instead of an IP address as the VirtualHost container name and the Listen directive binding if the domain name resolves in DNS to an IP address configured on the machine and Apache can bind to it.

14

Name-Based Virtual Hosts

As a way to mitigate the consumption of IP addresses for virtual hosts, the HTTP/1.1 protocol version introduced the `Host:` header, which allows a browser to specify the exact host that the request is intended for. This allows several hostnames to share a single IP address. Most browsers nowadays provide HTTP/1.1 support.

> Although `Host:` usage was standardized in the HTTP/1.1 specification, some older HTTP/1.0 browsers also provided support for this header.

A typical set of request headers from Microsoft Internet Explorer is shown in Listing 14.4. If the URL were entered with a port number, it would be part of the `Host` header contents as well.

LISTING 14.4   Request Headers

```
GET / HTTP/1.1
Accept: image/gif, image/x-xbitmap, image/jpeg, image/pjpeg,
➥ */*
Accept-Language: en-us
Accept-Encoding: gzip, deflate
User-Agent: Mozilla/4.0 (compatible; MSIE 5.01; Windows NT 5.0)
Host: host1.example.com
Connection: Keep-Alive
```

Apache uses the `Host:` header for configurations in which multiple hostnames can be shared by a single IP address—the many to one scenario outlined earlier this hour—thus, the description *name-based virtual hosts*.

The `NameVirtualHost` directive enables you to specify IP address and port combinations on which the server will receive requests for name-based virtual hosts. This is a required directive for name-based virtual hosts. Listing 14.5 has Apache dispatch all connections to 192.168.128.10 based on the `Host` header contents.

LISTING 14.5   Name-Based Virtual Hosts

```
NameVirtualHost 192.168.128.10
Listen 192.168.128.10:80
<VirtualHost 192.168.128.10>
```

LISTING 14.5 continued

```
        ServerName host1.example.com
        DocumentRoot /usr/local/www-docs/host1
</VirtualHost>
<VirtualHost 192.168.128.10>
        ServerName host2.example.com
        DocumentRoot /usr/local/www-docs/host2
</VirtualHost>
```

For every hostname that resolves in DNS to 192.168.128.10, Apache can support another name-based virtual host. If a request comes for that IP address for a hostname that is not included in the configuration file, say host3.example.com, Apache will simply associate the request to the first container in the configuration file; in this case, host1.example.com. The same behavior is applied to requests that are not accompanied by a Host header; whichever container is first in the configuration file is the one that gets the request.

An end user from the example.com domain might have his machine set up with example.com as his default domain. In that case, he might direct his browser to http://host1/ instead of the fully qualified http://host1.example.com/. The Host header would simply have host1 in it instead of host1.example.com. To make sure that the correct virtual host container gets the request, you can use the ServerAlias directive as shown in Listing 14.6.

LISTING 14.6 The ServerAlias Directive

```
NameVirtualHost 192.168.128.10
Listen 192.168.128.10:80
<VirtualHost 192.168.128.10>
    ServerName host1.example.com
    ServerAlias host1
    DocumentRoot /usr/local/www-docs/host1
</VirtualHost>
<VirtualHost 192.168.128.10>
    ServerName host2.example.com
    ServerAlias host2
    DocumentRoot /usr/local/www-docs/host2
</VirtualHost>
```

In fact, you can give ServerAlias a space-separated list of other names that might show up in the Host header so that you don't need a separate VirtualHost container with a bunch of common directives just to handle all the name variants.

14

HTTP 1.1 forces the use of the Host header. If the protocol version is identified as 1.1 in the HTTP request line (that is, GET / HTTP/1.1), the request *must* be accompanied by a Host header. In the early days of name-based virtual hosts, Host headers were considered a tradeoff: Fewer IP resources were required, but legacy browsers that did not send Host headers were still in use and therefore could not access all of the server's virtual hosts. Today, that is not a consideration; there is no statistically significant number of such legacy browsers in use.

The only reason to opt for IP-based and not use name-based virtual hosts is if there are virtual hosts that must use SSL. You can learn more about SSL and this limitation in Hour 17, "Setting Up a Secure Server."

Mass Virtual Hosting

In Listing 14.5, the DocumentRoots follow a simple pattern:

```
DocumentRoot /usr/local/www-docs/hostname
```

where *hostname* is the hostname portion of the fully qualified domain name used in the virtual host's ServerName. For just a few virtual hosts, this configuration is fine. But what if there are dozens, hundreds, or even thousands of these virtual hosts? The configuration file can become difficult to maintain. Apache provides a good solution for cookie-cutter virtual hosts with mod_vhost_alias. You can configure Apache to map the virtual host requests to separate content trees with pattern-matching rules in the VirtualDocumentRoot directive. This functionality is especially useful for ISPs that want to provide a virtual host for each one of their users. The following example provides a simple mass virtual host configuration:

```
NameVirtualHost 192.168.128.10
Listen 192.168.128.10:80
VirtualDocumentRoot /usr/local/www-docs/%1
```

The %1 token used in this example's VirtualDocumentRoot directive will be substituted for the first portion of the FQDN. mod_vhost_alias directives have a language for mapping FQDN components to filesystem locations. Even characters within the FQDN can be accessed.

If we eliminated all the VirtualHost containers and simplified our configuration to the one shown here, the server would serve requests for any subdirectories created in the /usr/local/www-docs directory. If the hostname portion of the FQDN is matched as a subdirectory, that's where Apache will look for content when it translates the request to a filesystem location.

Note that although virtual hosts normally inherit directives from the main server context, some of them, such as `Alias` directives, do not get propagated. For instance, the virtual hosts will not inherit this filesystem mapping:

```
Alias /icons /usr/local/apache2/icons
```

The `FollowSymLinks` flag for the `Options` directive is also disabled in this context. However, a variant of the `ScriptAlias` directive is supported.

The `VirtualScriptAlias` directive shown in the following snippet treats requests for any resources under `/cgi-bin` as containing CGI scripts:

```
NameVirtualHost 192.168.128.10
Listen 192.168.128.10:80
VirtualDocumentRoot /usr/local/vhosts/%1/docs
VirtualScriptAlias /usr/local/vhosts/%1/cgi-bin
```

Note that `cgi-bin` is a special token for that directive; calling the directory just `cgi` won't work; it must be `cgi-bin`.

For IP-based virtual hosting needs, there are variants of these directives: `VirtualDocumentRootIP` and `VirtualScriptAliasIP`. However, because the primary motivation of IP-based virtual hosts is for SSL and there's no pattern-matched path support for SSL resources such as certificates and keys, the uses are fairly limited.

Other Virtual Hosting Techniques

If you don't have access to the DNS configuration for the domains you want to host Web sites for, you still can have multiple independently maintained Web sites off of one Apache instance. This is a frequent occurrence in intranet Web server deployments. We can simply assign each `VirtualHost` its own TCP port, as shown in Listing 14.7.

LISTING 14.7   Assigning TCP Ports

```
Listen 192.168.128.10:8000
Listen 192.168.128.10:8001
Listen 192.168.128.10:8002

ServerName intranet.example.com
<VirtualHost 192.168.128.10:8000>
    DocumentRoot /usr/local/www-docs/host-8000
</VirtualHost>
<VirtualHost 192.168.128.10:8001>
    DocumentRoot /usr/local/www-docs/host-8001
```

14

Listing 14.7 continued

```
</VirtualHost>
<VirtualHost 192.168.128.10:8002>
    DocumentRoot /usr/local/www-docs/host-8002
</VirtualHost>
```

For this configuration, requests for `http://intranet.example.com:8000/`, `http://intranet.example.com:8001/`, and `http://intranet.example.com:8002/` are dispatched to their respective `VirtualHost` containers.

`ServerPath` enables the server to dispatch requests to `VirtualHost` containers by matching the leading path of the request, as shown in Listing 14.8. Because most browsers these days support the `Host` header, the `ServerPath` directive is seldom used.

Listing 14.8 `ServerPath` Example

```
NameVirtualHost 192.168.128.10
Listen 192.168.128.10:80
<VirtualHost 192.168.128.10>
    ServerName host1.example.com
    ServerPath /host1
    DocumentRoot /usr/local/www-docs/host1
</VirtualHost>
<VirtualHost 192.168.128.10>
    ServerName host2.example.com
    ServerPath /host2
    DocumentRoot /usr/local/www-docs/host2
</VirtualHost>
```

With the configuration shown in Listing 14.8, requests that are not accompanied by a `Host` header are dispatched according to the request's URI path. For instance,

```
GET /host1/qa/doc.html HTTP/1.0
```

will be dispatched to the `host1.example.com` container. Apache will look for

```
/usr/local/www-docs/host1/host1/qa/doc.html
```

to fulfill the request. This imposes a requirement on each virtual host; all content for `host1.example.com` must be deployed underneath its `DocumentRoot` in the subdirectory `host1`. The same holds true for `host2` and so on.

Security Considerations

Because each virtual host runs within the Apache process pool, all the CGIs that run within each virtual host run as the same operating system user. So, although the content might be independently maintained, a malicious user could conceivably access or interfere with another user's Web resources.

Apache 2.0 has a facility, suExec (for *set user-id execution*), and a companion module, mod_suexec, that enable safe setuid execution of CGI scripts. This means that scripts can be run under a different user than Apache itself is running as. However, this facility limits the directories in which setuid execution is permitted. New in Apache 2.0 is the Perchild MPM, which allows groups of processes in the Apache process pool to run as different users (as you learned in Hour 11, "Multi-Processing Modules"). At the time of this writing, the Perchild MPM is still experimental, but it is a promising development for the future of secure virtual host CGI execution.

Performance Considerations

The examples we've seen so far have had virtual hosts with only different ServerNames, DocumentRoots, and so forth. However, other directives such as CustomLog and ErrorLog (that you learned about in Hour 8, "Logging and Monitoring") can also be defined on a per virtual host basis. As the number of virtual hosts grows, the resources consumed by Apache grow considerably if each virtual host opens up two log files. Nonetheless, most virtual hosts usually require independent traffic analysis, so having all their traffic data mingled might be considered undesirable. mod_log_config enables you to use the %v formatting option to add the name of the host to the log entry, as shown in Listing 14.9.

LISTING 14.9 Using the %v Option

```
LogFormat "%h %l %u %t \"%r\" %>s %b %v" common
CustomLog logs/access_log
NameVirtualHost 192.168.128.10
Listen 192.168.128.10:80
<VirtualHost 192.168.128.10>
    ServerName host1.example.com
    ServerAlias host1
    DocumentRoot /usr/local/www-docs/host1
</VirtualHost>
<VirtualHost 192.168.128.10>
    ServerName host2.example.com
    ServerAlias host2
    DocumentRoot /usr/local/www-docs/host2
</VirtualHost>
```

14

Whether requested as `http://host1.example.com/` or `http://host1/` and
`http://host2.example.com/` or `http://host2/`, the `access_log` in Listing 14.9 will log
requests for the root resource of `host1` and then `host2` as shown here:

```
10.0.0.120 - - [08/May/2002:03:28:21 -0800] "GET /
➥HTTP/1.0" 200 806 host1.example.com
10.0.0.120 - - [08/May/2002:03:28:22 -0800] "GET /
➥HTTP/1.0" 200 672 host2.example.com
```

A trivial Perl script can process the `access_log` prior to log analysis so that each Web
site's traffic can be independently analyzed. Nonetheless, if CGIs are run in the individual virtual hosts, it might be advantageous to separate the `ErrorLogs` for each virtual
host. When a CGI encounters a runtime error and emits messages to `stderr`, Apache
writes the error message to the `ErrorLog`; often, this is the best debugging resource that a
CGI developer has. In Listing 14.10, each virtual host gets its own error log.

LISTING 14.10   Per Virtual Host Error Log Configuration

```
LogFormat "%h %l %u %t \"%r\" %>s %b %v" common
CustomLog logs/access_log
NameVirtualHost 192.168.128.10
Listen 192.168.128.10:80
<VirtualHost 192.168.128.10>
    ServerName host1.example.com
    ServerAlias host1
    DocumentRoot /usr/local/www-docs/host1
    ErrorLog logs/host1-error_log
</VirtualHost>
<VirtualHost 192.168.128.10>
    ServerName host2.example.com
    ServerAlias host2
    DocumentRoot /usr/local/www-docs/host2
    ErrorLog logs/host2-error_log
</VirtualHost>
```

Although this is convenient for the CGI developer, it could potentially tax the system
resources if the number of virtual hosts is high. Apache opens a number of file handles
for its internal operations; increasing the burden by opening a bunch of separate log files
and having log file writes going to a number of different log files simultaneously will
impede Apache's performance.

Because the process pool is shared—in addition to consuming log file resources—it is
possible for one virtual host to be greedy with operating system resources such as
memory and CPU time that have been allocated to Apache but which other virtual hosts

must also use. For high-traffic Web sites or Web sites that produce a lot of dynamic content through CGIs, it might turn out that running all the Web sites as virtual hosts in one Apache instance is not a good idea.

Running Multiple Apache Instances on a Machine

Given the security and performance considerations, it might be desirable not to run virtual hosts at all. If an application environment such as mod_perl or PHP is maintaining persistent database connections or has conflicting security requirements, it might be preferable to run entirely separate Apache instances. These applications often have different process pool requirements than the static content server processes.

Some caveats to running multiple instances are

1. The configuration file, log file, and content directories are usually maintained separately. If you are running multiple instances, you definitely don't want the PidFile directive writing the parent process ID for each instance to the same file!

2. The operating system memory must be sufficient to run multiple instances' process pools.

3. Applications running in separate instances might still be able to access each other's filesystem resources. The only surefire way to prevent that is to configure your operating system with chrooted or jailed resources, which is a fairly advanced operating system configuration.

Summary

Apache can be configured to handle virtual hosts in a variety of ways. Whether you need a large number of cookie-cutter virtual hosts, a varied set of different virtual host configurations, or the number of IP addresses you can use is limited, there's a way to configure Apache for your application. Name-based virtual hosting is a common technique for deploying virtual hosts without using up IP addresses. IP-based virtual hosting is still necessary when a virtual host is used for SSL. If you cannot change your DNS configuration, your only recourse is to use separate port numbers for your virtual hosts.

14

Q&A

Q **How can I migrate an existing name-based virtual host to its own machine while maintaining continuous service?**

A If a virtual host is destined to move to a neighboring machine, which by definition cannot have the same IP address, there are some extra measures to take. A common practice is to do the following:

1. Set the time-to-live of the DNS mapping to a very low number. This increases the frequency of client lookups of the hostname.

2. Configure an IP alias on the old host with the new IP address.

3. Configure the virtual host's content to be served by both name- and IP-address-based virtual hosts.

4. After all the requests for the virtual host at the old IP address diminish (due to DNS caches expiring their old lookups), the server can be migrated.

Q **Can I mix IP- and name-based virtual hosting?**

A Yes. If multiple IP addresses are bound, you can allocate their usage a number of different ways. A family of name-based virtual hosts may be associated with each; just use a separate `NameVirtualHost` directive for each IP. One IP might be dedicated as an IP-based virtual host for SSL, for instance, whereas another might be dedicated to a family of name-based virtual hosts.

Quiz

1. Which `VirtualHost` container gets a request if the connection uses `NameVirtualHost` but no `Host` header is sent?

2. Is the `ServerName` directive necessary in a `VirtualHost` container?

3. When is the `Host` header required?

4. When can a hostname be used instead of an IP address to bind a `VirtualHost` container?

Quiz Answers

1. Reading the configuration top-to-bottom, the first `VirtualHost` container is favored. The same behavior occurs if there is a `Host` header but no `VirtualHost` container that matches it.

2. Only when name-based virtual hosts are used. The Host header contents are compared to the contents of the ServerName directive. If a match isn't satisfied, the VirtualHost containers' ServerAlias directive value(s) are checked for matches.

3. If the request is sent with HTTP/1.1, the Host header must be sent. Apache sends a 400 Bad Request response if it gets a request that identifies itself as an HTTP/1.1 request without a Host header.

4. A hostname can be used for the VirtualHost container if it resolves in DNS to an IP address that Apache is bound to. If the DNS resolution does not match any of the server's IP address bindings, that VirtualHost won't get any requests. Although it is possible to use hostnames, it is recommended that you use IP addresses instead.

Related Directives

This section contains new directives introduced in this hour. You can consult the Apache reference documentation for comprehensive syntax information and usage.

- **NameVirtualHost:** Used to make Apache examine connections for its Host headers. This directive is required for name-based virtual hosting.

- **ServerName:** Required for name-based virtual hosts for matching against Host headers. Otherwise, the only significance is for server-generated self-referential URLs, such as those in error messages.

- **ServerAlias:** Used inside VirtualHost containers that are using name-based virtual hosts. A ServerAlias provides alternative names by which a virtual host can be accessed.

- **ServerPath:** Used to make Apache examine the URL paths match requests to VirtualHost containers.

- **VirtualDocumentRoot:** Used to map requests to a content tree with the hostname on a pattern-matching basis using mod_vhost_alias. There is an alternative directive, VirtualDocumentRootIP, that performs the pattern matching against the IP address for IP-based virtual hosting.

- **VirtualScriptAlias:** Used to map requests for cgi-bin to a content tree where CGI scripts can run. The directory path can be specified on a pattern-matching basis, similar to VirtualDocumentRoot. Also has an alternative, VirtualScriptAliasIP, that matches against the server's bound IP address.

14

Further Reading

The Apache Web site has a number of configuration examples for virtual hosting:

`http://httpd.apache.org/docs-2.0/vhosts/`

Configuring IP aliasing on Linux is explained at

`http://www.linuxdoc.org/HOWTO/mini/IP-Alias/`

For Solaris, you can find additional information at

`http://www.science.uva.nl/pub/solaris/solaris2.html#q4.10`

Documentation for the popular BIND DNS server is at

`http://www.isc.org/products/BIND/`

HOUR 15

Apache as a Proxy Server

This hour explains how to configure Apache as a forward proxy and a reverse proxy. You can use a forward proxy to allow multiple clients to access the Internet through a single, controlled point. You can use a reverse proxy to protect or load balance backend servers containing sensitive data. The caching filter in Apache allows for faster access for clients and reduced load on the servers. In this hour, you will learn how to

- Configure Apache as a forward proxy
- Configure Apache as a reverse proxy
- Add caching support to Apache

Introduction to Proxy Servers

Apache can be configured as a proxy server. A *proxy* is a program that performs requests on behalf of another.

There are different kinds of Web proxies. A traditional HTTP proxy, also called a *forward proxy*, accepts requests from clients (usually Web browsers), contacts the remote server, and returns the responses. Figure 15.1 shows how a forward proxy works.

FIGURE 15.1
Forward proxy.

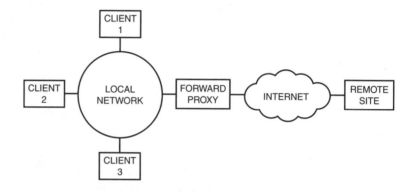

A reverse proxy is a Web server that is placed in front of other servers, providing a unified front end and offloading certain tasks, such as SSL processing, from the backend Web servers. Figure 15.2 shows how a reverse proxy works.

FIGURE 15.2
Reverse proxy.

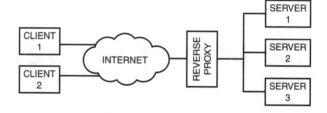

The proxy architecture in Apache is flexible and can be extended. Retrieved content can be cached, scanned for viruses, compressed, altered, and so on.

Enable Proxy Support for Apache

To enable proxy support in Apache, you need to enable the main proxy module and some or all of the three supported backends: HTTP, CONNECT, and FTP. The CONNECT option allows SSL connections to pass untouched via the proxy and is explained later in this hour. The FTP backend allows the proxy server to act as a gateway to access remote FTP servers via a normal HTTP browser.

Building Apache from Source

You can specify the following options at build time:

- `--enable-proxy:` Enable main proxy module
- `--enable-proxy-connect:` Enable CONNECT passthrough method

- **--enable-proxy-ftp:** Enable FTP backend support
- **--enable-proxy-http:** Enable HTTP backend support

Binary Installations

Most binary or vendor-supplied Apache servers already include support for mod_proxy. To enable it, you need to edit the configuration file and uncomment or add the appropriate LoadModule directives, as shown in Listing 15.1.

LISTING 15.1   Enabling Proxy Modules in the Apache Configuration File

```
LoadModule proxy_module modules/mod_proxy.so
LoadModule proxy_connect_module modules/proxy_connect.so
LoadModule proxy_http_module modules/proxy_http.so
LoadModule proxy_ftp_module modules/proxy_ftp.so
```

Apache as a Forward Proxy

Apache provides a standards-compliant forward proxy server that can proxy content from HTTP and FTP servers.

One advantage of a forward proxy is that it is a central place to control access to the Internet and log HTTP requests. A proxy server also can isolate the internal network from external machines. If the proxy server is combined with caching functionality, it can help speed up Internet access when several clients access the same resources.

Forward proxies became very popular years ago when most Internet connections happened over slow links and organizations wanted specific control over who had Internet access, but forward proxies are not widely used anymore.

Apache Forward Proxy Configuration

This section details how to configure Apache to act as a forward proxy.

Enabling Proxy Functionality

The ProxyRequests directive enables or disables the forward proxy functionality in Apache and takes an on or an off argument. This directive does not affect the reverse proxy functionality in Apache, which is explained later in the hour.

You generally do not want to provide access to your proxy to people outside your network because doing so is a potential security risk. That is, an attacker could use the proxy to retrieve documents from internal servers or to attack third-party servers, making the requests look as though they are coming from your network.

You can configure who has access to your forward proxy by using the following containers: `<Directory proxy:pattern>`, `<Proxy pattern>`, and `<ProxyMatch pattern>`. The *pattern* parameter specifies the resources that will be protected. You probably want to restrict access to all proxy functionality to unauthorized users, and you can do so using * as the pattern. Listing 15.2 shows you how to configure Apache to act as a forward proxy server and restrict proxy access to clients coming from the internal network.

LISTING 15.2 Enable Proxy Requests

```
ProxyRequests on

<Proxy *>
    Order deny,allow
    Deny from all
    Allow from 10.0.0.0/255.255.255.0
 </Proxy>
```

You can use the rest of access control directives explained in Hour 7, "Restricting Access."

The `AllowCONNECT` directive enables you to specify a list of ports that the proxy `CONNECT` method will be allowed to access, assuming that you enabled `CONNECT` support for your proxy server, either at build time or when loading the appropriate shared object.

The `CONNECT` method is a special HTTP method used to proxy SSL requests transparently through a proxy server. This is known as *tunneling*.

URL Blocking

The `ProxyBlock` directive enables you to block certain domains and URLs, preventing them from being accessed through the proxy. It takes a space-separated list of words, hosts, or domains. The proxy will block any URL containing them. The special value of `ProxyBlock *` will block access to all sites.

Proxy Hierarchy

Proxy servers can be arranged in hierarchies. This is especially useful for caching proxies. (Caching is covered later in the hour.)

ProxyRemote

You can specify which URLs to forward to a specific remote proxy server by using the ProxyRemote directive. Each ProxyRemote directive takes two arguments. The first argument is a URL scheme that the remote server supports, or a partial URL pattern that, if matched, means the current request should be forwarded to the remote server. The second argument is the URL for the remote server. For example, the directive

```
ProxyRemote http://some.example.com http://10.0.1.1:8000
```

means that proxy requests for some.example.com should in turn be handed over to the remote proxy server listening at address 10.0.1.1 and port 8000.

The special value of * for the first argument means the specified remote server should be contacted for all requests.

NoProxy

The NoProxy directive specifies which machines the proxy server should connect to directly, bypassing the remote proxy server specified by a ProxyRemote directive. The NoProxy directive takes a space-separated list of domains, hostnames, IP addresses, and/or subnets.

ProxyDomain

In certain situations, local clients will try to connect to resources using unqualified domain names. That is, users will type myserver in their browsers to access the myserver.example.com Web site. The ProxyDomain directive enables you to specify the default domain that should be appended to local names. The proxy server will then send a redirect to the client with the fully qualified domain name.

ProxyMaxForwards

The ProxyMaxForwards directive specifies the maximum number of chained proxies a request may travel before being discarded. This is useful to avoid infinite loops due to a faulty configuration.

ProxyVia

Usually, when a proxy server relays a request to the destination server or to another remote proxy server, it adds a Via: header containing information about itself. The ProxyVia directive enables you to configure this behavior.

`ProxyVia` can take one of four values:

- **On:** A `Via:` header with the proxy hostname will be added.
- **Full:** Same as `On`, but includes information about the Apache version.
- **Off:** The default behavior. It will not add its own `Via:` header, but will not modify any `Via:` header if already present.
- **Block:** No `Via:` header will be added and existing `Via:` headers will be removed.

Tuning

The `ProxyReceiveBufferSize` directive enables you to specify the size of the buffer, in bytes, for HTTP and FTP connections in order to increase throughput in large downloads. If you set this value to `0`, the default system buffer size will be used.

The `ProxyTimeout` directive enables you to specify the time in seconds that the proxy will wait for a request to a remote server to be successful. This directive can be used both for forward proxies and reverse proxies.

Configuring Client Support

This section describes how to add proxy support to the Internet Explorer and Mozilla browsers. This step is necessary to tell the browsers that instead of accessing the Web sites directly, they must use the proxy server instead. Most modern browsers have built-in proxy support and can be configured in a similar way.

Configuring Internet Explorer

Open the Internet Options dialog. You can get there from the Control Panel icon or by selecting Tools, Internet Options in the Internet Explorer menu bar.

You can then select the Connections tab and click on the LAN Settings button. A dialog will pop up. Click on the Use a Proxy Server for Your LAN check box and specify the address and port of your proxy server. This proxy server will be used to access all content. If you want to access servers in your same network directly, select the Bypass Proxy Server for Local Addresses check box. If you want to access specific remote servers directly, you can click on the Advanced button and enter the remote servers in the Exceptions text box. Figure 15.3 shows the steps involved.

Configuring Mozilla

You can configure your proxy settings on Mozilla by clicking on the Edit menu bar entry and selecting Preferences. You can access the proxy settings by clicking on Advanced and then on Proxies, as shown in Figure 15.4.

FIGURE 15.3

Proxy configuration for Internet Explorer.

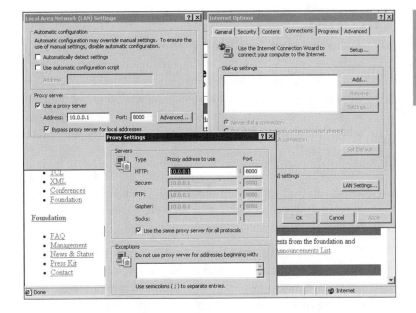

FIGURE 15.4

Proxy configuration for Mozilla.

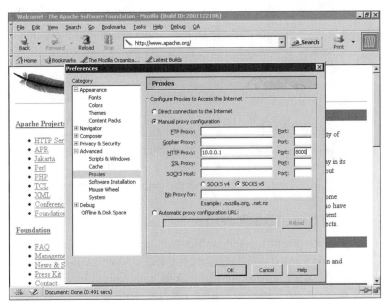

You can then select Manual Proxy Configuration and enter the address and port of the proxy server. If you want to contact certain servers directly, and bypass the proxy, you can enter those servers in the No Proxy For section.

Caching

Accessing or generating certain content can be very expensive in terms of server resources or network delay. You can configure Apache to save some of that data locally, in memory or disk, to speed up future access. Doing so is known as *caching*. In previous versions of Apache, cache control was tightly integrated with the proxy. In Apache 2.0, the cache functionality has been abstracted as a filter module (mod_cache) and can be used to cache not only content retrieved by the proxy, but also content generated by Apache itself.

Caching has several advantages, depending on the scenario. If several clients access the Internet through the same forward proxy, caching frequently accessed content can improve the speed of Web access and save bandwidth. This is useful when the link to the Internet is a slow one.

In a reverse proxy situation or when mod_cache is used in a Web server, caching can be used to speed up access to semi-static content, such as weather maps, delayed stock quotes, and movie schedules. This information has to be dynamically generated, but typically does not change for several minutes. Caching this type of content will reduce the load of the backend systems, decreasing response time and improving scalability.

Although caching can also be implemented at the application level, the caching modules in Apache provide additional flexibility that is particularly useful when the content generation code cannot be modified.

> At the time this book was written, caching support in Apache 2.0 was still in alpha state, and the caching modules were considered experimental. That means the directives and behavior discussed in this section might have changed by the time you read this.

Caching Backends

The mod_cache module enables two caching backend mechanisms: memory and disk. A memory-based cache is faster, but does not survive a server restart and is limited by the physical memory of the server. A disk cache is slower, but persists even if the server is stopped and restarted. The operating system disk-caching algorithm will also speed up disk accesses.

Building Apache from Source

If you are building Apache from source, you must pass the following arguments to the Apache configure script to add support for caching:

- **--enable-cache:** Enable dynamic caching main module
- **--enable-disk-cache:** Enable the disk caching backend
- **--enable-mem-cache:** Enable the memory caching backend

Binary Installations

Most binary or vendor-supplied Apache servers include support for caching. To enable it, you must edit the configuration file and uncomment or add the appropriate LoadModule directives, as shown in Listing 15.3.

LISTING 15.3   Enabling Caching Modules in the Apache Configuration File

```
LoadModule cache_module modules/mod_cache.so
LoadModule disk_cache modules/mod_disk_cache.so
LoadModule memory_cache_module modules/mod_mem_cache.so
```

Caching Configuration

You can use the CacheOn directive to enable or disable caching functionality globally by setting it to on or off. You can specify which URLs to cache with the CacheEnable and the CacheDisable directives, explained in the next section.

What to Cache

The CacheEnable directive accepts two parameters. The first parameter specifies the cache type, which is one of the currently available cache storage methods: mem for memory or disk for disk. The second parameter provides a partial URL prefix. Resources matching this prefix will be cached. The CacheDisable directive takes a single argument: a partial URL prefix specifying resources that will *not* be cached.

You can have fine-grained caching behavior control using these two directives.

How Long to Cache

This section explains several directives that can be used to control the lifetime of cache objects.

CacheMaxExpire

The CacheMaxExpire directive enables you to specify the maximum time in hours to cache a document, under any circumstance, before checking again to see whether the document has been updated. If an expiration value is not specified, it will default to a value of 24 hours. The CacheMaxExpireMin directive enables you to specify the value in minutes.

CacheLastModifiedFactor

If an object does not provide an expiry value, Apache takes a simple approach to estimate it. CacheLastModifiedFactor takes a numeric argument. The expiry value for the resource will be calculated multiplying that number by the value of the last-modified header provided by the remote server. That is, if the resource was modified 10 hours ago and the value of the directive is 0.5, the expiry value will be 5 hours.

CacheForceCompletion

This directive takes a percentage of download completion. If a client cancels a request (for example, the user presses the stop button in the browser) and this percentage has been reached, Apache will download and cache the response anyway.

CacheDefaultExpire

This directive takes a default expiry time in hours that will be used in a proxy environment when retrieving objects via protocols that do not support the concept of expiration time. It defaults to one hour.

Apache as a Reverse Proxy

A reverse proxy is a Web server that sits in front of other Web servers, known as *backend servers*. The reverse proxy Web server can be configured to pass certain requests to the backend servers and return the result to the clients as if it were the reverse proxy that generated the content. A reverse proxy is useful for several reasons:

- **Performance:** A reverse proxy can be used to ease the load on the backend servers. A reverse proxy can handle SSL requests for the backend servers, load balance requests, or cache frequently accessed content. Another common configuration scenario is to have the reverse proxy directly serve static content, such as images, and retrieve the dynamic content from the backend servers. This is especially useful when the backend servers are Java application servers not optimized for static content Web serving.
- **Security:** If the backend servers contain sensitive information, or have security problems, the reverse proxy can act as an HTTP-level firewall, isolating these

servers from direct Internet exposure. For example, versions of Microsoft Internet Information Server have had serious and widely publicized security flaws. A reverse proxy based on Apache, set up in front of servers running IIS, can block malicious attacks and provide a migration path to a fully Apache-based installation.

- **Unified front end:** A reverse proxy can provide a unified URL space to a variety of backend resources. This can be used to have unified logging, user management, and session tracking for a variety of backend architectures and servers.

Reverse Proxy Configuration

Reverse proxy support is included as part of the core mod_proxy module. Refer to the "Apache as a Forward Proxy" section of this hour for information on how to add proxy support to an Apache installation.

For the remainder of this section, rproxy.example.com will designate the machine running the reverse proxy and backend.example.com will refer to the backend machine providing the content.

Specifying Reverse Proxy URLs

You can use the ProxyPass and ProxyPassReverse directives to map URLs in the reverse proxy to URLs in the backend servers.

The ProxyPass directive has two syntaxes. If the directive is placed outside of a <Location> container, it takes two arguments. The first argument is the prefix to match. The second is the corresponding URL for a resource in the backend to retrieve whenever a request matches the first argument. The remaining part of the matched prefix will be added to the backend URL.

For example, the directive

```
ProxyPass /dynamic/ http://backend.example.com/
```

will cause a request for http://rproxy.example.com/dynamic/content/index.html to return the content from http://backend.example.com/content/index.html

If the ProxyPass directive is placed inside a <Location> container, it takes a single argument: the remote URL. The matching prefix will be taken from the value of the <Location> directive. The previous example could be rewritten as the following:

```
<Location /dynamic/>
ProxyPass http://backend.example.com/
</Location>
```

In certain situations, the backend server might issue redirects. These redirects will include a Location: header that contains a reference to the backend server (backend.example.com). The ProxyPassReverse directive will intercept these headers and rewrite them so that they include a reference to the reverse proxy (rproxy.example.com) instead.

The previous examples could be rewritten as follows:

```
ProxyPass /dynamic/ http://backend.example.com/
ProxyPassReverse /dynamic/ http://backend.example.com/
```

> Note that the ProxyPassReverse directive operates only at the HTTP header level. It will not inspect or rewrite links inside HTML documents.

Preventing URLs from Being Reverse Proxied

It is possible to prevent certain URLs from not being proxied by specifying an exclamation sign (!) as the remote site URL in ProxyPass directives. It is important that those directives are placed before other ProxyPass directives. For example, the following configuration will pass all requests to a backend site, except requests for images, which will be served locally:

```
ProxyPass /images/ !
ProxyPass / http://backend.example.com
```

The ProxyErrorOverride Directive

This directive takes a setting of on or off and enables you to intercept error messages from backend machines and replace them with the equivalent reverse proxy server error messages. This enables you to further hide the existence of the backend server and provide a consistent front end to different backend servers, even for error messages.

The ProxyPreserveHost Directive

When Apache is acting as a reverse proxy, the Host: header is modified in the proxy request to match the hostname specified in the ProxyPass directive. The original Host: header is placed in another header, X-Forwarded-Host, as will be explained in the next section. In certain situations, it is desirable to preserve the original value of the header. This can be done by setting ProxyPreserveHost on in the configuration file.

Additional Headers

Certain information about the request gets lost with a reverse proxy in place. The reverse proxy records some of that information in new headers that are added to the request to the backend server:

- **X-Forwarded-For:** IP address or hostname of the client
- **X-Forwarded-Host:** Original host requested
- **X-Forwarded-Server:** Hostname for the proxy server

Related Open Source and Commercial Products

The Squid proxy is another popular open source proxy that can be found at `http://www.squid-cache.org`.

The `mod_backhand` module (`http://www.backhand.org/mod_backhand/`) provides similar functionality to a reverse proxy, although at the time of this writing, it has not yet been ported to work with Apache 2.0.

Covalent Technologies (`http://www.covalent.net`) provides several modules for Apache 2.0 as part of its Enterprise Ready Server. Some of the modules allow passing arbitrary information to the backend server (such as SSL client certificate information) and others allow on-the-fly URL rewriting of the content served by the reverse proxy.

Netegrity (`http://www.netegrity.com`) has a secure reverse proxy product based on Apache that allows for additional nice features such as single sign on.

Summary

This hour explained configuration of Apache as a forward and reverse proxy and how to use Apache's built-in caching filter mechanism. It explained the benefits of using a proxy in different situations and provided detailed information of the available configuration directives. Advanced reverse proxy functionality can be achieved in combination with `mod_rewrite`, which is described in Hour 22. The filtering architecture of Apache allows additional compression or translation modules to be used in conjunction with the proxy functionality.

Q&A

Q Can I use absolute links in the backend server content?

A You can, but because HTML links will not be affected by `ProxyPassReverse` rules, you must make sure that equivalent links exist in the reverse proxy or that the reverse proxy has been configured to retrieve them from the backend server.

Quiz

1. What kind of information is lost due to the existence of the reverse proxy server?

2. How can you configure a reverse proxy so that *all* requests are passed to the back-end server?

Quiz Answers

1. The protocol used, either HTTP or HTTPS. In the case of HTTPS, all information related to certificates, algorithms, key lengths, and so on, is lost.

   The remote IP address, hostname, and port, and the reverse proxy host, address, and port are also lost.

   Some of the lost information is recorded in headers added by the reverse proxy server.

2. Answer:

```
ProxyPass / http://backend.example.com
ProxyPassReverse / http://backend.example.com
```

Related Directives

This section contains directives mentioned in this hour or that are related to topics discussed in this hour. You can consult the Apache reference documentation for comprehensive syntax information and usage.

Forward Proxy Directives

- **ProxyRequests:** Enable or disable forward-proxy engine
- **ProxyRemote:** Specify remote proxy server
- **ProxyBlock:** Restrict access to certain domains
- **AllowCONNECT:** Allow CONNECT method for SSL tunneling
- **ProxyReceiveBufferSize:** Tuning of buffer size for higher throughput
- **ProxyMaxForwards:** Prevent infinite loops due to faulty configurations
- **NoProxy:** Bypass remote proxy
- **ProxyDomain:** Domain to add to local names
- **ProxyTimeout:** Specify a timeout in seconds
- **ProxyVia:** Handling of the Via: header

Reverse Proxy Directives

- **ProxyPass:** Specify URLs to associate with backend servers
- **ProxyPassReverse:** Modify redirect requests from the backend server
- **ProxyPreserveHost:** Preserve the original Host: header in request to backend servers
- **ProxyErrorOverride:** Replace backend error messages

Caching Directives

- **CacheOn:** Enable caching functionality
- **CacheEnable:** Enable caching of specific URLs
- **CacheDisable:** Disable caching of specific URLs
- **CacheMaxExpire, CacheMaxExpireMin:** Maximum expiration time
- **CacheLastModifiedFactor:** Factor to determine the expiry time for resources
- **CacheForceCompletion:** Percentage of download before proxy will complete request even if client connection is aborted
- **CacheDefaultExpire:** Expiration time for protocols that do not support the concept

Further Reading

You can find a variety of resources related to proxy servers and caching at
http://directory.google.com/Top/Computers/Software/Internet/Servers/Proxy/.

Hour 22 deals with mod_rewrite, a module commonly used with the Apache reverse proxy. For example, the following article explains how to use both modules to provide a load balancing solution:
http://www.webtechniques.com/archives/1998/05/engelschall/.

The article refers to Apache 1.3, but the architecture can be applied to Apache 2.0 as well.

15

HOUR 16

Tuning Apache

You might encounter scalability and performance problems if the number of visitors to your Web site increases significantly. Although most bottlenecks in Web performance nowadays are tied to dynamic page generation and database access, some relate to the Web server. In this hour, you will learn

- Which operating system and Apache-related settings can limit the server scalability or degrade performance
- About several tools for load testing Apache
- How to fine-tune Apache for optimum performance
- How to configure Apache to detect and prevent abusive behavior from clients

Scalability

This section covers scalability problems and how to prevent them. This is more of a "don't do this" list, explaining limiting factors that can degrade performance or prevent the server from scaling. Later sections deal with proactive tuning of Apache for optimal performance.

Operating System Limits

Several operating system factors can prevent Apache from scaling. These factors are related to process creation, memory limits, and maximum simultaneous number of open files or connections.

 The Unix ulimit command enables you to set several of the limits covered in this section on a per-process basis. Please refer to your operating system documentation for details on ulimit's syntax.

Processes

Apache provides settings for preventing the number of server processes and threads from exceeding certain limits. These settings affect scalability because they limit the number of simultaneous connections to the Web server, which in turn affects the number of visitors that you can service simultaneously. These settings vary from MPM to MPM and are described in detail in Hour 11, "Multi-Processing Modules."

The Apache MPM settings are in turn constrained by OS settings limiting the number of processes and threads. How to change those limits varies from operating system to operating system. In Linux 2.0.x and 2.2.x kernels, it requires changing the NR_TASKS defined in /usr/src/linux/include/linux/tasks.h and recompiling the kernel. In the 2.4.x series, the limit can be accessed at runtime from the /proc/sys/kernel/threads-max file. You can read the contents of the file with

```
cat /proc/sys/kernel/threads-max
```

and write to it using

```
echo value > /proc/sys/kernel/threads-max
```

In Linux (unlike most other Unix versions), there is a mapping between threads and processes and they are similar from the point of view of the OS.

In Solaris, those parameters can be changed in the /etc/system file. Those changes don't require rebuilding the kernel, but might require a reboot to take effect. You can change the total number of processes by changing the max_nprocs entry and the number of processes allowed for a given user with maxuproc.

File Descriptors

Whenever a process opens a file (or a socket), a structure called a *file descriptor* is assigned until the file is closed. The OS limits the number of file descriptors that a given process can open, thus limiting the number of simultaneous connections the Web server can have. How those settings are changed depends on the operating system. On Linux systems, you can read or modify /proc/sys/fs/file-max (using echo and cat as explained in the previous section). On Solaris systems, you must edit the value for rlim_fd_max in the /etc/system file. This change will require a reboot to take effect.

You can find additional information at

http://httpd.apache.org/docs/misc/descriptors.html

Controlling External Processes

Apache provides several directives to control the amount of resources external processes use. This applies to CGI scripts spawned from the server and programs executed via Server Side Includes. Support for the following directives is available only on Unix and varies from system to system:

- **RLimitCPU:** Accepts two parameters: the soft limit and the hard limit for the amount of CPU time in seconds that a process is allowed. If the max keyword is used, it indicates the maximum setting allowed by the operating system. The hard limit is optional. The soft limit can be changed between restarts, and the hard limit specifies the maximum allowed value for that setting. If you are confused, check Hour 11 for a similar discussion with ServerLimit and MaxClients.

- **RLimitMem:** The syntax is identical to RLimitCPU but this directive specifies the amount (in bytes) of memory used per process.

- **RLimitNProc:** The syntax is identical to RLimitCPU but this directive specifies the number of processes.

These three directives are useful to prevent malicious or poorly written programs from running out of control.

Apache Settings

This section presents you with different Apache settings that affect performance.

File System Access

Accessing files on disk is expensive. You should try to minimize the number of disk accesses required for serving a request. Symbolic links, per-directory configuration files, and content negotiation are some of factors that affect the number of disk accesses:

- **Symbolic links**: In Unix, a *symbolic link* (or *symlink*) is a special kind of file that points to another file. It is created with the Unix ln command, and is useful for making a certain file appear in different places.

16

Two of the parameters that the `Options` directive allows are `FollowSymLinks` and `SymLinksIfOwnerMatch`.

By default, Apache won't follow symbolic links because they can be used to bypass security settings. For example, you can create a symbolic link from a public part of the Web site to a restricted file or directory not otherwise accessible via the Web. So, also by default, Apache needs to perform a check to verify that the file isn't a symbolic link. If `SymLinksIfOwnerMatch` is present, it will follow a symbolic link if the target file is owned by the same user that created the symbolic link. Because those tests must be performed for every path element and for every path that refers to a filesystem object, they can be expensive. If you control the content creation, you should add an `Options +FollowSymLinks` directive to your configuration and avoid the `SymLinksIfOwnerMatch` argument. In this way, the tests won't take place and performance isn't affected.

- **Per-directory configuration files**: As explained in Hour 4, "Getting Started with Apache," it is possible to have per-directory configuration files. These files, normally named `.htaccess`, provide a convenient way of configuring the server and allow for some degree of delegated administration. However, if this feature is enabled, Apache has to look for these files in each directory in the path leading to the file being requested, resulting in expensive filesystem accesses. If you don't have a need for per-directory configuration files, you can disable this feature by adding `AllowOverride none` to your configuration. Doing so will avoid the performance penalty associated with accessing the filesystem looking for `.htaccess` files.

- **Content negotiation**: As explained in Hour 9, "Content Negotiation and Environment Variables," Apache can serve different versions of a file depending on client language or preferences. This can be accomplished with file extensions, but for every request, Apache must access the filesystem repeatedly looking for files with appropriate extensions. If you need to use content negotiation, make sure that you at least use a type-map file, minimizing accesses to disk.

- **Scoreboard file**: This is a special file that the main Apache process uses to communicate with its children in certain older operating systems. You can specify its location with `ScoreBoardFile`, but most modern platforms do not require this directive. If this file is required, you might find improved performance if you place it on a RAM disk. A *RAM disk* is a mechanism that allows a portion of the system memory to be accessed as a filesystem. The details on creating a RAM disk vary from system to system.

Additionally, take a look at the optimizing performance section to see how `mod_file_cache` can be used to improve performance by mapping certain files into memory.

Network and Status Settings

A number of network-related Apache settings can degrade performance:

- **HostnameLookups:** When `HostnameLookups` is set to on or `double`, Apache will perform a DNS lookup to capture the hostname of the client, introducing a delay. The default setting is `HostnameLookups off`. If you need to use the hostnames, you can always process the request logs with a log resolver later, as explained in Hour 8, "Logging and Monitoring."

  Certain other settings can trigger a DNS lookup, even if `HostnameLookups` is set to `off`, such as when a hostname is used in `Allow` or `Deny` rules, as covered in Hour 7, "Restricting Access."

- **Accept mechanism:** As explained in Hour 11, Apache can use different mechanisms to control how Apache children arbitrate requests. The optimal mechanism depends on the specific platform and number of processors. You can find detailed tests and performance analysis at `http://research.covalent.net/projects/osdl1.html`. Additional information can be found at `http://httpd.apache.org/docs-2.0/misc/perf-tuning.html`

- **mod_status:** This module, explained in Hour 8, collects statistics about the server, connections, and requests, which slows down Apache. For optimal performance, disable this module, or at least make sure that `ExtendedStatus` is set to `off`, which is the default.

Load Testing Your Web Site

You can test the scalability and performance of your site with benchmarking and traffic generation tools. There are many commercial and open source tools, with varying degrees of sophistication. It is difficult to accurately simulate real-world request traffic because visitors have different navigation patterns, access the Internet using connections with different speeds, stop a download if it is taking too long, press the reload button repeatedly if they get impatient, and so on. That is why some tools record actual network traffic for later replay.

This section describes several tools that will help you discover performance problems and determine how your program handles high-traffic situations.

ApacheBench

The Apache server comes with a simple but useful load-testing tool, called ApacheBench, or ab. You can find it in the bin/ directory of the Apache distribution.

This tool enables you to request a certain URL a number of times and display a summary of the result.

The following command requests the main page of the www.example.com server 1000 times, with 10 simultaneous clients at any given time:

```
$/usr/local/apache2/bin/ab -n 1000 -c 10 http://www.example.com/
```

> If you invoke ab without any arguments, you will get a complete listing of command-line options and syntax.

The result will look similar to the following:

```
This is ApacheBench, Version 2.0.32 <$Revision: 1.87 $>
Copyright (c) 1996 Adam Twiss, Zeus Technology Ltd,
http://www.zeustech.net/org/
Copyright (c) 1998-2001 The Apache Software Foundation, http://www.apache.org/

Benchmarking www.example.com (be patient)
Completed 100 requests
Completed 200 requests
Completed 300 requests
Completed 400 requests
Completed 500 requests
Completed 600 requests
Completed 700 requests
Completed 800 requests
Completed 900 requests
Finished 1000 requests
Server Software:        Apache/2.0.32
Server Hostname:        www.example.com
Server Port:            80

Document Path:          /
Document Length:        8667 bytes

Concurrency Level:      10
Time taken for tests:   64.525026 seconds
Complete requests:      1000
Failed requests:        0
```

```
Write errors:           0
Total transferred:      8911000 bytes
HTML transferred:       8667000 bytes
Requests per second:    15.50 [#/sec] (mean)
Time per request:       0.645 - (mean)
Time per request:       0.065 - (mean, across all concurrent requests)
Transfer rate:          134.86 [Kbytes/sec] received

Connection Times (ms)
             min   mean[+/-sd] median   max
Connect:      19    62   59.7 45 727
Processing:  178   572  362.8 478 3151
Waiting:      18   114  176.9 74 1906
Total:       255   634  390.3 536 3301

Percentage of the requests served within a certain time (ms)
 50%    536
 66%    611
 75%    662
 80%    693
 90%    872
 95%   1436
 98%   2162
 99%   2461
100%   3301 (longest request)
```

These requests were made over the Internet to a sample server. You should get many more requests per second if you conduct the test against a server in the same machine or over a local network.

The output of the tool is self-explanatory. Some of the relevant results are the number of requests per second and the average time it takes to service a request. You can also see how more than 90% of the requests were served in less than one second.

You can play with different settings for the number of requests and with the number of simultaneous clients to find the point at which your server slows down significantly.

JMeter

JMeter is a complete Web testing solution written in Java and is part of the Apache Software Foundation projects. It enables you to load test different URLs and to script the requests programmatically.

Figure 16.1 shows a sample JMeter test run. You can find more information at http://jakarta.apache.org/jmeter/.

FIGURE 16.1

Sample JMeter test run.

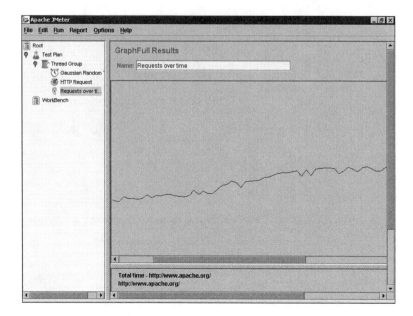

There are many additional Web performance tools, such as Siege `http://www.joedog.org/siege/index.shtml`. You can find many others at sites such as `http://freshmeat.net` and `http://sf.net`.

Tuning Apache for Performance

Although previous sections explained which settings might prevent Apache from scaling, the following are some techniques for proactively increasing the performance of your server.

Mapping Files to Memory

As explained previously, accesses to disk affect performance significantly. Although most modern operating systems keep a cache of the most frequently accessed files, Apache also enables you to explicitly map a file into memory so that access to disk isn't necessary. The module that performs this mapping is `mod_file_cache`. You can specify a list of files to memory map by using the `MMapFile` directive, which applies to the server as a whole. An additional directive, `CacheFile`, takes a list of files, caches the file descriptors at startup, and keeps them around between requests, saving time and resources for frequently requested files.

Distributing the Load

Another way to increase performance is to distribute the load among several servers. This can be done in a variety of ways:

- A hardware load balancer directing network and HTTP traffic across several servers, making it look like a single server from the outside.

- A software load balancer solution using a reverse proxy with mod_rewrite. Running Apache as a reverse proxy is covered in Hour 15, "Apache as a Proxy Server," and mod_rewrite is discussed in Hour 22.

- Separate servers providing images, large download files and other static material. For example, you can place your images in a server called images.example.com and link to them from your main server.

16

Caching

The fastest way to serve content is not to serve it! This can be achieved by using appropriate HTTP headers that instruct clients and proxies of the validity in time of the requested resources. In this way, some resources that appear in multiple pages but don't change frequently, such as logos or navigation buttons, are transmitted only once for a certain period of time.

Additionally, you can use mod_cache (described in Hour 15) to cache dynamic content so that it doesn't need to be created for every request. This is potentially a big performance boost because dynamic content usually requires accessing databases, processing templates, and so on, which can take significant resources.

Reduce Transmitted Data

Another way to reduce the load on the servers is to reduce the amount of data being transferred to the client. This in turn makes your clients' Web site access faster, especially for those over slow links. You can do a number of things to achieve this:

- Reduce the number of images.
- Reduce the size of your images.
- Compress big downloadable files.
- Pre-compress static HTML and use content negotiation, as explained in Hour 9.
- Use mod_deflate to compress HTML content, as described in Hour 12, "Filtering Modules." This can be useful if CPU power is available and clients are connecting over slow links. The content will be delivered quicker and the process will be free sooner to answer additional requests.

Network Settings

HTTP 1.1 allows multiple requests to be served over a single connection. HTTP 1.0 allows the same thing with keep-alive extensions. The KeepAliveTimeout directive enables you to specify the maximum time in seconds that the server will wait before closing an inactive connection. Increasing the timeout means that you will increase the chance of the connection being reused. On the other hand, it also ties up the connection and Apache process during the waiting time, which can prevent scalability, as discussed earlier in the hour.

The SendBufferSize directive, mentioned in Hour 11, can be useful to improve performance in specific situations.

Performance Tuning for Specific Apache Modules

You can take a number of steps to optimize content generation with specific Apache modules such as mod_perl, and you will need to consult your specific module documentation. You can find a mod_perl performance guide at http://perl.apache.org/guide/performance.html.

Loadable Modules

Using shared modules has a certain performance penalty associated with it—around 5%. If you want to improve performance further in your server, you might want to consider compiling all required modules statically into the server. In most cases, the flexibility that comes with loadable module support offsets the performance loss.

Preventing Abuse

Denial of service (DoS) attacks work by swamping your server with a great number of simultaneous requests, slowing down the server or preventing access altogether to legitimate clients. DoS attacks are difficult to prevent in general, and usually the most effective way to address them is at the network or operating system level. One example is blocking specific addresses from making requests to the server; although you can block those addresses at the Web server level, it is more efficient to block them at the network firewall/router or with the operating system network filters.

Other kinds of abuse include posting extremely big requests or opening a great number of simultaneous connections. You can limit the size of requests and timeouts to minimize the effect of attacks. The default request timeout is 300 seconds, but you can change it with the `TimeOut` directive. A number of directives enable you to control the size of the request body and headers: `LimitRequestBody`, `LimitRequestFields`, `LimitRequestFieldSize`, `LimitRequestLine`, and `LimitXMLRequestBody`.

To prevent abuse, the `mod_bwshare` module (referenced in Hour 24, "Additional Apache Modules and Projects") enables you to limit the number of files or bytes that a given client can download from the server.

Robots

Robots, *Web spiders*, and *Web crawlers* are names that define a category of programs that download pages from your Web site, recursively following your site's links. Web search engines use these programs to scan the Internet for Web servers, download their content, and index it. Normal users use them to download an entire Web site or portion of a Web site for later offline browsing. Normally these programs are well behaved, but sometimes they can be very aggressive and swamp your Web site with too many simultaneous connections or become caught in cyclic loops.

Well-behaved spiders will request a special file, called `robots.txt`, that contains instructions about how to access your Web site and which parts of the Web site won't be available to them.

The syntax for the file can be found at `http://www.robotstxt.org/`.

But sometimes Web spiders don't honor the `robots.txt` file. In those cases, you can use the Robotcop Apache 2.0 module, which enables you to stop misbehaving robots. The module can be found at `http://www.robotcop.org/`.

Troubleshooting

In certain occasions, you might need to troubleshoot your Apache installation. Although it occurs rarely, certain combinations of modules or development versions of Apache can cause some of the children to crash and core dump. You can specify where the core file is written with the `CoreDumpDirectory` directive. You can analyze the contents of this file to investigate what the cause of the crash is or to report a bug. This is an advanced topic and you can find information at `http://httpd.apache.org/dev/debugging.html`.

In other situations, you might need to troubleshoot the interaction of Apache with certain clients. The previous URL contains some links for tools that will help you achieve that. You can also find the TCPWatch GUI tool at `http://hathaway.freezope.org/Software/TCPWatch`.

Summary

This hour provided you with information on Apache and operating system settings that can affect scalability and performance. In most cases, however, the problems in Web site scalability relate to dynamic content generation and database access. Hardware-related improvements, such as high-quality network cards and drivers, increased memory, and disk arrays can also provide enhanced performance.

Q&A

Q How can I measure whether my site is fast enough?

A Many developers test their sites locally or over an internal network, but if you run a public Web site, chances are good that many of your users will access it over slow links. Try navigating your Web site from a dialup account and make sure that your pages load fast enough, with the rule of thumb being that pages should load in less than three seconds.

Q Is optimization always the best solution for scalability?

A It depends on the situation. If you adequately designed your Web infrastructure, you might be able to handle increased demand by simply adding a new machine behind a load balancer. This might be more cost-effective than spending the time to fine-tune your server or application code.

Quiz

1. Name some Apache settings that might limit scalability or affect Apache performance.

2. Name some operating system settings that might limit scalability.

3. Name some approaches to improve performance.

Quiz Answers

1. Some of the Apache settings that might affect scalability include the `FollowSymLinks`, `SymLinksIfOwnerMatch` arguments to the `Options` directive, enabling per-directory configuration files, hostname lookups, having a scoreboard file, and statistics collection with `mod_status`.

2. Some operating system settings that might affect scalability include limits for number of processes, open file descriptors, and memory allowed per process.

The following are some suggestions for improving performance: load distribution via a hardware load balancer or reverse proxy, data compression, caching, mapping files to memory, and compiling modules statically.

Related Directives

This section contains new directives introduced in this hour. You can consult the Apache reference documentation for comprehensive syntax information and usage.

16

Preventing Abuse

- **LimitRequestBody:** Limit the request body size
- **LimitRequestFields:** Limit the number of HTTP headers in the request
- **LimitRequestFieldSize:** Limit the size of the request headers
- **LimitRequestLine:** Limit the size of the first line of the request
- **LimitXMLRequestBody:** Limit the size of DAV requests

Network Settings

- **KeepAliveTimeout:** Time in seconds to wait before closing an inactive connection
- **Timeout:** Timeout for HTTP requests
- **SendBufferSize:** Size in bytes of the transmission buffer

Processes Limits

- **RLimitCPU:** Limit processing time
- **RLimitMem:** Limit memory
- **RLimitNProc:** Limit number of processes

File Related

- **MMapFile:** Map frequently used files to memory
- **CacheFile:** Cache file descriptors for frequently accessed files

Further Reading

The Scalable mailing list covers Web-related scalability issues including servers, disk arrays, and network interfaces. You can find archives of the list at
`http://archive.develooper.com/scalable@arctic.org/`.

An additional bandwidth control module can be found at
http://www.snert.com/Software/Throttle/, and an article explaining it can be found
at http://www.webtechniques.com/archives/2001/11/serv/. Unfortunately, at the
time this book was written, this module was available only for Apache 1.3.

You can find additional information about effective Web caching at
http://www.mnot.net/cache_docs/ and
http://linux.oreillynet.com/pub/a/linux/2002/02/28/cachefriendly.html.

Hour 17

Setting Up a Secure Server

This hour explains how to set up an Apache server capable of secure transactions. In this hour, you will learn

- The installation and configuration of the mod_ssl Apache module
- The SSL/TLS family of protocols and the underlying cryptography concepts
- What certificates are and how to create and manage them

The Need for Security

As the Internet became mainstream and the number of companies, individuals, and government agencies using it grew, so did the number and type of transactions that needed protection. Those include financial transactions, such as banking operations and electronic commerce, as well as exchange of sensitive information, such as medical records and corporate documents.

There are three requirements to carry on secure communications on the Internet: confidentiality, integrity, and authentication.

Confidentiality

Confidentiality is the most obvious requirement for secure communications. If you are transmitting or accessing sensitive information such as your credit card number or your personal medical history, you certainly do not want a stranger to get hold of it.

Integrity

The information contained in the exchanged messages must be protected from external manipulation. That is, if you place an order online to buy 100 shares of stock, you do not want to allow anyone to intercept the message, change it to an order to buy 1000 shares, or replace the original message. Additionally, you want to prevent an attacker from performing replay attacks, which, instead of modifying the original message, simply resend it several times to achieve a cumulative effect.

Authentication

You need to decide whether to trust the organization or individual you are communicating with. To achieve this, you must authenticate the identity of the other party in the communication.

The science of cryptography studies the algorithms and methods used to securely transmit messages, ensuring the goals of confidentiality, integrity, and authenticity. Cryptanalysis is the science of breaking cryptographic systems.

The SSL Protocol

SSL stands for Secure Sockets Layer and TLS stands for Transport Layer Security. They are a family of protocols that were originally designed to provide security for HTTP transactions, but that also can be used for a variety of other Internet protocols such as IMAP and NNTP. HTTP running over SSL is referred to as *secure HTTP*.

Netscape released SSL version 2 in 1994 and SSL version 3 in 1995. TLS is an IETF standard designed to standardize SSL as an Internet protocol. It is just a modification of SSL version 3 with a small number of added features and minor cleanups. The TLS acronym is the result of arguments between Microsoft and Netscape over the naming of the protocol because each company proposed its own name. However, the name has not stuck and most people refer to these protocols simply as SSL. Unless otherwise specified, the rest of this hour refers to SSL/TLS as *SSL*.

You specify that you want to connect to a server using SSL by replacing `http` with `https` in the protocol component of a URI. The default port for HTTP over SSL is 443.

The following sections explain how SSL addresses the confidentiality, integrity, and authentication requirements outlined in the previous section. In doing so, it explains, in a simplified manner, the underlying mathematical and cryptographic principles SSL is based on.

Confidentiality

The SSL protocol protects data from eavesdropping by encrypting it. Encryption is the process of converting a message, the *plaintext*, into a new encrypted message, the *cipher-text*. Although the plaintext is readable by everyone, the ciphertext will be completely unintelligible to an eavesdropper. Decryption is the reverse process, which transforms the ciphertext into the original plaintext.

Usually encryption and decryption processes involve an additional piece of information: a *key*. If both sender and receiver share the same key, the process is referred to as *symmetric* cryptography. If sender and receiver have different, complementary keys, the process is called *asymmetric* or *public key* cryptography.

Symmetric Cryptography

If the key used to both encrypt and decrypt the message is the same, the process is known as symmetric cryptography. DES, Triple-DES, RC4, and RC2 are algorithms used for symmetric key cryptography. Many of these algorithms can have different key sizes, measured in bits. In general, given an algorithm, the greater the number of bits in the key, the more secure the algorithm is and the slower it will run because of the increased computational needs of performing the algorithm.

Symmetric cryptography is relatively fast compared to public key cryptography, which is explained in the next section. Symmetric cryptography has two main drawbacks, however. One drawback is that keys should be changed periodically, to avoid providing an eavesdropper with access to large amounts of material encrypted with the same key. The other drawback is the key distribution problem: How to get the keys to each one of the parties in a safe manner? This was one of the original limiting factors, and before the invention of public key cryptography, the problem was solved by periodically having people traveling around with suitcases full of keys.

Public Key Cryptography

Public key cryptography takes a different approach. Instead of both parties sharing the same key, there is a pair of keys: one public and the other private. The public key can be widely distributed, whereas the owner keeps the private key secret. These two keys are

17

complementary; a message encrypted with one of the keys can be decrypted only by the other key.

Anyone wanting to transmit a secure message to you can encrypt the message using your public key, assured that only the owner of the private key—you—can decrypt it. Even if the attacker has access to the public key, he cannot decrypt the communication. In fact, you want the public key to be as widely available as possible. Public key cryptography can also be used to provide message integrity and authentication. RSA is the most popular public key algorithm.

The assertion that only the owner of the private key can decrypt it means that with the current knowledge of cryptography and availability of computing power, an attacker will not be able to break the encryption by brute force alone in a reasonable timeframe. If the algorithm or its implementation is flawed, realistic attacks are possible.

> Public key cryptography is similar to giving away many identical lockpads and retaining the key that opens them all. Anybody who wants to send you a message privately can do so by putting it in a safe and locking it with one of those lockpads (public keys) before sending it to you. Only you have the appropriate key (private key) to open that lockpad (decrypt the message).

The SSL protocol uses public key cryptography in an initial handshake phase to securely exchange symmetric keys that can then be used to encrypt the communication.

Integrity

Data integrity can be preserved by performing a special calculation on the contents of the message and storing the result with the message itself. When the message arrives at its destination, the recipient can perform the same calculation and compare the results. If the contents of the message changed, the results of the calculation will be different.

Digest algorithms perform just that process, creating message digests. A *message digest* is a method of creating a fixed-length representation of an arbitrary message that uniquely identifies it. You can think of it as the fingerprint of the message. A good message digest algorithm should be irreversible and collision resistant, at least for practical purposes. *Irreversible* means that the original message cannot be obtained from the digest and *collision resistant* means that no two different messages should have the same digest. Examples of digest algorithms are MD5 and SHA.

Message digests alone, however, do not guarantee the integrity of the message because an attacker could change the text *and* the message digest. Message authentication codes, or MACs, are similar to message digests, but incorporate a shared secret key in the process. The result of the algorithm depends both on the message and the key used. Because the attacker has no access to the key, he cannot modify both the message and the digest. HMAC is an example of a message authentication code algorithm.

The SSL protocol uses MAC codes to avoid replay attacks and to assure integrity of the transmitted information.

Authentication

SSL uses certificates to authenticate parties in a communication. Public key cryptography can be used to digitally sign messages. In fact, just by encrypting a message with your secret key, the receiver can guarantee it came from you. Other digital signature algorithms involve first calculating a digest of the message and then signing the digest.

You can tell that the person who created that public and private key pair is the one sending the message. But how can you tie that key to a person or organization that you can trust in the real world? Otherwise, an attacker could impersonate his identity and distribute a different public key, claiming it is the legitimate one. Trust can be achieved by using digital certificates. *Digital certificates* are electronic documents that contain a public key and information about its owner (name, address, and so on). To be useful, the certificate must be signed by a trusted third party (certification authority, or CA) who certifies that the information is correct. There are many different kinds of CAs, as described later in the hour. Some of them are commercial entities, providing certification services to companies conducting business over the Internet. Other CAs are created by companies providing internal certification services.

The CA guarantees that the information in the certificate is correct and that the key belongs to that individual or organization. Certificates have a period of validity and can expire or be revoked. Certificates can be chained so that the certification process can be delegated. For example, a trusted entity can certify companies, which in turn can take care of certifying its own employees.

If this whole process is to be effective and trusted, the certificate authority must require appropriate proof of identity from individuals and organizations before it issues a certificate.

By default, browsers include a collection of root certificates for trusted certificate authorities.

17

SSL and Certificates

The main standard defining certificates is X.509, adapted for Internet usage. An X.509 certificate contains the following information:

- **Issuer:** The name of the signer of the certificate
- **Subject:** The person holding the key being certified
- **Subject public key:** The public key of the subject
- **Control information:** Data such as the dates in which the certificate is valid
- **Signature:** The signature that covers the previous data

You can check a real-life certificate by connecting to a secure server with your browser. If the connection has been successful, a little padlock icon or another visual clue will be added to the status bar of your browser. With Internet Explorer, you can click the locked padlock icon to open a page containing information on the SSL connection and the remote server certificate. You can access the same information by selecting Properties, and then Certificates from the File menu. Other browsers, such as Netscape, Mozilla, and Konqueror provide a similar interface.

Open the `https://www.ibm.com` URL in your browser and analyze the certificate, following the steps outlined in the preceding paragraph. You can see how the issuer of the certificate is the Equifax Secure E-Business Certification Authority-2, which, in turn, has been certified by the Thawte CA. The page downloaded seamlessly because Thawte is a trusted CA that has its own certificates bundled with Internet Explorer and Netscape Navigator.

To check which certificates are bundled with your Internet Explorer browser, select Tools, Internet Options, Content, Certificates, Trusted Root Certification Authorities.

You can see that both issuer and subject are provided as distinguished names (DN), a structured way of providing a unique identifier for every element on the network. In the case of the IBM certificate, the DN is C=US, S=New York, L=Armonk, O=IBM, CN=`www.ibm.com`.

C stands for country, S for state, L for locality, O for organization, and CN for common name. In the case of a Web site certificate, the common name identifies the fully qualified domain name of the Web site (FQDN). This is the server name part of the URL; in this case, `www.ibm.com`. If this does not match what you typed in the top bar, the browser will issue an error.

Figure 17.1 shows the certificate information described earlier.

FIGURE 17.1

Certificate informa-tion.

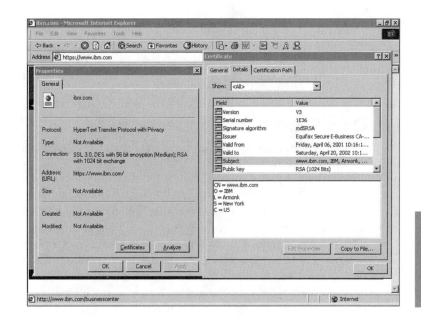

SSL Protocol Summary

You have seen how SSL achieves confidentiality via encryption, integrity via message authentication codes, and authentication via certificates and digital signatures.

The process to establish an SSL connection is the following:

1. The user uses his browser to connect to the remote Apache server.

2. The handshake phase starts, and the browser and server exchange keys and certificate information.

3. The browser checks the validity of the server certificate, including that it has not expired, that it has been issued by a trusted CA, and so on.

4. Optionally, the server can require the client to present a valid certificate as well.

5. Server and client use each other's public key to securely agree on a symmetric key.

6. The handshake phase concludes and transmission continues using symmetric cryptography.

Installing SSL

Now that you've learned all about SSL, you need to install SLL support for Apache. SSL support is provided by mod_ssl, a module that is included with Apache but is not enabled by default. mod_ssl, in turn, requires the OpenSSL library—an open source implementation of the SSL/TLS protocols and a variety of other cryptographic algorithms. OpenSSL is based on the SSLeay library developed by Eric A. Young and Tim J. Hudson. You can learn more about mod_ssl and OpenSSL in the Web sites noted in the reference section at the end of the hour.

OpenSSL

This section explains how to download and install the OpenSSL toolkit for both Windows and Unix variants.

Windows

At the time of writing this book, the Apache Software Foundation does not provide an SSL-enabled binary installer for Windows due to legal restrictions. That situation is likely to change soon, and you will be able to access precompiled SSL module and libraries. Check the Apache site for up-to-date information. The rest of the hour assumes that you have access to the openssl.exe command line utility, which will be included in the bin/ directory of the SSL-enabled Apache distribution. It is a utility for generating certificates, keys, signing requests, and so on.

Unix

If you are running a recent Linux or FreeBSD distribution, OpenSSL might already be installed in your system. Use the package management tools bundled with your distribution to determine whether that is the case or, otherwise, to install it.

If you need to install OpenSSL from source, you can download OpenSSL from http://www.openssl.org. After you have downloaded the software, you need to uncompress it and cd into the created directory:

```
# gunzip < openssl*.tar.gz | tar xvf -
# cd openssl*
```

OpenSSL contains a config script to help you build the software. You must provide the path to which the software will install. The path used in this hour is /usr/local/ssl/install, and you probably need to have root privileges to install the software there. You can install the software as a regular user, but to do so, you will need to change the path. Then you must build and install the software:

```
# ./config --prefix=/usr/local/ssl/install \
--openssldir=/usr/local/ssl/install/openssl
# make
# make install
```

If everything went well, you have now successfully installed the OpenSSL toolkit. The openssl command-line tool will be located in /usr/local/ssl/install/bin/.

This tool is used to create and manipulate certificates and keys and its usage is described in a later section on certificates.

mod_ssl

In the past, SSL extensions for Apache had to be distributed separately because of export restrictions. Although there are limitations in redistribution of binaries that need to be solved and clarified, these restrictions no longer exist for distribution of source code, and mod_ssl is bundled and integrated with Apache 2.0. This section describes the steps necessary to build and install this module. mod_ssl depends on the OpenSSL library, so a valid OpenSSL installation is required.

Unix

If you are using the Apache 2.0 server that came installed with your operating system, chances are that it already includes mod_ssl. Use the package management tools bundled with your distribution to install mod_ssl if it is not present in your system.

When you build Apache 2.0 from source, you must pass the following options to enable and build mod_ssl at compile time.

```
--enable-ssl --with-ssl=/usr/local/ssl/install/openssl
```

This assumes that you installed OpenSSL in the location described in previous sections.

If you compiled mod_ssl statically into Apache, you can check whether it is present by issuing the following command, which provides a list of compiled-in modules:

```
# /usr/local/apache2/bin/httpd -l
```

The command assumes that you installed Apache in the /usr/local/apache2 directory.

If mod_ssl was compiled as a dynamic loadable module, the following line must be added or uncommented to the configuration file:

```
LoadModule ssl_module modules/libmodssl.so
```

Managing Certificates

To have a working SSL server implementation, the first step is to create a server certificate. This section explains in detail how to create and manage certificates and keys by using the openssl command-line tool. For example, if you are using SSL for an e-commerce site, encryption prevents customer data from eavesdroppers and the certificate enables customers to verify that you are who you claim to be.

> The examples refer to the Unix version of the command-line program openssl. If you are running under Windows, you need to use openssl.exe instead and change the paths of the examples to use backslashes instead of forward slashes. The examples also assume that OpenSSL was installed in the path described earlier in the OpenSSL installation section.

Creating a Key Pair

You must have a public/private key pair before you can create a certificate request. Assume that the FQDN for the certificate you want to create is www.example.com. (You will need to substitute this name for the FQDN of the machine you have installed Apache on.) You can create the keys by issuing the following command:

```
# ./usr/local/ssl/install/bin/openssl genrsa -des3 -rand file1:file2:file3 \
    -out www.example.com.key 1024
```

genrsa indicates to OpenSSL that you want to generate a key pair.

des3 indicates that the private key should be encrypted and protected by a pass phrase.

The rand switch is used to provide OpenSSL with random data to ensure that the generated keys are unique and unpredictable. Substitute file1, file2, and so on, for the path to several large, relatively random files for this purpose (such as a kernel image, compressed log files, and so on). This switch is not necessary on Windows because the random data is automatically generated by other means.

The out switch indicates where to store the results.

1024 indicates the number of bits of the generated key.

The result of invoking this command looks like this:

```
625152  semi-random bytes loaded
Generating RSA private key, 1024 bit long modulus
.....++++++
.......................++++++
e is 65537 (0x10001)
Enter PEM pass phrase:
Verifying password - Enter PEM pass phrase:
```

As you can see, you will be asked to provide a pass phrase. Choose a secure one. The pass phrase is necessary to protect the private key and you will be asked for it whenever you want to start the server. You can choose not to protect the key. This is convenient because you will not need to enter the pass phrase during reboots, but it is highly insecure and a compromise of the server means a compromise of the key as well. In any case, you can choose to unprotect the key either by leaving out the -des3 switch in the generation phase or by issuing the following command:

```
# ./usr/local/ssl/install/bin/openssl rsa -in www.example.com.key \
    -out www.example.com.key.unsecure
```

It is a good idea to back up the www.example.com.key file. You can learn about the contents of the key file by issuing the following command:

```
# ./usr/local/ssl/bin/openssl rsa -noout -text -in www.example.com.key
```

Creating a Certificate Signing Request

To get a certificate issued by a CA, you must submit what is called a *certificate signing request*. To create a request, issue the following command:

```
# ./usr/local/ssl/install/bin/openssl req -new -key www.example.com.key
 -out www.example.com.csr
```

You will be prompted for the certificate information:

```
Using configuration from /usr/local/ssl/install/openssl/openssl.cnf
Enter PEM pass phrase:
You are about to be asked to enter information that will be incorporated
into your certificate request.
What you are about to enter is what is called a Distinguished Name or a DN.
There are quite a few fields but you can leave some blank
For some fields there will be a default value,
If you enter '.', the field will be left blank.
-----
Country Name (2 letter code) [AU]:US
State or Province Name (full name) [Some-State]:CA
Locality Name (eg, city) []: San Francisco
Organization Name (eg, company) [Internet Widgits Pty Ltd]:.
Organizational Unit Name (eg, section) []:.
Common Name (eg, YOUR name) []:www.example.com
Email Address []:administrator@example.com
Please enter the following 'extra' attributes
to be sent with your certificate request
A challenge password []:
An optional company name []:
```

It is important that the Common Name field entry matches the address that visitors to your Web site will type in their browsers. This is one of the checks that the browser will perform for the remote server certificate. If the names differ, a warning indicating the mismatch will be issued to the user.

The certificate is now stored in `www.example.com.csr`. You can learn about the contents of the certificate via the following command:

```
# ./usr/local/ssl/install/bin/openssl req -noout -text \
    -in www.example.com.csr
```

You can submit the certificate signing request file to a CA for processing. VeriSign and Thawte are two of those CAs. You can learn more about their particular submission procedures at their Web sites:

- **VeriSign:** http://digitalid.verisign.com/server/apacheNotice.htm
- **Thawte:** http://www.thawte.com/certs/server/request.html

Creating a Self-Signed Certificate

You can also create a self-signed certificate. That is, you can be both the issuer and the subject of the certificate. Although this is not very useful for a commercial Web site, it will enable you to test your installation of `mod_ssl` or to have a secure Web server while you wait for the official certificate from the CA.

```
# ./usr/local/ssl/install/bin/openssl x509 -req -days 30  \
-in www.example.com.csr -signkey www.example.com.key \
-out www.example.com.cert
```

You need to copy your certificate `www.example.com.cert` (either the one returned by the CA or your self-signed one) to `/usr/local/ssl/install/openssl/certs/` and your key to `/usr/local/ssl/install/openssl/private/`.

Protect your key file by issuing the following command:

```
# chmod 400 www.example.com.key
```

SSL Configuration

The previous sections introduced the (not-so-basic) concepts behind SSL and you have learned how to generate keys and certificates. Now, finally, you can configure Apache to support SSL. `mod_ssl` must either be compiled statically or, if you have compiled as a loadable module, the appropriate `LoadModule` directive must be present in the file.

If you compiled Apache yourself, a new Apache configuration file, named `ssl.conf`, should be present in the `conf/` directory. That file contains a sample Apache SSL configuration and is referenced from the main `httpd.conf` file via an `Include` directive.

If you want to start your configuration from scratch, you can add the following configuration snippet to your Apache configuration file:

```
Listen 80
Listen 443
<VirtualHost _default_:443>
ServerName www.example.com
SSLEngine on
SSLCertificateFile \
/usr/local/ssl/install/openssl/certs/www.example.com.cert
SSLCertificateKeyFile \
/usr/loca/ssl/install/openssl/certs/www.example.com.key
</VirtualHost>
```

With the previous configuration, you set up a new virtual host that will listen to port 443 (the default port for HTTPS) and you enable SSL on that virtual host with the SSLEngine directive.

You need to indicate where to find the server's certificate and the file containing the associated key. You do so by using SSLCertificateFile and SSLCertificateKeyfile directives.

Starting the Server

Now you can stop the server if it is running, and start it again. If your key is protected by a pass phrase, you will be prompted for it. After this, Apache will start and you should be able to connect securely to it via the https://www.example.com/ URL.

If you compiled and installed Apache yourself, in many of the vendor configuration files, you can see that the SSL directives are surrounded by an <IfDefine SSL> block. That allows for conditional starting of the server in SSL mode. If you start the httpd server binary directly, you can pass it the -DSSL flag at startup. You can also use the apachectl script by issuing the apachectl startssl command. Finally, if you always want to start Apache with SSL support, you can just remove the <ifDefine> section and start Apache in the usual way.

If you are unable to successfully start your server, check the Apache error log for clues about what might have gone wrong. For example, if you cannot bind to the port, make sure that another Apache is not running already. You must have administrator privileges to bind to port 443; otherwise, you can change the port to 8443 and access the URL via https://www.example.com:8443.

Configuration Directives

mod_ssl provides comprehensive technical reference documentation. This information will not be reproduced here; rather, I will explain what is possible and which configuration directives you need to use. You can then refer to the online SSL documentation bundled with Apache for the specific syntax or options.

Algorithms

You can control which ciphers and protocols are used via the SSLCipherSuite and SSLProtocol commands. For example, you can configure the server to use only strong encryption with the following configuration:

```
SSLProtocol all
SSLCipherSuite HIGH:MEDIUM
```

See the Apache documentation for a detailed description of all available ciphers and protocols.

Client Certificates

Similarly to how clients can verify the identity of servers using server certificates, servers can verify the identity of clients by requiring a client certificate and making sure that it is valid.

SSLCACertificateFile and SSLCACertificatePath are two Apache directives used to specify trusted Certificate Authorities. Only clients presenting certificates signed by these CAs will be allowed access to the server.

The SSLCACertificateFile directive takes a file containing a list of CAs as an argument. Alternatively, you could use the SSLCACertificatePath directive to specify a directory containing trusted CA files. Those files must have a specific format, described in the documentation. SSLVerifyClient enables or disables client certificate verification. SSLVerifyDepth controls the number of delegation levels allowed for a client certificate. The SSLCARevocationFile and SSLCARevocationPath directives enable you to specify certificate revocation lists to invalidate certificates.

Performance

SSLis a protocol that requires intensive calculations. mod_ssl and OpenSSL allow several ways to speed up the protocol by caching some of the information about the connection. You can cache certain settings using the SSLSessionCache and SSLSessionCacheTimeout directives. There is also built-in support for specialized cryptographic hardware that will perform the CPU-intensive computations and offload the main processor. The SSLMutex directive enables you to control the internal locking mechanism of the SSL engine. The SSLRandomSeed directive enables you to specify the mechanism to seed the random-number generator required for certain operations. The settings of both directives can have an impact on performance.

Logging

`mod_ssl` hooks into Apache's logging system and provides support for logging any SSL-related aspect of the request, ranging from the protocol used to the information contained in specific elements of a client certificate. This information can also be passed to CGI scripts via environment variables by using the `StdEnvVars` argument to the `Options` directive. `SSLLog` and `SSLLogLevel` enable you to specify where to store SSL-specific errors and which kind of errors to log. You can get a listing of the available SSL variables at `http://httpd.apache.org/docs-2.0/ssl/ssl_compat.html`.

The `SSLOptions` Directive

Many of these options can be applied in a per-directory or per-location basis. The SSL parameters might be renegotiated for those URLs. This can be controlled via the `SSLOptions` directive.

The `SSLPassprase` directive can be used to avoid having to enter a pass phrase at startup by designating an external program that will be invoked to provide it.

Access Control

The `SSLRequireSSL` directive enables you to force clients to access the server using SSL. The `SSLRequire` directive enables you to specify a set of rules that have to be met before the client is allowed access. `SSLRequire` syntax can be very complex, but itallows an incredible amount of flexibility. Listing 17.1 shows a sample configuration from the `mod_ssl` documentation that restricts access based on the client certificate and the network the request came from. Access will be granted if one of the following is met:

- The SSL connection does not use an export (weak) cipher or a NULL cipher, the certificate has been issued by a particular CA and for a particular group, and the access takes place during workdays (Monday to Friday) and working hours (8:00 a.m. to 8:00 p.m.).
- The client comes from an internal, trusted network.

You can check the documentation for `SSLRequire` for a complete syntax reference.

LISTING 17.1   `SSLRequire` Example

```
SSLRequire (    %{SSL_CIPHER} !~ m/^(EXP|NULL)-/ \
          and %{SSL_CLIENT_S_DN_O} eq "Snake Oil, Ltd." \
          and %{SSL_CLIENT_S_DN_OU} in {"Staff", "CA", "Dev"} \
          and %{TIME_WDAY} >= 1 and %{TIME_WDAY} <= 5 \
          and %{TIME_HOUR} >= 8 and %{TIME_HOUR} <= 20        ) \
          or %{REMOTE_ADDR} =~ m/^192\.76\.162\.[0-9]+$/
```

17

Reverse Proxy with SSL

Although at the time this book was written the SSL reverse proxy functionality was not included in mod_ssl for Apache 2.0, it is likely to be included in the future. That functionality enables you to encrypt the reverse proxy connection to backend servers and to perform client and server certificate authentication on that connection. The related directives are SSLProxyMachineCertificatePath, SSLProxyMachineCertificateFile, SSLProxyVerify, SSLProxyVerifyDepth, SSLProxyCACertificatePath, SSLProxyEngine, and SSLProxyCACertificateFile. Their syntax is similar to their regular counterparts. You can find more information about the Apache reverse proxy in Hour 15.

Problems with Specific Browser Versions

Some browsers have known problems with specific versions of the SSL protocol or certain features. Certain environment variables can be set to force specific behaviors. The following example, included in the default configuration file, is a workaround for bugs in the SSL implementation of Internet Explorer browsers.

```
SetEnvIf User-Agent ".*MSIE.*" nokeepalive ssl-unclean-shutdown \
downgrade-1.0 force-response-1.0
```

Summary

This hour explained the fundamentals of the SSL protocol and mod_ssl, the Apache module that implements support for SSL. You learned how to install and configure mod_ssl and the OpenSSL libraries, and how to use the openssl command-line tool for certificate and key generation and management. You can access the mod_ssl reference documentation for in-depth syntax explanation and additional configuration information. Bear in mind also that SSL is just part of maintaining a secure server, which includes applying security patches, OS configuration, access control, physical security, and so on.

Q&A

Q Can I have SSL with name-based virtual hosting?

A A question that comes up frequently is how to make name-based virtual hosts work with SSL. The answer is that you can't, at least currently. Name-based virtual hosts depend on the Host header of the HTTP request, but the certificate verification happens when the SSL connection is being established and no HTTP request can be sent. There is a protocol for upgrading an existing HTTP connection to TLS, but it is mostly unsupported by current browsers (see RFC 2817).

Q Can I use SSL with other protocols?

A `mod_ssl` implements the SSL protocol as a filter. Other protocols using the same Apache server can easily take advantage of the SSL.

Quiz

1. How can you prevent the prompting for a password at startup?

2. How can you use the `openssl` command-line tool to connect to an SSL-enabled server?

   The `openssl` command-line tool enables you to connect to SSL-enabled servers. Read the documentation and figure out how to do it. You can use the Unix man page for `openssl` or read the documentation at `http://www.openssl.org`.

Quiz Answers

1. You can use the `SSLPassPhrase` method to point to a program that will provide the pass phrase. The program should make the appropriate checks to make sure that it reveals the pass phrase only to Apache.

   Additionally, you could simply remove the password protection from the file containing the key, as described earlier in the hour. This has severe security implications, but it can be very convenient.

2.

   ```
   # openssl s_client -connect www.ibm.com:443
   ```

   You will see information related to the connection, certificates, ciphers, and so on. Then you can type

   ```
   GET / HTTP/1.0
   ```

   to get the contents of the index HTML page, similar to the way you learned in Hour 2, "Understanding Apache Internals," with `telnet`.

   You can configure many aspects of the connection, as explained in the documentation.

Related Directives

This section contains directives mentioned in this hour or that are related to topics discussed in this hour. You can consult the Apache reference documentation for comprehensive syntax information and usage.

Keys and Certificates

- **SSLPassPhraseDialog:** Alternative ways of specifying a pass phrase to decrypt key
- **SSLCertificateFile:** File containing server certificate
- **SSLCertificateKeyFile:** File containing server key
- **SSLCertificateChainFile:** File containing chain of certificates used to sign the server certificate
- **SSLCACertificatePath:** Path to a directory containing CA certificates for client authentication
- **SSLCACertificateFile:** Path to a file containing CA certificates for client authentication
- **SSLCARevocationPath:** Path to a directory containing CA for revoking client certificates
- **SSLCARevocationFile:** Path to a file containing CA for revoking client certificates
- **SSLVerifyClient:** Enable client certificate verification
- **SSLVerifyDepth:** Establish maximum depth to verify client certificates to

SSL Protocol

- **SSLProtocol:** Versions of SSL supported
- **SSLCipherSuite:** Ciphers supported
- **SSLEngine:** Enable SSL protocol engine
- **SSLRequireSSL:** Require client to connect to server using SSL
- **SSLRequire:** Require specific rules for client to connect

Performance

- **SSLMutex:** Locking mechanism
- **SSLRandomSeed:** Initialize random number generator
- **SSLSessionCache:** Specify an SSL-caching mechanism
- **SSLSessionCacheTimeout:** Caching sessions expiry time

Others

- **SSLOptions:** Control various aspects of SSL operation

Reverse Proxy

- **SSLProxyMachineCertificatePath, SSLProxyMachineCertificateFile, SSLProxyVerify, SSLProxyVerifyDepth, SSLProxyCACertificatePath, SSLProxyCACertificateFile:** Equivalent to their regular server counterparts, but related to the reverse proxy connection

Further Reading

An excellent, highly readable cryptography reference book is *Applied Cryptography: Protocols, Algorithms, and Source Code in C*, Second Edition, by Bruce Schneier; ISBN 0471117099.

A great book on the SSL protocol, and especially useful if you are programming with SSL libraries, is *SSL and TLS: Designing and Building Secure Systems*, by Eric Rescorla; ISBN 0201615983.

OpenSSL project: http://www.openssl.org

ModSSL project: http://www.openssl.org

OpenBSD, a free Unix server operating system with a focus on security: http://www.openbsd.com

Apache reference, by the original author of mod_ssl: http://www.apacheref.com

SSLv2 specification: http://home.netscape.com/eng/security/SSL_2.html

SSLv3 specification: http://home.netscape.com/eng/ssl3/draft302.txt

The following SSL-related RFCs can be obtained from http://www.rfc-editor.org/:

- Internet X.509 PKI: RFC 2459
- Transport Layer Security: RFC 2246
- Upgrading to TLS Within HTTP/1.1: RFC 2817

17

Part III
Extending Apache

Hour

Hour **18**

Extending Apache

Apache modules enable you to extend and add new functionality to Apache, such as access control, CGI processing, and encryption. Many of these modules have been described in previous hours, but this hour summarizes and categorizes all the available modules. Modules are compiled into the Apache server or you can build them as shared extensions. In this hour, you will learn about

- The Apache modules included in the distribution and their functionality
- The apxs tool for building modules as shared extensions
- The necessary command-line options to enable or disable compilation of specific modules

Modules Included with Apache

Modules, as you know by now, are pieces of code that extend the functionality of Apache. Apache comes with several standard modules. Many of them are compiled by default when building Apache as shown in Hour 3,

"Installing and Building Apache." You could also build a custom Apache server with only the modules you need. The configure script for Apache enables you to enable or disable specific modules. Table 18.1 provides you with a list of all modules shipped with Apache, whether they are compiled by default, and a brief description. The purpose of each module is explained in later sections.

> Binary Apache distributions from some vendors might not include some of these modules, and might include extra modules that are not part of the official Apache distribution.

TABLE 18.1   Apache Modules

Enabled by Default?	Module Name	Brief Description
Environment Variables		
Yes	mod_env	Environment variables
Yes	mod_setenvif	Environment variables based on client information
No	mod_unique_id	Unique identifier creation
Content Type Decisions		
Yes	mod_mime	Associate file extensions with MIME types
No	mod_mime_magic	Associate MIME types based on file contents
Yes	mod_negotiation	Negotiation of document versions
No	mod_charset_lite	Character set translation
URL Mapping and Manipulation		
Yes	mod_alias	Mapping of requests to filesystem resources and URL redirection
No	mod_rewrite	Advanced URL manipulation
Yes	mod_userdir	User homepages
No	mod_speling	Correct common URL typographical errors
No lation	mod_vhost_alias	Massive virtual hosting based on URL manipu-
Directory Handling		
Yes	mod_dir	Directory requests
Yes	mod_autoindex	Directory listings

TABLE 18.1   continued

Enabled by Default?	Module Name	Brief Description
Authentication and Access Control		
Yes	mod_access	Access control
Yes	mod_auth	Flat file user authentication
No	mod_auth_dbm	Database file user authentication
No	mod_auth_anon	Anonymous user authentication
No	mod_auth_digest	Digest authentication
HTTP Headers		
No	mod_headers	Header manipulation
No	mod_cern_meta	Legacy CERN support
No	mod_expires	Expiry header control
Yes	mod_asis	Send files without processing
Dynamic Content		
Yes	mod_include	Server-side includes
Yes	mod_cgi	CGI execution
Yes	mod_cgid	CGI execution for threaded MPMs
Yes	mod_actions	Associate requests with server processing
No	mod_suexec	Execute CGIs under different user IDs
No	mod_isapi	ISAPI extension support
No	mod_ext_filter	Allow external programs to act as filters
Monitoring		
Yes	mod_status	Status of the server
No	mod_info	Information about the server configuration
Logging		
Yes	mod_log_config	Logging configuration
No	mod_usertrack	User tracking via cookies
Proxy Support		
No	mod_proxy	Main proxy module
No	mod_proxy_connect	Support for SSL passthrough
No	mod_proxy_ftp	FTP proxy support
No	mod_proxy_http	HTTP proxy support

18

TABLE 18.1   continued

Enabled by Default?	Module Name	Brief Description
Loadable Module Support		
No	mod_so	Support for loadable module support
Caching		
No	mod_file_cache	Caching frequently accessed files
No	mod_cache	Caching filter
No	mod_disk_cache	Caching filter disk backend
No	mod_mem_cache	Caching filter memory backend
Document Authoring and Versioning		
No	mod_dav	DAV support
No	mod_dav_fs	DAV filesystem backend
Sample Modules		
No	mod_example	Sample module
No	mod_case_filter	Sample output filter
No	mod_case_filter_in	Sample input filter
Protocol Modules		
No	mod_echo	Sample echo protocol module
Yes	mod_http	HTTP support
Miscellaneous		
Yes	mod_imap	Server-side image maps
No	mod_ssl	SSL support
No	mod_deflate	Compression filter

Enabling or Disabling Modules

Modules that are enabled by default can be disabled at compilation time by using a configure switch like the following: --disable-*module*, with *module* being the name of the module without the mod_ prefix and replacing the underscore (_) with a dash (-). For example: --disable-cgi and --disable-asis.

Similarly, modules that are disabled by default can be enabled by using --enable-*module* script. For example: --enable-ext-filter and --enable-auth-digest.

If the server is compiled with shared module support, you can choose to build modules as shared extensions, as explained in Hour 3. You can then enable or disable specific modules by adding or removing `LoadModule` directives.

Environment Variables

Environment variables can be created or read by modules and passed to CGI scripts. These variables provide a simple but powerful mechanism to access data about the request and for module communication. For example, you could configure one module to set up a specific environment variable whenever a certain client accesses the server. Other modules can change their behavior, such as serving different content, depending on whether that environment variable exists and contains a specific value.

mod_env

This module allows setting or removing environment variables. Those variables are then available to CGI scripts, server-side includes, and other Apache modules such as PHP. You can learn more about mod_env in Hour 9, "Content Negotiation and Environment Variables."

mod_setenvif

Similar to mod_env, but the environment variables can be set or unset based on client information, such as the remote address or request headers. mod_setenvif is described in Hour 9.

mod_unique_id

Certain applications require a unique identifier for each request. When this module is present on the server, an environment variable containing that unique identifier will be created, which can in turn be used by other Apache modules or CGI programs.

Content Type Decisions

These modules enable you to determine the content type of different resources and to perform actions based on content type being requested. For example, you might want to process all image files through a certain filter or identify files ending in `.pl` extensions as CGI scripts.

mod_mime

This module determines the MIME type of a document by examining its file extension. This information will be added to the response headers, and can be used to associate that resource with Apache modules that can process it before sending the content to the client. You can learn more about this module in Hour 5, "Using Apache to Serve Static Content."

18

mod_mime_magic

The purpose of this module is similar to mod_mime, but instead of relying on a file extension, it tries to guess the MIME type by peeking at the first bytes of the file. This has a performance impact but can be useful in certain situations. Refer to Hour 5 for further information.

mod_negotiation

This module allows Apache to serve different versions of the same file based on file extensions, server settings, and client preferences. This is useful for maintaining a multi-lingual Web site, for example.

mod_charset_lite

This module tells Apache to translate the character set of a document to a different one; for example, from legacy EBCDIC to ASCII. In most cases, this is not necessary because the content is usually in ASCII. At the time of writing this book, this module is experimental, meaning that it is still in a development stage.

URL Mapping and Manipulation

URLs are used to access your Web site. The following modules enable you to perform actions based on the URL requested or even to modify it before passing it to other modules.

mod_alias

This module enables you to customize how the URLs of your Web site look. This module enables you to associate *(map)* directories in disk to certain URLs, redirect requests for nonexistent or obsolete content to the correct URL, and so on. Hour 5 covers this module configuration in detail.

mod_rewrite

This is a complex but powerful module that enables you to manipulate and rewrite the request URL. Hour 22 describes mod_rewrite and some of its applications, with sample configurations.

mod_userdir

This module allows Unix users to have their own homepages that can be accessed through a URL of the type: http://www.example.com/~user, with *user* being the user's Unix username. This module is explained in Hour 14, "Virtual Hosting."

mod_speling

This module can correct minor typos in URLs, such as links pointing to files with different cases, missing or transposed letters, and so on. Hour 5 covers this module.

mod_vhost_alias

This module provides support for dynamically configured mass virtual hosting. mod_vhost_alias is useful in situations in which you have to host and configure a great number of simple Web sites, as is common with some popular ISPs. This module is described in Hour 14.

Directory Handling

These modules enable you to specify the Apache behavior when a directory is requested, such as providing an HTML directory listing.

mod_dir

This module enables you to specify index files for directories and it handles common redirection problems associated with the trailing slash in directory names. This module is mentioned in Hour 5.

mod_autoindex

This module enables you to display directory listings in directories that do not have an index file. You can control every aspect of the listings, such as the ordering, icons, exclusion of certain files, and so on. Hour 5 covers this module.

Authentication and Access Control

The following modules enable you to restrict access to your Web site based on the identity of the user, the resource being accessed, or certain attributes of the request.

mod_access

This module can deny or grant access to resources based on the IP address, network, or hostname of a client, and on the existence of certain environment variables. Access control rules can be combined with the authentication modules described later in this hour. This module is explained in detail in Hour 7, "Restricting Access."

mod_auth

This module enables you to perform basic authentication, storing the username and group information in text files. This module is covered in Hour 7.

18

mod_auth_dbm

This module performs basic authentication, storing username and group information in database files, which allows the handling of a large number of users without significantly affecting performance. See Hour 7 for further information.

mod_auth_anon

This module allows anonymous user access to authenticated areas. This module is mentioned in Hour 7.

mod_auth_digest

This module supports digest authentication using the MD5 algorithm. This method of authentication is more secure than basic authentication, but is unsupported by most browsers. Check Hour 7 for more information.

HTTP Headers

The following modules enable you to add, remove, or modify headers of HTTP requests and responses. This can be useful for specifying content expiration, adding custom headers, and working around a specific browser limitation.

mod_headers

This module is able to add or remove arbitrary HTTP headers in both the request and response.

mod_cern_meta

Support for HTTP header metafiles, a legacy feature from the CERN Web server.

mod_expires

This module enables you to control the expiration time of resources, used for caching purposes. This is done via Expires: headers.

mod_asis

This module enables you to send files unprocessed directly to the client. This means that the files must contain their own HTTP headers. This is advanced functionality that is not required in normal scenarios and should be used with care.

Dynamic Content

The following modules enable you to create or modify content dynamically, either by inserting specific tags in the documents being served or by executing external programs.

mod_include

This module provides support for SSI (Server Side Includes), which allows the content of documents to be inserted inside others and provide basic dynamic processing capabilities. This makes it easy to provide a consistent look and feel across a Web site by using footer and header documents, for example. This module is explained in Hour 12, "Filtering Modules."

mod_cgi

This module implements the Common Gateway Protocol and allows content to be dynamically generated by external programs, such as Perl scripts. This module is covered in Hour 6, "Serving Dynamic Content with CGI."

mod_cgid

Provides equivalent functionality to mod_cgi, but for threaded MPMs. Apache creates an external daemon at startup, which in turn is in charge of spawning the CGI programs. Hour 6 explains this module.

mod_actions

This module enables you to associate HTTP request methods or resources of a particular MIME type with certain Apache modules or CGI scripts. The modules or programs can then process the content before sending it to the client. Check Hour 6 for additional information.

18

mod_isapi

This module provides ISAPI extension support. ISAPI is an API to extend the capabilities of the Microsoft IIS Web server.

mod_ext_filter

This module enables you to filter content served by Apache by using external programs, as explained in Hour 12.

mod_suexec

This module enables you to run CGI requests as a specified user and group. This can be useful in a server shared between different customers, but it has security implications..

Monitoring

The following modules are useful for monitoring the status of the server and accessing detailed configuration information.

mod_status

This module provides information about the runtime status of the server, such as the number of children, requests, uptime, and so on. This module is described in Hour 8, "Logging and Monitoring."

mod_info

This module provides information about the server, its modules, and their configuration. Hour 8 explains this module.

Logging

Logging modules enable you to save data about who accesses your Web sites and which resources they request, as well as recording errors.

mod_log_config

This module enables you to customize all aspects related to request logging. Everything related to the request, connection, authentication module, environment variables, and so on, can be logged. This module is explained in Hour 8.

mod_usertrack

This module allows basic user session tracking by using cookies. This is useful for finding out patterns of usage of the Web site for individual users. This is not as relevant as it used to be because most modern Web applications have their own session management.

Proxy Support

The Apache proxy module allows the server to act as a gateway for accessing other Web servers. The proxy module itself is modular and can be extended to support different backends, such as FTP.

mod_proxy

This module provides Apache with proxy capabilities. It is modular and extensible, allowing backends for protocols other than HTTP and being able to take advantage of Apache 2.0 filtering architecture for compressing and caching proxy data, for example. The following sections comprise a list of related modules. Apache proxy capabilities are covered in Hour 15, "Apache as a Proxy Server."

mod_proxy_connect

This module provides support for the SSL CONNECT method, which allows an HTTP proxy to tunnel SSL connections.

mod_proxy_ftp

This proxy module enables Apache to act as a proxy for FTP resources, allowing them to be accessed via a regular HTTP browser.

mod_proxy_http

This module provides an HTTP backend for the Apache proxy.

Loadable Module Support

Modules can be either compiled in or loaded dynamically, at runtime. The mod_so module enables dynamic loading of other modules.

mod_so

This module allows modules to be compiled as shared objects and be loaded dynamically by the Web server. This allows Apache to be extended without the need for recompilation.

Caching

Caching means saving the results of a request, usually for a dynamically generated resource. Future requests can use the cached response without incurring the penalty of generating the content over and over. The following modules provide different caching mechanisms for Apache.

mod_file_cache

This module enables you to cache frequently requested files in memory to increase performance of the Web server. This module is covered in Hour 16, "Tuning Apache."

mod_cache

This is a filtering module that is capable of caching any resource served or proxied by Apache. You can configure via rules whether to cache specific URLs. Several modules, described in the following sections, allow for storage of the cached objects. Hour 15 explains mod_cache and related modules.

mod_disk_cache

This module provides a disk-based caching storage mechanism for mod_cache.

mod_mem_cache

This module provides a memory-based caching storage mechanism for mod_cache.

18

Document Authoring and Versioning

The following modules provide support for the DAV publishing protocol. This protocol allows a client to access and manipulate content resources located on the server.

mod_dav

This module provides support for the HTTP-based WebDAV protocol, which is commonly used for sharing, editing, and publishing documents via a Web server. This module and the DAV protocol are covered in Hour 13, "Publishing Extensions."

mod_dav_fs

The mod_dav module can have different backends. This module is the default, filesystem–based backend.

Sample Modules

The purpose of the following modules is to serve as examples to other module authors, and they should not be enabled in a production server.

mod_example

This is a simple module that demonstrates the Apache API and should not be run for any other purpose.

mod_case_filter, mod_case_filter_in

Simple input filter and output filter sample modules that change the case of served content.

Miscellaneous Modules

The following are additional modules that do not fit in any of the previous categories.

mod_imap

This is a module that provides server-side image map support. That is, you click on a certain part of an image, the browser transmits the coordinates of the click to the server, and the server sends you to the correct URL. It works without requiring any CGI or dynamic component by defining the destination URLs in a file.

mod_ssl

This module provides Apache with support for the SSL/TLS protocol, which provides a security layer for the HTTP protocol. Hour 17 covers SSL module configuration.

mod_deflate

This module is a filter that can compress content on the fly, thus trading CPU usage for bandwidth reduction. This module is covered in Hour 12.

The Apache Extension Tool APXS

APXS stands for APache eXtenSion tool and is a useful script for compiling Apache modules. If Apache has been compiled with loadable module support, as explained in Hour 3, it is possible to add new functionality without the need to recompile the server. The apxs script is created at build time and contains information about how Apache was built, including server defaults and compiler flags. If you installed Apache from source in /usr/local/apache2, the apxs tool will be found at /usr/local/apache2/bin/apxs.

The apxs tool can be used with several options, but only a subset of them is important in most situations.

Usage

To compile and install a module with apxs, you just need to change your current directory to the one containing the module and type the following:

```
# apxs –c mod_example.c
```

The mod_example.so shared object will be created and you can then add it to your configuration file via the LoadModule directive. You can automate this step using the -i option, which will copy the shared object into the server modules directory, and the -a option, which will add the appropriate LoadModule directive into the configuration file.

> Depending on your system and the tools installed, the mod_example.so file might be created in the .libs/ subdirectory and/or have a different extension. The -a -i switches take care of this transparently.

If the module depends on additional object or source files, you can specify them in the command line and apxs will recognize and use them in the compilation process.

Additional Options

The apxs tool enables you to create a module template, change the output name of the resulting shared module, pass additional compiler flags, and so on. Check the apxs manual page for a detailed description.

18

Extending Apache with Third-Party Modules

In addition to the modules included in the Apache distribution, a variety of third-party modules, both commercial and open source, can be used to extend Apache. The build instructions vary with each module, and some of the most popular ones are covered in later hours.

Most operating system distributions that include Apache have packages for many of these third-party modules, and you can install them using the package manager for your operating system.

Summary

This hour's lesson explained how Apache can be extended using bundled modules, either by compiling them into the server or by using the apxs tool to build them as shared objects. The following hours will tell you how to extend Apache with other popular third-party modules such as PHP and mod_perl.

Q&A

Q I can't find the apxs utility mentioned in this hour. Where is it?

A If you are using the Apache that came installed with your Linux distribution, you might need to install a separate RPM package, apache2-dev, that includes the apxs utility. In addition, some Linux distributions rename it to apxs2, so users do not confuse it with the Apache 1.3 version.

Q Are there any benefits of compiling in modules instead of loading them dynamically with LoadModule?

A There are certain performance benefits, depending on the architecture, but they are usually offset by the flexibility that a shared module installation offers.

Quiz

1. Why is the apxs tool useful?
2. When is mod_cgid used instead of mod_cgi?

Quiz Answers

1. It enables you to add new modules to Apache without having to recompile the server. The only requirement is that the server is already compiled with loadable module support.

2. The mod_cgid module is used with threaded MPMs, such as the worker MPM.

Further Reading

The APXS manual page bundled with Apache provides extensive information.

Hour 3 provides information on MPM modules and basic compilation options.

For information on a particular module, you can refer to the hours mentioned in the directive descriptions of earlier sections. A complete module listing can be found at http://httpd.apache.org/docs-2.0/mod/index-bytype.html.

18

HOUR 19

PHP

PHP is a popular Web development language that works with a variety of Web servers, including Apache. This hour introduces the main features of PHP, helping you to determine whether it can be useful for your development needs. One of the strengths of PHP is the great number of extensions available for database connectivity, graphic creation, XML processing, and so on. This hour explains in detail how to build and integrate those extensions with PHP. In this hour, you will learn

- What PHP is and how it works
- How to download and configure PHP
- What PHP modules are available and how to enable them

Introduction to PHP

PHP is a server-side scripting language that can be embedded in HTML pages, similar to JSP (JavaServer Pages) and Microsoft ASP (Active Server Pages). The PHP engine is implemented as an Apache 2.0 filter, which processes pages containing PHP code before they are served to the client. PHP pages usually end with the .php extension.

A simple PHP page looks like the following:

```
<h1>Hello <?php $what="World!"; echo $what; ?>!</h1>
```

When a client requests this page from the Web server, it is processed by the PHP module, the embedded code is executed, and the result is substituted, as shown here:

```
<h1>Hello World!</h1>
```

This was just a simple example. A typical Web application might need to connect to databases, LDAP directories, or perform complex operations before returning a page. PHP provides an impressive number of extensions to ease these tasks. It is important to realize that PHP processing occurs in the server; the client gets to see only the final HTML.

PHP History

The inventor of PHP is Rasmus Lerdorf. He originally designed the language as a replacement for typical CGI development so that users could add dynamic features to their pages without having to know too much about programming. The current version of PHP is PHP 4, which is built on top of the Zend scripting engine, described later in the hour. Today, PHP is an incredible success by all measures: It runs on more than 7 million sites and is installed on more than 45% of all Apache Web servers, making it the most popular Apache module. More than 50 books in many languages cover PHP. The developer and user community grows daily.

PHP Architecture

PHP is a modular, extensible language. Figure 19.1 describes the PHP architecture.

PHP is implemented on top of the Zend scripting engine. The Zend engine is open source under the Q Public License (QPL), and is designed to be embedded and used in a variety of scenarios.

You can learn more about the QPL at
http://www.trolltech.com/products/download/freelicense/license.html.

Extension writers have access to PHP and Zend via well-defined APIs. Many of those extensions are wrappers around existing C libraries, which make the features provided by these libraries available to PHP developers. Database and directory connectivity, SNMP, and graphic generation and manipulation are some extension feature examples. This hour covers how to build and integrate many of them into your PHP installation.

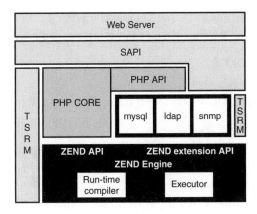

FIGURE 19.1

PHP architecture.

The SAPI (Server API) provides an abstraction layer that enables PHP to be embedded in a variety of Web servers, not only Apache.

The TSRM (Thread Safe Resource Manager) is a layer that provides thread-safe access to global data structures. This is necessary to integrate PHP into threaded Web servers.

PHP Advantages

Like any programming language, PHP has both advantages and disadvantages. We'll look at the advantages first.

Easy to Learn

PHP is really easy to learn. The short learning curve is especially appealing for Web designers and HTML coders who need to add dynamic content generation to their sites, but do not have a strong programming background. PHP enables them to easily and gradually add dynamic page generation features to their Web sites by mixing existing HTML with new PHP code.

Open Source

PHP is distributed under an Apache-style license that allows for both commercial and noncommercial use and development. A worldwide network of talented developers is continuously improving and enhancing PHP. You can fix bugs or customize the software to your specific needs (or pay someone to do so) because the source code is available. This is not possible with commercial, off-the-shelf products.

Community

PHP has a large base of users and developers. It is easy to find programmers fluent in the language. There are many online resources dedicated to PHP (Web sites, mailing lists,

19

and so on) that provide valuable information and support. Some of them are mentioned in the "Further Reading" section at the end of this hour.

Database Support

PHP provides extensive database support. It supports ODBC, open source databases such as MySQL and PostgreSQL, and commercial ones such as Microsoft SQL Server, Oracle, and DB2.

Multiplatform Support

PHP runs on a variety of operating systems and Web servers. PHP runs in most flavors of Unix and Windows as well as on Mac OS X, OS/2, and a variety of other operating systems. PHP supports different Web servers, ranging from the popular Apache, Microsoft IIS, and Netscape servers to less-known ones such as thttpd and AOLserver. This allows you to standardize on a common development language across a heterogeneous environment of systems and servers. You can build a solution with PHP on a specific platform/server/database combination, and then migrate to a different combination gradually, replacing one component at a time. You can develop your code on a Windows workstation running IIS and deploy it in on a Unix server running Apache with few or no changes.

Extensions

PHP has a great number of extensions and code samples for everything from XML manipulation to directory access. Programmers can leverage this body of existing code to put together advanced applications quickly.

Safe Mode

PHP allows execution of code in restricted environments. This option is very attractive to ISP and Application Server Providers, which can offer PHP to their clients without compromising security. These providers often want to serve multiple customers using a shared infrastructure.

Session Support

Most Web applications require keeping and managing state information between requests. PHP 4 offers native session management and an extension API so that users can provide their own backend storage mechanisms.

Rapid Development

PHP is compiled to a special byte code format before it is executed. That step is completely transparent to programmers and users, who can make changes to a PHP page and see the results immediately in their browsers. In comparison, Java servlet development requires longer compile/deployment cycles.

Commercial Support

Several companies provide support and services around PHP or bundle PHP as part of their server solution. Please refer to the resources at the end of this hour to learn more about these companies. You should consider their services if you use PHP in an enterprise environment, a mission-critical Web site, or need custom features added to the language.

It's Fun!

PHP is an exciting language to program in. You can leverage existing extensions and code to put together great Web sites quickly and easily.

PHP Disadvantages

You have learned about some of PHP's strong points, such as its open source nature, its ease of use, and the availability of a great number of extensions. However, PHP also has some weak points that you should keep in mind.

Code Maintenance

Web developers like the quick development cycle and the ability to mix PHP and HTML code. The short learning curve attracts people without a previous programming background. The result is that, as the functionality of a Web site expands, its architecture can grow organically into a mess of code and HTML, and its maintenance can become a nightmare.

Advanced Features

Language-wise, PHP lacks strong typing, full object-oriented support (such as multiple inheritance and private variables), and other capabilities present in other languages. On the other hand, many of these features are not needed in most of the Web applications for which PHP is used.

Dependency Tracking

Although PHP has a great number of extensions, they are in different stages of development and maturity. Even if these extensions are distributed with PHP and kept up to date with PHP releases, they depend on external libraries for database connectivity, and so forth. Hunting down which library version goes with which extension and making sure that different extensions work together can be time-consuming tasks. That is the reason several commercial vendors offer ready-to-run PHP distributions, often in conjunction with open source databases and the Apache Web server.

19

Corporate Acceptance

PHP is quite popular in the open source world and is technically superior to many of its commercial counterparts. However, it still lacks important momentum and mind share in corporate and enterprise environments. That means that if you work in a corporation and want to use PHP, you might be unable to do so, or might need to do significantly more explanation than if you chose to go with Java or C++. Zend Technologies and other PHP-centric companies are working hard evangelizing PHP. They are building the support and products necessary to make PHP a viable choice for enterprise customers.

Installation

This section will teach you the steps necessary to get a basic installation of PHP version 4 up and running on Apache 2.0 and how to test that it works.

Installation on Windows

At the time of this writing, there is no release of a PHP module for the Windows platform that runs on Apache 2.0. You will be able to download a Windows installer from http://www.php.net after one has been released. The steps will probably be be similar to the following:

1. Create a directory that will contain the PHP and related extension DLLs. Let's assume this directory is C:\PHP.

2. Modify the httpd.conf configuration file to load the Apache 2 SAPI module, using the LoadModule directive. For example, in Windows, the line will look something like this:

   ```
   LoadModule php4_module c:/php/sapi/apache2filter.dll
   ```

3. Copy the PHP.INI configuration file into the C:\windows or C:\winnt directory, depending on your Windows operating system. Edit it and change the settings of extension_dir to C:\PHP or wherever the extensions DLLs live.

4. Tell Apache which files must be processed by the PHP engine. To process all files ending with .php, you must place the following line in your httpd.conf file:

   ```
   AddType application/x-httpd-php .php
   ```

The PHPConfig utility enables you to configure different PHP.INI parameters on Windows. You can find it at http://www.analogx.com/contents/download/network/phpconf.htm.

PHP as a CGI Script

PHP can be run as a CGI script under Windows. This is not recommended for performance reasons, but it is the only alternative if the module for the Web server is not available. The following are the steps, assuming that you placed the PHP distribution files in `C:\PHP`:

```
ScriptAlias /php/ "c:/php/"
AddType application/x-httpd-php .php
Action application/x-httpd-php "/php/php.exe "
```

The first line allows Apache to execute CGI scripts on that directory. The second line associates an application type with the php file extension, and the last one associates that application type with the PHP executable. Notice that the paths contain forward slashes, as required by the Apache configuration file rules.

Running PHP as a CGI program has several security issues that you need to be aware of. You can find more information at `http://www.php.net/manual/en/security.cgi-bin.php`.

Testing That Installation Was Successful

You can test whether the installation was correct by creating a simple file with a php extension (such as `example.php`) and placing it in the `htdocs` directory. Include the following code in that file:

```
<? phpinfo() ?>
```

If PHP was installed successfully, either as a module or CGI program, you will see something similar to the page shown in Figure 19.2.

Installing on Unix

This section explains you how to install PHP 4 on Unix as an Apache 2 module. Installation of PHP as a CGI script is not covered in this hour because it is similar to the Windows CGI configuration and running PHP as a module is the preferred configuration.

Binary Installation

Most Linux and Unix distributions that come preinstalled with Apache already include a PHP module. Additionally, the PHP Web site provides binaries for Mac OS X. Use your package manager to find out whether the PHP package is already installed in your system; otherwise, download and install it. You can also check your distribution Web site and download the package from there. If you are using an RPM-based distribution (such

19

as Red Hat, SuSE, or Mandrake) you can install the downloaded package with the command-line rpm tool:

```
rpm -I mod_php*.rpm
```

You will need to become root to install the package. In most distributions, installing the package simply copies the binary libraries to the appropriate directory. So, you might still need to edit the configuration files to fully configure PHP.

FIGURE 19.2

Testing that the PHP installation was successful.

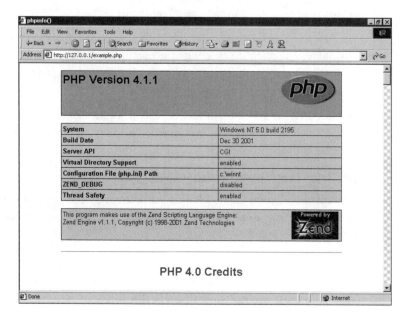

Source Code Installation

This section explains how to download, build, and install the PHP module.

Getting PHP

The PHP source code can be downloaded from the main PHP Web site at
http://www.php.net. The file you need is called php-4.x.y.tar.gz, where x.y is the
particular version of PHP. After you have downloaded the tarball, uncompress it and
change to the newly created directory:

```
# gunzip < php-4*.tar.gz | tar xvf -
# cd php-4*
```

The PHP directory structure contains the following important directories, as shown in
Table 19.1.

TABLE 19.1   PHP Directory Structure

Directory	Description
TSRM/	The Thread Safe Resource Manager.
Zend/	The code for the Zend scripting engine.
build/	The build-related scripts and Makefiles.
ext/	The extensions bundled with PHP for database access, XML manipulation, and so on. Each of the subdirectories contains a Makefile, and most of them have a README file that explains the purpose of the extension.
libs/	The directory where the PHP Apache module shared library will be placed when it is built.
main/	The core of the PHP code.
modules/	The directory where additional modules shared libraries will be placed.
pear/	The PEAR (PHP Extension and Application Repository) contains a collection of reusable library code similar to Perl's CPAN (http://www.cpan.org).
regex/	The regular expression library code.
sapi/	The server extension abstraction layer. Here you can find modules to interface PHP to Microsoft IIS, Netscape, and, of course, Apache.
scripts/	The miscellaneous scripts used by PHP developers.
rests/	The test suite.
Win32/	The Windows platform-specific code.

Compiling PHP

PHP, like many other open source projects, uses `autoconf` and `automake` tools to ease portability. The build scripts are able to find out by themselves most of the information they need to compile PHP, but you must pass certain parameters explicitly. PHP will be built as a loadable module, with the help of the Apache `apxs` tool, as explained in Hour 18, "Extending Apache."

The rest of this section assumes that you have installed Apache 2.0 in `/usr/local/apache2` and that you have root privileges. Apache must have been compiled with loadable module support enabled (`--enable-so` option). PHP will be installed under `/usr/local/php4`. If you want to build Apache and PHP as a regular user, you must change the paths provided later to paths that you have write permissions to.

Type the following in the directory created when you uncompressed the PHP 4 sources:

```
./configure --with-apxs2=/usr/local/apache2/bin/apxs --prefix=/usr/local/php4
```

19

You will see a rapid succession of messages while the configure script checks for the libraries it needs in your system and creates the Makefiles necessary for the build system. If everything goes well and the configure script finishes without throwing any errors, you can type the following to build PHP:

```
make
```

After the build finishes, you will have a `libphp4.so` file in the `libs/` directory.

To install the files, type

```
make install
```

This will perform the following tasks:

- Installs the shared library `libphp4.so` into the `/usr/local/apache2/modules` directory
- Adds a `LoadModule` directive into `/usr/local/apache2/conf/httpd.conf`
- Installs PHP header files, binaries, and the PEAR libraries into `/usr/local/php4`

The PHP module for Apache 2 is built as an Apache filter. To test that it works, you must enable PHP processing for the files containing the PHP code. Add the following to the `httpd.conf` file:

```
<Files *.php>
SetOutputFilter PHP
SetInputFilter PHP
</Files>
```

An alternative, traditional way of configuring PHP is the following:

```
AddType application/x-httpd-php .php
```

To test whether PHP is working correctly, create a file called `example.php` in the `/usr/local/apache2/htdocs` directory with the following contents:

```
<?php phpinfo(); ?>
```

Restart Apache and access the URL `http://127.0.0.1/example.php`. If PHP was installed correctly, you should see something similar to the page shown in Figure 19.2.

The Apache error file `/usr/local/apache2/logs/error_log` is the first place to look if you get an error or empty page. It will provide you with valuable information about what might have gone wrong. By far the most common issue is permissions: Make sure that the file `example.php` is readable by the user which Apache is running as.

Also make sure that Apache was built with loadable module support, as explained in Hour 3, "Installing and Building Apache." You can do so by issuing the following command:

```
/usr/local/apache2/bin/httpd -l
```

and looking for `mod_so.c` in the output. Make sure that PHP is being loaded by checking for the appropriate `LoadModule` directive in `httpd.conf`.

PHP Extensions

In the previous section, you learned how to build PHP as an Apache module and how to configure it to work with your Apache server. That was a basic installation. The PHP `configure` command allows many more flags to be passed to enable different language features and extensions. The following sections provide a selection of those flags. You can get a complete list by typing:

```
./configure --help | more
```

General Options

The following are general options that you can pass to the `configure` script.

```
--prefix=/some/path
```

Allows you to specify the path where PHP will be installed.

```
--with-apxs2=/path/to/apache2/bin/apxs
```

Builds shared Apache 2.0 module using the specified `apxs` utility.

```
--enable-debug
```

Enables debug symbols; useful for troubleshooting.

```
--without-pear
```

Does not install PEAR.

```
--enable-safe-mode
```

Enables the restricted safe mode by default. If you use this option, you will also be interested in `--with-exec-dir`, which specifies the executables allowed in safe mode.

```
--with-openssl
```

Includes OpenSSL support. OpenSSL is a library that provides SSL support, as explained in Hour 17, "Setting Up a Secure Server."

```
--with-curl
```

19

Includes curl support. Libcurl is a library that provides client-side support for a variety of protocols, including HTTP/HTTPS, FTP, Telnet, and more. You can learn more about curl at `http://curl.sourceforge.net/`.

`--enable-ftp`

Enables FTP support.

Graphics Support

The following commands are options that you can pass to the `configure` script to configure PHP graphics-related libraries.

`--with-gd=`/path/to/gd/install/dir

GD is a library that allows programmatic image creation and manipulation. It is useful for generating on-the-fly images and logos. You can learn more about GD at `http://www.boutell.com/gd/`.

The previous command line will build GD as part of PHP. If you want to create a shared library, you must pass the command line as

`--with-gd=shared,`/path/to/gd/install/dir

GD depends on additional libraries to support certain graphic formats. Associated configure options are

`--with-jpeg-dir=`/path/to/jpeg/install/dir

For libjpeg support.

`--with-png-dir=`/path/to/libpng/install/dir

For libpng support.

`--with-xpm-dir=`/path/to/libxpm/install/dir

For libXpm support.

`--with-t1lib=`/path/to/t1lib/install/dir

For t1lib, Adobe Type 1 fonts support.

GD allows the use of TTF (TrueType Fonts) to add text to images:

`--enable-gd-native-ttf`

Enables TrueType string function in GD.

`--with-freetype-dir=`/path/to/freetype2/install/dir

FreeType 2 support.

```
--with-ttf=/path/to/freetype/install/dir
```

Includes FreeType 1.x support.

An additional PHP module provides improved graphic manipulation using the imlib graphics library. You can find more information at `http://mmcc.cx/php_imlib/`.

Flash Animation

PHP provides Shockwave Flash support via two libraries: SWF and Ming. To install the SWF library:

```
--with-swf=/path/to/swf/install/dir
```

The SWF library can be found at `http://reality.sgi.com/grafica/flash/`.

To install the Ming library:

```
--with-ming=/path/to/ming/install/dir
```

The Ming library provides support for Flash generation and includes a PHP binding. It can be found at `http://opaque.net/ming`.

PDF Generation

PHP supports on-the-fly generation of PDF documents using the clibpdf and pdflib libraries:

```
--with-pdflib=/path/to/pdflib/install/dir
```

PDF support via the pdflib library requires a license for commercial usage. You can learn more about pdflib at `http://www.pdflib.com/pdflib/index.html`.

```
--with-cpdf=/path/to/clibpdf/install/dir
```

PDF generation support via the clibpdf library. You can learn more at `http://www.fastio.com/`.

Database Support

PHP supports a variety of database backends.

```
--with-mysql=/path/to/mysql/dir
```

Support for the MySQL (`http://www.mysql.com`) database. MySQL is a popular open source database. If the path is not specified, PHP includes built-in support and will use it instead.

19

`--with-pgsql=/path/to/pgsql/dir`

Support for the PostgreSQL database (`http://www.posgresql.org`).

XML Support

The following are options that you can pass to the `configure` script to configure PHP's XML-related libraries.

`--with-dom=/path/to/libxml/install/dir`

Includes DOM support via the libxml library, a C-based XML processing library distributed under the LGPL and the W3C IPR licenses. You can learn more about libxml at `http://xmlsoft.org/`.

`--disable-xml`

Disables built-in expat XML support (it is on by default).

`--enable-xslt`

Enables XSLT support.

`--with-sablot=/path/to/sablotron/install/dir`

Provides support for the Sablotron XSLT transformation engine. You can learn more about Sablotron at `http://www.gingerall.com/`.

`--with-expat-dir=/path/to/expat/install/dir`

Expat library required by Sablotron. You can find expat at `http://www.jclark.com/xml/expat.html`.

`--with-qtdom`

XML DOM support via the qt library that can be found at `http://www.trolltech.com/products/qt/`.

`--enable-wddx`

Enables wddx support, which is used when programming Web services.

Session Support

The following are options that you can pass to the `configure` script to configure PHP session support. This enables PHP scripts to keep track of user data between requests.

`--enable-trans-id`

Enables transparent ID propagation of session information (this can be done via cookies).

`--with-mm`

Enables shared memory support for session storage via the mm library. You can learn more about the mm library at `http://www.engelschall.com/sw/mm/`.

This section presented you with several configuration options to give you an idea of the capabilities of PHP. There are many more that provide support for additional databases, SNMP, CORBA, calendar functions, IMAP, Unicode, Java, LDAP, encryption, and more. You can get a comprehensive description of supported language features at `http://www.php.net/manual/en/`.

You can find additional extensions and PHP Web applications in Freshmeat at `http://freshmeat.net` and in the SourceForge PHP foundry at `http://sourceforge.net/foundry/php-foundry/`.

For example, the Vagrant charting extension `http://vagrant.sourceforge.net` provides support for programmatic generation of graphic charts.

Examples of Web applications based on PHP are Phorum (`http://phorum.org/`) for Web discussion boards and IMP (`http://www.horde.org/imp/`) for Web mail. Nuke (`http://phpnuke.org/`) and Midgard (`http://www.midgard-project.org/`) are content management/Web portal systems.

PHP Configuration

PHP can be configured either via the `php.ini` file located in `/usr/local/php4/lib/` (`C:\Windows\` on Windows platforms) or from inside the Apache configuration file. You can copy the file `php.ini-dist` from the build directory to `/usr/local/php4/lib/php.ini`. The `php.ini` consists of key/value pairs. The same settings can be specified in the Apache configuration file with the use of these directives:

`php_value name value`

Sets the value of the *name* variable to *value*.

`php_flag name on|off`

Sets a Boolean configuration option.

There are certain options, called *admin options*, that must be specified in the main Apache configuration file. They can be set using `php_admin_value` and `php_admin_flag`. These options are usually security related, such as `open_basedir` or `safe_mode_exec_dir`.

Some of the configuration options are relevant to PHP and others are for configuring specific PHP modules. The following is a selection of the available configuration options.

19

PHP Language

You can modify the way PHP can be mixed with HTML tags with the following options.

`short_open_tag` *boolean*

To include PHP code, you usually need to surround it with `<?php` or `<script>` tags. The `short_open_tag` directive enables you to use `<? ?>` tags in your code, although PEAR coding practices encourage you to use the `<?php` format.

`asp_tags` *boolean*

Allows use of ASP-style tags `<% %>` and constructs (`<%=$varname %>` to include the value of a variable.

`memory_limit` *integer*

`max_execution_time` *integer*

These two directives set the maximum amount of memory in bytes that a script is allowed to allocate, and the maximum time in seconds that a script is allowed to run before the script is terminated by the PHP engine, respectively. This helps to protect server resources from poorly written scripts.

`include_path` *string*

Specifies a list of directories where certain PHP functions (for including other files and so on) look for files.

Error Manipulation

`display_errors` *boolean*

Determines whether errors should be printed to the screen as part of the HTML output.

`error_log` *string*

Specifies the name of the file to which script errors should be logged. If the special value `syslog` is used, the errors are sent to the Unix system logger instead.

Output Manipulation

Apache transmits to the network the content created by the PHP script as it is being generated. You might want to add specific headers to a response, but are unable to do so because you have already sent part of the content. If you enable output buffering, PHP will cache the page, enabling you to set headers at any point on the page. PHP also provides hooks so that the content generated can be filtered or changed. As an example, PHP supports compression of the output of a script if the browser can understand compressed content, thus minimizing download time. PHP also provides the ability to append or prepend headers or footers to all generated pages, thus easing the task of creating a consistent, sitewide look and feel.

`auto_append_file` *string*

`auto_prepend_file` *string*

PHP makes it possible to append or prepend files to every page served. These files are parsed and interpreted as PHP scripts. If the name of the file is `none`, auto-prepending or appending is disabled.

`output_buffering` *boolean*

Enables or disables output buffering.

`output_handler` *handler*

Allows the specification of an output handler, such as `ob_gzhandler` for compression.

Security

It is possible to configure PHP to enhance the security of the installation, especially in environments with multiple or not fully trusted users. PHP allows a safe mode operation, which restricts the PHP/system functionality that the scripts can access, such as limiting access to only certain files or directories. It is possible to configure PHP to run as a CGI. This has advantages and risks from a security standpoint, such as the ability to use the Apache `suexec` wrapper. Many of the security issues need to be handled or complemented at the PHP level with safe coding practices. You can learn more at `http://www.php.net/manual/en/security.php`.

19

`safe_mode` *boolean*

Specifies whether to enable PHP's safe mode.

`safe_mode_exec_dir` *string*

Specifies that system calls executing external programs will work only with binaries in this directory.

`open_basedir` *string*

If present, this directive limits the files that can be opened by PHP to the ones contained under the specified directory path.

Dynamic Extension Support

You can either compile PHP extensions into the PHP executable, or you can choose to compile the extensions themselves as shared objects and load them from within the PHP engine.

```
enable_dl boolean
```

Enabled by default, this directive restricts the ability to load shared library code into PHP. The main reason to disable dynamic loading is security. Dynamic loading is not available when using PHP in safe mode.

```
extension_dir string
```

Specifies the directory in which PHP should look for dynamically loadable extensions.

```
extension string
```

Specifies which dynamically loadable extensions to load when PHP starts.

Summary

PHP, as are most other open source projects, is driven by the needs of the users and developers, who program PHP on a daily basis for their own projects. These projects range from personal home pages to high-profile financial sites.

PHP usage and number of extensions keep on growing. The language itself continues to evolve, and is starting to find applications outside the Web development field as a general-purpose scripting and embeddable language.

This hour explained how to install and configure PHP with Apache 2.0 and gave you an overview of the language's capabilities. Together with the hours on Tomcat and mod_perl, this hour will give you a good overview of the different development options for the Apache platform.

Q&A

Q How does PHP compare to other popular Web development languages such as Java and Perl?

A Although the three languages can provide similar functionality, Java is probably better suited for complex, transaction-oriented Web sites that need to interface with other enterprise systems. PHP is more oriented toward the creation of dynamic, publishing-oriented Web sites. It is not uncommon to find Web sites based on PHP in the front end and Java in the backend. Perl offers a set of features similar to PHP, but the learning curve is greater, although Perl has the advantage that it can be applied in other areas such as system administration.

Q What does PHP stand for?

A The original meaning of PHP was Personal Home Page because it was designed to provide users with a way of enhancing their home pages. The current meaning is PHP: Hypertext Processor, in the tradition of Unix recursive acronyms.

Quiz

1. What is the main advantage of running PHP as a module instead of as a CGI script?

2. What are the two ways of configuring PHP?

Quiz Answers

1. The main advantage is increased performance because PHP is loaded into the server and does not need to be launched as an external process for every request.

2. You can either use the `php.ini` file or add the configuration settings to Apache using the `php_value` and `php_flag` directives.

Related Directives

The only PHP-related directives that can appear in the `httpd.conf` file are `php_value` and `php_flag`. This hour describes many of the options available for these directives, and a comprehensive list can be found in the PHP manual.

Further Reading

The official PHP Web site can be found at `http://www.php.net`. There you will be able to download PHP and find related documentation. The PHP User Guide provides installation and configuration instructions as well as a comprehensive language reference guide.

Netcraft (`http://www.netcraft.com`) and SecuritySpace (`http://www.securityspace.com/s_survey/data/index.html`) provide figures on Apache and PHP usage.

19

Support

You can access PHP development and user mailing lists at `http://www.php.net/support.php`. Before asking your question, research the existing documentation and the Frequently Asked Question document. If you still cannot find an answer, consider posting to the mailing list, including as much detail as possible about your problem, what you tried and which errors you got, your operating system, and your server and PHP versions. This information will greatly increase the chances of getting a response and will help reduce the noise in the mailing list.

PHP Books

A comprehensive book list can be found at the PHP Web site `http://www.php.net/books.php`. The following books provide a good companion for learning the language:

- *PHP Fast & Easy Web Development*, by Julie C. Meloni, is a good introduction to the language.
- *PHP Developer's Cookbook*, by Sterling Hughes and Andrei Zmievski, is packed with useful practical examples.
- *PHP and MySQL Web Development*, by Luke Welling and Laura Thomson, is another good language tutorial that explains PHP alongside MySQL, a popular open source database commonly used together with PHP.

Web Sites

The following are popular Web sites that provide information on PHP:

- `http://www.phpbuilder.com`
- `http://www.zend.com`
- `http://www.phpwizard.net`
- `http://www.devshed.com/Server_Side/PHP/`

Commercial Vendors

Several vendors provide products based around PHP or include PHP as part of their server offering:

- **Zend** (`http://www.zend.com`) Founded by members of the core PHP team, Zend provides enterprise support and services around PHP. It also provides a development IDE and useful add-ons to the Zend engine for improved performance, source hiding, and script caching.

- **Covalent Technologies** (`http://www.covalent.net`) offers PHP as part of its Apache server solutions.

- **Synop** (`http://www.synop.com/`) provides products around PHP, including a development IDE and content management and site development solutions.

- **Nusphere** (`http://www.nusphere.com/`) provides Internet server solutions that include PHP, Perl, MySQL, and Apache.

Open Source Solutions

In addition to commercial companies, several open source projects provide bundles of Apache, PHP, databases, and so on. The following are some of them:

- **PHP4WIN** (`http://www.php4win.com/`) provides a PHP distribution for the Windows platform.

- **FoxServ** (`http://sourceforge.net/projects/foxserv/`) provides an installer for Linux and Windows.

- **PHPTriad** (`http://sourceforge.net/projects/phptriad/`) provides a packaged solution of PHP, MySQL, and several admin tools for the Windows platform.

19

HOUR **20**

mod_perl

The mod_perl module embeds a Perl interpreter inside the Apache Web server. This enables access to the Apache API from the Perl scripting language. In this hour, you will

- Learn how to download, build, and configure mod_perl
- Discover the capabilities of mod_perl 2.0 and compare it to previous versions based on Apache 1.3
- Learn how mod_perl extension modules such as Apache::ASP work, and how to run sample code that uses them

What Is mod_perl?

This commercial ran in the 1980s: Two dorks are walking opposing paths, each engrossed in his treat-eating endeavor. One is eating a chocolate candy bar; the other, a jar of peanut butter. They collide and are incensed that one's chocolate bar is in the jar of peanut butter, and peanut butter is smeared on the other's chocolate bar. "You got peanut butter on my chocolate!" said the one. "No, you got chocolate in my peanut butter!" replied the other. Then the voiceover comes on as they both smile with recognition that their collision was actually fortuitous: "It's two great tastes in one candy bar! Reese's Peanut Butter Cups."

In the 1990s, Perl and Apache enjoyed a similar collision. Perl's popularity was high due to its facilities for rapid development, object orientation, and powerful text processing. Perl was the de facto language of choice for Web application development, even though the only Web application framework in use at the time was CGI. The Apache Web server was also enjoying swelling popularity with its open APIs for extensibility. However, one problem with the API was that it was accessible only for C programmers.

One of the things that Perl is good at is taking a C API and wrapping it to expose the interfaces in the Perl language. This is exactly what mod_perl does. As a Perl interpreter embedded in Apache, it takes the request processing API that module programmers writing in C use and exposes it in Perl.

mod_perl 1.*x* versions have matured over the years and target the stable Apache 1.3.*x* API. mod_perl 2.0 is a complete redesign and works only with Apache 2.0 . This means that features a mod_perl 1.*x* user takes for granted might still be under development in mod_perl 2.0.

The mod_perl API

The mod_perl 1.*x* releases gave Perl programmers access to various aspects of the Apache 1.3 API. The entire request processing and server process lifecycles were exposed as various handler types that could be implemented in Perl. Joining these APIs in mod_perl 2.0 are filter and protocol handlers. In all, the process lifecycle, and request hooks and filters provide Perl programmers with access to much of the internals of Apache, making it possible to extend Apache functionality at well-defined points.

The complete list of mod_perl handlers covers the process model and API for Apache 2.0; for each request and process lifecycle event, there is a type of handler that can be run. These handlers are

- **PerlChildInitHandler:** With preforking process model, this type of handler can perform duties as child processes are created.
- **PerlOpenLogsHandler:** This type of handler is run as a process is created, and attempts to create a resource to record request handling events.
- **PerlPostConfigHandler:** After Apache parses its configuration files, this type of handler can operate on what was read.
- **PerlPreConnectionHandler:** This type of handler runs prior to Apache actually accepting a connection.

- **PerlProcessConnectionHandler:** This type of handler can implement protocols other than HTTP to handle a request, while still leveraging the Apache framework for access controls, content generation, logging, and so forth.

- **PerlInitHandler:** This is the first handler to run after the server has read a request's data and headers, but before anything is done with what was read. Inside a Location, Directory, or Files section, this acts as a PerlPostReadRequestHandler. Otherwise, it acts as a PerlHeaderParserHandler. So, the general usage is just PerlInitHandler, but the different configuration contexts allow for special uses.

- **PerlInputFilterHandler:** This type of handler can process request data and headers prior to other handlers using Apache's filter API.

- **PerlAccessHandler:** This type of handler gates access to the requested resource based on intrinsic characteristics of the connection, such as the host or network that the connection is coming from or the hour of the day in which the connection is received.

- **PerlAuthenHandler:** When a resource is password-protected, this type of handler can determine whether the user is who he claims to be.

- **PerlAuthzHandler:** This type of handler gates access to the requested resource by examining criteria of the authenticated user's attributes. The criteria can be anything about the user, such as group membership, the type of car she drives, or the letter of the alphabet that her username starts with.

- **PerlTypeHandler:** A type-checking handler that can set the MIME-type for the response. Apache's default type-checking is performed by mod_mime, and it uses filename extensions to set what ultimately ends up in the Content-type response header.

- **PerlFixupHandler:** This type of handler can perform any last-stop operation before response data is accessed or calculated.

- **PerlOutputFilterHandler:** This type of handler can use Apache's filtering API to process response data that another module has produced.

- **PerlResponseHandler:** In mod_perl 1.x, this was just PerlHandler, a handler that programmatically generated response data. This is the most common type of handler; this type of handler would, for instance, format data from a database query or rewrite a file's contents to produce output.

- **PerlLogHandler:** After a request has been served, the request and response attributes can be logged. This type of handler performs the recording of the event.

- **PerlTransHandler:** This type of handler takes the URI from the read request and maps it to a resource. A PerlTransHandler can also alter the URI; it can decide to

20

apply other handlers and it can run a subrequest with the modified request attributes.

Some of these handlers are new to mod_perl 2.0, and the way they are enabled in the server has also been updated. Under mod_perl 1.*x*, you had to decide at compile time whether you wanted certain types of handlers disabled or enabled. With mod_perl 2.0, there is a new directive, PerlOptions, that provides a finer level of granularity for whether a specific type of handler can be active. For instance,

```
PerlOptions -PerlProcessConnectionHandler
```

disables PerlProcessConnectionHandlers from being active.

mod_perl 2.0 has also been updated to take advantage of new Apache features, such as threaded multi-processing modules (MPMs) and the Apache Portable Runtime (APR). Many of the performance constraints that mod_perl 1.*x* had to work under can be addressed by using a threaded MPM, which allows sharing of expensive resources such as database connections and Perl interpreters. Taking advantage of the threading features will definitely require the latest and greatest version of Perl; support for multithreading has been one of the most active areas of Perl development in recent years.

The Perl build itself requires you to have threading options selected at compile time. Although compiling and installing Perl is outside the scope of this hour, you should be aware that before Perl is compiled, the sources are configured with a script in the distribution called Configure. To enable threads in Perl 5.6.*x*, you will need to use the -Dusethreads precompile configuration option to the Configure script. However, at the time this book is being written, no released version of Perl has all the threading facilities working reliably in a cross-platform fashion. In addition to threads, APR functions, such as those provided to Apache (and discussed in Hour 2, "Understanding Apache Internals") are accessible to mod_perl 2.0 application developers. Between threading and APR, a lot of new programming territory is opened up by mod_perl 2.0!

A variety of mod_perl-specific Perl modules, which provide page templating, authentication, logging, and session management, are available on the Comprehensive Perl Archive Network (CPAN). Taken together, these modules provide the framework for a highly functional application server. Many of them require updating to run under mod_perl 2.0; it might be a long time before the majority of them are compatible with both mod_perl 1.*x* and 2.0. For instance, at the time this book is being written, two popular templating packages, HTML::Mason and AxKit, are not compatible with mod_perl 2.0.

HTML::Mason is a templating system that emphasizes breaking up application logic and page layout into reusable components. It bears some similarity to JSP in that it exposes the programming language to the component author and provides caching. In addition, it provides a rich framework for cascading templates. AxKit is an XML/XSLT page generation system that emphasizes presentation flexibility through XSLT transformation. Both these packages are good reasons to use mod_perl. Check with the module author or, if the module has a help resource, check it for compatibility updates.

> CPAN is found at http://www.cpan.org/.
>
> You can find more information about HTML::Mason at http://www.masonhq.com/.
>
> You can find more information about AxKit at http://www.axkit.org/.

The most common use of mod_perl is CGI acceleration, and this facility is compatible with mod_perl 2.0 so long as the Apache::compat module is used as well. Apache::compat provides mod_perl 2.0 with compatibility with the mod_perl 1.x APIs. If you adhere to some programming practices, a Perl CGI can enjoy a tenfold or even hundredfold performance improvement running under mod_perl as compared to the performance running the same code by mod_cgi. We'll provide examples of CGI acceleration later in the hour.

Although space constraints don't permit us to cover *everything* that can be done with mod_perl (recall the length of the handler list earlier in the hour), we'll get you started by getting mod_perl installed and working through some illustrative examples. mod_perl is such a rich and powerful tool that we'll be able to touch on only a fraction of its capabilities. At the end of the hour, we'll provide resources for delving deeper into mod_perl's vast facilities.

Building and Installing mod_perl

The mod_perl distribution is available on CPAN, from CVS, or from the mod_perl Web site at http://perl.apache.org/.

The mod_perl 2.0 release requires

- Perl 5.6 or higher
- The Apache 2.0 source distribution
- The CGI.pm and LWP Perl modules distributions

> These instructions assume that you have an Apache 2.0 installation as well as the latest Perl 5.6.x and CGI.pm distributions installed.

20

Installing `mod_perl` from CPAN

One of the useful tools that comes with Perl is the CPAN module, a library that provides programmatic access to the CPAN repository.

This is what we will do to install `mod_perl` from CPAN:

1. Start the CPAN shell:

   ```
   perl -MCPAN -e shell
   ```

   If this is your first time using CPAN, the CPAN shell will ask for some initialization parameters. When that's done, it drops down to a prompt that takes commands for querying the archive contents, and getting and even installing Perl modules.

2. Give the CPAN shell the arguments it needs to build `mod_perl`:

   ```
   cpan> o conf makepl_arg "MP_APXS=/usr/local/apache2/bin/apxs
   ➥ MP_INST_APACHE2=1"
   ```

3. Install the module:

   ```
   cpan> install  Apache2
   ```

The CPAN shell performs the following tasks:

- Downloads the distribution
- Untars it
- Compiles `mod_perl`
- Installs the `mod_perl` Perl code to your Perl library
- Installs the `mod_perl` Apache module to your Apache distribution's modules directory

> You'll need root privileges to install libraries to Perl's system library. If you need the CPAN shell to install the libraries to an alternative location, consult the online documentation for the CPAN module by typing **perldoc CPAN** from your login shell.

That is the minimal default installation procedure.

> An easy way to express build options, such as those in step 2, is to create the file `makepl_args.mod_perl` in your home directory or in the parent directory of the Apache and `mod_perl` source trees. This file can parameterize the

> options desired for mod_perl (which includes options that can be passed to the Apache build itself, if you're doing a static compile). The INSTALL file in the mod_perl distribution provides details about driving options to mod_perl and Apache with makepl_args.mod_perl.

We'll be making other references to installing Perl modules off of the CPAN. When we do, the process will be just like the one for installing mod_perl, except that step 2 won't be required—it was a special step needed specifically for installing mod_perl. You can skip the next section, "Installing from CVS," to continue your installation from the CPAN.

Installing from CVS

Because Apache and mod_perl are undergoing a lot of change, it might be desirable (for instance, to pick up the latest bug fixes) to build from CVS. Review Hour 3, "Installing and Building Apache," for details of the Apache build process and accessing CVS. The following discussion assumes that there is an Apache built from the CVS tree installed in /usr/local/apache2.

In the parent directory of your checked-out httpd-2.0 tree, check out the mod_perl tree to a directory right next to it.

1. Get the CVS tree:

   ```
   cvs co -d :pserver:anoncvs@cvs.apache.org:/home/cvspublic co modperl-2.0
   ```

2. Prepare the build:

   ```
   cd modperl-2.0
   perl Makefile.PL MP_APXS=/usr/local/apache2/bin/apxs MP_INST_APACHE2=1
   ```

3. Do the build:

   ```
   make
   ```

4. Install into the Perl library:

   ```
   make install
   ```

To pick up the latest fixes to mod_perl at a later time, you'll only need to type

```
cvs up -PAd
```

at the top of your CVS tree and re-do steps 2 through 4.

Both CPAN and CVS Installations

Whether using a CPAN release or CVS, you'll need to configure Apache to actually use mod_perl. This means loading the Apache module binary itself and specifying Perl

20

libraries that hook into the Apache API. Configure Apache to load the mod_perl module by adding the following line to your server's httpd.conf:

```
LoadModule perl_module modules/mod_perl.so
```

You'll know that this modification is successful when something like this is in the error_log:

```
[Fri Apr 26 20:29:49 2002] [notice] Apache/2.0.36
➥(Unix) mod_perl/2.0.0 Perl/v5.6.1 configured -- resuming normal operations
```

Hello World with mod_perl

Now that Apache is successfully loading mod_perl, the next step is to get mod_perl to load its Perl modules. Add the following to httpd.conf:

```
PerlRequire /usr/local/apache2/conf/startup.pl
<Location /hello-world>
  SetHandler modperl
  PerlResponseHandler Apache::HelloWorld
</Location>
```

The file /usr/local/apache2/conf/startup.pl referred in the PerlRequire line can contain any Perl code that is useful for initialization; going forward, we'll refer to it as just startup.pl. We'll use it to extend mod_perl's search path—it is in that path that mod_perl looks for Perl modules to load as applications. After it can find the libraries we need, we'll load them as well. For instance, simply put the following in that file:

```
use lib qw(/usr/local/apache2/apps);
use Apache2 ();
use Apache::compat;
1;
```

The Location directive in the previous example configures Apache to have mod_perl handle requests for /hello-world and to have it use a Perl module called Apache::HelloWorld perform the logic.

Create the directory /usr/local/apache2/apps/Apache and put a file in there named HelloWorld.pm (shown in Listing 20.1).

LISTING 20.1 HelloWorld.pm

```
1: package Apache::HelloWorld;
2:
3: use strict;
4: use Apache::RequestRec (); #for $r->content_type
5: use Apache::RequestIO ();  #for $r->puts
6:
```

LISTING 20.1   continued

```
 7: sub handler {
 8:     my $r = shift;
 9:     $r->content_type('text/plain');
10:     $r->puts("Hello World, this is the " . __PACKAGE__ . " application');
11:     0;
12: }
13:
14: 1;
```

Restart your server and request that URL; for instance,
`http://modperl.example.com/hello-world` (substitute your host for
modperl.example.com). The response you should expect is

`Hello World, this is the Apache::HelloWorld application`

Congratulations, you've deployed your first `mod_perl` application! Notice the directory
hierarchy for the `mod_perl` handlers corresponds to their Perl packages. Because the
apps subdirectory we made for our `mod_perl` applications is in Perl's search path
(`@INC`)—we saw to that in line 1 of `startup.pl`—`Apache::HelloWorld` goes in the
directory `/usr/local/apache2/apps/Apache`. If we had a handler called
`Calc::Graph::PieChart::ThreeDee`, we would put the code in a file called
`ThreeDee.pm` in `/usr/local/apache2/apps/Calc/Graph/PieChart` with

`package Calc::Graph::PieChart;`

as the package declaration.

CGI Acceleration

Traditionally, one of the popular motivations for using `mod_perl` is to overcome the performance limitations of running Perl Web applications using the CGI API, instead of
writing to the Apache API as our `HelloWorld` example did.

`mod_perl` 1.*x* users have long enjoyed using a `PerlHandler` module, `Apache::Registry`,
that loads a CGI script and wraps a subroutine around it for persistent execution. The
benefit comes from doing away with the startup/shutdown penalty that CGIs normally
suffer from. The Perl interpreter is persistent because it's running in the Apache process.
The Perl interpreter, in turn, doesn't need to rerun the parsing and compilation phases of
CGI execution—that becomes merely a first-hit penalty. Finally, connections to databases
can be persistent if the Perl interpreter is persistent, which significantly speeds up
database-driven Web applications.

20

Over the years, variants of `Apache::Registry` and utility modules that work with them have been developed. For `mod_perl` 2.0, a new generation of modules is under development. `ModPerl::Registry` and other modules that relate to it are similar to the way `Apache::Registry` relatives relate to it. However, at the time of this writing, these modules are not fully operational. Fortunately, the compatibility module that we've previously mentioned, `Apache::compat`, allows most of the modules from the `mod_perl` 1.*x* generation to run under `mod_perl` 2.0, and that's what we'll use for these examples.

> These examples require having `mod_perl` 1.*x* installed, which in turn depends on building against an Apache 1.3.*x* source tree. Eventually, as `mod_perl` 2 matures, this requirement will go away. Fortunately, the build steps are very similar to the build steps you followed in the earlier discussion of building `mod_perl` 2.0. The examples in this section assume that the `mod_perl` 1.*x* libraries are installed in Perl's system library and therefore do not require you to manipulate Perl's search path. Look for updates to `ModPerl::Registry` and its relatives that will obviate this requirement.

The first step is to add the things we need to the `startup.pl` we created when we first set up `mod_perl`:

```
use lib qw(/usr/local/apache2/apps);
use Apache::compat ();
use Apache ();
use Apache::SubRequest ();
1;
```

Our examples will go in the `cgi-bin` directory that comes in the Apache distribution. We'll `mod_perl`-enable it by adding the handler directives, turning on the `ExecCGI` option, and flagging Apache that our scripts will generate their HTTP headers (as conventional CGIs do, at least for the MIME type). So, now the entry looks like this:

```
PerlModule Apache::Registry
<Directory "/usr/local/apache2/cgi-bin">
    AllowOverride None
    Options +ExecCGI
    Order allow,deny
    Allow from all
    SetHandler perl-script
    PerlHandler Apache::Registry
    PerlSendHeader On
</Directory>
```

Restart the server to make the changes effective. Set the Unix file system permissions on the `printenv` script that comes with Apache so that it is executable (by default, it's not executable when you install Apache). Just as with running CGIs under mod_cgi, as described in Hour 6, "Serving Dynamic Content with CGI," Apache::Registry and its related modules expect the script to have the executable bit set.

```
chmod +x /usr/local/apache2/cgi-bin/printenv
```

The code for printenv (see Listing 20.2) is a straightforward iteration through all the environment key-value pairs.

LISTING 20.2 printenv

```
 1: #!/usr/bin/perl
 2: ##
 3: ##  printenv -- demo CGI program which just prints its environment
 4: ##
 5:
 6: use strict;
 7:
 8: print "Content-type: text/plain\n\n";
 9: foreach my $var (sort(keys(%ENV))) {
10:     my $val = $ENV{$var};
11:     $val =~ s|\n|\\n|g;
12:     $val =~ s|"|\\"|g;
13:     print "${var}=\"${val}\"\n";
14: }
```

Note that we've modified this slightly so that it is *strict safe*, which we'll discuss shortly.

Now access the CGI, for instance by navigating to http://modperl.example.com/cgi-bin/printenv (substitute your host for *modperl.example.com*).

This will display a dump of all the environment variables. The environment is identical to a standard CGI environment except that there's an additional variable, MOD_PERL. You know the script has been served by mod_perl's Apache::Registry script and not Apache's built-in mod_cgi when you see an environment entry that looks like this:

```
MOD_PERL="mod_perl/2.0.0"
```

This demonstrates the simplest case for running a CGI under mod_perl. More complex examples that use CPAN libraries, handle form input, and so forth run similarly. However, there are a number of caveats:

- **Clean up resources:** Be sure to close database connections and file handles that are opened in the script. Relying on Perl to clean up is a safe shortcut under a conventional CGI, but it's a dangerous practice under persistent mod_perl execution, so do your own tidying up.

20

- **Be strict safe:** All variables should be lexically scoped. Variables that are not declared lexically scoped by being initialized with Perl's my operator might leak values from one request to another. This is due to the code that is cached by mod_perl. An easy way to enforce lexical scoping is to begin all Apache::Registry scripts with the strict pragma.

- **Use strict;:** The Perl compiler won't operate on the script if the strict pragma is in effect and there are variables that aren't scoped properly.

One of the Perl online documents that is installed when you install mod_perl discusses this in further detail. Type

```
perldoc mod_perl_traps
```

to review the issues relating to running CGIs under mod_perl.

There are times when code that was never meant to run as anything other than a CGI must be put under mod_perl execution. If the amount of work required to make a CGI strict safe is high, Apache::PerlRun provides a nice alternative. This request handler uses the persistent Perl interpreter that's running in the Apache process, but it makes no effort to cache the compilation of the script; every request goes through a full compile, run, and data-flush cycle. It's still significantly faster than running a straight CGI; the Perl interpreter does not need to be started and shut down with every request.

To enable Apache::PerlRun, change the Directory entry slightly, so that instead of the handling being performed by Apache::Registry, it's Apache::PerlRun. Change the entry to the following:

```
PerlModule Apache::PerlRun
<Directory "/usr/local/apache2/cgi-bin">
  AllowOverride None
  Options +ExecCGI
  Order allow,deny
  Allow from all
  SetHandler perl-script
  PerlHandler Apache::PerlRun
  PerlSendHeader On
</Directory>
```

The output is identical, but it removes the requirement that the code be strict safe; "dirty" CGIs are okay under Apache::PerlRun.

Page Components and Templating

In the last few years, CGI-style Web application has all but disappeared; it has largely been replaced by page component and templating systems. A component system uses page fragments to assemble a complete HTML document for the browser to render. The browsers don't see the code that links the components together—all the processing is done on the server. Page templating provides not only boilerplating of the formatting and layout code in the HTML, but also provides placeholders for programmatic data display. Usually, these two concepts go together to provide page-centric Web application development.

The most basic component system for Apache is `mod_include` and its support for server side includes (SSI), which is covered in Hour 12, "Filtering Modules." Although SSIs are fine for composing a page of fragments and dealing with environment variables, they are severely deficient as far providing a programmatic framework for handling data. PHP is another component and templating system. PHP has its own language implemented, which has proven to be a mixed blessing; PHP is discussed in detail in Hour 19. For those who want to architect a component system in Perl, `mod_perl` has been a godsend. In fact, it is so easy to build a component system to run under `mod_perl` that there are arguably too many of them on the CPAN. In this section, we'll focus on one of the more popular ones.

For flexibility and power, `Apache::ASP` is difficult to beat. `Apache::ASP` provides an implementation of Microsoft's Active Server Pages (ASP). Be aware that although Microsoft ASP logic is typically developed with VBScript, `Apache::ASP` logic is implemented in Perl. Although this isn't necessarily a good portability solution, if you like the ASP API but dislike VBScript and like serving your pages with Apache, `Apache::ASP` might be just what you're looking for. It provides access to all the Apache request object data and all of Perl's built in functions, and is easily extended with more modules off of the CPAN.

We'll set up a simple `Apache::ASP` application by loading it in the `httpd.conf`, creating a directory to hold our `Apache::ASP` documents (`mkdir /usr/local/apache2/asp`), another directory for its internal application state maintenance (`mkdir /usr/local/apache2/asp_statedir`), and setting up a Directory container for it. This application simply echoes back any form variables that are submitted to it.

This is how you specify that you want content in this directory to accessed under the `/asp` namespace and that it should be handled by the `Apache::ASP` module:

```
PerlModule  Apache::ASP
Alias /asp /usr/local/apache2/asp
<Directory /usr/local/apache2/asp>
    Options Indexes FollowSymLinks
    Order allow,deny
    Allow from all
  <Files ~ (\.asp)>
```

20

```
    SetHandler  perl-script
    PerlHandler Apache::ASP
    PerlSetVar  Global .
    PerlSetVar  StateDir /usr/local/apache2/asp_statedir
  </Files>
</Directory>
```

Now deploy the following page in the asp directory in a file called form.asp (see
Listing 20.3).

LISTING 20.3   form.asp

```
 1: <!DOCTYPE HTML PUBLIC "-//IETF//DTD HTML//EN">
 2: <html>
 3:   <head>
 4:     <title>Apache::ASP form dump</title>
 5:   </head>
 6:
 7:   <body bgcolor="#ffffff">
 8:     <h1>Apache::ASP form dump</h1>
 9:     <form method="POST">
10:     <table border="1" cellpadding="3">
11:       <tr><td colspan="4" bgcolor="lightgrey"><b>Text Fields</b></td></tr>
12:       <tr>
13:         <td>
14:           Username:<br><input type="text" name="username" size="15">
15:         </td>
16:         <td>
17:           Password:<br><input type="password" name="password" size="15">
18:         </td>
19:         <td>
20:           Biography<br>
21:           <textarea name="biography" rows="3" cols="14"></textarea>
22:         </td>
23:         <td> </td>
24:       </tr>
25:       <tr><td colspan="4" bgcolor="lightgrey"><b>Selectors</b></td></tr>
26:       <tr>
27:         <td>Your Computer Peripherals: <br>(Check All That Apply)<br>
28:           <input type="checkbox" name="peripherals" value="wifi">
                ➥ Wireless 802.11b<br>
29:           <input type="checkbox" name="peripherals" value="dvd">
                ➥DVD Drive<br>
30:           <input type="checkbox" name="peripherals" value="cdburner">
                ➥ CD Burner
31:         </td>
32:         <td>Your Preferred Web Browser: <br>(Pick One)<br>
33:           <input type="radio" name="browser" value="netscape">
                ➥ Netscape Navigator<br>
34:           <input type="radio" name="browser" value="mozilla">Mozilla<br>
```

LISTING 20.3   continued

```
35:                <input type="radio" name="browser" value="msie">
                   ➥Internet Explorer<br>
36:                <input type="radio" name="browser" value="other">Other
37:        </td>
38:        <td>Your Hobbies: <br>(Check All That Apply)<br>
39:          <select multiple name="hobbies" size="4">
40:            <option value="apache">Hacking Apache
41:            <option value="surfing">Surfing
42:            <option value="mosh">Moshing
43:            <option value="gliding">Hang Gliding
44:          </select>
45:        </td>
46:        <td>My Favorite Programming Language: <br>(Pick One)<br>
47:          <select name="language">
48:            <option value="perl">Perl
49:            <option value="tcl">Tcl
50:            <option value="java">Java
51:            <option value="python">Python
52:            <option value="php">PHP
53:            <option value="ruby">Ruby
54:          </select>
55:        </td>
56:     </tr>
57:     <tr>
58:       <td colspan="4" align="left">
59:          <input type=button value="Clear" name="clearbutton"
                   ➥ onClick="alert('Clear Clicked')">
60:          <input type=submit name="submitbutton" value="Submit">
61:          <input type=reset name="resetbutton" value="Reset">
62:       </td>
63:     </tr>
64:   </table>
65:   </form>
66:   <% if(%{$Request->{Form}}) { %>
67:
68:   <hr size=1>
69:
70:   Your username is <tt><%=$Request->Form('username')%></tt> <br>
71:   Your password is <tt><%=$Request->Form('password')%></tt> <br>
72:   Your biography is <tt><%=$Request->Form('biography')%></tt> <br>
73:   Your computer peripherals are <tt>
74:     <% for my $p ($Request->Form('peripherals')) { %>
75:        <%= $p %>
76:     <% } %>
77:   </tt><br>
78:   Your web browser is <tt><%=$Request->Form('browser')%></tt> <br>
79:   Your computer peripherals are <tt>
80:     <% for my $i ($Request->Form('hobbies')) { %>
```

20

LISTING 20.3 continued

```
81:        <%= $i %>
82:     <% } %>
83:     </tt><br>
84:     Your programming language is <tt><%=$Request->Form('language')%></tt> <br>
85:     <% } %>
86:
87:     <hr>
88:     <address><a href="mailto:webmaster@example.com">Example</a></address>
89:     </body>
90:  </html>
```

Now access this from your Web browser: http://modperl.example.com/asp/form.asp
(substitute your host for modperl.example.com).

Apache::ASP also supports XML-like tags that map to Perl functions for request processing and producing output, similar to the taglibs that JSP developers are accustomed to.
Because Perl modules can be accessed directly in your ASP code, you can take advantage of CGI.pm's facilities for programmatic form widget generation.

Before installing Apache::ASP, you must install some CPAN modules such as MLDBM,
MLDBM::Sync, and Digest::MD5.

Other modules, such as Time::HiRes (for debugging), HTML::FillInForm (for filling values on form widgets), and XML::Sablotron (for XSLT transformations), can enhance
your Apache::ASP installation's capabilities.

To install these modules, refer to the CPAN installation process we used earlier to install
mod_perl. You won't have to recompile Apache or mod_perl, but acquiring, compiling,
and installing the modules is greatly streamlined by the CPAN module.

A number of other page component assembly and templating systems are available for
mod_perl. Some other popular component and template systems include

- HTML::Mason
- HTML::Embperl
- HTML::Template
- Template Toolkit

There are others, and each one has strengths and weaknesses in terms of how much simplicity or power it exposes to the page developer. Sometimes it is advantageous to sand-
box the page developer to limit the amount of trouble he can get into; other times, it's
preferable to expose the full power of the underlying programming language to the page

developer. Although many of these modules have been in use for a long time under
mod_perl 1.*x*, their level of compatibility with mod_perl 2.0 varies considerably (even
with Apache::compat).

Access, Authentication, and Authorization

Some of the other problems that mod_perl can solve easily are complex authentication
and authorization requirements. Hour 7, "Restricting Access," covers the basics of
authentication and authorization.

Suppose that you have resources that are accessible to a user larry only during the hours
of 9 a.m. to 5 p.m., curly only from 5 p.m. to 1 a.m., and to moe on the graveyard shift
from 1 a.m. to 9 a.m.

Our module, StoogeAuthz, will handle authenticating our three stooges and these crazy
authorization requirements for us. First, we'll configure httpd.conf:

```
PerlModule Apache::StoogeAuthz
<Location /stooges>
  AuthName "stooge stuff"
  AuthType Basic
  PerlAuthenHandler Apache::StoogeAuthz
  PerlSetVar StoogeAuthz_passwd_file /usr/local/apache2/conf/stooge_passwd
  PerlSetVar StoogeAuthz_day_user larry
  PerlSetVar StoogeAuthz_swing_user curly
  PerlSetVar StoogeAuthz_graveyard_user moe
  require user larry curly moe
</Location>
```

Then we'll create the password file /usr/local/apache2/conf/stooge_passwd by using
the htpasswd utility that comes with Apache:

```
htpasswd -c -s /usr/local/apache2/conf/stooge_passwd larry
```

```
htpasswd -s /usr/local/apache2/conf/stooge_passwd curly
```

```
htpasswd -s /usr/local/apache2/conf/stooge_passwd moe
```

20

We want the -c option only the first time—to create the password file.
Further, we're using SHA1 encryption, so we need the -s option.

Remember to create the stooges directory (mkdir
/usr/local/apache2/htdocs/stooges) so that we don't get a 404 error.

Finally, we'll deploy our Apache::StoogeAuthz module by placing a file StoogeAuthz.pm with the code in Listing 20.4 in /usr/local/apache2/apps/Apache.

LISTING 20.4   StoogeAuthz.pm

```
 1: package Apache::StoogeAuthz;
 2:
 3: # standard Perl stuff
 4: use strict;
 5: use FileHandle;
 6: use constant DEBUG => 1;
 7:
 8: # mod_perl libraries
 9: use Apache::Log ();
10: use Apache::Const -compile => qw(OK AUTH_REQUIRED FORBIDDEN SERVER_ERROR
11:           DECLINED);
12:
13: # other CPAN modules
14: use MIME::Base64;
15: use Digest::SHA1;
16:
17: # uses SHA1 encrypted passwords to authenticate
18: # and the time of day to authorize
19:
20: # these are the parameters that configure this module
21: my $param = {
22:    StoogeAuthz_passwd_file => undef,
23:    StoogeAuthz_day_user => undef,
24:    StoogeAuthz_swing_user => undef,
25:    StoogeAuthz_graveyard_user => undef
26: };
27:
28: # this is the actual request handler, Apache gives it a
29: # request object as an argument
30: sub handler {
31:    # get our request object
32:    my $r=shift;
33:     # populate our parameters with what was configured in
34:    # httpd.conf
35:    while(my($key, $val) = each %$param) {
36:       $val = $r->dir_config($key) || $val;
37:       $key =~ s/^StoogeAuthz_//;
38:       $param->{$key} = $val;
39:    }
40:    # if not configured don't handle the request
41:    if (! $param->{passwd_file}) {
42:        return Apache::DECLINED;
43:    }
44:    my($passwd_lookup,$user_found);
```

LISTING 20.4   continued

```
45:    # here the dialog pops up and asks you for username and password
46:    my($res, $passwd_sent) = $r->get_basic_auth_pw;
47:    return $res if $res; # e.g. HTTP_UNAUTHORIZED
48:    # mod_perl 1.x programmers are accustomed to $r->connection->user
49:    my $user_sent = $r->user;
50:    # open our password file
51:    my $pwfile = new FileHandle $param->{passwd_file}, "r";
52:    if (defined $pwfile) {
53:        while (my $entry = <$pwfile>) {
54:            chomp $entry;
55:            if ($entry =~ /^${user_sent}:(.*)/) {
56:                        $passwd_lookup = $1;
57:                        $user_found += 1;
58:                        last;
59:                }
60:        }
61:        if (! $user_found) {
62:            $r->log_reason("No such user found: $user_sent");
63:            $r->note_basic_auth_failure;
64:            return Apache::AUTH_REQUIRED;
65:        }
66:        undef $pwfile; # close the password file
67:    } else {
68:        $r->log_reason("Couldn't open password file:
           ➥$param->{passwd_file}");
69:        return Apache::SERVER_ERROR;
70:    }
71:    # SHA1 encrypt the password the user gave
72:    my $passwd_sent_sha='{SHA}' .
73:                    encode_base64(Digest::SHA1::sha1($passwd_sent));
74:    chomp($passwd_sent_sha);
75:    if ($passwd_sent_sha ne $passwd_lookup) { # passwords don't match
76:        $r->log_reason("Password doesn't match for user: $user_sent, " .
77:                       "$passwd_sent_sha ne $passwd_lookup");
78:        $r->note_basic_auth_failure;
79:        return Apache::AUTH_REQUIRED;
80:    }
81:    # ok, we're authenticated but not yet authorized
82:    print STDERR "User authenticated: $user_sent\n" if DEBUG;
83: # get the time local to the machine hosting Apache,
84: # not the browser!
85:    my($sec,$min,$hour) = localtime();
86:    if ($hour >= 9 && $hour < 17) {
87:        if ($param->{day_user} eq $user_sent) {
88:            return Apache::OK;
89:        } else {
90:            $r->log_reason("user $user_sent is denied access during " .
91:                           "the day shift, you must be " .
92:                           "$param->{day_user} to access");
```

LISTING 20.4 continued

```
 93:                return Apache::FORBIDDEN;
 94:                    }
 95:        }
 96:        if ($hour >= 17 || $hour < 1) {
 97:                if ($param->{swing_user} eq $user_sent) {
 98:                    return Apache::OK;
 99:                } else {
100:                $r->log_reason("user $user_sent is denied access during " .
101:                                    "the swing shift, you must be " .
102:                                    "$param->{swing_user} to access");
103:                return Apache::FORBIDDEN;
104:                }
105:        }
106:        if ($hour >= 1 && $hour < 9) {
107:                if ($param->{graveyard_user} eq $user_sent) {
108:                    return Apache::OK;
109:                } else {
110:                $r->log_reason("user $user_sent is denied access during " .
111:                                    "the graveyard shift, you must be " .
112:                                    "$param->{graveyard_user} to access");
113:                return Apache::FORBIDDEN;
114:                }
115:        }
116:      return Apache::OK;
117: } # handler
118:
119:
120: 1;
```

mod_perl 2.0 has a nicer API for adding new directives to the Apache vocabulary than mod_perl 1.*x* (which required compiling XS binary extensions for your Perl code). This should obviate the need for PerlSetVar directives in httpd.conf and accessing $r->dir_config() in the module code. However, at the time of this writing, some components of mod_perl 2.0's are unimplemented, such as Apache::ModuleConfig. Therefore, using PerlSetVar and dir_config() from the mod_perl 1.*x* API and leveraging Apache::compat is an easy way to start using established and stable mod_perl 1.*x* APIs under mod_perl 2.0.

Architecting a Scalable mod_perl Infrastructure

Under mod_perl 1.*x*, servers often suffered from performance constraints that stemmed from the preforked process model of Apache. For instance, applications that required a database connection and wanted to enjoy the benefits provided by Apache::DBI's persistent database connections had to have a database connection per Apache process per database resource. Additionally, much of the time for an Apache process handling a request is spent sending data over high-latency networks, which further ties up resources that might be better spent performing templating logic. In essence, "smart" Apache processes that know how to talk to databases and perform complex operations are bogged down by dumb jobs, such as bleeding data down to the browser. For busy Web sites with a large process pool, this is a big problem.

For mod_perl 2.0 installations using the preforked MPM, these issues remain. However, threaded MPM installations can at least mitigate the resource connection issue. Several new directives allow mod_perl 2.0 to manage the number of Perl interpreters active within an Apache instance. The Perl interpreters can be maintained in a pool that mod_perl can check out, make use of, and then return to the pool, much as you would check out, use, and return materials from a public library. These directives include

- **PerlInterpStart:** Number of Perl interpreters to start
- **PerlInterpMax:** Maximum number of running Perl interpreters
- **PerlInterpMaxSpare:** Maximum number of spare Perl interpreters
- **PerlInterpMinSpare:** Minimum number of spare Perl interpreters
- **PerlInterpMaxRequests:** Maximum number of requests per Perl interpreter
- **PerlInterpScope:** Scope for which the selected interpreter should be held; one of request, connection, handler, subrequest

The pool management API itself has been abstracted for programmatic manipulation of the number of thread items using the Apache::TIPool module. An experimental Perl module for handling database connection pools, Apache::DBIPool, is distributed with mod_perl 2.0 as a minimal reference implementation. However, at the time of this writing, there are no production-quality modules on the CPAN that implement the Apache::TIPool API for database connection management.

The interim solution to the database connection problem, as well as the high-latency client resource consumption problem, is to put a proxy tier in front of the mod_perl server. The proxy tier can have a large process pool to handle high traffic, but can be connected to the mod_perl applications via a high-speed network to minimize the resources that that more constrained process pool must consume.

Summary

Writing Web applications as logic that runs inside the Web server process offers many performance benefits. The standard APIs that Apache exposes for C programmers are

20

nice, but lack the rapid development characteristics of a scripting language. mod_perl wraps the C API and exposes it to Perl programmers for a variety of application uses. You can write your own Apache modules in Perl, and can even perform the same duties as most of the modules written in C that are distributed with Apache. You can leverage existing modules available on the CPAN to provide templating, logging, session management, and authentication functionality. Although mod_perl is not an application server per se, it provides all the raw materials of one. Many Web sites are running on cobbled-together application frameworks built on top of mod_perl and CPAN modules. You can dramatically accelerate your CGIs with a few simple changes to your httpd.conf. Finally, mod_perl's new thread item API provides many interesting possibilities for resource pooling. Although there are other scripting language modules that hook into the Apache API, none provides the rich set of tools and mature code base that mod_perl does. Chocolate and peanut butter taste pretty good together!

Q&A

Q Does the Perl interpreter run in the Apache process or does it run externally under mod_perl?

A Running the Perl process externally is a model used by FastCGI. There's a similar API, SpeedyCGI, (see http://sourceforge.net/projects/speedycgi/) that performs similar duties. In contrast, mod_perl runs in process and therefore enables intimate access to Apache's internals; mod_perl's rich API then is dependent upon running inside the Apache instance.

Q Are there other language modules that do what mod_perl does?

A Various modules have been developed over the years for similarly exposing Apache's C API for Python, Tcl, and even Java. However, none of these projects has ever enjoyed the popularity of mod_perl. An interesting development in Apache 2.0 is having access to mod_perl objects from inside PHP. For instance, in a PHP page, you can get mod_perl's Apache request object like so

```
<?
  $perl = new Perl;
  $r = $perl->call("Apache::request");
?>
```

and then perform operations on it as you would from with a Perl handler!

Q Can I use mod_perl applications with my Java servlets?

A Traditionally, these have been separate realms of application development. However, with Apache 2.0's filtering API, it is conceivable that your mod_perl application could represent HTTP responses to mod_jk or vice versa. For instance, a mod_perl response in XML can be filtered through a Java servlet that performs XSLT styling with the Apache filtering API.

Q How do I set up mod_perl on Windows?

A This is a thorny issue because it requires compiling mod_perl for Windows, usually with Microsoft Visual Studio, and having that compile match the compile of Apache. There are mod_perl hackers who regularly post compiled distributions of mod_perl; you'll need to use the same version of Apache that they compiled against to use their distributions. One place to get mod_perl, as well as a number of mod_perl-related CPAN modules, compiled to work with Apache binaries posted by the Apache Software Foundation (see http://httpd.apache.org) and the Perl distribution from ActiveState (http://www.activestate.com/) is http://theoryx5.uwinnipeg.ca/. Check there for the latest developments regarding running mod_perl on Windows.

Quiz

1. Why is using the strict pragma important for mod_perl development?

2. Is it necessary to use all the CPAN modules like AxKit and Apache::ASP to benefit from mod_perl?

3. Can Apache be configured to handle other network protocols besides HTTP with mod_perl?

Quiz Answers

1. When you have use strict; in your Perl code, you ensure that you don't have any undeclared or accidental global variables in your code. These might not be a problem in a CGI, but they can wreak havoc in mod_perl's persistent execution model.

2. Nope. If your Web site is burdened with a lot of CGI requests, you can get immediate benefit just by using Apache::Registry or one of the other modules that come with the mod_perl distribution and enable CGI acceleration.

3. Yes. The PerlProcessConnectionHandler component of the API allows Perl to do all the protocol-level handling. For instance, you could write a Perl module to handle mail server duties such as SMTP or POP3. You could even invent your own network protocol and leverage Apache for its other server framework APIs and enjoy the rapid development benefits of Perl!

20

Further Reading

Writing Apache Modules with Perl and C, Lincoln Stein and Doug MacEachern, 1999, O'Reilly and Associates.

This book has not been updated to include all the new APIs in Apache 2.0 and mod_perl 2.0. However, it provides a rich discussion of the APIs as they existed in Apache 1.3.*x* and mod_perl 1.*x* that still has some applicability to the next generation.

mod_perl Developer's Cookbook, Geoffrey Young, Paul Lindner, and Randy Kobes, 2002, Sams

Although not updated for mod_perl 2.0, this book provides a rich set of solution-oriented examples of using mod_perl 1.*x* APIs.

http://perl.apache.org/

The home for all things mod_perl. Watch this site for news and updated releases of mod_perl. This site also provides searchable archives of mailing lists as well as subscription information, so use it as your gateway to the vast mod_perl community.

http://perl.apache.org/~dougm/

Doug MacEachern, the author of mod_perl, often posts items of special interest to mod_perl developers here. Bleeding-edge build patches, examples, and technical notes can be found here, but you'll need to snoop around—there's no table of contents for Doug's stealth Web site.

HOUR **21**

Tomcat and Apache

This hour gives an introduction to the Tomcat Java servlet and JavaServer
Pages (JSPs) container reference implementation. Servlets and JSPs are used
to run Java-based Web applications.

In this hour, you will learn

- How server-side Java works
- How to configure Tomcat to work with Apache
- How to run basic servlets and JSPs using Tomcat

A Little History of Java Servlets

Although some Web content is static, in that it doesn't change much if at all
from one request to another, there are few software applications under development these days that aren't Web-enabled. The earliest Web applications
were common gateway interface (CGI) programs whose application logic
was typically coded in a scripting language, as described in Hour 6,
"Serving Dynamic Content with CGI." However, as needs grew from simply
providing a Web-based user interface to existing applications to entirely
Web-based applications, so also grew the need for programming

environments suitable for developing these applications. When Sun Microsystems introduced the Java programming language in 1995, it focused on providing a richer browser-based interface using embedded graphical applications or *applets*. However, applets never really seemed to solve the richer-interface-needed problem very well. Nonetheless, Java's strengths as a language drove its popularity, much to the chagrin of its early proponents, for *server*-based applications. Java offers a fully object-oriented programming construct that lends itself to sophisticated design patterns, while avoiding the platform-specific concerns of older OO languages such as C++.

The Java Servlet API was developed to provide an environment for server-based Web applications. The early implementations of this API included the Apache JServ project as well as Sun's Java Web Server. As the API underwent revision and was joined with the JavaServer Pages API specification in 1999, Sun donated the Java Web Server code to the Apache Software Foundation and JServ development was retired. That donation eventually bore fruit as Tomcat 3.0, the reference implementation for Servlet API version 2.2 and JSP API version 1.1. At the time this book is being written, the latest version of the API's are Servlet API version 2.3 and JSP version 1.2, and Tomcat 4.0 is the reference implementation for these specifications.

Servlets are Java programs that run on the server side, waiting for requests, processing them, and providing responses. Compare this to CGIs, which are launched, marshal any resources they need, perform their processing, and then cease execution. Servlets are launched either when the servlet engine starts up or when the first request for the servlet arrives. When they are running, servlets can remain loaded for the lifetime of the servlet engine, thereby avoiding the startup and shutdown penalty of CGI execution.

JSPs are Java's answer to other page-oriented application environments such as Microsoft's Active Server Pages and PHP. A JSP is authored like an HTML page with embedded Java code and special tags that are processed by the JSP container. However, a JSP is not parsed and processed with each request. Upon first request, a JSP is converted on the fly to Java servlet source code and compiled into Java virtual machine (JVM) bytecode that is cached for efficient future execution cycles.

Servlet Container Integration with Apache

Servlet engines run their applications within a Java process or Java virtual machine. Java is compiled to bytecode that is portable among JVMs; code compiled for a JVM running on Windows will execute equally well on a JVM running on Linux. A servlet engine is referred to as a servlet *container*. A container provides Java objects that represent HTTP requests and responses that will be passed to the running servlets for processing. Although it is possible for Tomcat to run standalone and serve HTTP requests directly,

Apache does a better job at tasks such as handling static content and SSL connections, and Tomcat is commonly used alongside an Apache server. Unlike mod_perl and PHP, which run as modules inside the Apache process, a JVM is external and requires a mechanism to connect to the Web server. That's where the JServ protocol helps out.

Tomcat inherited the Apache JServ protocol (AJP) from the JServ project. AJP is a protocol for connecting an external process to a servlet container. It is the responsibility of an Apache module, mod_jk, to speak this protocol to the servlet container. We'll cover downloading mod_jk and setting it up later in this hour. The protocol has undergone a number of revisions; Tomcat 4.0 and the current version of mod_jk use AJP 1.3, which is typically referred to as ajp13.

Figure 21.1 shows a typical setup, with the Apache Web server listening on port 80 for HTTP requests and Tomcat running in another process listening for ajp13 connections on port 8009. The Web server need not listen on port 80; we'll shortly configure mod_jk and Tomcat to use another port to illustrate how the ajp13 protocol connection is configured.

FIGURE 21.1
The Apache Web server and Tomcat communicate request and response data over the ajp13 protocol.

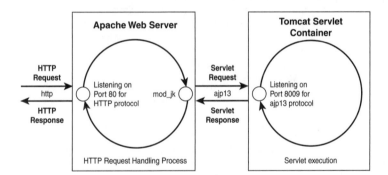

Installing and Running Tomcat

Tomcat 4.0 requires Java 2 Standard Edition (J2SE) 1.2 or higher. If you have only an older Java Development Kit (JDK 1.1.8 is still widely deployed), you must upgrade. The J2SE runtime for Windows, Linux, and Solaris can be downloaded from Sun; support for these and other platforms might be available from other vendors. The Tomcat 4.0 distribution can be downloaded from the Apache Jakarta project (see the "Further Reading" section at the end of this hour for download URLs). The source code for Tomcat is freely available from the Jakarta project Web site. However, most users don't need to compile Tomcat; it is written entirely in Java, so if you have the required Java runtime, the precompiled binaries will run.

In addition to using ajp13 to connect Tomcat to Apache, it also can be run as a standalone Web server. The HTTP support built into Tomcat is not especially robust,

21

particularly in comparison to the Apache Web server, but for simple development purposes or lightweight Web server demands, it's perfectly adequate. After Tomcat is installed, we'll use its HTTP support to verify that it is running.

At the time of this writing, Tomcat 4.0.4 is the most recent release. There are different packages available for the newest J2SE distribution (1.4), but the installation and startup are similar. The Tomcat startup script expects the environment variable JAVA_HOME to be set to the directory where the Java runtime is installed.

Installing on Unix

For Unix and Linux users, you can simply set the environment variable in your shell, download the latest binary distribution (Listing 21.1 assumes that you've downloaded jakarta-tomcat-4.0.4.tar.gz), uncompress and unpack it in the directory you want it installed in, and run the startup script.

LISTING 21.1   Steps to Install Tomcat

```
export JAVA_HOME=/usr/local/j2se1.3
export CATALINA_HOME=/usr/local/jakarta-tomcat-4.0.4
cd /usr/local
gunzip < jakarta-tomcat-4.0.4.tar.gz | tar xvf -
cd jakarta-tomcat-4.0.4/bin
./catalina.sh start
```

> The version of tar included in Solaris and other Unix systems does not correctly handle tarballs with paths that exceed a certain length. That is the case with the Tomcat tarball, so you might need to download and use gtar instead. gtar is an equivalent utility that can be found at ftp://gatekeeper.dec.com/pub/GNU/tar/.

Now you should be able to access the Tomcat HTTP server on port 8080, for instance, by navigating to http://localhost:8080/ (if not accessing from localhost, change the hostname accordingly) as shown in Figure 21.2.

> To make sure that the JAVA_HOME and CATALINA_HOME environment variables are set the next time you log in, set them in your login script. For example, if you are using the bash shell, you can put the export commands shown earlier in the .bash_profile file in your home directory.

FIGURE 21.2

The Tomcat splash screen.

Installing on Windows

Windows users must go into the properties for the My Computer icon, select the Advanced tab, and click Environment Variables. Click New and set the JAVA_HOME environment variable's value to the path in which the Java runtime is installed. In Figure 21.3, JAVA_HOME is set to C:\j2sdk1.4.0.

FIGURE 21.3

Setting JAVA_HOME in Windows.

21

Although doing so is not necessary, setting `Path` to `%Path%;%JAVA_HOME%\bin` at this stage makes compiling and running Java code from the Windows command shell much more convenient.

Assuming that you've downloaded `jakarta-tomcat-4.0.4.exe`, double-click it to launch the Windows installer. After an informational message about detecting the `JAVA_HOME` setting and agreeing to the Apache license, you will see a software component selection menu as shown in Figure 21.4.

FIGURE 21.4

Tomcat component selection menu.

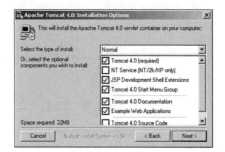

On Windows NT, 2000, or XP, you will probably want your Tomcat server to run as a Windows service, so click the second check box from the top to enable this feature. After selecting the path in which Tomcat should be deployed, the files are installed and a Start Menu folder is created as shown in Figure 21.5.

FIGURE 21.5

The installed Tomcat folder.

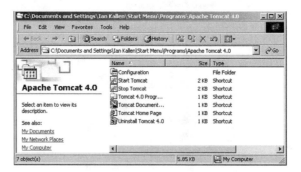

To start your server, click the Start Tomcat icon. Windows NT, 2000, and XP users can also start their server from the Windows Service Manager, provided the option shown in

Figure 21.4 was selected. Just as in the Linux case shown in Figure 21.2, you should be able to access Tomcat's HTTP server on port 8080.

Connecting the Apache Web Server to Tomcat

In addition to the Tomcat distribution, the Jakarta project has a separate distribution that you can download, jakarta-tomcat-connector, which has the full source code for mod_jk and other connectors. Precompiled binaries of Apache 2.0 mod_jk for Windows and Linux are available as well from the Jakarta Web site. On Linux and Unix systems, the module binary is typically a file named mod_jk.so; on Windows, it's usually named mod_jk.dll.

> The packaging for mod_jk binaries varies greatly, sometimes on a month-to-month basis. Consult the Jakarta Web site for the latest news about what packages are available.

After you have the module binary, put it in the modules subdirectory of your Apache installation's server root. On a typical Unix installation, the httpd.conf configuration addition shown in Listing 21.2 loads and enables mod_jk.

LISTING 21.2   Apache Directives to Configure mod_jk

```
LoadModule jk_module modules/mod_jk.so
JkWorkersFile conf/workers.properties

JkMount /examples/*.jsp ajp13
JkMount /examples/servlet/* ajp13
Alias /examples /usr/local/jakarta-tomcat-4.0.4/webapps/examples
<Directory /usr/local/jakarta-tomcat-4.0.4/webapps/examples>
  Order allow,deny
  allow from all
  Options indexes
</Directory>
<Directory /usr/local/jakarta-tomcat-4.0.4/webapps/examples/WEB-INF>
  deny from all
</Directory>
```

21

The JkWorkersFile directive refers to a separate file that configures the ajp13 protocol communication parameters; an example called workers.properties is distributed with mod_jk. For a basic setup, the default values shown in Listing 21.3 for workers.properties are typically fine. The file format uses name/value pairs, in which the name and value are separated by an equal sign. workers.tomcat_home might be the only value that you have to set; it should agree with the value you previously set for CATALINA_HOME. If you need to set up more than one installation of Tomcat on your machine, you'll need to adjust the worker.ajp.port parameter in workers.properties to make sure that mod_jk is connecting to the correct Tomcat installation; your Tomcat installations will not be able to start up sharing port numbers.

LISTING 21.3   workers.properties

```
workers.tomcat_home=/usr/local/jakarta-tomcat-4.0.4
workers.java_home=$(JAVA_HOME)
ps=/
worker.list=ajp13
worker.ajp13.port=8009
worker.ajp13.host=localhost
worker.ajp13.type=ajp13
```

Should you need to alter the values from their defaults, the workers.properties file in the mod_jk distribution is annotated with comments that explain the values' use.

The JkMount directives in Listing 21.2 make all HTTP requests that Apache receives with a URL that begins with /examples/servlet, or has a .jsp file extension and begins with /examples, go through mod_jk to Tomcat. It would not be sufficient simply to have

```
JkMount /examples/* ajp13
```

and be done with it. Any inline links to binary files such as images would be subject to mod_jk's handling, which we do not want to do. The JkMount directive must specify content that Tomcat is to actually *process*: JSPs and servlets. The reason you need the Alias directive and Directory container is to enable Apache to serve images or other non-servlet and non-JSP content.

You typically won't need to change anything in the Tomcat configuration file, but it is a critical third component in getting Tomcat and Apache to work together.

You can find the `server.xml` Tomcat configuration file in the Tomcat distribution's `conf` subdirectory. Inside `server.xml`, you should see the XML container shown in Listing 21.4.

LISTING 21.4   Portion of `server.xml` That Configures AJP 1.3

```
<!-- Define an AJP 1.3 Connector on port 8009 -->
<Connector className="org.apache.ajp.tomcat4.Ajp13Connector"
           port="8009" minProcessors="5" maxProcessors="75"
           acceptCount="10" debug="0"/>
```

The critical thing to notice is that the `port` attribute in Listing 21.4 agrees with the `worker.ajp13.port` in Listing 21.3. After the `httpd.conf`, `workers.properties`, and `server.xml` files are configured and activated, start up Tomcat and Apache. You should be able to access your Tomcat content not only by using Tomcat's HTTP listener on port 8080, but also by using Apache's HTTP listener on its regular port. For instance, `http://localhost/examples/jsp/` (change your hostname accordingly if not installing to `localhost`) should serve the Tomcat JSP examples from Apache.

Java Web Applications

One of the key concepts in the servlet and JSP specifications is that of a Web application or Webapp. A *Webapp* is a path under which an application and its content are accessible. The `/examples` path that comes with Tomcat is a Webapp. It consists of application components such as JSPs and servlets, static content such as HTML and images, metadata that can configure how the application components operate, and other resources such as tag library descriptors.

A Webapp follows a specific directory layout structure and has metadata descriptions that follow standard formats. Webapp directory layouts and metadata descriptors are not proprietary to Tomcat, but are part of the servlet and JSP specifications. The directory layout follows the form shown in Figure 21.6.

Because the `WEB-INF` directory contains application data, it is crucial that it be secured against malice and mischief. The contents of the `WEB-INF` directory must not be exposed by the Apache server's `Alias` directive that maps the Webapp context path to the physical filesystem path. The final `Directory` container shown in Listing 21.2 accomplishes this with its `deny` directive.

21

FIGURE 21.6
Webapp directory structure.

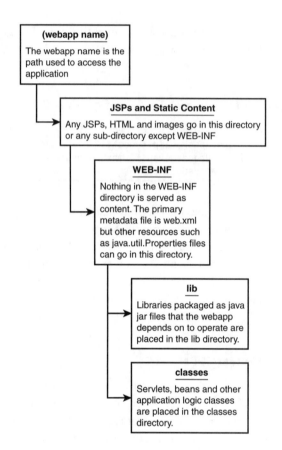

> **(webapp name)**
> The webapp name is the path used to access the application

> **JSPs and Static Content**
> Any JSPs, HTML and images go in this directory or any sub-directory except WEB-INF

> **WEB-INF**
> Nothing in the WEB-INF directory is served as content. The primary metadata file is web.xml but other resources such as java.util.Properties files can go in this directory.

> **lib**
> Libraries packaged as java jar files that the webapp depends on to operate are placed in the lib directory.

> **classes**
> Servlets, beans and other application logic classes are placed in the classes directory.

Build Your Own Webapp

Now that you know the anatomy of a Webapp, you can build one for yourself. Although the servlet and JSP APIs enable a number of powerful application concepts that are beyond the scope of this book, the resources at the end of this hour should provide a good starting point for further exploration. Start with a servlet in a bare bones Webapp that simply dumps the context, request, and system parameters when requested.

In the Tomcat webapps directory, create a subdirectory for your Webapp and make that your current directory. Type the following in your shell:

```
mkdir sams-webapp
cd sams-webapp
```

Create the metadata directory and make that your current directory. Type the following in your shell:

```
mkdir WEB-INF
cd WEB-INF
```

Now create the source code and binary directories for your servlet code and make the source directory your current directory. Type the following in your shell:

```
mkdir classes src
cd src
```

Windows users can create the same directory structure using the Windows Explorer interface.

To create the PropertiesDump example Java servlet, save the code in Listing 21.5 in a file called `PropertiesDump.java`. You can download this and other code listings from the book at `http://apacheworld.org`.

LISTING 21.5   PropertiesDump Servlet

```
1: import java.io.IOException;
2: import java.io.PrintWriter;
3: import java.util.Enumeration;
4: import javax.servlet.*;
5: import javax.servlet.http.*;
6:
7: /**
8:  * The PropertiesDump servlet displays JVM, servlet container and
9:  * webapp properties and parameters in an HTML page.
10:  */
11:
12: public class PropertiesDump extends HttpServlet {
13:
14:     public void doGet(HttpServletRequest request,
➥HttpServletResponse response)
15:         throws ServletException, IOException
16:     {
17:         PrintWriter out = response.getWriter();
18:         HttpSession session = request.getSession();
19:         response.setContentType("text/html");
20:
21:         out.println("<!DOCTYPE HTML PUBLIC \"-//IETF//DTD HTML//EN\">");
22:         out.println("<html>");
23:         out.println("<head>");
24:         out.println("<title>Properties Dump Servlet</title>");
25:         out.println("</head>");
26:         out.println("<body bgcolor=\"white\">");
27:         out.println("<h1>Properties Dump Servlet</h1>");
28:
```

21

LISTING 21.5   continued

```
29:         // web-app/servlet/init-param
30:         out.println("<b>Servlet init parameters:</b><br>");
31:         out.println("<blockquote>");
32:         Enumeration e = getInitParameterNames();
33:         while (e.hasMoreElements()) {
34:             String key = (String)e.nextElement();
35:             String value = getInitParameter(key);
36:             out.println(key + " = " + value + "<br>");
37:         }
38:         out.println("</blockquote>");
39:
40:         // web-app/context-param
41:         out.println("<b>Context init parameters:</b><br>");
42:         out.println("<blockquote>");
43:         ServletContext context = getServletContext();
44:         Enumeration enum = context.getInitParameterNames();
45:         while (enum.hasMoreElements()) {
46:             String key = (String)enum.nextElement();
47:             Object value = context.getInitParameter(key);
48:             out.println(key + " = " + value + "<br>");
49:         }
50:         out.println("</blockquote>");
51:
52:         // attribute values set by the servlet container
53:         out.println("<b>Context attributes:</b><br>");
54:         out.println("<blockquote>");
55:         enum = context.getAttributeNames();
56:         while (enum.hasMoreElements()) {
57:             String key = (String)enum.nextElement();
58:             Object value = context.getAttribute(key);
59:             out.println(key + " = " + value + "<br>");
60:         }
61:         out.println("</blockquote>");
62:
63:         // extra attributes that might be set elsewhere in the
64:         // request if more than one servlet has handled the request
65:         out.println("<b>Request attributes:</b><br>");
66:         out.println("<blockquote>");
67:         e = request.getAttributeNames();
68:         while (e.hasMoreElements()) {
69:             String key = (String)e.nextElement();
70:             Object value = request.getAttribute(key);
71:             out.println(key + " = " + value + "<br>");
72:         }
73:         out.println("</blockquote>");
74:
75:         // browser and server software and deployment metadata
76:         out.println("<b>Request properties:</b><br>");
77:         out.println("<blockquote>");
```

LISTING 21.5   continued

```
78:          out.println("Servlet Name: " + getServletName() + "<br>");
79:          out.println("Protocol: " + request.getProtocol() + "<br>");
80:          out.println("Scheme: " + request.getScheme() + "<br>");
81:          out.println("Server Name: " + request.getServerName() + "<br>");
82:          out.println("Server Port: " + request.getServerPort() + "<br>");
83:          out.println("Server Info: " + context.getServerInfo() + "<br>");
84:          out.println("Remote Addr: " + request.getRemoteAddr() + "<br>");
85:          out.println("Remote Host: " + request.getRemoteHost() + "<br>");
86:          out.println("Character Encoding: " +
➥ request.getCharacterEncoding() + "<br>");
87:          out.println("Content Length: " +
➥ request.getContentLength() + "<br>");
88:          out.println("Content Type: "+ request.getContentType() + "<br>");
89:          out.println("Locale: "+ request.getLocale() + "<br>");
90:          out.println("Default Response Buffer: " +
➥   response.getBufferSize() + "<br>");
91:          out.println("Request Is Secure: " + request.isSecure() + "<br>");
92:          out.println("Auth Type: " + request.getAuthType() + "<br>");
93:          out.println("HTTP Method: " + request.getMethod() + "<br>");
94:          out.println("Remote User: " + request.getRemoteUser() + "<br>");
95:          out.println("Request URI: " + request.getRequestURI() + "<br>");
96:          out.println("Context Path: " + request.getContextPath() + "<br>");
97:          out.println("Servlet Path: " + request.getServletPath() + "<br>");
98:          out.println("Path Info: " + request.getPathInfo() + "<br>");
99:          out.println("Path Trans: " + request.getPathTranslated() + "<br>");
100:          out.println("Query String: " + request.getQueryString() + "<br>");
101:          out.println("</blockquote>");
102:
103:          // form data submitted
104:          out.println("<b>Parameter names in this request:</b><br>");
105:          out.println("<blockquote>");
106:          e = request.getParameterNames();
107:          while (e.hasMoreElements()) {
108:              String key = (String)e.nextElement();
109:              String[] values = request.getParameterValues(key);
110:              out.print(key + " = ");
111:              for (int i = 0; i < values.length; i++) {
112:                  out.print(values[i] + " ");
113:              }
114:              out.println("<br>");
115:          }
116:          out.println("</blockquote>");
117:
118:          // HTTP request header names and values
119:          out.println("<b>Headers in this request:</b><br>");
120:          out.println("<blockquote>");
121:          e = request.getHeaderNames();
122:          while (e.hasMoreElements()) {
```

21

LISTING 21.5   continued

```
123:                  String key = (String)e.nextElement();
124:                  String value = request.getHeader(key);
125:                  out.println(key + ": " + value + "<br>");
126:              }
127:          out.println("</blockquote>");
128:
129:          // HTTP cookie names and values
130:          out.println("<b>Cookies in this request:</b><br>");
131:          out.println("<blockquote>");
132:          Cookie[] cookies = request.getCookies();
133:          if (cookies != null) {
134:              for (int i = 0; i < cookies.length; i++) {
135:                  Cookie cookie = cookies[i];
136:                  out.println(cookie.getName() + " = "
137:                              + cookie.getValue() + "<br>");
138:              }
139:          }
140:          out.println("</blockquote>");
141:
142:          // data stored in the HttpSession
143:          out.println("<b>Session data in this request:</b><br>");
144:          out.println("<blockquote>");
145:          out.println("Requested Session Id: " +
146:                          request.getRequestedSessionId() + "<br>");
147:          out.println("Current Session Id: " + session.getId() + "<br>");
148:          out.println("Session Created Time: " +
➥ session.getCreationTime() + "<br>");
149:          out.println("Session Last Accessed Time: " +
150:                          session.getLastAccessedTime() + "<br>");
151:          out.println("Session Max Inactive Interval Seconds: " +
152:                          session.getMaxInactiveInterval() + "<br>");
153:          out.println("Session values: ");
154:          Enumeration names = session.getAttributeNames();
155:          out.println("<blockquote>");
156:          while (names.hasMoreElements()) {
157:              String name = (String) names.nextElement();
158:              out.println(name + " = " + session.getAttribute(name) +
➥ "<br>");
159:          }
160:          out.println("</blockquote>");
161:          out.println("</blockquote>");
162:
163:          // JVM System properties
164:          out.println("<b>Java Virtual Machine Properties:</b><br>");
165:          out.println("<blockquote>");
166:          Enumeration sysProps = System.getProperties().propertyNames();
167:          while (sysProps.hasMoreElements()) {
168:              String name = (String)sysProps.nextElement();
169:              out.println(name + "= " + System.getProperty(name) + "<br>");
```

LISTING 21.5 continued

```
170:
171:            }
172:            out.println("</blockquote>");
173:
174:            out.println("</body>");
175:            out.println("</html>");
176:       }
177: }
```

The PropertiesDump servlet has one method, doGet(), that handles an HTTP get request by overriding the default doGet() method inherited from the parent class, HttpServlet. The doGet() method's two arguments are the HttpServletRequest and HttpServletResponse objects supplied to it when the servlet container invokes it. Lines 17 and 18 access those objects first. Line 17 creates a PrintWriter, out; all the servlet's output goes through out. Line 18 gets an HttpSession object, session, from the request. Lines 29 through 38 access any initialization parameters for the servlet that are defined in the Web app's configuration file, web.xml. The format and contents of this file will be explained shortly. Lines 40 through 50 access any initialization parameters for the entire Web app, which are also configured in web.xml. Lines 63 through 73 access any extra attributes that are set within the request. The servlet API allows one servlet to hand off a request to another servlet (or JSP); attributes can be set to provide communication between the different points in the handling sequence. Lines 75 through 101 call various HttpServletRequest object methods that access server and browser software character-istics and intrinsic request attributes. Lines 103 through 115 access any HTML form data submitted to the servlet; if you compose an HTML form that uses the GET method, you can set the form's action attribute to link to the servlet's URL to see all the form's names and values displayed. Lines 118 through 127 display all the request headers that the browser sent to the Web server. Lines 129 through 140 display all the HTTP cookie name/value pairs sent by the browser. Lines 142 through 161 display the HTTP session metadata and the session data that is stored. Finally, 163 through 172 display all the JVM System properties.

The next step is to compile the servlet into Java bytecode from the source directory's parent directory. Windows users should open a command shell and type

```
cd C:\Program Files\Apache Tomcat 4.0\webapps\sams-webapp\WEB-INF
```

Or, on Unix:

```
cd /usr/local/jakarta-tomcat-4.0.4/webapps/sams-webapp/WEB-INF
```

Then compile the servlet by typing

```
javac -classpath "c:\Program Files\Apache Tomcat 4.0\common\lib\servlet.jar";
➥"c:\Program Files\Apache Tomcat 4.0\webapps\sams-webapp\WEB-INF\src" -d
➥ classes src\PropertiesDump.java
```

21

Or, on Unix:

```
javac -classpath
/usr/local/jakarta-tomcat-
➡4.0.4/common/lib/servlet.jar:/usr/local/jakarta-tomcat-
➡4.0.4/webapps/sams-webapp/WEB-INF/src
-d classes src/PropertiesDump.java
```

Next, you want to make the servlet accessible via the URL /sams-web/servlet/ properties so that the user doesn't need to see the class name used for the code and the servlet container knows where to find the class. To do this, you need to create a simple web.xml in the WEB-INF directory as shown in Listing 21.6.

LISTING 21.6   Sample web.xml

```
<?xml version="1.0" encoding="ISO-8859-1"?>

<!DOCTYPE web-app
    PUBLIC "-//Sun Microsystems, Inc.//DTD Web Application 2.3//EN"
    "http://java.sun.com/dtd/web-app_2_3.dtd">

<web-app>
    <servlet>
        <servlet-name>PropertiesDump</servlet-name>
        <servlet-class>PropertiesDump</servlet-class>
    </servlet>
    <servlet-mapping>
        <servlet-name>PropertiesDump</servlet-name>
        <url-pattern>/servlet/properties</url-pattern>
    </servlet-mapping>
</web-app>
```

The servlet container tag associates a servlet-name to a servlet-class; the servlet-mapping container tag associates the url-pattern to the servlet-name.

Next, restart Tomcat, either in the Windows service manager or using the catalina.bat command with the stop argument, depending on whether you're running Tomcat as a Windows service.

The output from a request for the PropertiesDump servlet might look something like the output shown in Figure 21.7.

Note that Servlet init parameters and Context init parameters are empty. You can modify the web.xml and make parameters available to just the configured servlet or to any servlet in the Webapp, as shown in Listing 21.7. You will need to restart Tomcat again for the changes to take effect.

LISTING 21.7   Modified `web.xml`

```xml
<?xml version="1.0" encoding="ISO-8859-1"?>

<!DOCTYPE web-app
    PUBLIC "-//Sun Microsystems, Inc.//DTD Web Application 2.3//EN"
    "http://java.sun.com/dtd/web-app_2_3.dtd">

<web-app>
    <context-param>
        <param-name>example-context-param</param-name>
        <param-value>Some Context Value</param-value>
    </context-param>
    <servlet>
        <servlet-name>PropertiesDump</servlet-name>
        <servlet-class>PropertiesDump</servlet-class>
        <init-param>
            <param-name>example-servlet-param</param-name>
            <param-value>Some Servlet Value</param-value>
        </init-param>
    </servlet>
    <servlet-mapping>
        <servlet-name>PropertiesDump</servlet-name>
        <url-pattern>/servlet/properties</url-pattern>
    </servlet-mapping>
</web-app>
```

FIGURE 21.7

*PropertiesDump
servlet output.*

The servlet now has values to display for itself and the Webapp context, as shown in Figure 21.8.

The PropertiesDump servlet is a complete walkthrough of the data available to servlet and JSP authors. The full scope of the servlet and JSP APIs is a huge topic, but this should provide a good starting point.

21

FIGURE 21.8

PropertiesDump servlet with context and servlet parameter values.

Accessing SSL Variables

If you've built your server with SSL support, there are security parameters that the Apache Web server is aware of for the HTTPS requests it handles. Because Tomcat runs in a separate process, however, it doesn't have direct access to this data that something in-process—such as an Apache module, mod_perl, or PHP application—has. mod_jk can make that data available with the following directives:

- **JkExtractSSL:** Can be set to off or on; it enables or prevents mod_jk from sending SSL information to Tomcat. The default is on.

- **JkHTTPSIndicator:** Sets an HttpServletRequest attribute name that indicates whether SSL is on. The default attribute name is HTTPS.

- **JkSESSIONIndicator:** Sets an HttpServletRequest attribute name by which the SSL session ID can be accessed. The default attribute name is SSL_SESSION_ID.

- **JkCIPHERIndicator:** Sets an HttpServletRequest attribute name by which the type of SSL cipher used in the request can be accessed. The default attribute name is SSL_CIPHER.

- **JkCERTSIndicator:** Sets an HttpServletRequest attribute name by which the type of SSL client certificate used in the request can be accessed. This may be useful, for instance, for certificate-based authentication within the Web app. The default attribute name is SSL_CLIENT_CERT.

Although Tomcat's standalone HTTP listener can be set up to use SSL, Apache's superior performance as an HTTP server makes using it for SSL the more common choice for production Web servers.

Building `mod_jk`

If for whatever reason you can't use one of the `mod_jk` binaries available at the Jakarta Web site, you will have to download the `jakarta-tomcat-connectors` source distribution yourself to build it. At the time of this writing, there were no less than three different ways to build `mod_jk`. Although the shell script and autoconf-generated Makefile methods should work, they've fallen into disrepair from time to time. So, the method used here will use Jakarta Ant to build `mod_jk`.

Ant is a Java build tool from the Jakarta group that performs compilation, packaging, and other tasks for software development projects. It uses XML files that describe what tasks it should perform for a project. Ant can be compared to `make` except that it's especially well suited for Java development, whereas `make` is not. The default name for the XML file is `build.xml`; we'll use a `build.xml` shortly to perform some builds. Values that Ant depends on, such as the location of certain libraries, can be defined in the `build.xml` or in external file parameters, typically called `build.properties`. Now that you know what Ant is, download and unpack the binary distribution and set the `ANT_HOME` environment variable to the directory where you unpacked Ant, as shown in Listing 21.8.

LISTING 21.8   Unpacking the `jakarta-ant` Distribution

```
cd /usr/local
gunzip < jakarta-ant-1.4.1-bin.tar.gz | tar xvf -
```

Unix users can use the `ant` shell script in `ANT_HOME`'s `bin` subdirectory to run Ant. Unfortunately, the Ant distribution doesn't have quite everything we need. We'll have to supplement our Ant distribution with an extra library, `jkant`, to build `mod_jk`. Sources for `jkant` come with the connectors installed in Ant's `lib` directory. First, we'll need to unpack the `jakarta-tomcat-connectors` distribution with the commands shown in Listing 21.9.

LISTING 21.9   Unpacking the `jakarta-tomcat-connectors` Distribution

```
cd /usr/local
gunzip < jakarta-tomcat-connectors-4.0.4-src.tar.gz | tar xvf -
```

You need to build first the required library:

```
cd jakarta-tomcat-connectors-4.0.4-src/util
$ANT_HOME/bin/ant
```

21

Then you'll need to edit the `build.xml` file found in `jakarta-tomcat-connectors-4.0.4-src/jk/` to set the locations for where Tomcat is installed by setting the value for `tomcat40.home`. Then you can type

```
cd jakarta-tomcat-connectors-4.0.4-src/jk/
$ANT_HOME/bin/ant
```

to build the `jkant` jar. Copy it to your Ant distributions by typing

```
cp ../jk/build/WEB-INF/lib/jkant.jar $ANT_HOME/lib
```

At last, you're ready to build `mod_jk` itself! Type

```
cd /usr/local/jakarta-connectors-4.0.4-src/jk/native
```

Edit the `build.xml` so that the `apache2.home` and `apxs20` properties point to where Apache 2.0 and its `apxs` script are installed. Next, invoke Ant again by typing

```
$ANT_HOME/bin/ant
```

This will build `mod_jk.so`. Presuming that your Apache 2.0 installation is in `/usr/local/apache2`, you can install `mod_jk` by typing

```
cp ../build/WEB-INF/jk/apache2/mod_jk.so /usr/local/apache2/modules
```

> The build systems for `mod_jk` change frequently. The preceding procedure seemed to be the most reliable method at the time this book was written. Building `mod_jk` for Windows requires Microsoft Visual Studio. At the time of this writing, the procedure for building `mod_jk` on Windows is not documented. However, you should consult the Jakarta Tomcat site for the latest information. Remember that you can always download a Windows binary from the Jakarta Web site.

Summary

Java servlets and JSPs provide a rich programming framework for running server-side Java applications. These applications, or Webapps, run inside a servlet container, Tomcat, outside of the Apache process. Hooking up Tomcat and Apache requires setting up a connector module, `mod_jk`, to turn an HTTP request that Apache sees and turn them into an `HttpServletRequest` Java object that Tomcat uses for input. Conversely, the `HttpServletResponse` Java object that Tomcat produces is purveyed as an HTTP response by Apache. The communication between `mod_jk` and Tomcat happens over a protocol, AJP 1.3. `mod_jk` knows what requests to route to Tomcat by how the `JkMount` directives are specified. Hour 24, "Additional Apache Modules and Projects," introduces several other useful Apache Java projects that can be useful in server-side Web development.

Q&A

Q **When I try to access a Webapp context with `mod_jk` set up in my server, I get an error that says `handler "jakarta-servlet" not found for:`. What does that mean?**

A This error is most commonly caused by `mod_jk` being unable to connect to Tomcat. Check that

- Tomcat is running.
- The value for `worker.ajp13.port` in `workers.properties` agrees with the `port` attribute specified in Tomcat's `server.xml`. Look for the `Connector` with the `className` attribute to set `org.apache.ajp.tomcat4.Ajp13Connector`.

Q **How can I debug my `mod_jk` configuration?**

A Add the following lines to your `httpd.conf`:

```
JkLogFile logs/jk.log
JkLogLevel debug
```

When activated in your server configuration, these directives will make `mod_jk` write extensive messages to `jk.log`, including any ajp13 connection failures and other error conditions.

Q **Is there an easier way to reload a Webapp than restarting Tomcat?**

A Yes, Tomcat comes with a manager Webapp that can load, unload, disable, and re-enable other Web apps. The manager's usage is detailed in the Tomcat documentation, and in the comments found in the Tomcat `conf` directory's `web.xml`.

Quiz

1. Must you create an `Alias` and `<Directory>` container for the Webapp directories?
2. Can you define attribute names/values that are shared by all servlets and JSPs in a Webapp?
3. What is the primary advantage of running an application as a Java Webapp as compared other methods such as `mod_perl` and PHP?

21

Quiz Answers

1. No, this is necessary only if there is content in the Webapp that Apache is to serve that is not generated by Java.

2. Yes, use the `context-param` container in the Webapp's `web.xml` as shown in Listing 21.7.

3. Because the Java code is executed in a separate process space, it can be scaled independently of the HTTP work that the Apache Web server is performing. In contrast, PHP and `mod_perl` run in-process with Apache and cannot be scaled independently of Apache itself.

Related Directives

This section contains new directives introduced in this hour. You can consult the Jakarta Tomcat reference documentation for comprehensive syntax information and usage.

- **JkMount:** Takes a URL pattern and a protocol (for example, ajp13).
- **JkWorkersFile:** Takes a path (absolute or server root–relative) to the properties file (typically named `workers.properties`) that configures `mod_jk`'s communication with Tomcat.
- **JkExtractSSL:** Enables/prevents `mod_jk` from sending SSL information to Tomcat.
- **JkHTTPSIndicator:** Sets an `HttpServletRequest` attribute name that indicates whether SSL is on.
- **JkSESSIONIndicator:** Sets an `HttpServletRequest` attribute name by which the SSL session ID can be accessed.
- **JkCIPHERIndicator**: Sets an `HttpServletRequest` attribute name by which the type of SSL cipher used in the request can be accessed.
- **JkCERTSIndicator:** Sets an `HttpServletRequest` attribute name by which the type of SSL client certificate used in the request can be accessed.
- **JkLogFile, JkLogLevel:** Sets up debug file and debug level.

Further Reading

The Jakarta Web site has links for the Tomcat and Ant software distributions, documentation and mailing lists:

```
http://jakarta.apache.org/index.html
```

The full servlet API is available online and can be downloaded in Java's javadoc format from

`http://java.sun.com/products/servlet/index.html`

The full JSP 1.2 and servlet 2.3 specifications are available online and may be downloaded in PDF format from

`http://jcp.org/aboutJava/communityprocess/final/jsr053/index.html`

The full JSP API javadocs and news about other JSP API related developments are found at `http://java.sun.com/products/jsp/index.html`

Java Tools for Extreme Programming: Mastering Open Source Tools, including Ant, JUnit, and Cactus by Richard Hightower and Nicholas Lesiecki provides a good introduction to using Ant and other tools for effective Java software development practice.

21

Hour **22**

Dynamic URI Resolution with `mod_rewrite`

This hour introduces a unique Apache module: `mod_rewrite`. `mod_rewrite` provides the Apache administrator with a variety of tools for content delivery and redirection needs that in other circumstances would require a dedicated module, a CGI, or some other additional application code. In this hour, you will learn

- What `mod_rewrite` is
- How to use `mod_rewrite`'s directives to transform requests using regular expressions
- When to use `mod_rewrite` instead of `mod_alias`

Basic Redirects and Aliases Review

Although most modern Web servers have at least some facility for extending the server's capabilities—either through an application programming interface (API) such as Apache's module API or at a minimum with common

gateway interface (CGI) applications—Apache has a unique additional facility with
`mod_rewrite`.

`mod_rewrite` enables you to alter the processing of incoming requests based on a collection of rules that can take into account elements such as the request URL and the existence of a certain environment variable. Additionally, the syntax used in the configuration examples relies on regular expressions. The hour's end has pointers to further reading; regular expression pattern matching is a tremendous topic on its own!

Rules-Driven Content Mapping and Redirection

Hour 5, "Using Apache to Serve Static Content," discussed URL mapping with `mod_alias`. You saw that if you want to make content in `/usr/local/qa-documents` accessible with the URI path `/qa-docs`, you could do so using the `Alias` directive:

```
Alias /qa-docs /usr/local/qa-documents
```

When the Web server reads a request line with a matching leading URI path, such as

```
GET /qa-docs/schedules/milestone_1.html HTTP/1.0
```

The translation phase resolves the URI path to the file system location:

```
/usr/local/qa-documents/schedules/milestone_1.html
```

Figure 22.1 illustrates the basic URI resolution process.

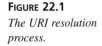

FIGURE 22.1
The URI resolution process.

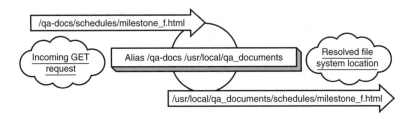

`mod_alias`' `Redirect` directives are composed similarly to its `Alias` directives. In a local redirect case, when content is reorganized, there will be significant visitors to the old URL and it is not desirable for them to get 404 responses. For instance, if content is moved around in such a way that documents previously accessible as `/qa-docs` move to `http://qa.example.com/docs`, the redirect would be expressed like this:

```
Redirect /qa-docs http://qa.example.com/docs
```

The preceding line performs an external redirect and Apache will send a 302 Moved Temporarily response. You will see later in the hour how mod_rewrite supports internal redirects. In that case, Apache will retrieve the updated content and return it to the user transparently.

Figure 22.2 shows the browser/server HTTP exchange in a redirect case.

FIGURE 22.2

Redirection.

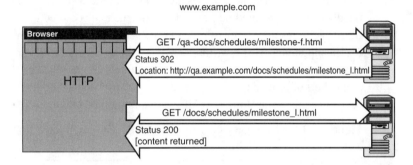

Variations of the mod_alias directive syntax, AliasMatch and RedirectMatch, support regular expressions for the source URI path argument.

Links to other Web sites are easily logged by using the RedirectMatch syntax. Although most clickthrough tracking systems use a CGI or Java servlet to keep track of the navigation, we'll rely on log analysis with this directive syntax:

```
RedirectMatch ^/redirect/(.+) http://$1
```

Suppose that a link to MyYahoo! must be tracked. Simply linking directly to http://my.yahoo.com/ is not an option. Use the RedirectMatch facility; when the browser requests

```
http://www.example.com/redirect/my.yahoo.com/
```

the server will log a 302 response that can be counted when the log file is processed. From the browser's perspective, the redirect to http://my.yahoo.com/ is followed.

To summarize, with standard content aliases and redirects, the only request parameter used to resolve the URI is the request line itself. In contrast, mod_rewrite enables us to access server configuration and HTTP request variables for sophisticated rule sets to drive URI resolution.

Zen and the Art of `mod_rewrite`

Just about all Web servers provide tools for mounting various physical file system resources to a Web server's virtual file system. They all work the same way, more or less. A map is maintained of URI paths that point to physical file system locations. `mod_rewrite` takes this to a new extreme. The full range request header, and environment and server configuration variables are exposed to the configuration file instrumentation for handling request resolution. This information can be accessed to manipulate how URIs are translated to resources, rewriting paths along the way using pattern matching as a basic text manipulation. This rewriting behavior is what the module is named for. A number of built-in functions and conditional logic constructs are provided as well. `mod_rewrite` stops short of providing a complete programming language, but nonetheless provides a rich toolset for controlling how URIs are transformed into delivered resources.

Figure 22.3 shows a `mod_rewrite`-driven URI resolution logic flow.

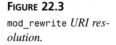

FIGURE 22.3
`mod_rewrite` *URI resolution.*

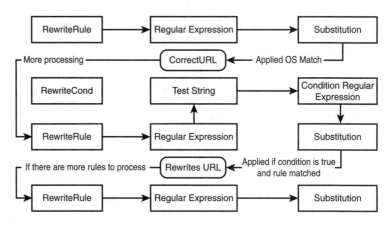

> The pattern-matching directives provided by `mod_alias` and the logical constructs provided by `mod_rewrite` are two features that are often overlooked when comparing other Web servers to Apache. These features are among the things that distinguish Apache's flexible and powerful configuration language from those of the others.

Although all the details of regular expression usage are beyond the scope of this text, we'll refer to resources in the "Further Reading" section of this hour that provide lots of regular expression learning tools. It's worth noting that there are different flavors of regular expressions. Through Apache 1.3, the Web server's pattern matching was limited to simple regular expressions. Apache 2.0 uses the Perl Compatible Regular Expression

(PCRE) library, which provides the full power of Perl 5–style regular expressions to the Web server configuration.

> The PCRE library implements extensions to conventional regular expressions; the same extensions implemented by Perl 5 itself. NFA-style regular expressions, the type used in Apache 1.3, and Perl 5 regular expressions are discussed in detail by Jeffrey Friedl's book, *Mastering Regular Expressions*. See the "Further Reading" section at the end of this hour.

Super-Charge Your Redirects

Regular expression–driven URI resolution to file system resources using `AliasMatch` is a powerful feature. However, it might be desirable to have attributes of a request, in addition to the request line itself, dictate how the URI is resolved to an HTTP response. We'll start with a fairly simple illustration. Suppose that your Web site is using Server Side Includes (SSI) and it's been configured to use the `.shtml` extension for SSI processing. You don't want your content to have `.shtml` extensions anymore so that all your URLs can standardize on `.html` instead. You could rename all your files, but you would also have to go into each file and change

```
<!--#include virtual="/includes/footer.shtml" -->
```

to

```
<!--#include virtual="/includes/footer.html" -->
```

in all the content. Changing all the content might be very painstaking. A faster solution would be to use `mod_rewrite`'s `RewriteRule` directive set with something like this:

```
1: RewriteEngine on
2: RewriteRule (/.*)\.shtml$ $1.html
```

Line 1 turns on `mod_rewrite` processing. Line 2 captures any requests that end with `.shtml` and rewrites them as such that `/docs/qa/milestone_1.shtml` ends in `html`. Well, that's fine if that's the page you're accessing from a browser, but what about the includes? The `RewriteRule` will be applied to subrequests as well. When `mod_include` looks for `/includes/footer.shtml`, `mod_rewrite` will step in and ensure that `/includes/footer.html` is found.

Suppose now that a Web site was developed using Microsoft ASP to look up document data in a database, but the records have a low modification rate. It is therefore highly inefficient to access the data with URLs like

```
http://www.example.com/poordesign.dll?PAGEDB::PAGENAME::DISPLAY
```

where the arguments after question mark are used to dynamically access data. It's much more efficient to materialize the data as pages that can be statically accessed (and incrementally updated as data changes). However, it's not acceptable to have users who have bookmarked URLs to get 404s. The solution is to export the pages to static files and configure Apache with mod_rewrite to resolve the URLs to those files. Listing 22.1 shows a few mod_rewrite directives that rewrite the request data according to the original request's QUERY_STRING data.

LISTING 22.1   Directives to Map QUERY_STRING Data to File Names

```
1: RewriteEngine On
2: RewriteMap downcase int:tolower
3: RewriteCond %{QUERY_STRING} PAGEDB::([A-Z]+)::DISPLAY
4: RewriteRule ^/poordesign\.dll$ /${downcase:%1.html} [L]
```

The first line in Listing 22.1 turns on mod_rewrite. Later examples won't explicitly turn it on like this, but it's important to note that even if mod_rewrite is loaded in the server, it is not activated unless this directive precedes the actual rewriting configuration directives. The RewriteEngine directive is needed only once in the configuration file. The second line uses the RewriteMap directive to associate mod_rewrite's internal tolower function to the logical name downcase. The name choice is arbitrary; using pepperoni instead of downcase would work equivalently, it would just be less descriptive.

The third line uses the RewriteCond directive to look at the QUERY_STRING portion of the request (all the stuff after the question mark) and regular expression pattern match it against the pattern that follows. The RewriteCond directive gates further execution of mod_rewrite directives; if the condition evaluates to false, the subsequent mod_rewrite directives are not processed. The pattern has a set of parentheses around a portion of it; the captured text is available in the RewriteRule that follows on the fourth line as the variable %1. If there had been more captured patterns, they would have been available as %2, %3, and so on, for each set of parentheses. The fourth line is where it all comes together. If /poordesign.dll is matched, the downcase function is applied to the URI of the request, and appended with the .html suffix. The square brackets at the end are for flags; in this case, we give the L flag to indicate that this is the last rule to process. If the document were on the file system as /spinnaker.html, it could be accessed as

```
http://www.example.com/poordesign.dll?PAGEDB::SPINNAKER::DISPLAY
```

The prior example manipulated the request characteristics to parameterize the resolution of the request to local content. We could easily extend the example to perform a full redirect, and force the browser to issue a new request for the target content, by adding R to the flag part of the RewriteRule.

22

To add this flag, you need to modify the fourth line of Listing 22.1 to read

```
RewriteRule ^/poordesign\.dll$ /${downcase:%1.html}? [L,R]
```

The browser is redirected to `http://www.example.com/spinnaker.html`.

Note also the question mark at the end of the destination URL. If that were absent, the browser would have redirected to

```
http://www.example.com/spinnaker.html?PAGEDB::SPINNAKER::DISPLAY
```

which would work with static content. But freed of the `QUERY_STRING`, the URL looks much better.

Random Acts

One of the interesting features of `RewriteMap` is the built-in randomizer. Instead of writing a CGI or Java servlet to handle random URL redirection, `mod_rewrite` provides a very simple facility for doing this. You can use `RewriteMap`'s randomizer with its build `rnd` function and then, by having your `RewriteRule` reference it, the syntax would look like this:

```
RewriteMap surprise rnd:/usr/local/apache2/conf/random_url.txt
RewriteRule /random http://${suprise:url}.apache.org/ [R,L]
```

The `RewriteMap` directive associates `surprise` with the `rnd` function and the function's output is used to construct the destination URL.

Suppose that the contents of the map file, `/usr/local/apache2/conf/random_url.txt`, are simply this:

```
url httpd|jakarta|perl|xml
```

When the browser requests `http://www.example.com/random`, the server will look up the line that begins with `url` in the map file and randomly return one of the pipe-delimited options. The redirection will ultimately point to `http://httpd.apache.org/`, `http://jakarta.apache.org/`, `http://perl.apache.org/`, or `http://xml.apache.org/`.

Dynamic Content

The same principle can be applied to content that is included in a page as a Server-Side Include (SSI). Perhaps it is desirable to have a rotating SSI component. This is often accomplished with banner ad management software by using a CGI or Java servlet. However, the low-budget solution is to use `mod_rewrite` in conjunction with mod_include, explained in Hour 12, "Filtering Modules." On the page with the rotating component, use the normal SSI syntax:

```
<!--#include virtual="/surprise-component" -->
```

When Apache performs its subrequest to handle the URI /surprise-component, mod_rewrite can step in to do its magic with this syntax:

```
RewriteMap surprise rnd:/usr/local/apache2/conf/random_component.txt
RewriteRule ^/surprise-component /${surprise:component} [PT,L]
```

The contents of the map file /usr/local/apache2/conf/random_component.txt are simply

```
component component1.inc|component2.inc|component3.inc
```

As the page is reloaded, the contents of /component1.inc, /component2.inc and /component3.inc are randomly included where the SSI tag appears.

Using mod_rewrite for Authorization

Apache has a rich set of modules that provide a wide variety of options for authenticating users, that is, determining who they are, as described in Hour 7, "Restricting Access." However, the facilities for authorizing users and determining what they can access are comparatively limited. Besides connection characteristics such as the connection IP address or domain name, the only other options are the Require directive's group specification.

Suppose that a directory structure designed to have a common area available to all users as well as a set of private user-specific directories is set up like this:

- **/users/** is accessible to all logged in users.
- **/users/jones** is accessible only to the user logged in as jones.
- **/user/smith** is accessible only to the user logged in as smith.
- **/user/foo** is accessible only to the user logged in as foo.

To accomplish this for only three users, it's relatively straightforward to configure, as shown in Listing 22.2.

LISTING 22.2 Configuration of Three User-Specific Access Controlled Directories Without Using mod_rewrite

```
1: <Directory "/usr/local/apache2/htdocs/users/">
2:     AuthUserFile /usr/local/apache2/etc/passwd
3:     AuthType Basic
```

22

LISTING 22.2   continued

```
 4:     AuthName "Secret Stuff"
 5:     require valid-user
 6: </Directory>
 7: <Directory "/usr/local/apache2/htdocs/users/smith">
 8:     AuthUserFile /usr/local/apache2/etc/passwd
 9:     AuthType Basic
10:     AuthName "Secret Stuff"
11:     require user smith
12:     satisfy all
13: </Directory>
14: <Directory "/usr/local/apache2/htdocs/users/jones">
15:     AuthUserFile /usr/local/apache2/etc/passwd
16:     AuthType Basic
17:     AuthName "Secret Stuff"
18:     require user jones
19:     satisfy all
20: </Directory>
21: <Directory "/usr/local/apache2/htdocs/users/foo">
22:     AuthUserFile /usr/local/apache2/etc/passwd
23:     AuthType Basic
24:     AuthName "Secret Stuff"
25:     require user foo
26:     satisfy all
27: </Directory>
```

The common directory permits access to all users in the password file, whereas the smith user is the only user who can access the smith directory, jones the jones directory, and foo the foo directory. Simple, right? Well, if the user population is undergoing a lot of change, has grown very large, or both, this would be an unwieldy configuration file!

As you can see, this would be difficult to scale to dozens or hundreds of users. Programmatically matching the logged-in usernames to directory names would be preferable. The password file should be the only piece that has to grow or withstand a high rate of change. Fortunately, we can fulfill these requirements with mod_rewrite. The example in Listing 22.3 doesn't access a RewriteMap that uses internal functions; it runs an *external program*, a Perl script named auth-check to handle the directory to username matching.

LISTING 22.3   mod_rewrite Directives to Provide User-Specific Access Controls

```
1: RewriteMap auth prg:/usr/local/apache2/bin/auth-check
2: <Directory "/usr/local/apache2/htdocs/users">
3:     AuthUserFile /usr/local/apache2/etc/passwd
```

LISTING 22.3   continued

```
 4:    AuthType Basic
 5:    AuthName "Secret Stuff"
 6:    require valid-user
 7:    satisfy all
 8: </Directory>
 9:
10: # look ahead in the request process for the REMOTE_USER
11: RewriteCond %{LA-U:REMOTE_USER} (.+)
12: # send the URI's that look like /foo/something to our mapping
13: # program and who we've logged in as
14: RewriteRule ^/users/(([^/]+)/.* ${auth:$1:%1}
15: # if the mapping program said OK, go to our original REQUEST_URI
16: RewriteRule OK  %{REQUEST_URI} [S]
17: # otherwise, treat it as forbidden
18: RewriteRule NOT - [F]
```

The auth-check program is a simple Perl script, as shown in Listing 22.4.

LISTING 22.4   The auth-check Program

```
1: #!/usr/bin/perl
2: $|++;
3: while (<STDIN>) {
4:     chomp;
5:     my($dir,$user)=split(':', $_);
6:     my $return = ($user eq $dir) ?  "OK\n" : "NOT\n";
7:     print $return;
8: }
```

There's a lot going on in Listing 22.3, so hold on to your seats. The RewriteMap (line 1) defines an auth "function" that mod_rewrite will keep running as a co-process. The Directory container (line 2) ensures that Apache will require authentication for the parent directory, /users, and that all authorization conditions must be met to permit access. The RewriteCond directive (line 11) enables capture of the name the user logged in as. The first RewriteRule captures the directory the user is accessing, and inputs it and the username into the auth function. The next rules get the output of the auth function, either OK or NOT, and either rewrite the URL back to the original REQUEST_URI value or forbid access, respectively.

The Perl script in Listing 22.4 simply turns off output buffering (line 2) and gets lines of input from standard input (line 3). Then it splits the line of input on the colon character into the $dir and $user variables (line 5), and finally returns either OK or NOT depending on a simple text equality test of $dir and $user. It runs continuously, waiting for input from Apache.

 Recent versions of Apache 1.3 provide some facilities, by using the `Require` directive, for allowing access only if the logged-in username matches the owner of the file. That functionality might be ported to Apache 2.0 eventually. In that case, the preceding `mod_rewrite` code would not be necessary, although it is still a good example of `mod_rewrite`'s capabilities.

Flexible Proxying

The semantics and issues of forward versus reverse HTTP proxying were discussed in Hour 15, "Apache as a Proxy Server," but it's worth noting `mod_rewrite`'s solutions for complex proxying problems as well. Maybe this is reminiscent of an aptitude test, but here it goes: What `mod_alias` is to mapping URIs to file system resources, `mod_proxy` is to mapping URIs to remote HTTP resources. However, as you saw, `mod_alias` provides some pattern matching features with `AliasMatch` and `RedirectMatch`, whereas `mod_proxy` does not.

To set up a reverse proxy on www.example.com with `mod_proxy`, the typical directives would look like the following:

```
ProxyPass /qa-docs http://qa-host.example.com/docs
ProxyPassReverse /qa-docs http://qa-host.example.com/docs
```

The same behavior can be generated with `mod_rewrite` by using the `RewriteRule` directive:

```
RewriteRule /qa-docs http://qa-host.example.com/docs [P]
```

The P flag tells `mod_rewrite` not to redirect, but to pass-through the request back to the origin server, qa-host.example.com. To the browser, the appearance is maintained of the response coming from www.example.com.

Note that `mod_rewrite` has no proxying facility of its own. `mod_rewrite` must be present for the P flag to have any effect. But it provides a clearer definition of the expected behavior in only one directive, instead of two.

Dynamic Proxying and Load Balancing

The reverse proxying and random rotation capabilities can be combined for traffic distribution in a large infrastructure environment. Suppose that the architecture is like the one in Figure 22.4. The front end server doesn't handle any file system access or CGI execution; it simply passes the traffic through.

FIGURE 22.4

Server architecture with a front end reverse proxy and backend content servers.

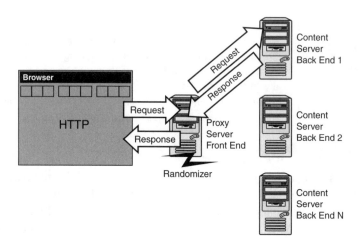

Why is this valuable? Typically, a Web server's process resources are tied up by network I/O handling high-latency end users. To continue handling requests as fast as they're coming in, a Web server can be tuned to have a larger process pool, but the more each process resource is tied up, the more that process is unavailable to handle more requests.

By dividing up the duties between front end and backend Web servers, the infrastructure can distribute the burden among more machines. In this architecture, the backend Web servers are freed to access filesystem resources, run CGIs, and perform other local resource-demanding tasks. The front end Web server is dedicated to handling the high network latency end users. A high-speed connection between the front and back ends makes the whole system perform with a very high utilization threshold. The backend configurations are configured as normal. However, the front end, with mod_proxy and mod_rewrite, is configured with directives like

```
RewriteMap backends rnd:/usr/local/apache2/conf/backend_servers.txt
RewriteRule (.*) http://${backends:server|backend1}.example.com/$1 [P]
```

where /usr/local/apache2/conf/backend_servers.txt is a text file that looks like this:

```
server backend1|backend2|backend3|backend4|backend5|backend6
```

Virtual Hosting

Perhaps the server must have a set of cookie-cutter virtual hosts, with paths that resolve with a fixed pattern. Maintaining a lengthy configuration file with repeated

<VirtualHost> sections might be error prone. Suppose that foo.example.com, bar.example.com, and so on, all resolve in DNS to 192.168.100.10. (We could use other domains, but we'll stick to example.com for a generic reference to different hostnames.) Depending on how your operating system is configured, it might suffice to put the hostname IP mappings in your /etc/hosts file. Listing 22.5 shows how mod_rewrite can perform our cookie cutter virtual hosting.

LISTING 22.5   Virtual Hosting with mod_rewrite

```
 1: <VirtualHost 192.168.100.10:80>
 2:    <Directory /usr/local/apache2/docs>
 3:    Options Indexes FollowSymLinks
 4:    </Directory>
 5:    RewriteEngine On
 6:    RewriteMap downcase int:tolower
 7:    RewriteMap vhost txt:/usr/local/apache2/conf/vhost_map.txt
 8:    # the /icons alias is shared by all virtual hosts
 9:    RewriteCond %{REQUEST_URI} !^/icons/
10:    # make sure the Host: header wasn't empty
11:    RewriteCond   %{HTTP_HOST}  !^$
12:    # make sure FOO.EXAMPLE.COM is handled the same as foo.example.com
13:    RewriteCond   ${downcase:%{HTTP_HOST}}  ^(.+)$
14:    RewriteCond   ${vhost:%1}  ^(/.*)$
15: </VirtualHost>
```

The contents of the map file (/usr/local/apache2/conf/vhost_map.txt) that is read on line 7 are simply

```
foo.example.com:80 /usr/local/apache20/docs/foo
bar.example.com:80 /usr/local/apache20/docs/bar
foo.example.com /usr/local/apache20/docs/foo
bar.example.com /usr/local/apache20/docs/bar
```

For port 80 virtual hosts, it's important that the map file keys have both the plain version of the hostname and the port-number-appended version. If the first map file key had been simply foo.example.com, lookup on it could have failed because the HTTP Host: request header might have the full hostname and port number in it. For virtual hosts on different ports, this is not an issue: The plain hostname is never sent; the hostname with the port number appended always is.

Note that when the number of keys to look up in a map file is high, mod_rewrite supports looking them up in a dbm database. This is advantageous because looking up records in a dbm database is faster with negligible slowdowns as the data set grows, whereas looking up records in a text file linearly degrades performance as the number of records grows. Simply specify

```
RewriteMap vhost dbm:/usr/local/apache2/conf/vhost_map
```

instead of

```
RewriteMap vhost txt:/usr/local/apache2/conf/vhost_map.txt
```

However, you will be required to programmatically maintain the database in
/usr/local/apache2/conf/vhost_map. There are libraries for a number of different languages to support this, so check the Apache URL Rewrite Guide resource in the "Further Reading" section at the end of the hour for sample code to generate a dbm from a text file.

Virtual hosting environments can be complicated to operate and maintain. Typically there are a variety of content maintainers, and there might be more complex content serving requirements than the one outlined earlier, which only supports static file system content.

For more information about mass virtual hosting applications, refer to Hour 14, "Virtual Hosting," for a discussion of mod_vhost_alias.

Summary

As you have seen, mod_rewrite offers a lot of power and flexibility! If you are familiar with regular expressions, you have seen the range of URI-to-resource resolution possibilities broaden. If regular expressions are new to you, we hope this will motivate you to learn more about using them so that you can make full use of mod_rewrite.

Q&A

Q Does mod_rewrite provide conditional application of URI transformation?

A Yes, the RewriteCond directive enables you to test for textual patterns in a variety of request and server configuration parameters. These tests can control the flow of rewrite rule application and can be additive to provide complex conditions under which rewrite rules should be applied.

Q How do I debug my rewrite rules?

A After the RewriteEngine On declaration, use these additional directives:
```
RewriteLog /path/to/logfile
RewriteLogLevel X
```

where X is a number in the range inclusive of 1 through 9. The higher the number, the "noisier" the log's verbosity. The RewriteLog is really the best insight to what's happening; it can provide traces of pattern matches and rule application decisions.

Q When should `mod_rewrite` be used and when should `mod_alias` be used?

A `Alias` and `ScriptAlias` directives are essential to provide the basic URI-to-filesystem-resource resolution. You can make `mod_rewrite` look up how to do the resolution, but that's relatively consumptive of CPU and other operating system resources.

22

Quiz

1. Which Web servers have a configuration-driven dynamic request-rewriting module?
2. Which `RewriteMap` function provides a randomizer?
3. How many times is the `RewriteEngine` directive needed in the configuration file?

Quiz Answers

1. Although other Web servers might have APIs for manipulating request attributes, only Apache 1.3.x and Apache 2.0 have `mod_rewrite`, a module for putting the logic for that manipulation in the server configuration.
2. The `RewriteCond`'s `rnd` function allows a `RewriteRule` to pick a bit of text out randomly.
3. For `mod_rewrite`'s other directives to be put into effect, the `RewriteEngine` need appear only once with its value set to on.

Related Directives

This section contains directives mentioned in this hour or that are related to topics discussed in this hour. You can consult the Apache reference documentation for comprehensive syntax information and usage.

- **`Redirect`:** Matches the leading part of a path to redirect the browser to a destination URL.
- **`RedirectMatch`:** Similar to `Redirect`, but can use other parts of the requested path on a pattern-matching basis to calculate a destination URL for a redirect.
- **`RewriteEngine`:** Enables `mod_rewrite`. Without this directive, other `mod_rewrite` directives are not acted on.
- **`RewriteCond`:** Sets up a true or false condition to check whether a request or server variable has a successful pattern match. If `RewriteCond` returns true, subsequent `mod_rewrite` directives are processed.

- **RewriteMap:** Provides a lookup resource to perform a function on input text. The function might be looking up a value in a text or dbm file, modifying text with an internal function such as changing case, or running an external program to perform processing.
- **RewriteRule:** Substitutes request text with pattern matching and applies substitutions from input matches, `RewriteCond` matches, and `RewriteMap` results.
- **RewriteLog:** Enables logging of the `mod_rewrite` processing. Typically used only for debugging purposes.
- **RewriteLogLevel:** Adjusts the verbosity of the `RewriteLog` log file. With many `RewriteRule`, `RewriteCond`, and `RewriteMap` directives, setting `RewriteLogLevel` to the noisiest level, `debug`, `mod_rewrite`'s debugging is voluminous.

Further Reading

Mastering Regular Expressions, Jeffrey E.F. Friedl, 1997, O'Reilly & Associates, Inc.

Apache Module `mod_rewrite` at

`http://httpd.apache.org/docs-2.0/mod/mod_rewrite.html`

Apache 1.3 URL Rewriting Guide at

`http://httpd.apache.org/docs-2.0/misc/rewriteguide.html`

Additional information about regular expressions can be found at

`http://directory.google.com/Top/Computers/Programming/Languages/`
`Regular_Expressions/FAQs,_Help,_and_Tutorials/`

HOUR 23

Migrating to Apache 2.0

The majority of the current Web servers are Apache 1.3 servers, followed at a distance by Microsoft IIS and IPlanet servers. It is likely that Apache 2.0 will replace many of them in the future, but the transition will happen gradually and in the meantime, Apache 2.0 will have to coexist with them.

In this hour, you will learn

- How to determine when it makes sense to migrate to Apache 2.0, maintain a mixed environment, or preserve the existing servers
- How to migrate to Apache 2.0 from previous versions of Apache, and what the main differences with those versions are
- How to migrate to Apache 2.0 from commercial servers such as Microsoft IIS and IPlanet

Apache 1.3

Apache 1.3 is the predecessor of Apache 2.0 and is the most popular server on the Internet at the time this book was written. Some versions, such as Apache 1.3.12 and 1.3.20, have been found more stable than others, and thus are more widely deployed. This section describes the architecture of Apache

1.3 and how it compares to Apache 2.0, and provides you with advice on how to transition to Apache 2.0.

Apache 1.3 runs both on Unix and Windows. Like Apache 2.0, the server is open source and extensible via modules, and that is one of the reasons of its success. However, Apache 1.3 lacks features of Apache 2.0 such as MPMs, filtering, and protocol modules.

The only available Apache 1.3 process model on Unix is Prefork. As mentioned in Hour 11, "Multi-Processing Modules," this makes the server robust, but it does not scale as well as a threaded server. Apache 1.3 runs as a threaded server on Windows, but support for this operating system is inferior to Windows support in 2.0 because, at the time, there was no Apache Portable Runtime abstraction layer and the integration with the Unix code left a lot to be desired.

Migrating to Apache 2.0

Before you migrate a given Apache 1.3 installation to Apache 2.0, you must consider the pros and cons of migrating. These issues include performance, functionality, Windows support, and protocol modules.

Performance

In most Unix systems, the Worker MPM available with Apache 2.0 can provide greater scalability than a process-based server. This is especially true for platforms that have heavy processes, such as AIX, and for high-traffic sites that serve static content.

Improved Functionality

Apache 2.0 offers major new functionality such as filtering and new options for existing directives. Modules that in the past had to be downloaded separately, such as mod_dav and mod_ssl, are now bundled with the server, which eases installation.

Most third-party modules for Apache 2.0 have improved greatly from their 1.3 counterparts. For example, mod_perl 2.0 offers significant advantages in terms of functionality and memory footprint, as described in Hour 20, "mod_perl."

Improved Windows Support

If you are running Apache 1.3 on Windows, you are strongly encouraged to upgrade. Apache 2.0 offers significantly increased performance and stability thanks to the Apache Portable Runtime. For the first time, this version of the server is considered as stable as its Unix counterparts.

Protocol Modules

Hour 24, "Additional Apache Modules and Projects," mentions two protocol modules: mod_pop3 for remote mail access and mod_ftp for implementing an FTP server. The number of available protocol modules will increase over time as Apache 2.0 matures. This capability is especially interesting for system administrators who need to maintain different servers because they can consolidate the administration of services and users.

Reasons Not to Migrate to Apache 2.0

Although Apache 2.0 has many exciting features, there are some scenarios in which migrating from an existing Apache 1.3 installation might not be the best option. If your current Apache 1.3 servers are working just fine, don't have performance issues, and provide the desired functionality, it is probably not a good idea to rush to Apache 2.0 or any other server.

Many more modules have been developed for Apache 1.3 than currently exist for Apache 2.0, and unsupported modules can be a migration obstacle. Those modules can either be in-house modules designed for 1.3 or third-party modules that have yet to be ported. Possible solutions for this problem are explained in the following section.

Migration Help: Apache 1.3 to Apache 2.0

The following is some advice on how to migrate existing Apache 1.3 installations to Apache 2.0.

Configuration Changes

The Apache 2.0 configuration format is the same as in Apache 1.3, but some directives are no longer relevant and the syntax of others has changed. Covalent Technologies provides a free Perl script that can be used to help with the migration of existing Apache 1.3 configuration files. The script, named `confconv.pl`, can be downloaded from

`http://apache.covalent.net/tools/index.php`

The script takes care of several configuration changes, such as commenting out the following deprecated directives:

`ServerType`: Apache 1.3 offered the option of not running the server continuously and instead starting and terminating it for every request by the `inetd` Unix daemon. This is no longer an option in Apache 2.0.

`ClearList`, `AddModule`: In Apache 1.3, the module order was important to determine how certain requests would be processed. These two directives enabled you to explicitly determine that order, but are no longer necessary because in Apache 2.0 the modules can organize themselves.

`Port`: The `Port` directive no longer exists and has been replaced by the `Listen` directive.

The following directives have a different meaning depending on the MPM and their settings must be carefully examined: StartServers, MaxClients, MaxRequestsPerChild, MinSpareServers, and MaxSpareServers.

For example, the number of start servers is less in the Worker MPM than in Prefork because each Worker process has, in turn, several threads.

Apache Modules

Many popular Apache modules have versions for both Apache 1.3 and 2.0 and can thus ease the transition. These include third-party modules (such as PHP, mod_perl, and connector modules for Tomcat), bundled modules (such as mod_cgi, mod_dav, and mod_ssl), and commercial modules (such as the BEA WebLogic connector module and the Covalent SNMP module).

Running Both

Sometimes it is necessary to maintain a mixed 1.3/2.0 environment, usually because of the need to run modules that are not yet ported to 2.0.

It is possible to run Apache in a reverse proxy configuration. Apache 2.0 can serve the static content and content generated by supported modules and pass other requests to a backend Apache 1.3 running unsupported modules.

Microsoft Internet Information Server

Microsoft Internet Information Server (IIS) is the dominant Web server for the Windows family of operating systems. The reasons for the success are multiple, primarily based around ease of use and integration with other Microsoft products. MS IIS comes preinstalled with the operating system or is available as an option at installation time. It provides an easy-to-use GUI for configuring the server and an SNMP interface for monitoring.

IIS is tightly integrated with other Microsoft technologies, such as the Microsoft FrontPage Web publishing tool, Microsoft Active Server Pages (ASP) for server-side development, and more recently, the .NET Framework. In addition to being an HTTP server, IIS also includes an FTP server that can be controlled from the same GUI interface as the Web server.

Third-party developers can extend Microsoft IIS via modules using the Internet Server Application Programming Interface (ISAPI). This is similar to the Apache API, but is not as comprehensive.

The following sections provide you some advice on whether it makes sense to migrate from IIS to Apache 2.0.

Migration to Apache 2.0

Several good reasons exist for migrating from IIS to Apache 2.0 running on Windows or Unix, but the two main reasons are increased security and stability.

Security

For the past few years, serious vulnerabilities affecting Microsoft IIS have been discovered periodically. These security flaws allow remote attackers to gain full control of the machine. Several Internet worms, such as Nimda and Code Red, have been developed that exploit these bugs, take over the server, and use it to scan other networks looking for additional vulnerable servers to infect. Those worms do not affect Apache, but their attack attempts will appear in your logs, as described in Hour 8, "Logging and Monitoring."

In contrast, although Apache is not guaranteed to be bug-free, the number of security flaws found in Apache over the years has been much lower and the flaws relatively minor, such as not being remotely exploitable. If you are processing sensitive information, such as credit card information, in your Web site, this can be a major incentive to migrate to a more secure server platform.

Stability

Although it has improved over the years, IIS has traditionally endured memory leaking and stability problems under high Web traffic. This has forced administrators to reboot the machines periodically.

Part of the problem is not with the Web server software, but with the underlying Windows operating system, which is not as robust as Unix server platforms. Apache cannot solve this problem, but its cross-platform nature gives you a migration path in case you need it.

Standardization

Many companies have in place a mixture of machines, operating systems, and server software. This drives up the costs of management, support, and administrator's training. Because Apache 2.0 supports both Unix and Windows, one way to simplify your server infrastructure would be to adopt Apache across all your platforms.

Development

Even if your main hosting infrastructure is Unix-based, having a Windows version of Apache 2.0 can be beneficial for programmers using Windows-based development environments. Because many Apache modules such as PHP and mod_perl and Java-based projects have been ported to Windows, developers can develop and test locally on their machines and deploy on a Unix server.

Features

The great number of third-party Apache modules available and the built-in functionality provide a number of features not available in other servers, such as IIS. Extensive URL rewriting and page redirection capabilities are good examples.

Reasons Not to Migrate from IIS

The following are several reasons why you might want to stick with an IIS-based solution. Many of these problems are addressed in the "Migration Help: IIS to Apache 2.0" section later this hour.

The main reason is expertise. System administrators and programmers who are familiar with IIS and related technologies, such as ASP, will need to overcome a learning curve that can be quite steep in some cases. This is due to the fact that many people go all the way, and migrate not just the Web server but also move to a different platform altogether, such as Solaris or Linux.

If you have a significant amount of legacy code, you might not be able to migrate easily and you will need to keep up separate servers, as described in the "Migration Help: IIS to Apache 2.0" section.

Finally, if you are satisfied with your current IIS installation, don't experience performance or stability problems, and keep up to date with security patches, there is no reason to change to Apache or any other Web server.

Migration Help: IIS to Apache 2.0

In case you decide to migrate from IIS to an Apache solution running on Windows or Unix, there are some tips you need to remember. One of the big advantages of Apache and many other open source technologies described here is that they run both on Unix and Windows. They can work and interoperate with a variety of other Windows technologies, including IIS, so the transition can be staged as opposed to an all-or-nothing approach.

GUI Configuration

The first thing that people coming from a Windows background notice about Apache is that it does not come with a GUI. Third-party GUI configuration tools are available for Apache as described in Hour 10, "Apache GUIs." Some of these tools, such as Comanche, work on both Unix and Windows.

Development

Most Web development in the Windows platform is based on Active Server Pages technology. You can consider a number of alternatives, ranging from environments that enable you to host your ASP pages unchanged to functionally equivalent open source technologies such as PHP.

ASP Engines

A number of products provide support for ASP on both Unix and Windows platforms, although with some limitations that might or might not affect you.

Instant ASP from Halcyon Software and Sun Chili!Soft ASP are two such products. You can learn more about them at `http://www.halcyonsoft.com` and `http://www.chilisoft.com`. They are Java-based and run on both Windows and a variety of Unix platforms.

23

Although most ASP developers use VBScript, ASP itself is language-independent and you can write ASP pages using Perl. Hour 20 covered `Perl::ASP`, an Apache `mod_perl` module for doing just that.

PHP

PHP is the open source equivalent to Active Server Pages, and was introduced in Hour 19. PHP has the added advantage of running on both Apache and IIS, enabling you to provide a flexible, staged migration plan or to standardize on a common development language across different Web servers.

PHP on Windows supports access to COM objects, Active Data Objects, connection to Microsoft SQL Server, and many other Windows technologies. These can be used to easily interoperate with existing code from PHP projects.

Java

If your development framework is Java-based, the migration from one platform to another is relatively easy. The Apache Tomcat servlet and JSP container and most application servers such as WebLogic can work with either Apache or IIS and with either Windows or Unix. Tomcat is described in Hour 21, "Tomcat and Apache."

Additional Software

When developing on Windows, Microsoft SQL Server is commonly used. There are a number of open source alternatives, such as MySQL (`http://www.mysql.org`) and PostgreSQL (`http://www.postgresql.org`). These databases have ODBC, JDBC drivers, and provide connection libraries for most languages.

Extending the Server

If you have developed proprietary IIS modules, you will be glad to know that `mod_isapi` provides an ISAPI compatibility layer for 2.0 to ease migration of your extensions. The module is included in the standard Apache 2.0 distribution.

Consolidated Server

IIS bundles other servers, such as an FTP server. This comes up every so often on comparative reviews as a checkbox that Apache does not fulfill. This is kind of silly because Apache is just a Web server, and a number of other FTP servers are available both for Unix and Windows.

However, this changes with Apache 2.0 because a commercial FTP protocol module integrates and takes advantage of the Apache framework, as explained in Hour 24.

Reverse Proxy

Even if you need to keep running IIS servers, you will benefit from placing an Apache reverse proxy in front of them. The proxy can be configured to block malicious requests and attacks directed to the backend IIS servers. You can then gradually migrate functionality from those IIS servers to Apache.

Many companies have policies in place standardizing on certain software packages or vendors, such as Microsoft IIS, regardless of whether they make sense for a given project. In response, some developers have gone so far as to tweak Apache so that the `Server:` headers, error responses, and so on, are identical to what MS IIS would answer, thus misleading the "standardization police" into thinking they are running IIS. I am not suggesting here that you go to these extremes, but sometimes advocating open source Apache over other servers from Microsoft or IPlanet can be an uphill battle. In those situations, companies with Apache-based products such as IBM and Covalent can provide the commercial support and services that would make Apache acceptable for your management.

IPlanet

IPlanet servers run on a variety of Unix-based and Windows operating systems. IPlanet is the new name for the Netscape server division after its acquisition by Sun. Although the installed base of IPlanet servers has been decreasing steadily over the past years, it is still popular with certain segments of the market, such as financial services companies. The IPlanet Web server is based on a threaded architecture and provides functionality found in other servers such as SSL, flexible logging, authentication, and so on. The IPlanet Web server is part of an integrated family of servers including directory, calendaring, and application servers.

Similar to the IIS ISAPI and the Apache API, IPlanet Web servers can be extended via modules using NSAPI (Netscape Server API) .

IPlanet provides GUI management tools, although they are somewhat difficult to use and some people resort to configuring the server using text files directly.

Migrating to Apache 2.0 from IPlanet

The two main reasons people mention for migrating from IPlanet servers are the lack of a clear product roadmap and the fact that IPlanet has dropped support of older, but widely deployed, server versions. When facing a new upgrade cycle, IT managers are looking for less costly and less risky alternatives, such as Apache. Even if commercial backing is a requirement, IPlanet servers tend to be considerably more expensive than Apache-based commercial servers.

IPlanet servers integrate and work nicely with other IPlanet products, such as the IPlanet Application Server. However, IPlanet has failed to grow a substantial developer community and thus lacks a solid base of third-party modules. Apache is an open, vendor-neutral platform that supports many more modules than IPlanet does, both commercial and open source; for example, to connect to competitive application servers. Finally, Apache runs in more operating systems than IPlanet.

Reasons Not to Migrate from IPlanet

There are not many reasons, either technical or business-wise, not to jump on the Apache 2.0 bandwagon. One of them is if you are using the IPlanet Web server as part of a larger IPlanet solution, including application servers and directory services. Another one is if you have an existing working setup that meets your needs, based on IPlanet. You might want to test drive an Apache-based solution in case you need to migrate in the future, but there is no reason to migrate to Apache or any other server if you have a working system.

Migration Help: IPlanet to Apache 2.0

Apache can match most IPlanet features—you just need to map IPlanet configuration to the equivalent Apache directives. Covalent provides a migration guide that can help you with the process.

Apache can integrate with IPlanet directory servers via the LDAP module described in Hour 24. PHP has been ported to the NSAPI architecture and is available for IPlanet servers, so as with the IIS case, it can be used to ease the transition.

Most of the development in IPlanet environments is based on CGI or Java. Both technologies are available for Apache and the transition should be straightforward.

General Migration Advice

To summarize, the main advantages of choosing Apache 2.0 as your Web server platform are that it is an open, vendor-neutral platform that is scalable and secure. All these features have made Apache the de facto standard in Web servers, with all major application server and Web development vendors providing modules that work with Apache.

Probably the best migration advice is to introduce Apache 2.0 gradually in your environment, and move forward as you gain experience with the server. You can start by configuring Apache 2.0 to serve parts of your Web site. For example, you could set up an Apache 2.0 server in charge of delivering images, and change your links to point to it. Or you could set up a reverse proxy for more fine-grained control.

Summary

This hour compared Apache 2.0 to a variety of other Web servers, taking into account both technical and business considerations. The hour provided advice in migrating to the Apache 2.0 platform, with an emphasis on gradual, phased approaches.

Q&A

Q Why do you insist in a gradual approach to migration?

A Most Web servers are not an end in themselves, but rather exist to provide a service. Stability and availability are the most important qualities for a successful Web site. When migrating to a new, better platform, you need to integrate with the existing functionality or port it. A gradual approach, substituting one server or service at a time, in a controlled manner, minimizes the chances of downtime. If something goes wrong, you can easily revert to the previous configuration.

Q How can Apache integrate in the Microsoft .NET Framework?

A Although .NET runs traditionally with IIS, the interface to the Web Server has been abstracted. It is entirely possible to write an Apache module that integrates Apache as the Web server component in .NET, although no such module exists at the time of this writing. Combined with projects such as Mono (`http://go-mono.com`), an open source implementation of .NET, Apache could provide an entire .NET environment in Unix systems.

Halcyon Software, mentioned earlier in the hour, also provides a cross-platform runtime environment for the .NET Framework.

Further Reading

Covalent (`http://www.covalent.net`) provides several white papers on migrating from IIS and IPlanet to Apache 2.0.

The following is a link to the "Migration of Linux-Apache-MySQL-PHP Platform to Windows 2000" guide from Microsoft (although I have never met anyone who has migrated an Apache server to a Microsoft solution):

`http://www.microsoft.com/TechNet/prodtechnol/iis/deploy/depovg/miglamp.asp`

Seriously.

23

Hour **24**

Additional Apache Modules and Projects

Apache's architecture and its open source license allow it to be extended via commercial and open source modules, different from the ones included in the distribution. In addition, the Apache Software Foundation is the home of a variety of other Web-related projects that you will find useful.

In this hour, you will learn about

- Additional Apache 2.0 modules
- Other Apache Software Foundation projects
- Web resources covering the Apache server

Apache 2.0 Modules

Apache's modular architecture is one of its strengths. A great number of modules exist for previous versions of Apache. Many of them have already been ported to Apache 2.0 and take advantage of its new architecture, such as `mod_perl`, PHP, and the connector modules for Tomcat. Those modules have already been covered in this book, so this section covers only additional modules currently available for Apache 2.0. At the time of this writing, the number of available Apache 1.3 modules is much greater, but this will likely change as Apache 2.0 is widely adopted.

LDAP

The `mod_auth_ldap` module provides authentication services against an LDAP server. LDAP stands for Lightweight Directory Access Protocol, a protocol used to access data stored in directory servers. Companies keep a variety of information, usually employee-related, in directories so that it can be accessed and reused by a variety of applications such as e-mail clients and Web servers. This module can authenticate and authorize users, and can also interoperate with the FrontPage Extensions module. You can grant or deny access based on a specific combination of user and group attributes and a variety of other filters. You can find documentation about this module at `http://httpd.apache.org/docs-2.0/mod/mod_auth_ldap.html`.

The `mod_auth_ldap` module works in conjunction with the `mod_ldap` module, which provides connection pooling and caching services for other LDAP modules, such as the previously mentioned `mod_auth_ldap`. You can find documentation about the `mod_ldap` module at `http://httpd.apache.org/docs-2.0/mod/mod_ldap.html`.

The code for both modules can be obtained via CVS. The repository can be browsed here: `http://cvs.apache.org/viewcvs.cgi/httpd-ldap`.

POP3

One of the advantages of Apache 2.0 is its multi-protocol architecture, which allows different protocols to be implemented as plug-ins of the main server.

The `mod_pop3` module implements POP3 (Post Office Protocol version 3), a client protocol used to retrieve mail from a central server. This allows Apache to act as a mail server for most mail clients. The `mod_pop3` module can take advantage of the Apache layered architecture and offer secure access using the SSL protocol, which can be inserted as a filter. You can find this protocol module at `http://cvs.apache.org/viewcvs.cgi/httpd-pop3/`.

Mailing List Archiving

The `mod_mbox` module provides a Web interface to Unix mailbox files. This is particularly useful for archiving mailing lists. Unlike other archiving software, `mod_mbox` does not create a myriad of smaller files, but keeps a single file and generates the listings on the fly. You can find this protocol module at `http://cvs.apache.org/viewcvs.cgi/httpd-mbox/`.

Bandwidth Management

The `mod_bwshare` module enables you to control how individual clients access your Web site. It monitors the amount of bandwidth used by clients, number of files downloaded, and other parameters, and enables you to slow them down or disconnect them if they exceed certain limits. You can use `mod_bwshare` to prevent faulty or malicious clients from slowing down your server or making it unavailable for other clients. The `mod_bwshare` module can be found at `http://www.topology.org/src/bwshare/`.

Extending Apache with C++

The Apache Web server is written in C, and extending it with C++ code can be tricky. The `mod_cplusplus` module makes it easy to extend Apache with modules coded in C++. It exposes the server's internal structures and request and filtering phases through an object-oriented API. This module can be found at `http://modcplusplus.sourceforge.net`.

24

mod_snake

The `mod_snake` module enables you to extend Apache with modules written in the Python language, in a similar way to what `mod_perl` does for Perl. It enables you to write filters, accelerate existing CGI scripts, and even build new protocol handlers using Python. `mod_snake` works both with 2.0 and 1.3 versions of Apache.

You can find more information about this module at `http://modsnake.sourceforge.net`.

You can learn more about Python at `http://www.python.org`.

Tcl

The Tcl Apache project provides several modules to extend Apache with the Tcl scripting language, in a similar way to `mod_snake` and `mod_perl`. It also provides support for embedding Tcl in HTML pages, in a similar way to how PHP works.

The advantages of using Tcl as a development language are that it is lightweight, extensible, and easy to learn. You can learn more about the Tcl Apache project at `http://tcl.apache.org` and about Tcl at `http://tcl.activestate.com`.

Another Tcl module that works with Apache 2.0, together with a well-documented application development framework, can be found at `http://www.websh.com`.

XSLT Module

This Apache 2.0 module allows XML stylesheet processing of documents using the libxml and libxslt libraries. XML stylesheets enable you to transform XML documents into other formats. mod_xslt enables you to transform a source XML document into different HTML documents, depending on the stylesheet applied. This allows you to support browsers with different capabilities, or easily change the look and feel of your Web site. You can download the mod_xslt module from http://www.mod-xslt.com/.

mod_mya

This module provides basic authentication services, in a similar way to how the modules described in Hour 7, "Restricting Access," do. However, this module stores its user and group information in a MySQL database. This enables you to share authentication information across a variety of servers. You can find more information about this module at http://www.fractal.net/mod_mya.tm.

mod_bakery

This is an authorization module that works using encrypted cookies. Once a client has successfully authenticated, a secure cookie (that cannot be tampered with) is issued and will be transmitted by the client browser with every request. The session information is stored in a common MySQL backend database and can thus be shared by different Web servers, CGI programs, Apache modules, and so on. You can find this module at http://www.fractal.net/mod_bakery.tm.

mod_v2h

This is a mass virtual hosting module that uses the MySQL database as its backend. It is similar in functionality to Apache's mod_mass_vhost, described in Hour 14, "Virtual Hosting." You can find more information about this module at http://www.fractal.net/mod_v2h.tm.

Commercial Modules

A number of vendors provide commercial modules for the Apache 2.0 platform, mostly targeted for enterprise environments.

BEA

BEA WebLogic is a Java application server commonly used in enterprise environments. Although WebLogic can answer HTTP requests on its own, that is not usually how it is deployed. Instead, a Web server such as Apache is placed in front of the application server and connects to it using a special connector module. Requests for static content are served directly by the Web server, and requests for dynamic content are relayed to the backend application server.

BEA bundles an Apache 2.0 connector module with WebLogic that provides that functionality. It can talk to a cluster of backend application servers and even load-balance requests among them. The module is aware of sessions and can redirect requests to the backend server that created a specific session, and failover to other servers if that server is unavailable. You can specify request patterns and locations that will be sent to the application server and even modify the request URLs.

The threaded architecture of Apache allows the module to keep a pool of connections to the application server, increasing performance and responsiveness.

The Apache connector module is part of the WebLogic distribution, which you can download at http://www.bea.com.

Enterprise Ready Server

The Apache 2.0–based server offering from Covalent includes several proprietary modules, which are described in the list that follows. You can find more information about these modules at http://www.covalent.net.

- **mod_snmp:** This module adds Simple Network Management Protocol (SNMP) capabilities to the Apache Web server. This protocol is commonly used to manage network servers and equipment from a central console such as HP OpenView or Tivoli. With this module, you can easily monitor Apache performance in real time, including server uptime, load average, number of errors in a certain period of time, number of bytes and requests served, and many other metrics.

- **mod_covalent_auth:** This module provides a common framework for authentication and authorization against LDAP directories, NIS, databases, and a variety of other backends.

- **mod_ftp:** This module is built on top of the Apache multi-protocol framework and provides support for the File Transfer Protocol (FTP). It integrates and takes advantage of other Apache modules capabilities, such as authorization, logging, and SSL support.

24

ASF Projects

This section covers a selection of Apache Software Foundation projects that are not directly related to the Apache HTTP server, but are useful Web development tools. Many other projects can be found at http://www.apache.org.

Java and Apache

The Jakarta community (http://jakarta.apache.org) is the home of several Java-based projects. The goal of the Jakarta Project is to provide and maintain commercial-quality server solutions based on the Java platform that are developed in an open and cooperative fashion.

Most of these server solutions relate to Web technologies. The Apache Java community is a dynamic and active one, and has produced a great number of projects covering many different areas, from XML processing to database connectivity. This section will show you some of the most interesting ones.

Tomcat

Tomcat, described in Hour 21, "Tomcat and Apache," is the reference implementation for the servlet and JavaServer Pages specifications. This is the most widely known Jakarta project and is used as the basis for a variety of commercial and open source projects. You can find it at http://jakarta.apache.org/tomcat/.

Ant

Ant is a build tool, similar to the Unix tool make, which was used in previous hours to compile Apache and its modules. Instead of using Makefiles, Ant reads XML descriptions of the tasks to carry out. Ant can be extended via Java, and many other Jakarta projects use it for their building system. You can find out more about Ant at http://jakarta.apache.org/ant/index.html.

Taglibs

The JavaServer Pages technology enables developers to provide extra functionality by adding custom tags. The Taglibs project intends to be a common repository for these extensions. You can find this project at http://jakarta.apache.org/taglibs/.

Struts

Struts provides a Model-View-Controller (MVC) framework for development of large JSP- and servlet-based applications. The Model of the framework is composed of server objects, maintaining the internal state of the application. The JSPs represent the View part. Struts servlets are the Controller component, taking requests from the client, changing the state of the application, and updating the view by delivering the appropriate JSP. You can find more about Struts at http://jakarta.apache.org/struts/.

James

James (Java Apache Mail Enterprise Server) provides a mail solution based on the JavaMail API and supports a variety of protocols such as SMTP, POP3, and IMAP. The James homepage can be found at http://jakarta.apache.org/james.

Avalon

The Avalon project provides a common framework for developing and maintaining Java server-side applications. It hosts a set of components and practices that can be reused for a variety of projects. It contains a variety of subprojects that provide support for logging, pooling, data access, management extensions, and other commonly needed functionality in server-side development. You can find more information at http://jakarta.apache.org/avalon/.

Jakarta Commons

Although the aim of the Commons project is code reuse, it approaches the problem differently than the Avalon project. Its goal is to create a collection of small, stable, mostly self-contained components (as opposed to a framework) that are useful for a variety of tasks, such as database access, HTTP client, Bean manipulation, and XML processing. This project can be found at http://jakarta.apache.org/commons/.

The Apache XML Project

The Apache XML Project provides a variety of tools for creating, parsing, and manipulating XML documents. The following are several well-known and useful XML projects.

XML Parsers

The Xerces project provides XML parsers for Java and C++, and bindings for a variety of scripting languages. It provides support for XML standards such as the Simple API for XML (SAX), Document Object Model (DOM), XML namespaces, XML schemas, and others. It keeps track of W3C standards and drafts and aims for full compliance. You can find Xerces at http://xml.apache.org/xerces-j/.

The Crimson project provides support for XML parsing via the JAXP interface http://xml.apache.org/crimson/index.html.

XML Manipulation

Xalan is an XSLT processor available for Java and C++. XSL is a stylesheet language for XML, and the T stands for transformation. Xalan enables you to define stylesheets to

describe how an XML document will be transformed in a different document (XML-based or not). You can find more information about Xalan at
`http://xml.apache.org/xalan/`.

The Jakarta Formatting Object Processor project is a more publishing-oriented solution and enables you to take an XML document and provide output documents in PDF, PostScript, and a variety of other formats. It can be found at
`http://xml.apache.org/fop/`.

Cocoon is a complete publishing framework that integrates many other Apache technologies and can run in many open source and commercial servlet containers and application servers. You can find more information about Cocoon at
`http://xml.apache.org/cocoon/`.

Apache Resources

This section presents you with a variety of Apache resources that can help you improve your Apache knowledge and keep you informed of the latest Apache developments.

Apache Support

Before using any of these forums, make sure that you read the relevant Apache documentation, such as the Frequently Asked Questions (FAQ) document, and search the mailing list archives for similar questions. If, after doing that, you still have not found an answer, you might want to post or mail your question. Provide details on the Apache version you are using, operating system information, and a detailed explanation of the problem. Include any entries you get in the `error_log` file and any relevant configuration file snippets. List all the previous steps you took to solve the problem and how they failed. This will help you get an answer quicker and avoid wasting everyone's time.

Mailing Lists

There are several mailing lists related to the Apache HTTP server.

The `announce@httpd.apache.org` mailing list is used for news of server releases, security issues, and other important releases. It is a very low-traffic list and you certainly want to be subscribed to it to keep up to date with Apache.

The `users@httpd.apache.org` mailing list is a user support forum.

The `dev@httpd.apache.org` is the developer's mailing list. Do *not* post user-related questions to this list.

You can find information about how to subscribe to these mailing list and pointers to the archives at `http://httpd.apache.org/lists.html`.

Apache Bug Database

You can report bugs online at the following address:
http://httpd.apache.org/bug_report.html.

Before doing so, make sure that you follow the instructions described in that page so that bug reports are not duplicated or invalid.

Apache Newsgroups

The newsgroups comp.infosystems.www.servers.unix and comp.infosystems.www.servers.ms-windows cover different servers, among them Apache. A popular way of accessing newsgroups is through the Google groups Web interface at http://groups.google.com.

Apache News

These are the main news Web sites covering Apache:

- **Apache Today:** http://www.apachetoday.com
- **Apache Week:** http://www.apacheweek.com
- **Slashdot Apache section:** http://slashdot.org/index.pl?section=apache

Finally, you can find information related to Apache and this book at http://apacheworld.org.

ApacheCon

The Apache Software Foundation holds annual or semiannual conferences. These events are a great opportunity to find out about the latest developments in the Apache world, and provide a forum where developers and users can exchange experiences. The official Apache conferences Web site can be found at http://www.apachecon.com.

Commercial Support

Apache is an open source project and there is a great amount of freely available information and peer-based support. However, in certain situations, such as in enterprise deployments, you might require commercial support. You can usually obtain commercial support from your server software or operating system vendor. Third-party commercial support, consulting, and training services are available from Covalent Technologies (http://www.covalent.net) and Red Hat (http://www.redhat.com).

Additional Modules

There is no central repository for Apache modules. You can find most Apache modules in one of the Web sites mentioned in this section.

24

The Apache module repository is the closest to a central directory of modules. It can be found at `http://modules.apache.org`.

Freshmeat (`http://freshmeat.net`) is a news site and project catalog of free software projects. A number of Apache modules and Apache-related projects can be found there.

Several Apache-related projects are hosted in the SourceForge Web site, which provides mailing lists, documentation, bug tracking, and many other services. You can find it at `http://sourceforge.net`.

The Apache Overview Howto, by one of the authors of this book, provides a comprehensive list of Apache projects and modules: `http://www.linuxdoc.org/HOWTO/Apache-Overview-HOWTO.html`.

Summary

This hour provided you with an overview of additional modules and programs that extend or work with Apache. Hopefully, the software described here and included with Apache itself will address most of your Web server–related needs. If not, remember that Apache is open source, so you can always build your own module!

By now, you should have a pretty good understanding of the capabilities of Apache and how to configure the server to meet your specific needs. In addition to the information presented in this book, Apache includes an excellent reference documentation that you can use to learn about specific syntax details. Apache, like many other successful open source projects, is continuously being improved and the resources mentioned in this hour will help you keep up to date with new Apache developments.

Q&A

Q Will my Apache 1.3 modules work with Apache 2.0?

A No, the APIs have changed considerably between versions. You will need to wait until the module authors release an Apache 2.0 version. You can, however, apply an intermediate solution: Run Apache 2.0 as a reverse proxy server, forwarding requests that require processing by 1.3 modules to an Apache 1.3 server in the backend. Reverse proxies are covered in Hour 15, "Apache as a Proxy Server."

Q Why do most of the third-party Apache modules run only on Unix?

A Although previous versions of Apache did run on Windows, they were not considered of the same quality as their Unix counterparts. This means that most people involved with Apache, either as users or developers, were running the server on

Unix. Although that is still the case, the new MPM architecture in Apache 2.0 and the Apache Portable Runtime make it possible to have a great Web server for Unix *and* Windows. This, together with the constant security problems of IIS, will translate into more and more people considering migrating to Apache on the Windows platform, and encourage development or porting of Windows modules.

24

APPENDIX A

The Apache Software License

The following is the Apache Software License, under which the Apache server is released.

The Apache Software License, Version 1.1

Copyright © 2000-2001 The Apache Software Foundation. All rights reserved.

Redistribution and use in source and binary forms, with or without modification, are permitted provided that the following conditions are met:

1. Redistributions of source code must retain the above copyright notice, this list of conditions and the following disclaimer.

2. Redistributions in binary form must reproduce the above copyright notice, this list of conditions and the following disclaimer in the documentation and/or other materials provided with the distribution.

3. The end-user documentation included with the redistribution, if any, must include the following acknowledgment:

"This product includes software developed by the Apache Software Foundation (`http://www.apache.org/`)."

Alternately, this acknowledgment may appear in the software itself, if and wherever such third-party acknowledgments normally appear.

4. The names "Apache" and "Apache Software Foundation" must not be used to endorse or promote products derived from this software without prior written permission. For written permission, please contact apache@apache.org.

5. Products derived from this software may not be called "Apache," nor may "Apache" appear in their name, without prior written permission of the Apache Software Foundation.

THIS SOFTWARE IS PROVIDED "AS IS" AND ANY EXPRESSED OR IMPLIED WARRANTIES, INCLUDING, BUT NOT LIMITED TO, THE IMPLIED WARRANTIES OF MERCHANTABILITY AND FITNESS FOR A PARTICULAR PURPOSE ARE DISCLAIMED. IN NO EVENT SHALL THE APACHE SOFTWARE FOUNDATION OR ITS CONTRIBUTORS BE LIABLE FOR ANY DIRECT, INDIRECT, INCIDENTAL, SPECIAL, EXEMPLARY, OR CONSEQUENTIAL DAMAGES (INCLUDING, BUT NOT LIMITED TO, PROCUREMENT OF SUBSTITUTE GOODS OR SERVICES; LOSS OF USE, DATA, OR PROFITS; OR BUSINESS INTERRUPTION) HOWEVER CAUSED AND ON ANY THEORY OF LIABILITY, WHETHER IN CONTRACT, STRICT LIABILITY, OR TORT (INCLUDING NEGLIGENCE OR OTHERWISE) ARISING IN ANY WAY OUT OF THE USE OF THIS SOFTWARE, EVEN IF ADVISED OF THE POSSIBILITY OF SUCH DAMAGE.

This software consists of voluntary contributions made by many individuals on behalf of the Apache Software Foundation. For more information on the Apache Software Foundation, please see `http://www.apache.org/`.

Portions of this software are based upon public domain software originally written at the National Center for Supercomputing Applications, University of Illinois, Urbana-Champaign.

INDEX

autoconf tool, compiling PHP (Unix), 309

automake tool, compiling PHP (Unix), 309

Avalon, Jakarta project (ASF), 405

awstats, log analysis, 139

AxKit, 327

B

backend servers, 242-244

backend storage

database file-based access control authentication, 113

digest-based authentication, 115

file-based authentication, 111

functions, authentication modules, 110

backends

authorization (modules), 403

caching, 240

proxy servers, enabling, 234

backslash (\), 56

balancing, load balancing (mod_rewrite directive), 381-382

bandwidth, managing, modules, 401

basic authentication, 108

batch file CGIs, testing (Windows configurations), 97

BEA WebLogic, 29, 403

BeOS, MPMs, 184

beta, Apache versions (naming), 38

binaries, 158

Comanche, 163

downloading (Apache installations), 43

installing

Apache installtions (Unix), 43-44

caching, 241

installation methods (selecting), 38

Linux, 95

Perl installations, 95

PHP, Unix, 307

proxy servers, 235

Solaris, 96

scripts, 54

server binary, commands, 64

Unix, 40

binary installer, 45

bind to port, troubleshooting, 68

Block value, ProxyVia directive, 238

blocks, <IfDefine SSL> (SSL directives), 275

bookmarks, icons (static content), 83

BOS MPM (Multi-Processing Module), 27

boxes. *See also* check boxes

dialog boxes, Internet Options, 238

text boxes, Exceptions, 238

browser authentication, AuthType directive, 110

BrowserMatch directive (environment variables), 146

browsers

access, environment variables, 117

Apache, accessing, 66

digest authentication, 109

mod_deflate limitation, 193

SSL protocols (secure servers), 278

Vary: header (content negotiation), 152

browsing, directives, 56

buckets, 190

buffers, TCP buffers (Prefork MPMs), 177

bug databases, support resource, 407

build directories, 55

build scripts, compiling PHP (Unix), 309

build.xml file (Jakarta Ant), 365-366

build/ (PHP directory), 309

building

Apache

CVS (concurrent versioning system), 44-45

source, 234, 241

configure script (CVS), 45

loadable modules, 55

mod_jk module, 365-366

mod_perl module, 328-329

source code, installation methods (selecting), 38

Crimson project (XML project), 405

crit, LogLevel directive option, 133

cryptography, public key or symmetric, 265

CSS (Cascading Style Sheets), mod_deflate limitation, 193

curl support (PHP extensions), 312

custom installation, Apache (Windows), 46

customized messages, error message replacement, 74

CustomLog directive, 129-131, 227

CVS (concurrent versioning system)
    building, 44-45
    clients, 44
    configurations (mod_perl module), 329
    mod_perl module, 329
    Web site, 44, 400

D

-D, httpd option, server binary, 64

data, transmitted data (performance), 257

database file-based access control authentication, 113-114

database support (PHP extensions), 313

databases
    bug databases, support resource, 407
    dbm database, keys (mod_rewrite directive), 383
    HTTP requests, logging, 130
    lock databases
        DAV configurations, 206
        error messages (mod_dav installations), 213
        paths, 206
    logging to, 138
    MySQL, sharing authentication (modules), 402
    PHP benefit, 304
    storing, 138

DAV (Document Authoring and Versioning)
    access, restricting, 207
    clients
        Microsoft, 209-211
        resources, accessing metadata, 205
        servers, managing files, 205
        Unix, 211-212
    configuring, 206-208
    directives, 207
    error messages, 213
    extensions, choosing, 214
    Microsoft FrontPage, 214
    modules, 296
    projects, 212-213
    protocols, HTTP methods, 205
    read-only access, 207

repositories, meta information, 208

servers, 207, 211

support, Web folders, 209

DavDepthInfinity directive, advanced DAV configurations, 208

DavLockDB, lock databases (DAV configurations), 206

DAVMinTimeout directive, advanced DAV configurations, 208

dbm databases, keys (mod_rewrite directive), 383

dbmmanage, user mangement (database file-based access control authentication), 113

dbmmanage.pl, user mangement (database file-based access control authentication), 113

debug, LogLevel directive option, 134

debugging
    CGI executions, configurations, 94
    mod_ext filter module, 198
    symbols (PHP extensions), 311

DebugLevel argument (ExtFilterOptions directive), 198

default
    arguments, AcceptMutex directive, 178
    schemas, directives, 57

AuthType directive, authentication modules, 110

AuthUserFile directive, users file (backend storage), 111

BrowserMatch (environment variables), 146

browsing, 56

building, 72

CacheDefaultExpire, cache expirations, 242

CacheDisable, caching functionality, 241

CacheEnable, caching functionality, 241

CacheFile directive, mapping files (memory), 256

CacheForceCompletion, cache expirations, 242

CacheLastModifiedFactor, cache expirations, 242

CacheMaxExpire, cache expirations, 242

CacheMaxExpireMin, cache expirations, 242

CacheOn, caching functionality, 241

ChildPerUserId (Perchild MPMs), 181

comments, 56

configuration files, 56-57

configuring, 136

controlling
Perchild MPMs, 181
Prefork MPMs, 176-178
Windows MPMs, 183
Worker MPMs, 180

CoreDumpDirectory, 179-183, 259

CustomLog directive, 129-131, 227

DAV, 207

DavDepthInfinity, advanced DAV configurations, 208

DAVMinTimeout, advanced DAV configurations, 208

DefaultCharset directive, character sets, 149

DefaultType directive, MIME type (defining), 79

Deny directive, access control rules, 116

DirectoryIndex directive (directory listings), 80

enabling, 235

ErrorDocument directive, error messages, 74

ErrorLog, 227

external processes, operating systems (scalability), 251

ExtFilterDefine directive, external filtering configuations, 197

filter configurations, 191

ForceType directive, MIME type, 79

formatting directives, 126-128

Group, 177, 180-182

Header directive, headers (managing), 147

HostNameLookups directive, conditional logging, 131

IdentityCheck directive, conditional logging, 131

Include, configuration files, 60

IndexOption directive, directory listings, 81

IndexOrderDefault directive, directory listings, 82

JkCERTSIndicator directive, 364

JkCIPHERIndicator directive, 364

JkExtractSSL directive, 364

JkHTTPSIndicator directive, 364

JkMount, 354

JkSESSIONIndicator directive, 364

JkWorkersFile, 354

KeepAliveTimeout directive, network settings (performance), 258

LanguagePriority directive (content negotiation), 151

limiting (Prefork MPMs), 177, 180

LimitRequestBody directive, preventing abuse (performance), 259

LimitRequestFields directive, preventing abuse (performance), 259

LimitRequestFieldSize directive, preventing abuse (performance), 259

H

Halcyon Software, Instant ASP (ASP engine), 393

handlers
cgi-script content handler, CGI content, 92
configuring, 80
content handlers, static content, 80
mod_perl module, 324-326

handling directories, modules, 291

hardware load balancer (performance), 257

Header directive, headers (managing), 147

header modification, hook, 28

headers
Accept: (client negotiation), 150
Accept-Charset: (client negotiation), 150
Accept-Encoding: (client negotiation), 150
Accept-Language: (client negotiation), 150
CGI (Common Gateway Interface), 94, 102
Content-Language: HTTP header (character sets), 149
Content-Type: (character sets), 149
directory listings, 82
files, 55
Host: (name-based virual hosting), 222-223

Host:, ProxyPreserveHost, 244

HTTP (Hypertext Transfer Protocol), 10
environment variables, 145
headers, 78, 89, 257
managing (modules), 292
request, 13
response, 13
manging, 147
request headers,
name-based virtual hosting (syntax), 222
reverse proxy configurations, 244
Server header, server identification, 75

Hello World, Perl modules (loading), 330-331

Help
Apache 1.3 migrations, 389-390
Apache 2.0, IIS (Internet Information Server) migration, 392-394

hiding files, directory listings, 82

hierarchies, proxy (forward proxy configurations), 236-238

hooks, 28, 33, 189

Host header, name-based virtual hosting, 223

hosting, Web hosting, 204. *See also* **virtual hosting**

HostnameLookups, network setting (scalability), 253

HostNameLookups directive, conditional logging, 131

hostnames, resolving (managing logs), 137

hosts, virtual hosts, 160, 166

Host: header, ProxyPreserveHost directive, 244

Host: header (name-based virtual hosting), 222

.htaccess, per-directory configuration files, 61, 252

htdocs directory, 55, 307

HTML::Mason, 326

HTML::Embperl, page component and templating system, 338

HTML::Mason, page component and templating system, 338

HTML::Template, page component and templating system, 338

htpasswd utility
authentication, 339
user password files (managing), 112

HTTP (Hypertext Transfer Protocol)
backends, proxy servers, 234
basic authentication, DAV protocols, 205
forward proxy, 235-239
headers, 257, 292
accessing (environment variables), 145
CGI reponses, 89
MIME types, 78

X-Z